3RD Edition

UK Government
& Politics

Philip Lynch and Paul Fairclough

Editor: Eric Magee

Philip Allan Updates, an imprint of Hodder Education, an Hachette UK company, Market Place, Deddington, Oxfordshire OX15 0SE

Orders
Bookpoint Ltd, 130 Milton Park, Abingdon, Oxfordshire, OX14 4SB
tel: 01235 827827
fax: 01235 400454
e-mail: uk.orders@bookpoint.co.uk
Lines are open 9.00 a.m.–5.00 p.m., Monday to Saturday, with a 24-hour message answering service. You can also order through the Philip Allan Updates website: www. philipallan.co.uk

ISBN 978-0-340-98663-9

First published 2004
Second edition 2005
Third edition 2010

Impression number   5   4   3   2   1

Year   2014   2013   2012   2011   2010

Printed in Italy

Environmental information
Hachette UK's policy is to use papers that are natural, renewable and recyclable products and made from wood grown in sustainable forests. The logging and manufacturing processes are expected to conform to the environmental regulations of the country of origin.

P01766

Contents

Introduction

This textbook is designed to meet the needs of AS students of government and politics. It provides comprehensive, accessible and up-to-date coverage of all the key topics on the AQA, Edexcel and OCR specifications (see the exam specifications grid at the end of this introduction). Our aim is that you should need few other resources when studying the subject. However, politics is, by its nature, ever-changing. You should therefore enhance your understanding and keep up to date by following the news in the mainstream media and by reading subject-specific magazines such as *Politics Review*.

Each of the 11 chapters in this book provides comprehensive coverage of the topic under consideration. You don't have to read the chapters in order, but can start reading wherever you or your teacher(s) decide to begin the course. To enable you to make connections between topics, there are references in the chapters to the other places in the book where a particular issue is discussed in more detail. In addition, you can use the detailed contents pages and the index (at the back of the book) to lead you to the section containing the information you require.

This new edition also benefits from a number of special features designed to focus your attention on the ideas, issues and debates that really matter at AS:

> **Concepts explained** and **Key terms** Concepts listed in the specifications and other key political terms, explained on the page where they appear.
> **Distinguish between** Summaries clarifying the differences between similar or commonly confused political concepts or features.
> **Viewpoint** Both sides of a controversial question set out.
> **What you should know** A bullet-point summary of the main points made in each chapter.
> **UK/US comparison** Explanations of differences between the UK and the USA in a given area to enhance your knowledge of the topic.
> **Exam focus** Questions of varying length at the end of each chapter to test your knowledge and understanding. These will help you prepare for the kinds of questions that appear on your AS papers.

Although everything you need to achieve a high grade is provided between these covers, we have also included weblinks and further reading sections to help you extend your reading.

PowerPoints summarising key knowledge and arguments for each chapter, and web-based tasks to help you revive and consolidate your knowledge for each chapter are available online. Go to www.hodderplus.co.uk/philipallan.

Philip Allan Updates produces a number of other resources that can be used in conjunction with this textbook. These include:

UK Government & Politics Annual Survey, Paul Fairclough and Eric Magee (2010 survey ISBN: 978-0-4441-1043-2). Published each February since 2006, the *Annual Survey* provides a digest of the main issues and events in UK politics during the preceding year.

AS UK Government & Politics Exam Revision Notes (3rd edition), Patrick Walsh-Atkins (ISBN: 978-0-340-99081-0). Condensed, bullet-pointed revision notes that cover all the core AS topics, updated for 2010.

A–Z UK Government & Politics Handbook, Paul Fairclough and Eric Magee (ISBN: 978-0-340-99111-4). A dictionary of UK government and politics that provides an excellent reference point for those studying the subject at AS.

AS UK Government & Politics Teacher Resource Pack (3rd edition), Neil McNaughton (ISBN: 978-0-340-99082-7). Updated following the 2010 general election, this allows teachers to integrate the most up-to-date politics into their teaching.

Politics Review magazine. An online archive of issues back to 1993 is also available.

AS Student Unit Guides, for AQA and Edexcel, Units 1 and 2.

Visit www.philipallan.co.uk.

What is politics?

Before starting to study UK government and politics it is helpful to define some of the key terms and concepts you are going to encounter. A student of English literature or chemistry would probably have little difficulty in offering a 'definition' of their chosen subject, but it is less easy to explain precisely what politics is. This is hardly surprising, given the range of definitions and interpretations in common usage.

Dictionary definitions of politics

1   The academic study of how a people, a nation or a state is governed.
2   A public profession concerning matters of government. Involving the acquisition of status and the exercise of power and authority.
3   Activities relating to the organisation of a state, relations between the state and other states, and between the state and its citizens.

The first definition, of course, relates to what we are all engaged in as students of politics. The second describes the public face of politics so often portrayed in the media: the personal rivalries, the adversarial 'knockabout' of prime minister's questions, the ambition, and the potential for sleaze and impropriety in high office. This second take on politics is at the heart of what the US satirist Ambrose Bierce meant when he mischievously defined politics as 'a means of livelihood effected by the more depraved portion of our criminal classes'.

However, it is the third definition of politics that is of most interest to you as you begin your studies. This is because it focuses on 'process' as opposed to 'personality': the bigger picture of how a state is organised and operates rather than the intrigue of day-to-day intra- and inter-party politics.

Politics as the art of conflict resolution

In adopting this third description as a working definition of politics we are essentially defining politics as the art of conflict resolution. It is accepted that conflict is an essential (by which we mean ever-present as opposed to desirable) feature of human existence. Such conflict may result from a number of interconnected factors:

➤ **Scarcity of resources** where certain goods are in short supply and conflict results from arguments over the distribution of the available resources.

➤ **Ideological differences** where individuals hold fundamentally different perspectives on the way in which society should be organised.

Concepts explained

Power

Power is the ability to do something or make something happen. It can be sub-divided into four forms.

➤ **Absolute power** is the unlimited ability to do as one wishes and this exists only in theory.

➤ **Persuasive power** is the ability to persuade others that a course of action is the right one.

➤ **Legitimate power** involves others accepting an individual's right to make decisions, perhaps as a result of an election.

➤ **Coercive power** means pressing others into complying using laws and penalties.

In a democracy, governments exercise legitimate power, with elements of persuasive and coercive power.

Authority

Authority is the right to take a particular course of action. The German sociologist Max Weber (1864–1920) identified three sources of authority:

➤ **Traditional authority** based on established traditions and customs).

➤ **Charismatic authority** based on the characteristics of leaders.

➤ **Legal-rational authority** granted by a formal process such as an election.

In the UK only parliament has the authority to make and unmake laws. This legal-rational authority is legitimised through free and fair elections.

Authority and power may be held independently of one another: a bomb-wielding terrorist may have power without authority; a teacher might have authority without genuine power; and a police officer in a tactical firearms unit may have power and authority.

> **Differences in approach** where individuals may share the same ideological perspective but adopt different approaches in seeking to achieve their common goals.
> **Divisions of labour and power** where individuals are unhappy about their own position within society and therefore seek to challenge the status quo.

The study of politics must therefore involve a focus on how the beliefs and interests of different groups in society are dealt with in a manner that is acceptable to the vast majority, if not to all. More precisely, it involves an examination of the way in which *power* is divided up between individuals, between individuals and the state and between the various institutions that make up the state. In essence then, our working definition of politics can be summed up in the title of Harold Laswell's 1936 book, *Politics: Who Gets What, When and How.*

A time of change

There were great changes in UK government and politics in the opening years of the twenty-first century. A decade that had dawned with fears that the so-called 'millennium bug' would bring civilisation to its knees gave way to the far more real threats posed by global recession and global terrorism.

New Labour continued its reforms, with the Human Rights Act and the Freedom of Information Act coming into force in October 2000 and January 2005 respectively. But the attacks of 9/11 and 7/7 actually led to far greater controls of individual liberties in the UK than had been the case at any time since the end of the Second World War. The Labour Party had entered government with a bang, following a landslide victory at the 1997 general election, and had gone on to win a historic third consecutive term in government in 2005. It left office with a whimper in 2010 amid accusations that it had mismanaged the nation's finances in the face of the most serious economic downturn since the Great Depression of the 1930s, and taken the nation into what many had come to regard as an 'unwinnable war' in Afghanistan.

The emergence of the Conservative–Lib Dem coalition government in the wake of the 2010 general election — the first coalition government in the UK since 1945 — served to reinforce the sense that this was a decade in which many of the assumptions upon which the study of UK government and politics had traditionally been based needed to be reassessed.

Exam specifications

The table below shows you how you can use this book in conjunction with the specifications of the three main UK awarding bodies: AQA, Edexcel and OCR.

Chapter	AQA	Edexcel	OCR
1 Democracy and participation	**AS Unit 1 (GOVP1)** Participation and voting behaviour	**AS Unit 1 (6GP01)** Democracy and political participation	**AS Unit 1 (F851)** [Implicit throughout unit but not as a core 'topic']
2 Elections and voting	**AS Unit 1 (GOVP1)** Participation and voting behaviour Electoral systems	**AS Unit 1 (6GP01)** Elections	**AS Unit 1 (F851)** Electoral systems and referenda UK parliamentary elections Voting behaviour in the UK
3 Political parties: structure	**AS Unit 1 (GOVP1)** Political parties	**AS Unit 1 (6GP01)** Party policies and ideas	**AS Unit 1 (F851)** Political parties (mandatory topic)
4 Political parties: policies and ideas	**AS Unit 1 (GOVP1)** Political parties	**AS Unit 1 (6GP01)** Party policies and ideas	**AS Unit 1 (F851)** Political parties (mandatory topic)
5 Pressure groups	**AS Unit 1 (GOVP1)** Pressure groups	**AS Unit 1 (6GP01)** Pressure groups	**AS Unit 1 (F851)** Pressure groups (mandatory topic)
6 The constitution	**AS Unit 2 (GOVP2)** The British constitution	**AS Unit 2 (6GP02)** The constitution	**AS Unit 2 (F852)** The constitution
7 Parliament	**AS Unit 2 (GOVP2)** Parliament	**AS Unit 2 (6GP02)** Parliament	**AS Unit 2 (F852)** The legislature (mandatory topic)
8 The prime minister and the core executive	**AS Unit 2 (GOVP2)** The core executive	**AS Unit 2 (6GP02)** The prime minister and cabinet	**AS Unit 2 (F852)** The executive (mandatory topic)
9 Judges and civil liberties	**AS Unit 2 (GOVP2)** The British constitution	**AS Unit 2 (6GP02)** Judges and civil liberties	**AS Unit 2 (F852)** The judiciary
10 Devolution and local government	**AS Unit 2 (GOVP2)** Multi-level governance	**AS Unit 2 (6GP02)** The constitution	**AS Unit 2 (F852)** The constitution
11 The European Union	**AS Unit 2 (GOVP2)** Multi-level governance	**AS Unit 2 (6GP02)** The constitution	**AS Unit 2 (F852)** The European Union

Acknowledgements
We would like to thank Kay Moxon for her helpful and constructive reviewing of the manuscript of this book.

Chapter 1

Democracy and participation

Key questions answered in this chapter

➤ What is democracy and what forms can it take?

➤ What is the difference between direct democracy and representative (or indirect) democracy?

➤ How effectively do citizens participate in politics in the UK?

➤ How democratic is the UK?

➤ What attempts have been made to enhance democracy and participation in the UK and how successful have they proven?

What is democracy?

Democracy is 'rule by the people' or 'people power'. The term has its origins in the Greek word *dēmokratia* — a union of *dēmos* (meaning 'the people') and *kratos* (meaning 'power'). Put simply, democratic systems of government give citizens a say in choosing the politicians, and in some cases even the policies, that will shape their everyday life.

However, this broad definition of democracy can cause problems, for while it is often used when referring to political systems such as those operating in the UK and the USA, it might also be said to apply to countries where the power of the people is channelled in a manner that some might consider to be 'undemocratic': for example, in 'single-party states' such as the former East Germany (German Democratic Republic) and North Korea (Democratic People's Republic of Korea). A further problem with the term 'democracy' is that the word *demos* could just as easily be translated as 'the mob', leaving democracy as little more than 'mobocracy', 'mob rule' or 'anarchy' (literally, 'no government').

Such confusion over the precise meaning and application of the term 'democracy' has resulted in a situation where it is now common to use the word not in isolation but rather prefixed with a 'qualifier' that serves to describe both the style of democracy in operation and the way in which it operates in practice. Thus we commonly refer to the UK not simply as a 'democracy', but as a **liberal democracy** or a 'representative democracy'.

Concepts explained

Liberal democracy Liberal democracy is a style of democracy incorporating free and fair elections with a belief in the importance of certain key rights and responsibilities.

Liberal democracies extend the right to vote (the franchise) widely among citizens.

They guarantee freedom of speech and allow the people to assemble and petition for the redress of grievances.

Key terms

➤ **Democracy** Rule by the people or 'people power'.

➤ **Liberal democracy** A style of democracy incorporating free and fair elections with a belief in the importance of certain key rights and responsibilities.

Direct democracy and representative democracy

Direct and representative democracy

Direct democracy

➤ Under a direct model of democracy, citizens are afforded a direct input into the policy-making process. In western democracies, a degree of direct democracy is often achieved through the use of referendums, where citizens are given the opportunity to vote on whether a specific proposal is adopted or rejected.

Representative democracy

➤ In a representative (or indirect) democracy, citizens elect representatives who enact laws on their behalf. Under the representative model there is no obligation on the part of those elected to seek further approval from citizens before they introduce new policies. Representatives are held accountable through the ballot box at the next election. They are therefore free to legislate independently once returned to office.

Direct democracy

Direct democracy is said to have its origins in classical Athens (*c.* 500 BC), where the city-state's 40,000 free men had the right to attend assembly meetings at which certain policies or actions could be approved or rejected. Attendance at such meetings was not compulsory, though a quorum of around 6,000 citizens was required on certain key votes.

Voting at the assembly is often said to have involved those present casting coloured stones into a clay urn in order to indicate their preference, with the vessel being broken apart and the stones counted at the end of the process. However, in reality most votes would have been conducted through a simple show of hands.

New England 'town hall meetings'

A more contemporary example of direct democracy in action would be the 'town hall meetings' still held in New England states such as Maine and Massachusetts in the USA. As was the case in ancient Athens, however, modern town hall democracy commonly operates on a small scale with hundreds or thousands involved as opposed to tens of thousands.

Representative democracy

It is clear that direct democracy in it purest sense is simply not practical in a modern state comprising millions of citizens. Even the Athenian model presented a problem for those counting hands at assembly meetings, and the form of direct democracy practised at New England town hall meetings is commonly limited to areas with eligible populations of under 10,000. As a result, most modern democracies practise an 'indirect' or **representative** form of democracy.

Edmund Burke summed up what many see as the essence of representative democracy in Britain in a speech he made to his Bristol constituents in 1774: 'Your representative owes you not his industry only but his judgement,' Burke argued, 'and he betrays you if he sacrifices it to your opinion.'

The Burkean view, therefore, is that citizens elect individuals to represent them in a legislature and that such individuals are expected to represent the interests of their constituents until the following election. Crucially, however, they are not simply delegates sent with specific instructions or orders to follow. As a result, our elected representatives might at times make decisions that are contrary to our wishes.

Viewpoint Is representative democracy desirable?

YES
- Elected representatives are often better educated and more articulate than the general public.
- They have access to relevant research and are able to educate themselves on the merits and demerits of a particular course of action before casting their vote in parliament.
- Representative democracy allows parliament to implement policies that are necessary but unpopular — the kinds of things that would not secure support if put to a public ballot.
- Representative government allows for 'joined-up government' where individual policies are decided not in isolation but with full consideration of potential knock-on effects for other areas of policy.

NO
- Elected representatives often enjoy lengthy terms in office (up to 5 years in the case of UK MPs), meaning that they cannot easily be held publicly accountable for the decisions they make.
- Many MPs simply toe the party line and do as the whips tell them, rather than thinking for themselves and/or representing the interests of their constituents.
- Representative democracy limits the opportunities for popular participation between elections. It is also said to contribute to political apathy.
- Representative democracy has a tendency towards elitism, where those returned to the legislature are drawn from a narrow range of social backgrounds and those from different backgrounds or with less centrist views are not properly heard.

Key terms

➤ **Direct democracy** Where citizens are given a direct input into the decision-making process.
➤ **Representative democracy** Where citizens elect representatives to formulate legislation and take other decisions on their behalf.

Referendums

As we have seen, direct democracy in its purest form is impossible to achieve on a large scale in a modern democratic state — yet orthodox representative democracy can all too easily become remote and unresponsive to the needs of citizens. It is this paradox that has led many democratic states to employ elements of direct democracy, while holding to the representative model.

The classic modern tool of direct democracy is the **referendum**. Outside of the UK, referendums are used to resolve a wide range of issues. In Eire, for example, a 1995 referendum legalised divorce, whereas in Switzerland, where they average around four referendums per year, the people approved a decision to join the United Nations by 55% to 45% in 2002.

Key term

➤ **Referendum** A vote on a single issue put to a public ballot by the government of the day. Referendums offer a degree of direct democracy. They are generally framed in the form of a simple 'yes/no' question. They are rarely used in the UK but are employed more widely in countries such as Switzerland. UK-wide referendums have been promised before the UK adopts the euro and the coalition government has promised a referendum in May 2011 on the alternative vote for Westminster elections.

Distinguish between

Referendums and initiatives

Referendums

➤ Regular referendums are called by those in power either when they want to legitimise a certain course of action or where they are constitutionally required to hold a referendum due to the nature of the proposed changes. In a referendum, matters such as the question which is to be put to the public ballot are left largely in the hands of elected politicians.

Initiatives

➤ Initiatives give ordinary citizens the opportunity to call a public ballot on a question of their own choosing, often by collecting a predetermined number of signatures on a petition and thereby triggering a referendum. Many US states allow such ballot initiatives, and although not all of these measures pass into law, many do. For example, California's Proposition 8 (2008) banned same-sex marriage and an initiative proposed in 2010 aimed to legalise cannabis (see Box 1.1). Many other countries have similar provisions in their constitutions. In New Zealand, for example, the Citizen's Initiated Referenda Act (1993) required support of only 10% of the electorate for a non-binding referendum to be initiated.

Box 1.1 The initiative process in California

In order to qualify for a public vote on changing a regular law in California, petitions must secure a number of signatures equal to at least 5% of the total number of votes cast for state governor at the previous election. In 2010 the target was 433,971 signatures.

On 24 March 2010, an initiative proposing the Regulate, Control and Tax Cannabis Act of 2010 received enough signatures to qualify it for the November 2010 ballot.

This proposal would make it legal for those over the age of 21 to possess, cultivate and transport cannabis for personal use as well as allowing local governments to regulate and tax the commercial production and sale of cannabis.

Viewpoint Do referendums enhance democracy?

- Referendums offer a more direct form of democracy. They encourage participation by allowing citizens to have a real input into key decisions that matter to them.
- They provide a way of focusing or renewing the mandate on a particular issue or legitimising major constitutional changes.
- They can prevent dangerous divisions within political parties over controversial issues. This prevents governments from collapsing and thereby provides for greater continuity in government.
- They could be used to provide a clear and final answer where parliament is deadlocked.
- They can provide a means by which tricky moral questions are resolved.

- Referendums are inconsistent with representative democracy and undermine the doctrine of parliamentary sovereignty.
- They can result in a 'tyranny of the majority' or even a tyranny of a very organised minority, where turnout is low.
- Excessive use of referendums can result in voter fatigue and declining turnout.
- Most issues are too complicated to be condensed into a simple 'yes/no' question.
- Different levels of funding and media access between the 'yes' and 'no' camps might mean that the referendum is not played out on a level playing field.
- Governments can schedule referendums and phrase questions in a way that makes a favourable result more likely.
- Decisions are not always considered final. Governments sometimes go back again and again until they get the result that they want.

Referendums and the UK system of government

Are referendums compatible with the UK system of government? In the 1940s, the then prime minister Clement Attlee described referendums as 'a tool of demagogues and dictators', concluding that the referendum was 'a device so alien to all our traditions'. It seems appropriate, therefore, to use his words as a way of providing a starting point for our discussion.

'A tool of dictators and demagogues'

Attlee's first criticism was firmly rooted in the age in which he was writing. Whereas recent years have witnessed the rise of referendums in the UK as a means by which a government's mandate can be renewed or focused, Attlee would have been more familiar with the way in which totalitarian leaders such as Adolf Hitler had employed such devices as a means of legitimising courses of action that (a) had already been determined and (b) were clearly not democratic. However, even in the modern era there is an argument that referendums can result in a kind of tyranny of the majority, and that the majority in question may be ill-equipped to understand precisely what is being asked of them.

'A device so alien to all our traditions'

Attlee's second criticism can be interpreted in a number of ways. Taken literally, it was simply a statement of reality — the fact that referendums were simply not a feature of the UK political landscape in the 1940s, when Attlee was writing, or for that matter in the 1950s or 1960s. However, the comment also hints at a deeper meaning: the notion that the UK is essentially a 'representative' as opposed to a 'direct' democracy.

As we have seen, under the representative model of democracy — sometimes referred to as the 'trustee' or 'Burkean' model — MPs are elected to represent the interests of constituents to the best of their ability. Crucially, however, those who represent us at Westminster are not simply delegates — issued with instructions outlining the way in which they are expected to act in the legislature. MPs are instead expected to apply their judgement to the questions of the day and be prepared to go against the will of the people where they judge a particular course of action to be in the broader interests of those whom they serve. While individual MPs are ultimately held accountable to their constituents at election time, the majority party is generally seen as being free to use its mandate in seeking to bring into law those policies it set out in its election manifesto. The doctrine of parliamentary sovereignty ensures that no further authority need be sought from the general public before these measures are brought on to the statute books. Within a representative democracy, therefore, referendums would appear to be at best unnecessary and at worst unhelpful.

The UK experience

While the UK still has no formal list of circumstances in which referendums are legally required, it has long been accepted that referendums might provide a way of legitimising major constitutional changes. In the nineteenth century, A. V. Dicey referred to the referendum as a kind of 'people's veto', and modern UK leaders such as the former prime minister Tony Blair have largely accepted this premise: 'in the case of major constitutional change,' Blair remarked in 1995, 'there is clearly a case for that decision to be taken by the British people'. It is no surprise, therefore, that the programme of constitutional reform embarked upon by New Labour in 1997 resulted in as many referendums being held in the party's first 2 years in office as had taken place in total up to that juncture.

Although the public reaction to the increased prevalence of referendums in recent years has been largely positive, the UK experience of referendums thus far has highlighted a number of problems. They are divided here into five broad categories: topic; wording; timing; funding; and turnout.

Topic

At the time of writing in 2010, there had only been one UK-wide referendum, the ballot held on continued membership of the EEC (now the European Union) in 1975, although the whole UK has since been promised votes ahead of electoral reform, the proposed UK adoption of the euro and, more recently, the ratification of the EU Constitution. Whereas referendums in other parts of the world have been held on issues ranging from the legal status of marijuana to the rights of aborigines, all nine referendums sanctioned by the UK Parliament since 1973 (see Table 1.1) have related directly to the distribution of power between supranational, national and subnational institutions.

Whereas such changes inevitably fall within the definition of 'major constitutional reform' identified by Blair, it is noteworthy that other equally significant changes, such as reform of the House of Lords, have not been legitimised by a public vote. The sense remains, therefore, that governments are inclined to offer referendums only on those issues where they have a direct interest in doing so, or where they are relatively certain of the outcome. This was certainly a criticism levelled at Harold Wilson's decision to go to the people in 1975 over continued membership of the EEC, an issue on which his Labour administration was deeply divided.

Although Margaret Thatcher's reaction to that vote — declaring that referendums served only to 'sacrifice parliamentary sovereignty to political expediency' — is better applied to that one referendum than in general terms, the problem of precisely what

Table 1.1 UK referendums, 1973–2007

Date	Who voted	Question (paraphrased)	% yes	% no	% turnout
1973 (Mar.)	N Ireland	Should NI stay in the UK?	98.9	1.1	58.1
1975 (June)	UK	Should UK stay in the EEC?	67.2	32.8	63.2
1979 (Mar.)	Scotland	Should there be a Scottish Parliament?	51.6	48.4	63.8
1979 (Mar.)	Wales	Should there be a Welsh Parliament?	20.3	79.7	58.3
1997 (Sept.)	Scotland	Should there be a Scottish Parliament?	74.3	25.7	60.4
		With tax-varying powers?	63.5	36.5	
1997 (Sept.)	Wales	Should there be a Welsh Assembly?	50.3	49.7	50.1
1998 (May)	London	A London mayor and London Assembly?	72.0	28.0	34.0
1998 (May)	N Ireland	Approval for the Good Friday Agreement	71.1	28.9	81.0
2004 (Nov.)	North East	A regional assembly for the North East?	22.0	78.0	48.0

kinds of issue require a referendum in the UK is hard to resolve. Most other countries have codified constitutions that clearly set out the circumstances in which a referendum must be held, or at least leave the decision to a supreme court. However, in the UK, such decisions are entirely left to the whim of the party in office, as seen in 2008 with the decision not to offer a referendum in respect of the Lisbon Treaty.

Wording

The precise form of words presented to the public in a referendum can also prove controversial. The wording of the 1975 referendum on whether or not the UK should remain in the EEC was said to have been phrased in such a way as to encourage a positive response. Critics of referendums also criticise the way in which the precise details of the proposal are arrived at: for example, the decision to offer the Welsh an 'assembly' with 'secondary legislative powers' in 1997, while at the same time offering the possibility of a Scottish 'parliament' with 'primary legislative' and 'tax-varying powers'.

Although the Electoral Commission was granted the authority to comment on the intelligibility of questions posed in all future referendums under the 2000 Political Parties, Elections and Referendums Act — see Box 1.2 — the then deputy prime minister, John Prescott, was quick to confirm that the government (through its control of parliament) would retain the final say.

Box 1.2 The Electoral Commission's Question Assessment Guidelines

➤ The question should prompt an immediate response.

➤ Words and phrases used in the question should not have positive or negative connotations.

➤ Words and phrases used in the question should not lead voters in a particular direction.

➤ Words and phrases used in the question should not be loaded.

➤ The question should not contain 'jargon'.

➤ The language used in the question should be consistent.

➤ Words and phrases used in the question should reflect the language used and understood by the voter.

➤ The question should not provide more information than is necessary to answer the question meaningfully.

➤ The question should not be longer than necessary.

➤ The question should be well structured.

Source: Electoral Commission.

Timing

When considering the issue of timing, critics of referendums often highlight the possibility of ballots being scheduled close to events that might skew the result in favour of the outcome desired by the government of the day. However, the reality in recent years has been somewhat different: namely, that the New Labour administrations in office between 1997 and 2010 singularly failed to schedule those referendums promised. For example, although Tony Blair was clearly a supporter of UK entry into the euro, the lack of support among the broader public meant that the referendum promised in the run-up to the 1997 general election did not take place thereafter. While the need to meet the EU's 'convergence criteria' was initially offered in explanation of this failure to name a date for the ballot, there has been little progress in the last decade — even when the criteria were largely met, for a time, and other countries were allowed to 'work around' the various tests and enter the Eurozone.

Funding

In past referendums, concerns have been raised over the different levels of funding available to the 'yes' and 'no' camps. This was certainly true of the campaigns surrounding the 1975 referendum on EEC membership, where the 'yes' camp was said to have outspent the 'no' camp by 3 to 1.

Again, such concerns were addressed by the report of Lord Neill's Committee on Standards in Public Life (1998) and by the subsequent creation of the Electoral Commission. Under the Political Parties, Elections and Referendums Act (2000), future referendums in the UK should be state funded, with the 'yes' and 'no' campaigns each receiving a £600,000 public grant.

Turnout

The paradox of referendums is that, while such devices are championed as a means of encouraging political participation and enhancing legitimacy, turnout at UK referendums is often very low, bringing both of these stated goals into question. Though the latter problem can be addressed by the application of thresholds (i.e. by requiring a fixed percentage of the electorate to give a 'yes' vote, as opposed to a majority of those turning out), such artificial hurdles can create problems of their own; as seen in the Scottish devolution referendum in 1979. The reality is stark. Turnout at the nine referendums called by the Westminster Parliament has averaged just 57.5% — almost 2% below the level reached at the 2001 general election. While low turnout at referendums is disappointing in itself, the problem is made worse still when the results in such referendums are marginal. The Welsh devolution referendum of September 1997 is a case in point, with only 50.3% of the 50.1% who turned out favouring the establishment of the National Assembly of Wales.

Local referendums

While attention understandably often focuses on the nine referendums called by the Westminster Parliament between 1973 and 2004, we should not ignore the increasing use of such devices at local level since the 1990s, both in approving structural changes to the local government in some areas and in seeking to authorise policies such as the congestion charge.

Establishing directly elected mayors

The Greater London Authority, comprising a directly elected mayor of London and a 25-member assembly, was established following a regional referendum in the capital in 1998. Since then there have been more than 30 separate referendums on the question of whether or not to establish directly elected local mayors in places as distant as the Isle of White and Hartlepool.

The election of the Hartlepool FC mascot, H'Angus the Monkey (otherwise known as Stuart Drummond) as mayor of Hartlepool in 2002 brought widespread criticism. How, it was argued, could an individual initially campaigning on a platform of giving free bananas to schoolchildren be placed in charge of a £106 million municipal budget? However, Drummond's performance in office and subsequent re-election in 2005 and 2009 led many to reconsider their position.

H'Angus the Monkey, otherwise known as Stuart Drummond

Although turnout at some of these local mayoral referendums has caused concern — ranging between 10% and 64% — the widespread use of such public polls has clearly added to the sense that referendums are now part of the UK's democratic architecture.

Congestion charges

The congestion charge initiative originated with central government, but it was largely left to local authorities to adopt and implement. Whereas the first mayor of London, Ken Livingstone, used his

Table 1.2 Congestion charge referendums

Year	Place	Turnout	'Yes'	'No'
2005	Edinburgh	61.7%	25.6%	74.4%
2008	Manchester	53.2%	21.2%	78.8%

considerable executive powers over London transport to introduce the charge in the capital, efforts to do so in Edinburgh (2005) and in Manchester (2008) involved seeking public approval for the introduction of such charges through a local referendum (see Table 1.2).

While some regard the holding of these referendums and the resounding 'no' votes that resulted as a welcome exercise of 'pure democracy' or 'people power', others have been more circumspect. In the case of Edinburgh, the cost of developing the proposals rejected in the referendum was estimated at £9 million — a considerable sum of money simply to write off on the basis of what may well have been a knee-jerk reaction to the prospect of paying a new 'tax'. The rejection of charges in Manchester appeared to have

Box 1.3 **Public confusion over the congestion charge**

Ali Abbas from Manchester Friends of the Earth group said, 'I'm disappointed at a missed opportunity. It was a great chance for us to make a huge improvement to our transport and to help to tackle greenhouse emissions. When we asked people why they wouldn't vote for it they told us that 'we won't vote for it because the transport is so bad'. But our argument was 'if you vote for it, the transport will get better'.

Source: 'C-charge: a resounding "NO"', *Manchester Evening News*, 12 December 2008.

been prompted by similar concerns — particularly an unwillingness to pay the charge before the public transport infrastructure was in place (see Box 1.3).

In both Edinburgh and Manchester, the 'no' votes effectively prevented the improvements in transport infrastructure that those on all sides of the funding argument accepted were necessary. In the case of Manchester, the 'no' vote was particularly significant as the transport secretary Geoff Hoon had already conceded that there was 'no Plan B' for improving transport infrastructure in the city. As Lord Peter Smith, chairman of the Greater Manchester Authorities, commented to the *Manchester Evening News*, the result was 'very clear...this is not just a vote "no" for congestion charging, it is a vote "no" to improvements on the trams, railways and buses and there will now be no improvements'.

Should the UK use more referendums or provide for initiatives?

Despite the promise of a number of referendums in recent years, the vast majority of English people in 2010 who were under the age of 50 had never had the opportunity to vote in a major UK referendum. The nine referendums called by the Westminster Parliament between 1973 and 2010 focused on an extraordinarily narrow range of issues. The way in which such ballots have been conducted and the low levels of turnout witnessed have raised issues of legitimacy that go beyond simply questioning whether or not such devices are compatible with our representative democracy.

However, while there is no great clamour for the adoption of the kind of **initiative** process seen in many US states and in some European countries, public support for the wider use of referendums appears to be increasing. This greater public acceptance of referendums, allied to the prospect of further constitutional reform, makes it likely that such devices will be used, or at least offered, a good deal more in the coming years.

Should the UK allow recalls of elected officials?

A **recall** election is a procedure that allows registered voters to petition for a public vote to remove an elected official from office before the end of his or her term. In most cases,

Key terms

➢ **Initiative** A process by which citizens can call a referendum, normally by collecting a predetermined number of signatures on a petition.

➢ **Recall** A device that allows citizens to unseat an elected official before the end of their term in office.

> ### Box 1.4 Recalls in California
>
> In the US state of California, a recall of a state-wide official such as the governor would require a number of signatures equal to at least 12% of the total votes cast in the last election for the office in question. Those organising the 2003 recall of California governor Gray Davis claimed that the Democrat had 'mismanaged state finances', 'threatened public safety by cutting services' and been 'slacking off' in his job, having allegedly 'gone two years without calling a cabinet meeting'.
>
> Source: P. Fairclough, 'Direct democracy in the USA: referendums, initiatives and recalls', *Politics Review*, vol. 13, no. 4, April 2004.

recalls are permitted only where there is evidence of corruption, negligence or, in some cases, incompetence. Although recalls have not traditionally been available to voters in the UK, the 2009 MPs' expenses scandal led to calls for the introduction of such a system.

The right to recall elected officials is available to citizens in around one in three US states, although successful recalls are relatively rare. One reason for this is that recall petitions normally have to secure the support of a predetermined number of votes before they can qualify for a ballot (see Box 1.4).

Problems with recalls

Although the recall process can make politicians more accountable to voters, it also undermines the principle of representative democracy. For example, when the 'Recall Gray Davies' campaign was launched in California in February 2003 (see Table 1.3), the Democrat governor was only weeks into his second term in office, having been convincingly re-elected the previous November. There was even evidence that the campaign had been organised and funded by disgruntled Republicans.

Table 1.3 The 2003 California gubernatorial recall and subsequent special election

Recall of Gray Davies		Votes	% vote
'For'		4,536,262	55.3%
'Against'		3,668,076	44.7%
Votes for new governor (top 5 candidates of 135)			
A. Schwarzenegger	Republican	3,850,804	48.7%
C. M. Bustamante	Democrat	2,504,481	31.7%
T. McClintock	Republican	1,053,907	13.4%
P. M. Camejo	Green	218,843	2.8%
A. Huffington	Independent	44,200	0.6%

Source: P. Fairclough, 'Direct democracy in the USA: referendums, initiatives and recalls', *Politics Review*, vol. 13, no. 4, April 2004.

Political culture and participation

What is political culture?

The nature of political participation within a given state will be influenced, in part, by the prevailing **political culture**.

> ### Concepts explained
>
> **Political culture** The ideas, beliefs and attitudes that shape political behaviour within a given area. It describes the way in which citizens collectively view the political system and their status and role within it.

Political culture and participation in the UK

UK political culture was traditionally said to be defined by three characteristics:

➤ **Homogeneity** — the belief that citizens shared a common heritage and identity; a sense of togetherness that transcended what divided them.

➤ **Consensus** — where UK citizens accepted the basic 'rules of the game'. These rules include the need for toleration, pragmatism, peaceful negotiation and compromise.

➤ **Deference** — the idea that people deferred to an elite that was regarded as being 'born to rule', that there was a natural willingness to accept an ingrained, class-based inequality and a rigid social hierarchy.

Such defining features were said to favour certain, perhaps more passive, forms of political participation. For example, one would hardly expect to see high levels of direct action in a society where most citizens shared a common view of what was needed, accepted the rules of the game and were deferential towards those holding positions of authority.

In the second half of the twentieth century, however, UK political culture underwent something of a transformation. Successive waves of immigration, the rise of Scottish and Welsh nationalism, and the decline of the Church of England all played their part in creating a situation in which the UK was increasingly said to be characterised more by multiculturalism than by homogeneity. At the same time, the postwar consensus broke down in the 1970s with the rise of politicians such as Margaret Thatcher. In recent years, this decline in consensus has been reflected in the proliferation of single-issue campaigns, the rise of direct action and increased support for nationalist parties. It is probably also fair to say that the UK has become a less deferential society. Where the power of the ruling elite was once perpetuated by the veil of secrecy and mystery that surrounded it, the rise of modern, less deferential media has done much to demystify such individuals and institutions. Unthinking deference towards the ruling elite has, as a result, declined significantly.

Political participation in the UK

Political participation can be broadly categorised into its electoral and non-electoral forms.

Electoral participation

Those who are eligible and registered to vote in a given election are referred to collectively as the electorate. Under the Representation of the People Act (1969), the **franchise** was extended to virtually all citizens aged 18 or over. The effect of this Act and other changes dating back to the Great Reform Act (1832) was significantly to increase the number of individuals eligible to vote.

➤ In 1831, only 5% of adults were able to vote. This represented 450,000 individuals from a population of around 25 million.

➤ By 1969, 99% of adults were able to vote. This represented around 40 million individuals from a population of 58 million.

Key terms
➤ **Franchise** The franchise is the right to vote as established by parliamentary statute. The vast majority of adult UK citizens have the right to vote. Exceptions include current members of the House of Lords, those convicted of offences relating to elections, and those detained in secure mental health facilities or prison. The franchise was extended significantly with the Representation of the People Act (1969), which reduced the voting age from 21 to 18.
➤ **Political participation** Collectively refers to the range of ways in which citizens can involve themselves in the political process.

In the UK, voters are legally required to register to vote. Around 95% of the voting age population (VAP) were registered to vote ahead of the 2005 general election. One should remember, however, that British citizens living abroad also retain the right to vote. In addition, not all of the UK VAP is entitled to vote. For example, you cannot vote in parliamentary elections if you are:
➤ a European Union citizen from an EU country other than the UK or Ireland, although European citizens can vote in European Parliament elections and local elections in any EU country in which they are living
➤ a member of the House of Lords
➤ a convicted criminal serving a custodial sentence
➤ convicted of a corrupt or illegal electoral practice
➤ suffering from a severe mental illness

Turnout
One of the most obvious ways in which an individual can participate in a political system is to vote. Levels of **turnout** are, therefore, one important measure of political participation (see Table 1.4).

Key term
➤ **Turnout** The percentage of registered voters who cast a ballot in a given election.

Table 1.4 General election turnout, 1945–2005

Year	%	Year	%	Year	%	Year	%
1945	72.8	1964	77.1	1979	76.0	2001	59.4
1950	83.9	1966	75.8	1983	72.7	2005	61.4
1951	82.6	1970	72.0	1987	75.3	2010	65.1
1955	76.8	1974 (Feb.)	78.8	1992	77.7		
1959	78.7	1974 (Oct.)	72.8	1997	71.4		

Low turnout is a problem because it brings into question the government's **legitimacy** and the strength of its electoral **mandate**. In 2005, for example, the Labour Party secured a Commons majority of 65 with the support of only 35.2% of the 61.4% of eligible voters who turned out to vote. This was equivalent to 21.6% of the electorate.

When considering turnout one should, however, remember three things. First, the national turnout figure masks massive regional variations. In the 2001 general election, for example, independent Dr Richard Taylor won on a 68.0% turnout in Wyre Forest, despite a record low turnout of only 59.4% nationwide. Similarly, although the national turnout in 2010 was 65.1%, there was a significant gulf between the highest constituency turnout (77.3% in East Renfrewshire) and the lowest (44.3% in Manchester Central). This variation is referred to as **differential turnout**. Turnout also varies significantly according to age and social class.

Concepts explained

Legitimacy The legal right or authority to exercise power. A government claims legitimacy as a result of the mandate it secures at a general election.

Mandate The right of the governing party to pursue the policies it sets out in its general election manifesto.

➤ The doctrine of the mandate gives the governing party the authority to pursue its stated policies but does not require it to do so or prevent it from introducing proposals not included in its manifesto.

➤ In its 1997 general election manifesto, New Labour promised both to remove the rights of hereditary peers to sit and vote in the House of Lords and to move towards a more democratic and more representative second chamber. It largely delivered on the first of these pledges with the House of Lords Act (1999).

Differential turnout Where the national turnout figure recorded at a given election masks differences in turnout by constituency or by region. A number of factors might account for differential turnout:

➤ how marginal an individual seat or election is (is there a chance to make a real change?)
➤ the electoral system in operation (do people think that their vote will count?)
➤ local or national issues and controversies
➤ the 'intensity' of the campaign
➤ media attention (lesser or greater media activity in one constituency or in a given election may affect turnout)

Second, turnout varies considerably according to variables such as age, gender, social class and ethnicity. Older voters, women, those in higher social classes and Caucasian voters are statistically more likely to turn out and vote. For example, only 44% of eligible voters in the 18–24 age category cast a ballot at the 2010 general election, compared to the 76% turnout figure recorded for the over-65s. At the same election, just 57% of those in the DE social classes cast a ballot, compared to a 76% turnout in the AB categories.

Third, turnout varies significantly between different types of election. So-called 'second order' elections such as local elections and elections to the European Parliament often witness far lower levels of turnout than general elections (see Table 1.5).

What factors might account for variable turnout?

➤ **Type of election.** Voters are more likely to turn out to vote when they value the institutions to which individuals are seeking to be elected. This may account for the relatively low levels of turnout witnessed at local elections.

➤ **Political apathy or disengagement.** The POWER Report suggested that increasing numbers of voters were coming to the conclusion that elections made little difference, particularly where the main UK political parties were seen to be converging ideologically.

➤ **'Hapathy'.** A proportion of those who abstain do so because they are happy with the status quo and do not, therefore, feel the need to cast a ballot.

➤ **The relative value of a vote.** Those living in safe seats may feel that there is little point in their voting because the result is already a foregone conclusion. Those in marginal seats may be more likely to turn out and cast a ballot.

➤ **The electoral system in operation.** Some voters may be more inclined to cast a ballot where they think that their vote will be counted. Some argue that turnout would be higher at UK general elections if they were contested under a proportional electoral system as opposed to a 'winner-takes-all' system such as first-past-the-post.

Table 1.5 Turnout at UK elections, 2005–09

Election	Year	Turnout (%)
General	2010	65.1
General	2005	61.4
European Parliament	2009	34.5
Scottish Parliament	2007	52.4
Welsh Assembly	2007	43.5
Northern Ireland Assembly	2007	62.3
Greater London Assembly	2008	44.5
London mayor	2008	44.6
English local	2009	39.2
London boroughs	2006	39.5
Metropolitan boroughs	2008	34.1
County councils	2009	35.0
Unitary councils	2009	41.4
Shire district councils	2009	39.0
Scottish unitary councils	2007	52.8
Welsh unitary councils	2008	44.8
Northern Irish district councils	2005	62.8

Source: Edmund Tetteh and Richard Cracknell, *Turnout*, House of Commons Standard Note SN/SG/2633.

Key term

➤ **Political apathy** A state of passivity or indifference towards political institutions and their associated processes, linked to a decline in political participation.

➤ **The role of the mass media.** Intense media coverage can have the effect of stimulating turnout in a particular election or constituency, particularly where polling published in the media appears to suggest that the contest is close and every vote might matter.

Distinguish between

Political apathy and 'hapathy'

Political apathy

➤ Political apathy is a state of passivity or indifference which is often linked to low turnout in elections. Although passivity need not necessarily carry negative connotations, apathy is generally seen as something that can have a corrosive effect on democracy.

'Hapathy'

➤ Hapathy is the idea that voters may abstain from voting as a result of happiness with (as opposed to indifference towards) the way in which they are being governed. Research conducted on behalf of the Electoral Commission in 2005 showed that 29% of those who described themselves as 'satisfied with democracy' did not cast a vote at the 2005 general election whereas 59% who were 'dissatisfied with democracy' still turned out.

Weblinks

www.parliament.uk/commons/lib/research/rp2005/RP05-033.pdf — a research paper on the 2005 general election, including evidence on political participation: turnout, candidacy, etc.

Non-electoral participation

Studies of political participation often focus on electoral participation defined in narrow terms: that is, electoral turnout. If we adopt a more inclusive definition of electoral participation, we might include other activities: for example,

Tony Foggon/Alamy

➤ **Canvassing and leafleting.** Large numbers of volunteers are mobilised at grassroots level in support of each party's election campaign. While some of these individuals are paid-up members of the party they are working for, many are not.

➤ **Organising election events and fundraising activities.** Most election campaigns are funded locally, the major exception being those in marginal constituencies at general elections.

Key term

➤ **Canvassing** Where local party activists go from door to door in an effort to assess (i.e. canvass) the strength of support and win over floating voters.

Although the Political Parties, Elections and Referendums Act (2000) imposed a £30,000 per-constituency spending limit on candidates at general elections, it is generally up to local activists to raise the funds needed by collecting donations from local party backers and organising fundraising events in support of their chosen candidate.

➤ **Staffing campaign offices.** Every candidate is required to name an election agent (or 'official agent'). This individual acts as 'campaign manager', liaising with the returning officer in the constituency and managing the official records of campaign revenue and expenditure. The major parties often employ professional election agents, whereas independent candidates and those representing smaller parties tend to rely on a volunteer to perform this role, or even act as their own agent. The agent manages the candidate's campaign team — those who staff the campaign office in the run-up to the campaign and perform specific roles on election day. This team includes counting agents and party 'tellers' who stand outside polling stations in an effort to gauge support for their chosen party on the day of the election, thereby allowing their preferred candidate to target their 'get-out-the-vote' strategies.

It is also important to remember that there are many forms of non-electoral participation: for example,

➤ **Writing to one's elected representatives or meeting with them in person.** MPs are expected to work as advocates for constituents facing particular difficulties. Constituents may write to their MP asking for advice or support in relation to a particular problem, or seek to meet the MP in person. Although many MPs do not live in the constituencies they represent in parliament, most take the time to hold surgeries at their constituency offices. For example, while the Respect MP for Bethnal Green and Bow, George Galloway, was widely criticised for spending several weeks in the Big Brother House in 2006, he routinely held a weekly surgery at his constituency office in London.

➤ **Having an ongoing membership of and/or involvement in a political party.** While the memberships of the main UK political parties have fallen significantly in recent years (see Table 1.6), such organisations still provide a significant avenue for political participation. Even those who are not themselves a member of a political party may attend meetings organised by a party, and some parties actively seek to involve non-members when selecting their parliamentary candidates. This was seen with the Conservatives' use of an open primary in Totnes in 2009 and their use of open selection meetings in many other constituencies ahead of the 2010 general election.

➤ **Engaging in political protest or organised pressure group activity.** As party memberships have fallen, so involvement in pressure group activity of all shades has risen. There has been a particular increase in less formal, protest activity and in ethical, consumer-based campaigns.

Is there a participation crisis in the UK?

There has been a great deal of debate about the alleged **participation crisis** in the UK since the historically low levels of turnout at the 2001 and 2005 general elections. Some commentators have highlighted other areas where political participation has declined, such as falling party membership.

The POWER report

Although it was criticised at the time for the fact that its conclusions did not appear to be based squarely on empirical evidence, the 2006 **POWER inquiry** probably still offers us the most accessible recent snapshot of political participation in the UK.

Key terms

➤ **Participation crisis** The view that declining levels of political participation in the UK threaten to undermine its democratic systems.

➤ **POWER inquiry** An inquiry into the state of political participation in the UK initiated by the Joseph Rowntree Trust. The inquiry resulted in the publication of the POWER report: *Power to the People: The Report of POWER — An Independent Inquiry into Britain's Democracy*. The report's main conclusion was that the popular disillusionment with democratic institutions and the main political parties demanded immediate attention.

The changing nature of political participation

Recent years have witnessed a move away from traditional forms of participation, such as voting and party membership, towards membership of mainstream pressure groups and involvement in protest movements, consumer campaigns and direct action. This participatory shift was recognised by the POWER inquiry (see Boxes 1.5 and 1.6).

Weblinks

www.parliament.uk/commons/lib/research/briefings/snpc-03948.pdf — a short set of briefing notes on the POWER inquiry.

www.powerinquiry.org — the official POWER inquiry site with links to the POWER report in pdf.

Box 1.5 Declining participation in formal politics

The area of decline is in formal politics: turnout for general elections has declined very significantly since 1997; turnout for other elections has remained stubbornly low for years; party membership and allegiance has declined very severely over the last thirty years; elected representatives are held in very low esteem and widely distrusted. POWER's own research and experience over the last eighteen months has established that the level of alienation felt towards politicians, the main political parties and the key institutions of the political system is extremely high and widespread.

Source: *Power to the People: The Report of POWER — An Independent Inquiry into Britain's Democracy*, 2006 (executive summary)

Box 1.6 Increased participation in pressure groups and political protest

Contrary to much of the public debate around political disengagement, the British public are not apathetic. There is now a great deal of research evidence to show that very large numbers of citizens are engaged in community and charity work outside of politics. There is also clear evidence that involvement in pressure politics — such as signing petitions, supporting consumer boycotts, joining campaign groups — has been growing significantly for many years. In addition, research shows that interest in 'political issues' is high.

Source: **Power to the People: The Report of POWER — An Independent Inquiry into Britain's Democracy**, 2006 (executive summary)

Although such changes in participation were already well under way by 2000, they gathered pace after this, with low turnouts in the 2001, 2005 and 2010 general elections and a rise in 'the politics of protest' over fuel duty, fox hunting, globalisation and the war in Iraq.

Declining party membership

The sharp decline in individual party membership in the last 30 years has been matched by the steep rise in pressure group membership. In 2009, for example, the Royal Society for the Protection of Birds (RSPB) had more than twice as many members as the three main UK political parties combined (see Table 1.6 and Box 1.7). Indeed, whereas membership of the main UK parties continued to spiral downwards during the first decade of the twenty-first century, the RSPB's membership increased by 130,000 in the year 2008–09 alone. Thus, as Noreena Hertz remarked in the *Independent* back in 2001, 'It's not about apathy': 'while voting is waning, alternative forms of political expression…are all on the rise.'

In his 2009 book, *Trust: How We Lost it and How to Get it Back*, Blair's biographer Anthony Seldon made the link between declining levels of public trust in formal politics and this decline in party membership. While it is difficult to prove that such a causal link exists, this line of reasoning appears plausible in light of the

Table 1.6 Individual party membership (000s)

Year	Conservative	Labour	Liberal Democrat
1951	2,900	876	–
1983	1,200	295	145*
1987	1,000	289	138*
1992	500	280	101
1997	400	405	87
2001	311	272	73
2005	300	198	73
2008	250	166	60

*SDP–Liberal Alliance.

Source: John Marshall, **Membership of UK Political Parties**, House of Commons Library, 2009.

Box 1.7 The Royal Society for the Protection of Birds

➤ Over 1.2 million members.

➤ A staff of over 1,300 and over 8,800 volunteers.

➤ An income of over £50 million per year.

➤ A UK headquarters, three national offices and nine regional offices.

➤ A local network of 175 local groups and more than 110 youth groups.

anecdotal evidence compiled by the POWER inquiry. It might also be argued that the loss of trust identified by Seldon is one aspect of the declining deference identified earlier in this chapter.

The rise of consumer campaigns

As well as the growth in more conventional pressure group activity, in the last two decades there has also been a significant increase in the number of individuals involved in politically motivated consumer boycotts, social movements and other kinds of less formal political participation. For example, recent research has demonstrated that the percentage of individuals who have boycotted products for ethical reasons rose from 4% in 1984 to 31% in 2000 — with 28% also admitting to having bought certain goods for political ethical or environmental reasons in 2000.

Does political participation matter?

On a simple level, participation clearly matters because low levels of political participation undermine the legitimacy of political institutions and processes. In the case of low electoral turnout, it brings the governing party's mandate into question. In a similar vein, low levels of turnout at referendums undermine all the main arguments commonly advanced in favour of their wider use.

However, there is evidence to suggest that the damage done by low levels of political participation may extend beyond the theoretical, impacting not only on the legitimacy of government, but also on its quality and effectiveness. In an article in *Politics Review* in 2009, Paul Whiteley highlighted the link between political participation and government effectiveness in 37 countries. The

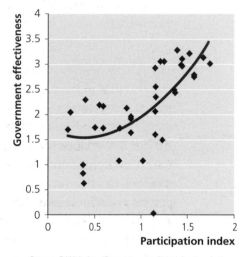

Source: P. Whiteley, 'Democracy and participation: is there a participation crisis?', **Politics Review**, vol. 19, no. 1, September 2009.

Figure 1.1 The relationship between political participation and government effectiveness in 37 countries, 2004

evidence (see Figure 1.1) would appear to suggest that countries with high levels of political participation are more likely to enjoy effective government. Note that each diamond on the graph represents a single country.

Addressing the participation crisis

Efforts to address falling levels of participation in formal politics have generally fallen into two broad categories:

➢ those that attempt to deal with the problem of electoral turnout head-on, generally by making it easier to vote
➢ those that try to get to the root of the problem by considering some deeper problems affecting democracy in the UK

Tackling the issue of low turnout

Two initiatives have already been trialled with a view to tackling the issue of low voter turnout 'head-on':

➤ encouraging a greater take-up of postal voting
➤ experimenting with SMS text voting and web-based voting

Such initiatives have brought mixed results. Although the extension of postal voting has certainly increased turnout, particularly at local elections, it has also led to allegations of voter fraud and intimidation, particularly where a significant number of voters are registered at a single address. In a sense, therefore, what has been gained in terms of turnout (i.e. the 'size' of the vote) has been lost in terms of the 'quality' of the vote, with the principle of a secret ballot being brought into question.

Trials of SMS text voting and web-based voting between 2000 and 2007 faced similar criticisms, the result being that such trials are now unlikely to be extended more widely.

A number of other proposals have also been made, most notably:

➤ making voting compulsory for those eligible, as in Australia
➤ lowering the minimum voting age from 18 to 16

Compulsory voting

Many countries require eligible voters not only to register to vote (as is the case in the UK) but also to cast a ballot on election day. In Australia, this requirement is included in the Commonwealth Electoral Act (1918), which was amended in 1924 to make voting at federal elections compulsory. The Act states that 'it shall be the duty of every elector to vote at each election'. Those non-voters who cannot supply a 'valid and sufficient reason' for their failure to cast a ballot are subject to a small fine.

The introduction of compulsory voting in Australia had an immediate and significant effect on electoral turnout. Australia had experienced sharply falling turnouts at the start of the 1920s, with only 59.4% casting a ballot in the 1922 elections to the House of Representatives (compared to 71.6% in 1919). Turnout at the first election held after the introduction of compulsory voting, in 1925, rose to 91.4%. Whereas only 61.4% of registered voters cast a ballot in the 2005 UK general election, the 2007 elections to the Australian House of Representatives saw a turnout of 94.8%.

Despite the obvious benefits it brings in terms of electoral turnout, compulsory voting is criticised by some civil liberties groups, which argue that the right not to cast a ballot should be protected. Forcing eligible citizens to vote runs the risk of repeating problems seen with postal voting: specifically, that while the numbers of ballots will increase, the quality of the vote will not. Some people will be voting simply because of their desire to avoid a fine, as opposed to participating more purposefully in the democratic process.

Weblinks

www.aec.gov.au — click on 'Voting' and scroll down to 'Compulsory voting' to access the relevant page from the Australian Electoral Commission website.

Viewpoint Should voting be made compulsory?

YES

- Voting is a civic duty comparable to other duties that citizens perform (e.g. paying taxes, attending school, completing jury service).
- It teaches the benefits of political participation.
- Parliament reflects more accurately the 'will of the electorate'.
- Governments must consider the total electorate in policy formulation and management, rather than simply focusing on those who are likely to turn out.
- Candidates can concentrate their campaigning energies on issues, rather than encouraging voters to attend the poll through 'get out the vote' activities.
- The voter is not actually compelled to vote for any single candidate because voting is by secret ballot. They can choose to leave their ballot paper blank or spoil their ballot.

NO

- It is undemocratic to force people to vote (i.e. an infringement of liberty).
- The ill informed and those with little interest in politics are forced to the polls.
- It may increase the number of **donkey votes** when used alongside a preferential voting system.
- It may increase the number of **informal votes**.
- It can serve to increase the number of safe, single-member constituencies — encouraging political parties to concentrate on the more marginal seats.
- It takes time and money to determine whether or not those who have failed to cast a ballot have done so for a valid reason or reasons.

Source: Australian Electoral Commission.

Key terms

> **Donkey votes** Under a preferential voting system, votes which are simply numbered 1, 2, 3, 4, etc. in order vertically down the list of available candidates. A 'reverse donkey' is one where candidates are numbered up the ballot paper.

> **Informal votes** Ballots which are completed incorrectly under a system of compulsory voting.

Reducing the voting age

The idea of reducing the voting age from 18 to 16 found some favour with the Labour prime minister Gordon Brown, although this seems unlikely to improve the national turnout figure.

Younger voters are statistically less likely to cast a ballot than those who are older. For example, only 44% of eligible voters in the 18–24 age category cast a ballot at the 2010 general election, compared to the 76% turnout figure recorded for over-65s. Reducing the voting age from 18 to 16 would increase the number of voters, but the percentage turnout figure would almost certainly fall (Box 1.8). This move would also raise the issue of whether those who are in many cases still not eligible to pay certain taxes should have a say in the make-up of the government that would set them.

The debate over reducing the voting age

In recent years there has been pressure for a reduction in the voting age from 18 to 16. The Electoral Reform Society argues for this and has organised a coalition on the issue. This resulted in the launch of the Votes at 16 campaign on 29 January 2003. Professor Robert Blackburn stated in his book *The Electoral System in Britain* that 'the argument against any further age reduction in voting rests simply upon grounds that some arbitrary age limit has to be drawn, and that many 16 and 17 year old people are unlikely to have gained the necessary political maturity to be able to express a considered political judgement.' The academic David Denver has argued that turnout would fall as a result of lowering the voting age since young people are the least likely to vote. However, at the age of 16 an individual is able to leave school, get married, join the armed forces and pay tax.

Source: I. White, **Reduction in Voting Age**, House of Commons Standard Note SN/PC/1747, 2009.

Weblinks

www.votesat16.org.uk — the site of the Votes at 16 campaign.

Addressing perceived flaws in UK democracy

The second broad approach to tackling low levels of participation in formal politics has been to find ways of enhancing the UK's democratic institutions and processes as a means to reignite public interest in them.

This approach is the one advocated by the POWER report, among others (see Box 1.9), and also provides the focus for the last section of this chapter.

Box 1.9 **Recommendations of the POWER inquiry**

➤ A rebalancing of power away from the executive and unaccountable bodies towards parliament and local government.

➤ The introduction of greater responsiveness and choice into the electoral and party systems.

➤ Allowing citizens a much more direct and focused say over political decisions and policies.

Source: **Power to the People: The Report of POWER — An Independent Inquiry into Britain's Democracy**, 2006 (executive summary).

Is the UK democratic?

Assessing the UK's democratic credentials is made hard by the fact that there are so many different perspectives on precisely what democracy should be. Few would argue that the UK perfectly fits the definition of a **pluralist democracy**. It makes more sense, therefore, for us to use the model of a liberal democracy for the purposes of our discussion here.

The main features of UK democracy

UK democracy has the following features:

➤ multilevel government where policies can, in theory at least, be developed and implemented by those best placed to understand the needs of the people (**subsidiarity**)

Concepts explained

Pluralist democracy

A system of government that encourages participation and allows for free and fair competition between competing interests.

In a pluralist democracy:

➤ there will be a diverse range of competing interests
➤ there will be numerous access points — points of leverage where pressure groups can exert influence
➤ no single group will be able to exclude any other from the political process

Some argue that the UK is a pluralist democracy. Others, however, maintain that the UK system of government is in fact dominated by elites: that members of a particular social class, those of a particular educational background, or those who move in particular social circles (virtuous circles) dominate the higher levels of government, industry and the media. Although the range of available access points has been increased both by UK membership of the EU and as a result of devolution, the term 'pluralist democracy' still appears more applicable to the USA than to the UK.

Subsidiarity

The principle that decisions should be taken at the lowest tier of government possible.

An approach designed to enhance local accountability and local democracy.

Limited by the extent to which it is practical and economically viable to deal with certain issues at a local level.

Key terms

➤ **Pluralist democracy** A system of government which encourages participation and allows for free and fair competition between competing interests.
➤ **Subsidiarity** The principle that decisions should be taken at the lowest tier of government possible.

➤ a system of free and fair elections, incorporating a wide franchise and operating under a secret ballot
➤ the protection of basic rights and liberties under the rule of law
➤ the existence of a wide range of political parties and pressure groups, providing numerous avenues for political participation and representation

A critique of UK democracy

Critics of the UK system are also able to point to a number of deficiencies in our democratic arrangements and practice:

➤ the use of the first-past-the-post system at general elections
➤ the failure properly to reform parliament
➤ low levels of voter turnout and widespread disillusionment with other traditional

forms of participation, such as membership of political parties and mainstream pressure groups
- the rise of (often extreme) single-issue pressure groups, and groups that seek to destabilise or even overthrow the state
- the absence of a proper separation of powers and the tendency towards executive dominance (or 'elective dictatorship')
- the transfer of government power away from elected bodies towards unelected quangos and free-standing agencies
- the absence of a properly drafted bill of rights incorporated within a codified and entrenched constitution

Has the UK become more democratic since 1997?

Although the reforms introduced by New Labour in the wake of its landslide victory at the 1997 general election have gone some way towards addressing those concerns identified, there is still considerable debate over precisely how much progress has been made.

On the positive side

- All but 92 of the 759 peers who had held the right to sit and vote in the upper Chamber prior to the House of Lords Act (1999) have been removed.
- A better separation of powers has resulted from changes to the role of Lord Chancellor and the creation of the UK Supreme Court under the Constitutional Reform Act (2005).
- The passage of the Human Rights Act (1998) and Freedom of Information Act (2000) have provided a clearer outline of the rights available to citizens.
- Devolution and the introduction of directly elected local mayors in many areas have brought government closer to the people, enhancing local democracy and local accountability.
- The increased use of referendums from 1997 is said to have enhanced democracy by giving those changes approved greater legitimacy.

On the negative side

- The UK experienced historically low levels of turnout at the 2001, 2005 and 2010 general elections.
- Lords reform stalled after 1999 and significant reforms to the House of Commons have failed to materialise.
- There has been an erosion of civil liberties since the attacks in the USA on 9/11 (2001) and London on 7/7 (2005).

Enhancing future UK democracy

In many cases, future changes to the way in which democracy operates in the UK will build upon the successes and failures outlined above under 'positive' and 'negative'.

Some of these ideas — for example, the possibility of making greater use of referendums, initiatives or recalls — have already been dealt with in this chapter. Others — for example, devolving power to the English regions — will be discussed in their proper context in later chapters. However, it is worth focusing on two areas that do not receive a great deal of coverage elsewhere in this book, namely:

➤ the extension of experiments in e-democracy
➤ greater use of citizens' juries and citizens' assemblies (or 'citizens' conventions') as a way of engaging citizens and enhancing the legitimacy of the policy-making process

Embracing e-democracy

The term **e-democracy** refers to the greater use of the internet, mobile phones and other electronic media as a means of enhancing the operation of existing political institutions and processes. It seeks to address the decline in some forms of political participation by making it far easier for citizens to engage with decision makers and shape the political agenda. While the term is commonly used when referring to initiatives taken by central government, e-democracy also refers to initiatives started by citizens and pressure groups (see Box 1.10). Although there appears to be little prospect of the 2000–07 trials in e-voting being rolled out more widely, e-democracy can be seen in a number of other initiatives, some government led and others citizen led (see Box 1.11).

> **Key term**
> ➤ **e-democracy** The greater use of the internet, mobile phones and other electronic media as a means of enhancing the operation of existing political institutions and processes, and encouraging greater political participation.

Box 1.10 Defining e-democracy

There is no single definition for e-democracy: it can broadly be described as the use of new Information and Communication Technologies (ICT) to increase and enhance citizens' engagement in democratic processes. Traditionally, initiatives have been categorised as follows, although the boundaries are becoming increasingly blurred:

➤ **top-down**: initiatives by the government, or local authorities, often with the goals of lowered costs, or increased efficiency, transparency and convenience;

➤ **bottom-up**: initiated by citizens and activists at the grassroots level. These generally aim to increase transparency, accountability or convenience as well as to inform, educate and campaign.

In each category activities can be either:

➤ **one-way** processes: such as dissemination of information from the government to citizen;

➤ **two-way** processes: such as public opinion polls, or consultation on draft bills. Such two-way, interactive forms of web-based e-democracy are often referred to as Web 2.0 applications.

Source: Postnote no. 321, 'E-democracy', Parliamentary Office of Science and Technology, 2009.

Box 1.11   Examples of e-democracy in the UK

www.parliamentlive.tv (top-down, one-way)
This website carries live and archived coverage of all public proceedings in parliament.

www.writetothem.com (bottom-up)
This website allows members of the public to identify any of their elected representatives by postcode and contact them via email or fax for free. The site sent some 174,750 messages in 2007, with more than 50% being from people who had never written to an elected representative of any kind.

http://theyworkforyou.com (bottom-up, two-way)
This website provides a searchable, annotatable version of what is said in parliament. Used by over 100,000 visitors a month, it provides information on a range of different measures of activities by MPs, such as parliamentary appearances and voting patterns.

http://forums.parliament.uk (top-down, two-way)
Parliament is developing its capacity to run online consultations on behalf of parliamentary select committees. The most popular consultation to date was on 'Human reproductive technologies and the law', in 2004, when 627 messages were posted by 333 registered users (59% of whom had never contacted their MP before).

http://petitions.number10.gov.uk (bottom-up, two-way)
This 10 Downing Street website was built to allow members of the public to petition the prime minister about whatever issues they see fit. One of the most popular petitions, on road pricing, received over 1.8 million signatures.

Source: Postnote No. 321, 'E-democracy', Parliamentary Office of Science and Technology, 2009.

Weblinks

www.parliament.uk/documents/upload/postpn321.pdf — a four-page briefing paper from the Parliamentary Office of Science and Technology, which addresses the issue of e-democracy.

Citizens' juries and citizens' assemblies

A citizens' jury is a panel of citizens convened to hear evidence and deliver their verdict on a government proposal or a specific policy area. Citizens' juries are used widely outside the UK, most notably in the USA and Germany, and were championed by the prime minister Gordon Brown in 2007 as a means of enhancing political participation. Crucially, such juries do not have final say on a given policy. Their feedback is considered by a panel of specialists and, ultimately, those politicians serving in government posts, who make the final decision over policy.

Weblinks

www.parliament.uk/commons/lib/research/briefings/snpc-04546.pdf — a research briefing from the House of Commons Library on the subject of citizens' juries.

Gordon Brown taking part in the first citizens' jury event in Bristol, September 2007

A citizens' assembly (or 'citizens' convention') is similar to a citizens' jury in the sense that it looks to involve a representative cross-section of the population in the policy-making process, in a way that is more meaningful than the kind of consultation routinely undertaken at the Green Paper stage of a legislative proposal. Where assemblies differ from juries is, first, that they involve a lot more people (hundreds or thousands as opposed to tens) and, secondly, that they are often given more power to decide upon a particular course of action, which can subsequently be put to a public vote through a referendum. This means that politicians are, in a sense, absenting themselves from the decision-making process.

It is likely that such citizens' assemblies will be used to provide the kind of 'public conversation' that the leaders of the three main UK parties have advocated ahead of the next wave of constitutional reform.

Box 1.12 What makes a good citizens' assembly?

Citizens' assemblies have been successful where it has been established from the outset that their findings will be put straight to a referendum, without amendment or modification by government. In these cases the assembly was seen to be independent and consequently the public and media bought into the process. Where it is not clear what the outcome will be or the assembly merely reports to Parliament as in the Netherlands, the assembly is dismissed as yet another consultation exercise that is unlikely to lead to change. Deliberative techniques on their own are not enough, the assembly has to be seen to be independent and have the power to propose change.

Source: A. Runswick, *A Guide to Involving Citizens in Constitutional Reform*, Unlock Democracy, 2007.

Weblinks

www.unlockdemocracy.org.uk/wp-content/uploads/2007/07/citizens-assembly-briefing.pdf
— a briefing paper on citizens' assemblies from the pressure group Unlock Democracy.

www.parliament.uk/commons/lib/research/briefings/snpc-04482.pdf — a research briefing
from the House of Commons Library on the subject of citizens' assemblies.

❯ What you should know

❯ Democracy is 'rule by the people' or 'people power', but this can mean different things to different people. Consequently, it has become common practice to prefix the term 'democracy' with another word as a way of affording it greater meaning. Thus the UK is said to be a liberal democracy because it incorporates free and fair elections with a commitment to the protection of certain key liberties and freedoms.

❯ Liberal democracies such as the UK and the USA tend to operate under a representative (or 'indirect') form of democracy, where the citizens elect politicians to make decisions on their behalf. This is a result of the fact that direct democracy (where citizens have a direct input into decision making) is regarded as impractical in a modern democracy with a large population and a wide franchise. However, the increasing use of referendums in the UK is an example of the way in which elements of direct democracy can operate alongside the representative model. A purer form of direct democracy operates in the form of the town hall meetings held in small towns in several New England states in the USA.

❯ The term 'political participation' refers collectively to the various ways in which citizens can involve themselves in the political process. Political participation covers all manner of activities, from voting at an election or joining a political party, to taking part in pressure group activity or boycotting certain products on ethical grounds. In recent years the UK has witnessed a decline in the more formal (or traditional) aspects of political participation, such as voting, and a rise in less formal, more spontaneous activity such as direct action.

❯ Many commentators regard this participatory shift as a major threat to UK democracy and have therefore looked for ways to halt and reverse the trend. The more notable proposals have included the introduction of compulsory voting, the lowering of the voting age and the extension of experiments in e-democracy (or 'digital democracy').

❯ In some respects the UK has become more democratic in recent years as a result of the removal of the right of most hereditary peers to sit and vote in the House of Lords, and the passage of the Human Rights Act (1998) and the Freedom of Information Act (2000). However, in other areas there is still significant room for improvement: parliamentary reform is incomplete; the inequities of the first-past-the-post system suggest the need for reform; and scrutiny of the executive needs to be enhanced.

UK/US comparison

Democracy and participation in the USA

➤ Whereas UK political culture was traditionally said to be characterised by homogeneity, deference and consensus, US political culture is based on principles such as individualism, liberty and a belief in limited government.

➤ The USA is far more diverse than the UK. It comprises 50 states covering six different time zones. The US population of over 300 million individuals encompasses all races and religions. This multi-variance is key to any understanding of US political culture.

➤ Like the UK, the USA is said to be a liberal democracy, but it is also widely seen as a pluralist democracy. This is due both to the availability of numerous access points and to the expectation of open competition between competing interests.

➤ Political power in the USA is fragmented 'vertically', under the federal system, and 'horizontally', through the entrenched separation of powers and the system of checks and balances. This fragmented system provides numerous access points, allowing greater political participation and providing for greater government accountability. This contrasts with the UK's unitary system and its partial fusion of powers.

➤ Whereas the fusion of powers present in the UK system is said to favour executive dominance (or 'elective dictatorship'), the US system is far more prone to gridlock — particularly where there is divided government: that is, where one of the two main parties controls the White House and the other controls all or part of the bicameral Congress.

➤ The US system has a long-established rights culture rooted not only in the Bill of Rights but also in subsequent constitutional amendments such as the Fourteenth Amendment (guaranteeing equal protection under the law). The rights of US citizens are also protected in regular congressional statutes (e.g. the 1964 Civil Rights Act) and through the rulings of the US Supreme Court. The UK was traditionally said to operate under a system of negative rights, but the passing of the Human Rights Act (1998) and other measures is said to have enhanced the protection of civil liberties.

➤ While both the UK and the USA are seen as operating under the representative model of democracy, many US citizens also have the opportunity to get involved more directly in policy making. While the US Constitution does not provide for US-wide direct democracy, the majority of states hold referendums and many also allow initiatives and recalls. Small towns in some US states also operate a more primitive form of direct democracy in the form of New England town hall meetings.

➤ Although electoral turnout is often lower in the USA than in the UK, this is partly explained by the fact that US turnout is commonly calculated as a percentage of the voting age population, as opposed to a percentage of registered voters — the measure used in the UK.

➤ The USA is widely seen as a participatory democracy with far higher levels of pressure group membership and involvement in grassroots activities such as campaigning, canvassing and 'get out the vote' campaigns than are seen in the UK.

Further reading

Fairclough, P. (2004) 'Direct democracy in the USA: referendums, initiatives and recalls', *Politics Review*, Vol. 13, No. 4.

Lynch, P. (2010) 'UK Update: Recall of MPs', *Politics Review*, Vol. 19, No. 3.

POWER report (2006) *Power to the People: The Report of the POWER Commission — An Independent Inquiry into Britain's Democracy*, POWER Commission.

Qvortrup, M. (2008) 'Referendums in the UK', *Politics Review*, Vol. 18, No. 2,.

Weir, S. (2006) 'Democracy in Britain', *Politics Review*, Vol. 16, No. 1.

Whiteley, P. (2009) 'Democracy and participation: is there a participation crisis in the UK?', *Politics Review*, Vol. 19, No. 1.

Whiteley, P. (2010) 'Enhancing democracy: how might participation be improved?', *Politics Review*, Vol. 19, No. 3.

Wildbore, H. (2008) 'Does Britain need a bill of rights?', *Politics Review*, Vol. 17, No. 4.

Exam focus

Short-answer questions (around 5 minutes each)

Explain, using examples, the meaning of each of the following terms:

1 Democracy
2 Direct democracy
3 Representative democracy
4 Political participation

Mid-length questions (around 10 minutes each)

Outline two arguments 'for' and two arguments 'against' each of the following:

1 Referendums
2 Recalls
3 e-democracy
4 Compulsory voting

Mini-essays (around 25–30 minutes each)

Write a mini-essay in response to each of the following questions:

1 'Referendums should be used more widely in the UK.' Discuss.
2 'The UK is experiencing a participation crisis.' Evaluate the arguments in support of this view.
3 To what extent would you regard the UK system as being truly democratic?
4 Critically assess the various changes proposed as a means of making the UK more democratic.

Chapter 2

Elections and voting

Key questions answered in this chapter
- ➤ What are the functions of elections?
- ➤ What are the advantages and disadvantages of the first-past-the-post system?
- ➤ How do the other electoral systems used in the UK operate?
- ➤ How important is social class in determining voting behaviour?
- ➤ How significant are issues, leaders and the perceived competence of parties?

Elections are at the heart of the democratic process. Voting in an election is the main form of political activity for many people. Through the electoral process, governments are chosen and then held accountable for their record in office. Political parties issue **manifestos** that outline the policies they would introduce if they gained power. The victorious party is expected to deliver those pledges in government.

Key term
- ➤ **Manifesto** A document in which a political party sets out its policy programme at an election.

Functions of elections

Elections have a number of functions:
- ➤ **Representation.** In a representative democracy, elections enable a large group (the electorate) to select a smaller group (representatives) to act on their behalf. In a direct democracy, by contrast, all eligible citizens take part in decision making.
- ➤ **Choosing a government.** In the UK parliamentary system, general elections determine the composition of the House of Commons rather than the executive. However, because the majority party in the Commons forms the government, general elections normally determine which party takes power.

Elections and referendums

Elections

➤ These are required by law and must take place within a specified period.

➤ They are a feature of representative democracy — citizens choose representatives to make decisions on their behalf.

➤ They determine who holds political office and, in the case of a general election, who forms the government.

➤ Citizens vote for candidates in single-member, or multi-member, constituencies, with most candidates standing for a political party.

➤ An election campaign will cover many issues of public policy.

Referendums

➤ A referendum is a one-off vote on a specific issue of public policy.

➤ The choice offered to voters is normally a simple 'yes' or 'no' to a proposal.

➤ The decision to hold a referendum in the UK is taken by the government — there is no constitutional obligation to hold a referendum on particular issues.

➤ Referendums are an example of direct democracy — citizens make the decisions themselves.

➤ **Participation.** Voting is the key act of political participation for most citizens. But **turnout** in elections has fallen in the last decade.

Key term

➤ **Turnout** The proportion of the electorate that votes in an election.

➤ **Influence over policy.** In theory, elections allow citizens to have their policy preferences heard, but in reality, they have limited scope to influence decisions. Election defeat can, however, force a party to rethink unpopular policies (e.g. Labour's 1983 policy of unilateral disarmament).

➤ **Accountability.** Facing the electorate every 5 years is one of the ways by which the government is held accountable for its performance in office. Individual MPs may also be held accountable for their record. Following the 2009 expenses scandal, many MPs stood down rather than face the verdict of voters.

➤ **Citizen education.** Election campaigns provide citizens with information on major political issues and the policies of the main parties. In theory, this enables citizens to make an informed decision on how to vote, but in practice the information provided is imperfect.

➤ **Legitimacy.** Elections give legitimacy to the winning party and to the political system as a whole. By voting, even for a losing party, citizens give their consent to the system. The government can claim to be acting on the will of the people.

➤ **Elite recruitment.** Political parties nominate candidates for election, provide them with campaign resources — and expect loyalty from them if they become MPs.

Democratic theorists prioritise the role of the people in the political process. They focus on 'bottom-up' functions such as policy influence, participation and accountability. In a representative democracy, the government should act in accordance with the wishes of the people.

For elite theorists, elections provide authority and stability for the political system, allowing elites to get on with the task of governing, with only limited recourse to the expressed wishes of the people. They highlight 'top-down' functions such as legitimacy and elite recruitment. In a representative democracy, the political elite decides what is in the best interests of the people.

Concepts explained

Election

A competitive process in which a designated group of people, known as the electorate, select individuals who will fill particular posts. Elections to public office are a central feature of the democratic process. Here, the electorate consists of almost all of the adult population. Members of legislatures, and the executive in presidential systems, are chosen in elections.

Legitimacy

A contested concept, usually equated with rightfulness. A political system is legitimate when it is based on the consent of the people — winning an election gives a government legitimacy. Political actions are also legitimate if they follow from agreed laws and procedures. Citizens in a liberal democracy accept the legitimacy of a government, even if they did not vote for it, if it acts within its lawful powers.

Elections and democracy

In a liberal democracy, elections should be competitive, free and fair. A competitive election requires that voters have a meaningful choice between different political parties. Free elections require basic civil liberties such as freedom of speech and association, the right to join and stand for a party of one's choice, and a free press. The maxim 'one person, one vote, one value' is a key criterion for a fair election: each citizen should have one vote that is of the same worth as everyone else's. Electoral law should be free from bias and overseen by an impartial judiciary. The electoral system should also translate votes cast into seats won in the legislature in a reasonably accurate manner.

Weblinks

www.electoralcommission.org.uk — the Electoral Commission website provides information on the conduct of elections in the UK.

Representation

Choosing a **representative** is an important function of elections. But there are competing perspectives on **representation**:

- delegate model
- trustee model
- constituency representation
- party representation
- functional representation

Delegate model

A **delegate** is an individual selected to act on behalf of others on the basis of clear instructions. They should not depart from these instructions in order to follow their own judgement or preferences. Examples include trade union delegates who cast votes according to an earlier decision of the union leaders or membership. However, MPs are not expected to act as delegates, slavishly bound by the instructions of voters. There is unlikely to be a consensus among voters in a constituency on complex issues, while ascertaining the views of the majority on every issue would be difficult.

Trustee model

Edmund Burke MP (1729–97) proposed the **trustee** model. MPs are responsible for representing the interests of their constituents in parliament. Once elected, they are free to decide how to vote based on their own independent judgement of the merits of an issue. Burke's perspective had a strong elitist undercurrent. It assumed that MPs knew best because they had greater understanding of affairs of state.

Key terms

- **Representation** The process by which an individual or individuals act on behalf of a larger group.
- **Representative** (a) *noun:* an individual who acts on behalf of a larger group but is free to exercise their own judgement; (b) *adjective:* exhibiting a likeness or being typical.

Key terms

- **Delegate** An individual authorised to act on behalf of others but who is bound by clear instructions.
- **Trustee** An individual who has formal responsibility for the interests of another (in law, this will often be property).

Delegates and trustees

Delegates

- Delegates are given clear instructions on how they are to act on behalf of the people they represent.
- They must follow these instructions in full and must not adapt them based on their own judgement of the issues.
- They must not vote on the basis of their personal views or conscience.

Trustees

- Trustees should take account of the interests and values of the group they represent, but they are not bound by strict instructions from them.
- They are free to exercise their own judgement on issues and to vote accordingly.
- They may vote according to their conscience.

Constituency representation

MPs are expected to protect and advance the collective interests of the **constituency** they represent, and to represent the interests of individual constituents. They may lobby the government about developments in the constituency (e.g. the future of a factory or the proposed site of a wind farm). MPs receive numerous requests for help from constituents by post and email, and in person at constituency surgeries. They may then take up individual cases (e.g. on housing) with the relevant authorities.

> **Key term**
> **Constituency** A geographical territory for which representatives are chosen in an election.

The relationship between an MP and his or her constituents is often seen as important for a healthy democracy. It may also bring an active MP a 'personal vote' at a general election. However, few MPs will go so far as to defy their party whip in their pursuit of constituency interests.

Party representation

Political parties dominate elections. Almost all successful general election candidates are elected not for their personal beliefs and qualities, but because they represent a political party. Parties also provide candidates with campaign funding. In return, MPs owe loyalty to their party in parliament. This perspective also sees parties as representative of the interests of particular groups in society.

The winning party claims that it has a **mandate** from voters to enact the policy commitments set out in its manifesto.

Concepts explained
Mandate

A mandate is an authoritative instruction or command. The doctrine of the mandate gives the winning party the authority to press ahead with the programme it presented to the electorate. An election manifesto is seen as a promise of future legislative action, or a contract between a party and those who voted for it. The idea of the mandate also means that a government should not introduce a major policy change unless it has been presented to the electorate.

Descriptive representation

A final perspective, known as descriptive or functional representation, suggests that parliament should mirror the society it represents. Representation is equated with resemblance. Parliament should be a microcosm of the larger body: all major social groups should be present in numbers roughly proportional to their size in the electorate.

The underlying assumption is that only people with similar social characteristics (e.g. gender, ethnicity and social class) can identify with and represent the interests of particular groups. So, women understand motherhood better than men, and members of ethnic minorities have more experience of racism. Critics argue that individuals need not have suffered disadvantage or discrimination to regard these as reprehensible and demand reform. It is also problematic to assume that people belong to only one social group, and that groups are homogeneous.

The House of Commons does not resemble British society (see Chapter 7). Most MPs are middle class. A growing number are career politicians with little work experience outside politics. Women and ethnic minorities are also under-represented. In 2010, 22% of MPs were women and only 4% had a black and minority ethnic background.

Weblinks

www.fawcettsociety.org.uk — the website of the Fawcett Society, which campaigns for greater representation of women in parliament.

Elections in the UK

Elections take place at different levels in UK politics:

> **General elections.** These elect all 650 MPs who make up the House of Commons. A general election must be held if the parliament has run its full 5-year term, but the prime minister can call an earlier contest at a time of his or her choosing. This gives the governing party a distinct advantage over it rivals, as the prime minister can call an election at a favourable moment. The Conservative–Liberal Democrat coalition that took office in 2010 planned to introduce fixed-term parliaments of 5 years. A general election must also be called if the government is defeated on a motion of no confidence, as happened in 1979.

> **European Parliament elections.** The UK elects 73 Members of the European Parliament at elections held at fixed-term intervals of 5 years.

> **Elections to the devolved assemblies.** Elections to the Scottish Parliament, Welsh Assembly and Northern Ireland Assembly are held at fixed 4-year intervals.

> **Local elections.** Local councillors are elected for fixed 4-year terms. In some local authorities, all councillors face the electorate at the same time; in others, only a proportion of members (normally a quarter) are elected each year. Some towns and cities also have directly elected mayors. In London, there is an elected mayor and London Assembly.

> **By-elections.** If a constituency seat in the House of Commons, devolved assembly or English local authority becomes vacant because of the death or resignation of an elected member, a by-election is held to choose a new representative.

Significant parts of the UK polity are not elected:

> the head of state — the hereditary monarch
> the second chamber of the legislature — the House of Lords
> the judiciary
> public bodies such as quangos

Electoral systems

Electoral systems translate votes cast by citizens into seats in an assembly or a political office. There are four main types of electoral system:

➢ majoritarian (e.g. the alternative vote)
➢ plurality (e.g. simple plurality)
➢ proportional (e.g. the list system)
➢ mixed (e.g. the additional member system)

Majoritarian system

A **majoritarian system** is one in which the winning candidate must secure an absolute majority of the vote (i.e. 50% + 1 vote). Candidates are usually elected in single-member constituencies. The first-past-the-post system used for UK general elections is often described as a majoritarian system. This is not strictly accurate because the term is being used to reflect a system output, when it should describe its mechanics.

Plurality system

First-past-the-post is, in fact, a **simple plurality system** in which the winner needs only a plurality of votes cast (i.e. one more than their closest rival), not an absolute majority. Plurality systems share some of the characteristics of majoritarian systems. MPs are elected in single-member constituencies and both systems are non-proportional. Large parties tend to get a higher proportion of seats than their vote merits, while smaller parties whose support is thinly spread are under-represented.

Proportional representation

The term **proportional representation** (PR) covers many systems with similar features. They produce a close fit between votes and seats, although no system can deliver perfect proportionality. The **district magnitude** (i.e. the number of legislative seats per constituency) is a crucial factor — the larger the constituency, the more proportional the result. In the European Parliament elections in Great Britain, using the regional list system, a smaller party is more likely to win a seat in the southeast region (which elects 10 MEPs) than the northeast (3 MEPs).

PR systems use multi-member constituencies and electoral formulas. Some (e.g. the single transferable vote, STV) allow electors to vote for as many candidates as they wish in order of preference, but others (e.g. the regional list system) permit only a single vote.

Mixed system

A **mixed system**, such as the additional member system (AMS), combines elements of the plurality or majoritarian systems and proportional representation. Some MPs are elected in single-member constituencies. The remainder are elected by proportional representation in multi-member constituencies. These list seats produce 'additional members' that are allocated to parties on corrective lines.

Some people believe that the most important tasks of an electoral system are to produce a clear winner and a strong government, and to maintain a link between MPs and geographical constituencies. Majoritarian or plurality systems are appropriate in this case. Others argue that an electoral system should provide maximum choice for voters and reflect accurately the diversity of opinion among the electorate. PR systems fit the bill here.

Weblinks

www.politicsresources.net/election.htm — a gateway providing links to information on electoral systems and elections across the world.

Majoritarian and proportional representation systems

Distinguish between

Majoritarian systems

➤ In a majoritarian system, a candidate must secure an absolute majority of the vote to win; in a plurality system, they need only win more votes than the second-placed candidate.
➤ Candidates are elected in single-member constituencies.
➤ The outcome is not proportional — large parties take a higher proportion of seats than their share of the vote merits, while smaller parties are often under-represented.
➤ They tend to produce single-party governments with working parliamentary majorities.

Proportional representation systems

➤ Candidates are elected in multi-member constituencies.
➤ Electoral formulas are used to allocate seats in the legislative assembly.
➤ The outcome is proportional — there is a close fit between the share of the vote won by a party and the share of the seats it is allocated.
➤ They tend to produce coalition governments, as no single party wins a majority of seats.

Key terms

➤ **District magnitude** The number or representatives elected from a particular constituency.
➤ **Majoritarian system** An electoral system in which the winning candidate must achieve an absolute majority of votes cast in a single-member constituency.
➤ **Mixed system** An electoral system where a proportion of representatives are elected under a majoritarian/plurality system in single-member constituencies, and the others are elected as 'additional members' using a proportional system in multi-member constituencies.
➤ **Proportional representation** An electoral system using multi-member constituencies in which an electoral formula is used to match the percentage of seats won by each party to the percentage of votes they won.
➤ **Simple plurality system** An electoral system in which the candidate with the most votes in a single-member constituency wins.

Glenda Jackson and Gordon Brown at a party meeting in Kilburn before the May 2010 general election

Electoral systems in the UK

Five different electoral systems are currently in use in the UK:
- first-past-the post — a plurality system used for general elections
- supplementary vote — a majoritarian system used to choose directly elected mayors
- additional member system — a mixed system used for elections to the Scottish Parliament, Welsh Assembly and London Assembly
- regional list — a proportional system used for elections to the European Parliament
- single transferable vote — a proportional system used in Northern Ireland for elections to the Northern Ireland Assembly, local authorities and the European Parliament, and for local elections in Scotland

The Conservative–Liberal Democrat coalition that took power in 2010 has promised a referendum on a sixth system, the alternative vote, for Westminster elections.

First-past-the-post

The first-past-the post system (FPTP), also known as simple plurality, is the most significant electoral system in the UK because it is used for general elections. A variant of it, known as the block vote — in which constituencies elect more than one candidate — is used in local elections in England and Wales. FPTP operates as follows:
- A candidate requires a plurality of votes to win: that is, one more vote than the second-placed candidate. There is no requirement to obtain a majority of the votes cast. In contests involving three or more candidates, the winner may fall well short of an overall majority. Table 2.1 shows the 2010 result in Hampstead and Kilburn, a three-way marginal seat won by the Labour candidate, Glenda Jackson, with under one-third of the votes cast.

Candidate	Party	Vote	% vote
Glenda Jackson	Labour	17,332	32.8
Chris Philp	Conservative	17,290	32.7
Edward Fordham	Liberal Democrat	16,491	31.2
Bea Campbell	Green	759	1.4
Magnus Nielsen	UKIP	408	0.8
Victoria Moore	BNP	328	0.6
Tamsin Omond	The Commons	123	0.2
Gene Alcantara	Independent	91	0.2

Table 2.1 Result in Hampstead and Kilburn, 2010 general election

➤ Electors cast a single vote by placing a cross (an 'X') on the ballot paper next to the name of their favoured candidate.

➤ MPs are elected in single-member constituencies. Each of the 650 constituencies in the UK elects one representative to the House of Commons.

➤ Constituencies are of roughly equal size (70,000 electors). Constituency boundaries are determined by independent boundary commissions which review the size of the electorate in each constituency every 8–12 years. Differences in the size of constituencies are permitted if there are significant geographical factors. The most populous constituency, the Isle of Wight, has 40,000 more electors than the UK average and an electorate five times larger than the smallest constituency, Na h-Eileanan an Iar (the Western Isles). Constituencies in Scotland have fewer voters on average than those in England, but the over-representation was reduced when the number of Scottish constituencies was cut from 72 to 59 for the 2005 general election.

Characteristic features or outcomes of FPTP elections are:
➤ a two-party system
➤ a winner's bonus
➤ bias to the Labour Party
➤ discrimination against third parties and small parties
➤ single-party government

Two-party system

FPTP tends to foster a two-party system. It favours major parties with strong nationwide support, giving them a good chance of securing a parliamentary majority. But it disadvantages smaller parties whose support is spread thinly. There is little incentive for a faction within one of the main parties to break away and form a new party because small parties find it very difficult to win seats. The Social Democratic Party (SDP) was formed by disaffected Labour MPs in 1981. It fought the 1983 general election in an alliance with the Liberals, winning 25% of the vote but only 23 seats.

The UK's two-party system is in failing health. Support for the two main parties fell to 65% of the electorate in 2010 as the Liberal Democrats won 23% of the vote and smaller parties polled a combined vote share of 12%. FPTP acts as a life support machine for the two-party system and disguises the advance of multi-party politics. But the Liberal Democrats entered government as part of a coalition with the Conservatives after the 2010 election delivered a hung parliament in which no party won an overall majority of seats.

Concepts explained

Party system

The set of political parties in a political system and the relationships between them. In a two-party system, only two main parties have a realistic chance of taking power. They will secure most votes and seats, and alternate in office as majority governments. In a two-and-a-half-party system, a smaller party exists alongside two major parties but is far from their equal. In a multi-party system, several parties are politically relevant — they win seats in the legislative assembly and are potential coalition partners. Coalition or minority government is the norm.

Winner's bonus

FPTP tends to exaggerate the performance of the most popular party, producing a winner's bonus or landslide effect. A relatively small lead over the second-placed party is often translated into a substantial lead in seats in parliament. The Conservatives won landslide victories in 1983 and 1987, with Labour doing likewise in 1997 and 2001 (see Table 2.2).

Table 2.2 UK general election results, 1945–2010

Year	Con vote %	Con seats	Lab vote %	Lab seats	Lib Dem vote %	Lib Dem seats	Others votes %	Others seats	Turnout %
1945	39.6	210	48.0	393	9.0	12	3.4	25	72.8
1950	43.4	298	46.1	315	9.1	9	1.4	3	83.9
1951	48.0	321	48.8	295	2.6	6	0.6	3	82.6
1955	49.7	345	46.4	277	2.7	6	1.2	2	76.8
1959	49.4	365	43.8	258	5.9	6	0.9	1	78.7
1964	43.4	304	44.1	317	11.2	9	1.3	0	77.1
1966	41.9	253	48.0	364	8.6	12	1.5	1	75.8
1970	46.4	330	43.1	288	7.5	6	3.0	6	72.0
1974 (Feb.)	37.9	297	37.2	301	19.3	14	5.6	23	78.8
1974 (Oct.)	35.8	277	39.2	319	18.3	13	6.7	26	72.8
1979	43.9	339	36.9	269	13.8	11	5.4	16	76.0
1983	42.4	397	27.6	209	25.4	23	4.6	21	72.7
1987	42.3	376	30.8	229	22.5	22	4.4	23	75.3
1992	41.8	336	34.2	271	17.9	20	6.1	24	77.7
1997	30.7	165	43.4	419	16.8	46	9.3	29	71.5
2001	31.7	166	40.7	413	18.3	52	9.3	28	59.4
2005	32.3	197	35.2	355	22.1	62	10.4	31	61.4
2010	36.1	307	29.0	258	23.0	57	11.9	28	65.1

Note: Liberal Democrats includes Liberals (1945–79) and SDP/Liberal Alliance (1983–87). Northern Ireland MPs are included as 'Others' from 1974.

Bias to Labour

Rather than simply favouring the winning party, FPTP has become biased in favour of Labour. Labour won a 167-seat majority in 2001 on a smaller share of the vote than the Conservatives managed in 1992, when a record 14 million votes delivered a 21-seat majority. The Conservatives fell 19 seats of an overall majority when winning 36% of the vote in 2010, whereas Labour had a majority of 66 in 2005 on a 35% vote share. There are a number of reasons for the bias towards Labour:

> **Differences in constituency size.** The electorate in constituencies won by Labour in 2010 was on average 3,800 lower than in those won by the Conservatives. This is largely because of population movement from inner-city constituencies to suburban and rural ones.

> **Differential turnout.** Turnout is lower in Labour-held seats — 61% in 2010, compared to 68% in seats won by the Conservatives. Labour wins seats with lower turnouts, while the Conservatives pile up wasted votes in safe seats.

> **Tactical voting.** Labour's total of seats was boosted by anti-Conservative tactical voting at the 1997, 2001 and 2010 general elections. But the Conservatives achieved slightly higher than average swings in their target seats by concentrating resources there.

The overall effect is that Labour's vote is more efficiently distributed — it needs fewer votes to win seats. By dividing the total vote for each party by the number of seats won, we find that in 2010 the Conservatives won one MP for every 35,000 votes, Labour one MP per 33,500 votes and the Liberal Democrats one MP for every 120,000 votes. On these figures, Labour is only just behind the Conservatives despite winning 49 fewer seats.

Discrimination against smaller parties

FPTP discriminates against third parties and smaller parties whose support is not concentrated in particular regions. There are no rewards for coming second or third; winning a plurality of votes in single-member constituencies is what counts. The Liberal Democrats have been consistent losers from FPTP, although they have increased their tally of seats through effective local campaigning. Small parties whose support is concentrated in a particular region — notably the Scottish Nationalist Party (SNP) and Plaid Cymru — fare better in terms of matching seats to share of the vote. The grip that the two main parties have had over seats at Westminster has been loosened to some extent, with the Liberal Democrats and smaller parties winning more seats in 2005 and 2010 than in other postwar elections. Their combined 85 MPs in 2010 made up 13% of the total, but this was still poor reward for 35% of the vote.

Single-party government

FPTP tends to produce single-party governments with working parliamentary majorities. Coalition governments and minority governments are rare at Westminster. Only the February 1974 and 2010 general elections did not deliver a majority of seats for one party.

A minority Labour government took office after the former, while the 2010 Conservative–Liberal Democrat coalition was the first coalition government since the Second World War. Four of the seven general elections held between 1910 and 1929 — when Britain had a three-party system — failed to produce a majority government, and a National Government of four and then three parties held power from 1931 to 1939.

Advantages of FPTP

Supporters of the first-past-the-post system point to a number of advantages.

Simplicity

FPTP is easy to understand and operate. The ballot paper is simple, electors only vote once and counting the votes is straightforward. Voters are familiar with the current system and, for the most part, view it as legitimate and effective.

Clear outcome

FPTP elections normally produce a clear winner. Even if no party secures a majority of the votes cast, the party securing the largest number of votes often achieves a majority of seats in the House of Commons.

Strong and stable government

By favouring the main parties and giving the winning party an additional bonus of seats, FPTP produces strong government. Single-party governments with working majorities exercise significant control over the legislative process. They can fulfil their mandate by enacting the policy commitments they made in their manifestos, and act decisively in times of crisis.

Responsible government

Voters are given a clear choice between the governing party, which is held responsible for its record in office, and a potential alternative government. The doctrine of the mandate obliges the winning party to put its proposals into effect.

Effective representation

Single-member constituencies provide a clear link between voters and their elected representative, with one MP responsible for representing the interests of the area.

Disadvantages of FPTP

Critics of FPTP respond by noting its disadvantages.

Disproportional outcomes

The number of parliamentary seats won by parties at a general election does not reflect accurately the share of the vote they achieved. A number of points can be mentioned here:
- The two main parties tend to win more seats than their vote merits, with the lead party given an additional winner's bonus.
- Third parties and small parties whose votes are spread thinly rather than concentrated in particular areas are under-represented.

> FPTP creates 'electoral deserts', or parts of the country where a party has little or no representation. The Conservatives won 17% of the vote in Scotland in 2010, but only one seat. Labour won only two of 58 seats in eastern England on almost 20% of the vote, and the Liberal Democrats polled 21% in the East Midlands but did not win a single seat.

> A party can, on occasion, win the most votes but receive fewer seats than its main rival. Twice in postwar politics, the party coming second in the popular vote gained more seats than its opponent. The Conservatives won more seats than Labour in 1951 despite trailing it in votes, and the roles were reversed in February 1974 when Labour got more seats despite the Conservatives outpolling them (see Table 2.2).

Plurality rather than majority support

Victorious candidates do not need to secure a majority of the votes cast. Two-thirds of MPs elected in 2010 did not achieve a majority in their constituency. Low turnout meant that a majority of MPs were supported by less than one in three of the electorate. Most voters are represented by an MP who is not from their chosen party. The general election of 1935 was the last time that a party won a majority of the popular vote. In 2010 the Conservatives and Liberal Democrats, who formed a coalition government, won a combined 59% of the vote.

Votes are of unequal value

FPTP does not meet the 'one person, one vote, one value' principle. Disparities in constituency size mean that votes are of different value. A vote cast in a small constituency is more likely to influence the outcome than one in a larger constituency. Many votes are wasted because they do not help to elect an MP. A **wasted vote** is:

> a vote for a losing candidate — 52% of all votes cast in 2005

> a vote for a winning candidate that was not required for him or her to win — 18% of votes in 2005

Limited choice

Voters are denied an effective choice because only one candidate stands on behalf of each party. They cannot choose between different candidates from the same party. Furthermore, many constituencies are **safe seats** in which one party has a substantial lead over its rivals that is unlikely to be overturned. Supporters of other parties have little prospect of seeing their candidate win. Voters whose favoured party is unlikely to win might engage in **tactical voting**. A tactical vote is one cast not for the voter's first-choice candidate, but for the candidate best placed to prevent a party they dislike from winning the seat.

Divisive politics

In the 1960s and 1970s, critics argued that FPTP brought **adversarial politics**. Small shifts in voting produced frequent changes of government. Parties were able to overturn policies introduced by their rivals, producing instability. From 1979 to 2010, FPTP contributed to long periods of one-party rule, first by the Conservatives then by Labour, without them winning majority support.

Weblinks

www.makemyvotecount.org.uk — website of a pro-electoral reform organisation that campaigns for a referendum on a new voting system.

Key terms

> **Adversarial politics** A situation often found in two-party systems in which the governing party is confronted by an opposition party that offers a different policy programme, and which is outwardly hostile towards the government even when in broad agreement with it.

> **Safe seat** A constituency that normally elects an MP from the same political party at every election.

> **Tactical voting** Voting for the candidate most likely to defeat the voter's least favoured candidate.

> **Wasted vote** A vote for a losing candidate in a single-member constituency, or a vote for a winning candidate that was surplus to the plurality required for victory.

Other electoral systems

The Blair governments undertook a major programme of electoral reform beyond, but not for, Westminster. Rather than impose a single blueprint, they introduced a range of new electoral systems — majoritarian, proportional representation and mixed systems (see Table 2.3).

Table 2.3 Electoral systems in the UK

Electoral system	Use in UK	Key features
First-past-the-post	General elections to the House of Commons	Simple plurality system; single-member constituencies; disproportional outcome.
Supplementary vote	Mayor of London and directly elected mayors	Majoritarian system; used to elect individuals; voters record two preferences; winning candidate has a majority.
Closed regional list	European Parliament elections in Great Britain	Proportional representation system; electors vote for a party in multi-member regions; proportional outcome.
Single transferable vote	Assembly, local and European Parliament elections in Northern Ireland Local government in Scotland	Proportional representation system; electors rank candidates in multi-member constituencies; proportional outcome.
Additional member system	Scottish Parliament Welsh Assembly London Assembly	Mixed electoral system; electors cast two votes — one for a constituency candidate elected by FPTP, one for a regional list candidate elected by PR; list candidates are allocated to parties on a corrective basis to produce a proportional outcome.

Alternative vote

The Conservative–Liberal Democrat coalition that took office in 2010 proposed to hold a referendum on replacing FPTP with the alternative vote (AV). AV is used to elect Australia's lower house, the House of Representatives. In the UK, it is used in Labour Party and Liberal Democrat leadership elections.

It has the following features:

➤ Representatives are elected in single-member constituencies.
➤ The winning candidate has to achieve an overall majority of the votes cast.
➤ Voters indicate their preferences by writing '1' beside the name of their first choice, '2' next to their second choice, and so on.
➤ If no candidate secures an absolute majority of first preferences, the lowest-placed candidate is eliminated, and the second preferences of his or her voters are transferred to the remaining candidates.
➤ The process continues until one candidate reaches the 50% + 1 vote threshold.

Advantages of AV

The advantages of AV are:

➤ Representatives are elected by majorities in their constituencies.
➤ The winning candidate must achieve broad support.
➤ The link between representatives and their constituencies is retained.

Disadvantages of AV

The disadvantages of AV are:

➤ It is not a proportional system, and can produce less proportional outcomes than FPTP. If used for the 1997 general election, AV would have given Labour an even larger majority and the Liberal Democrats more seats than the Conservatives.
➤ The candidate who secures most votes may not be elected when second preferences have been distributed — the least unpopular rather than most popular candidate may be elected.
➤ The second preferences of electors who voted for small extremist parties are taken into account.

Supplementary vote

The supplementary vote (SV) is a variant of AV. It has been used for the election of the mayor of London since 2000 (see Table 2.4), and for directly elected mayors in other towns and cities. The key features of SV are:

➤ The elector has one vote and records only his or her first and second preferences on the ballot paper.
➤ If no candidate wins a majority of first preferences, all but the top two candidates are eliminated, and the second preference votes for the remaining two eligible candidates are added to their first preference votes.
➤ The candidate with the highest total is elected.

Table 2.4 Election of mayor of London, 2008

Candidate	Party	First preference (%)	Second preference (%)	Final vote tally (%)
Boris Johnson	Conservative	43.2	12.9	53.2
Ken Livingstone	Labour	37.0	15.1	46.8
Brian Paddick	Liberal Democrat	9.8	32.0	
Sian Berry	Green	3.2	16.6	
Richard Barnbrook	BNP	2.9	6.4	
Others (5)		3.8	17.0	

Advantages of SV

The advantages of SV are:

➢ The winning candidate must achieve broad support.
➢ The second preferences of voters who supported minor parties are not counted.

Disadvantages of SV

The disadvantages of SV are:

➢ The winning candidate does not need to get a majority of first preference votes.
➢ If used for general elections, it would not deliver a proportional outcome.

Regional list

The regional list system of proportional representation has been used for elections to the European Parliament in England, Scotland and Wales (but not Northern Ireland) since 1999. Its key features are:

The mayor of London, Boris Johnson

➢ Representatives are elected in large multi-member regions. For European Parliament elections, there are 11 regions in Great Britain electing between three and ten MEPs.
➢ Political parties draw up a list of candidates, in the order in which they will be elected.
➢ Electors cast a single vote for a political party or independent. In the 'closed list' system used in Britain, electors can only vote for a party or for an independent candidate. They cannot choose between candidates representing the same political party. This gives political parties greater control over the electoral process, as they can position their favoured candidates at the top of the list. In an 'open list' system, voters can choose between candidates from the same party.
➢ Seats are allocated according to the proportion of votes won by each political party in the region.

Advantages of regional list

The advantages of the regional list system are:

> There is a high degree of proportionality. The size of the region (the 'district magnitude') matters — results are more proportional in regions electing a high number of representatives, but smaller parties are less likely to win seats in regions electing a small number of representatives.

> Political parties have used their lists to increase the number of women and ethnic minority candidates.

Disadvantages of regional list

The disadvantages of the regional list system are:

> In closed list systems, voters cannot choose between candidates from the same party.

> Parties control the order in which candidates are placed on the list, and can use this power to favour candidates who support the current leadership.

> The link between representatives and constituents is weakened in large multi-member constituencies.

Table 2.5 shows the outcome of the 2009 European Parliament elections in Great Britain. The result was largely proportional. However, the share of seats won by the four leading parties was higher than their share of the vote. The Greens won the same number of seats as the BNP and SNP, despite polling more votes. This is because the relatively small size of some regions still makes it difficult for a party whose vote is evenly distributed to win seats.

Table 2.5 Elections to the European Parliament, 2009 (GB only)

Party	Share of vote	Seats (share of seats)
Conservative	27.7	25 (36%)
UKIP	16.5	13 (19%)
Labour	15.7	13 (19%)
Liberal Democrat	13.7	11 (16%)
Green	8.6	2 (3%)
BNP	6.2	2 (3%)
SNP	2.1	2 (3%)
Plaid Cymru	0.8	1 (1%)
Others	8.5	0 (0%)

Single transferable vote

The single transferable vote (STV) is used in Northern Ireland for elections to the Northern Ireland Assembly, local government and the European Parliament. It is also used for local elections in Scotland — and for general elections in the Republic of Ireland. The main features of STV are:

> Representatives are elected in large multi-member constituencies. In elections to the Northern Ireland Assembly, 17 constituencies each elect six members.

> Voting is preferential — electors indicate their preferences by writing '1' besides the name of their first preference, '2' next to the name of their second choice and so on.

> Voting is also ordinal — electors can vote for as many or as few candidates as they like.

> A candidate must achieve a quota, known as the Droop quota, to be elected. Any votes in excess of this quota are redistributed on the basis of second preferences. The quota is calculated as follows:

$$\left(\frac{\text{total valid poll}}{(\text{seats} + 1)}\right) + 1$$

If no candidate reaches the quota on the first count, the lowest-placed candidate is eliminated and their second preferences are transferred. This process of elimination and redistribution of preferences continues until the requisite number of seats is filled by candidates meeting the quota.

Table 2.6 shows the result in the Upper Bann constituency in the 2007 elections to the Northern Ireland Assembly. Two candidates achieved the quota of 14% on the first count. Second preferences were then transferred across 12 counts before all six seats were filled. The second UUP candidate to be elected (Savage) scored fewer first preference votes than either Ward or McCrum, but overtook them when the second preferences had been transferred.

Table 2.6 Result in Upper Bann, 2007 Northern Ireland Assembly election

Candidate	Party	Status	Count	First preference votes	%
O'Dowd	SF	Elected	1	7,733	18.0
Simpson	DUP	Elected	1	6,828	15.9
Gardiner	UUP	Elected	9	5,135	12.0
Kelly	SDLP	Elected	8	4,689	10.9
Moutray	DUP	Elected	11	3,663	8.5
Ward	SF	Eliminated	12	3,118	7.3
McCrum	DUP	Eliminated	10	2,975	6.9
Savage	UUP	Elected	12	2,167	5.1

Advantages of STV
The advantages of STV are:
> It has a good record of delivering proportional outcomes, and ensures that votes are largely of equal value.
> Only a party or group of parties that wins more than 50% of the popular vote can form a government.
> Voters can choose between a large range of candidates, including different candidates from the same party.

Disadvantages of STV
The disadvantages of STV are:
> The system is less accurate in translating votes into seats than list systems or some versions of AMS.
> It uses large multi-member constituencies that weaken the link between individual MPs and their constituency.

> It is likely to produce a **coalition government** that may be unstable and can give disproportional influence to minor parties that hold the balance of power.

Key term
> **Coalition government** A government made up of more than one political party.

Additional member system

The additional member system (AMS) is a mixed electoral system. It has been used to elect the Scottish Parliament and Welsh Assembly since 1999, and the London Assembly since 2000. It is also used for general elections in Germany. The main features of AMS are:

> A proportion of seats in the legislative assembly are elected using FPTP in single-member constituencies; 73 out of 129 members of the Scottish Parliament (57%) are elected in single-member constituencies, as are 40 of the 60 members of the Welsh Assembly (67%).

> A smaller number of representatives — additional members — are elected in multi-member constituencies; 56 members of the Scottish Parliament (43%) and 20 members of the Welsh Assembly (33%) are elected in this way.

> Electors cast two votes: one for their favoured candidate in a single-member constituency, and one for their favoured party from a party list in a multi-member constituency

> List seats (additional members) are allocated on a corrective basis to ensure that the total number of seats for parties in the assembly is proportional to the number of votes they won. These seats are allocated using the d'Hondt rule (see Box 2.1).

> To win seats in the Greater London Assembly, a party must pass a threshold of 5% of the vote. There is no threshold for Scottish Parliament and Welsh Assembly elections.

Advantages of AMS

The advantages of AMS are:

> As a mixed system, it balances the desirability of constituency representation with that of fairness in election outcomes.

> The results are broadly proportional and votes are less likely to be wasted.

> Voters have greater choice. **Split-ticket voting** is allowed. Here, a voter uses their constituency vote to support a candidate from one party, and their list vote to support a different party.

Key term
> **Split-ticket voting** The practice of voting for candidates from different parties in an election where an elector is permitted to cast more than one vote.

Disadvantages of AMS

The weaknesses of AMS are:

> It creates two categories of representative in the legislative assembly, one with constituency duties and one without.

> Parties can have significant control over the party lists used to elect additional members.

> Smaller parties are often under-represented because multi-member seats elect relatively few representatives.

Box 2.1 The d'Hondt formula

The d'Hondt formula is a mathematical formula for allocating seats proportionally. It was invented by the nineteenth-century Belgian academic Victor d'Hondt. It is a highest average system that uses a divisor method rather than a quota. The formula does not deliver strict proportionality because it slightly favours large parties over smaller ones.

Under d'Hondt, the total votes of each party are divided by the number of seats it already has, plus the next seat to be allocated. Thus, the party totals are divided first by 1 (0 seats plus 1), then by 2 (1 seat plus 1) and so on. The first seat goes to the party with the largest number, the next seat to the next highest number and so on.

Table 2.7 shows the regional list election in Mid and West Wales in the 1999 Welsh Assembly election. The number of constituency seats won by each party in the region was taken into account in allocating the first list seat. The calculations for subsequent seats then took the list and constituency seats into account. The Conservatives won two of the four list seats, having failed to secure a constituency seat in the region.

Table 2.7 The regional list election in Mid and West Wales, 1999

	Con	Lab	Lib Dem	Plaid Cymru	Winner
Constituency seats won	0	2	2	4	
List votes	36,622	53,842	31,683	84,544	
First divisor	1	3	3	5	
First seat	36,622	17,947	10,561	16,910	Con
Second divisor	2	3	3	5	
Second seat	18,311	17,947	10,561	16,910	Con
Third divisor	3	3	3	5	
Third seat	12,207	17,947	10,561	16,910	Lab
Fourth divisor	3	4	3	5	
Fourth seat	12,207	13,460	10,561	16,910	Plaid Cymru

Source: J. Bradbury, 'Labour's bloody nose', *Politics Review*, Vol. 9, No. 2, November 1999, p. 7.

Table 2.8 shows the result of the 2007 elections to the Scottish Parliament. The SNP polled more constituency votes than Labour but won 16 fewer constituency seats. The SNP again won the highest share of the regional list vote and the list seats were allocated in a corrective way so that the SNP ended up with one more seat than Labour in the Scottish Parliament. The Conservatives also benefited from the distribution of list seats. Smaller parties and independents performed much better in the regional list contests than the constituency contests, picking up three seats.

Weblinks

www.electoral-reform.org.uk/votingsystems/systems.htm — the Electoral Reform Society's guide to electoral systems.

Table 2.8 Elections to the Scottish Parliament, 2007

Party	Share of constituency vote (%)	Constituency seats won	Share of regional list vote (%)	List seats won	Total seats
Conservative	16.6	4	13.9	13	17
Labour	32.2	37	29.2	9	46
Lib Dem	16.2	11	11.3	5	16
SNP	32.9	21	31.0	26	47
Green	0.1	0	4.0	2	2
Others	2.0	0	10.6	1	1

Impact of the new electoral systems

The new electoral systems have already had an impact on UK politics. The most significant effects are as follows:

> **Greater proportionality.** The results of the elections conducted under the new electoral systems have been more proportional than Westminster elections. The number of seats won by parties in the assemblies more closely matches the share of the vote they achieved. Smaller parties have had a greater chance of representation. However, no electoral system can translate votes into seats perfectly, and some systems perform this task better than others (see Box 2.2).

> **Multi-party systems.** The results of elections using PR and mixed electoral systems have confirmed that the UK has a number of party systems rather than a standard, nationwide two-party system. Many of these are multi-party systems. Labour has long won a majority of Scottish seats at Westminster, but has failed to do so in the devolved elections. Smaller parties that have been unable to make a breakthrough at Westminster (e.g. the Greens and UKIP) have won seats in the devolved assemblies and the European Parliament. UKIP came second in the 2009 European Parliament elections with 16% of the vote.

> **Minority and coalition governments.** None of the elections to the devolved assemblies has produced a clear winner. No party has won a majority of the popular vote or a majority of seats. The Scottish Parliament has seen two terms of a Labour–Liberal Democrat coalition, and one of a minority Scottish National Party government. In Wales, Labour has ruled as a minority government and in coalition with first the Liberal Democrats, and then Plaid Cymru. The Good Friday Agreement requires that the Northern Ireland executive includes the major unionist and nationalist parties.

Key term

> **Minority government**
A government formed by a political party that does not have an overall majority in the legislature.

> **Split-ticket voting.** Voting behaviour has become more complex. Minor parties and independent candidates have performed better in elections using the new

systems because electors recognise that a vote for a minor party is less likely to be wasted. One in five voters engaged in split-ticket voting in the 1999 Scottish Parliament elections (and more did so subsequently), by supporting a major party in the constituency vote but giving their list vote to another party.

Box 2.2 Deviation from proportionality

'Deviation from proportionality' is a measure of the proportionality of electoral systems. Table 2.9 shows that FPTP is the least proportional of the electoral systems used in the UK. STV is the most proportional. The AMS and list system have both produced results that are not greatly proportional. This is because the district magnitude (i.e. the number of legislative seats per constituency) of the regions is small, making it difficult for small parties to win seats.

Table 2.9 Deviation from proportionality under different electoral systems

Institution	Electoral system	Year of election	Deviation from proportionality (%)
House of Commons	FPTP	2010	23
European Parliament (GB only)	Regional list PR	2009	18
Scottish Parliament	AMS (57:43)	2007	13
National Assembly for Wales	AMS (66:33)	2007	19
Northern Ireland Assembly	STV	2007	7

Note: Deviation from proportionality is calculated by: calculating the difference between each party's percentage vote-share and seat-share, summing all deviations (ignoring minus signs) and halving the total.

Advocates of **electoral reform** see these outcomes as positive. However, the new systems have also brought problems:

➢ **Complexity.** A sizeable minority of voters have found the systems complex and the design of ballot papers has been criticised. In the 2007 Scottish Parliament elections, 146,000 ballots were rejected because they had not been completed correctly. In June 2004, voters in London took part in five contests on the same day, each using a different electoral system. In the mayoral election, 17% of second preference votes were rejected because the ballot paper was filled in incorrectly.

➢ **Constituency links.** Tensions between constituency and regional list members have arisen in the Scottish Parliament and Welsh Assembly. Whereas the former have a significant constituency workload, the latter do not have a clear link with their constituents and undertake less of this work. Candidates were barred from standing for both constituency and regional list seats in the 2007 Welsh Assembly elections, but are permitted to do so in Scotland.

Key term

➢ **Electoral reform** Changes made to an electoral system or a change from one electoral system to an alternative (in Britain, the term commonly refers to the campaign to replace FPTP with PR).

> **Low turnout.** Turnout in elections conducted under the new systems has often been low. Evidence from other countries shows that turnout in general elections conducted under PR elections is higher than that where FPTP is used. Turnout in second-order elections — that is, contests that do not determine the government — is normally lower than for general elections. But turnouts of 34% for the 2009 European Parliament election and 38% for the 2003 Welsh Assembly election were still disappointing.

Weblinks

www.ucl.ac.uk/constitution-unit/research/elections-parties/index.htm — click on 'Research' and then select 'Elections and parties' from the bullet list to access relevant reports by the Constitution Unit at University College, London, including its independent report (2002) on the new electoral systems.

Electoral reform

The campaign for electoral reform has a long history. The Proportional Representation Society, forerunner of the Electoral Reform Society, was formed in the 1880s. In 1918, a Speaker's Conference recommended that a mixed electoral system should replace FPTP. A bill introducing AV was passed by the House of Commons but rejected by the House of Lords in 1931.

Labour's interest in electoral reform revived in opposition in the 1980s and 1990s. John Smith committed a Labour government to holding a referendum on electoral reform for Westminster. Tony Blair included this pledge in Labour's 1997 manifesto, and commitments to introduce new electoral systems for the devolved assemblies, the European Parliament, and a mayor and assembly in London.

In 1997 the Blair government established an Independent Commission on the Voting System to examine the case for moving away from FPTP for general elections. It was chaired by Lord (Roy) Jenkins, a Liberal Democrat peer and former Labour cabinet minister. Jenkins recommended 'AV Plus', a hybrid of the AMS and alternative vote systems. Most MPs would have been elected in single-member constituencies using AV, with the remaining 20% elected from open lists in multi-member regions and allocated on a corrective basis.

But neither the Blair nor Brown government held the promised referendum on electoral reform. Blair's doubts about reform hardened after Labour's experience of coalitions with the Liberal Democrats in Scotland and Wales. He said that PR was unfair because it delivered undue influence to small parties holding the balance of power. Many Labour MPs were also unwilling to replace a system that had given them parliamentary majorities on a minority of the popular vote. The Labour government also rejected proposals for further electoral reform made by commissions it had created in Scotland and Wales. The Arbuthnot Commission (2007) had called for an open list system for the Scottish Parliament and the Richard Commission (2004) for STV for the Welsh Assembly.

In 2010, however, Gordon Brown declared his support for AV for general elections and pledged that, if re-elected, Labour would hold a referendum on its introduction. Electoral reform had not featured previously in Brown's constitutional reform agenda and a 2008 government review of the new electoral systems had not recommended changes for Westminster. The MPs' expenses scandal and the prospect of attracting Liberal Democrat support in the event of a hung parliament played a part in the change of position.

The Conservatives proposed to rectify the bias in the FPTP system by cutting the number of seats and redrawing boundaries so that constituencies are of more equal size. When the 2010 election produced a hung parliament, the Conservatives agreed to hold a referendum on AV as part of a coalition agreement with the Liberal Democrats. The Liberal Democrats' preferred system is STV, but they accepted the Conservative offer on AV even though it is not a proportional system. Research by the Electoral Reform Society suggested that the Liberal Democrats would have won an additional 22 seats if AV had been used for the 2010 general election, and 105 more under STV (see Table 2.10). The coalition agreement allows the Conservatives to campaign against AV in the referendum. It also proposes a reformed House of Lords elected by proportional representation.

Weblinks

www.electoral-reform.org.uk — the website of the Electoral Reform Society, a group advocating electoral reform, provides news and commentary.

Table 2.10 The 2010 general election under different voting systems

Party	First-past-the-post	Alternative vote	Single transferable vote
Conservative	307	281	246
Labour	258	262	207
Liberal Democrat	57	79	162
Others	28	28	35

Source: Electoral Reform Society, www.electoral-reform.org.uk.

Viewpoint Should there be electoral reform for Westminster elections?

YES

- FPTP fails to allocate seats fairly, producing outcomes that do not represent the views of the people.
- Votes are not of equal value under FPTP (many are wasted) and voters are often denied a meaningful choice.
- Governments with parliamentary majorities but no majority of the popular vote can bring about major changes — this raises questions of legitimacy.
- FPTP props up the two-party system when support for the main parties has declined and multi-party politics is becoming the norm.
- Electoral reform would help restore faith in parliament and would increase turnout.

NO

- FPTP delivers strong and stable government; proportional systems deliver coalition governments that are often weaker and unstable.
- Voters are provided with a clear choice between the government and the main opposition party.
- Majority governments have a clear mandate and are able to deliver their policy commitments without bowing to the demands of minor parties.
- Single-member constituencies provide a clear link between an MP and the people he or she represents.
- FPTP is understood and accepted by voters — there is little demand for electoral reform.

Voting behaviour

Two main approaches have been prevalent in studies of voting behaviour:

> - sociological approaches that focus on the social characteristics of voters, particularly **social class**, and their party loyalties
> - rational choice approaches that focus on decisions made by individual voters on political issues, the economy, party leaders and governing competence

Concepts explained

Social class

A social group defined by social and economic status. The working class consists of people in manual occupations and the middle class is made up of those with non-manual jobs. The traditional way that opinion pollsters categorise social class is: AB – professional and managerial; C1 – white collar (non-manual) workers; C2 – blue collar (manual) workers; and DE – semi-skilled, unskilled and those reliant on state benefits. Government statisticians use more complex typologies.

Class voting and partisanship

Sociological approaches made two main claims about the social characteristics of voters in the period 1945–70:

> - **Class voting.** A strong link existed between social class and voting. Most people voted for their 'natural' class party: that is, the party that best represented the interests of their social group. A majority of the working class (i.e. manual workers) voted for the Labour Party, while most of the middle class (i.e. non-manual workers) backed the Conservatives. There were, however, some exceptions. At a time when the working class was the largest social group, the Conservatives would not have won power without the support of a sizeable minority of working-class voters.
> - **Partisanship.** Most voters had stable, long-term feelings of positive attachment to one of the main parties. This party identification developed through **socialisation** or social learning in the home (most people voted for the same party as their parents), school, workplace and neighbourhood.

Both class voting and partisanship have declined since 1970. Two trends have been apparent:

➤ **Class dealignment.** The relationship between social class and voting has weakened, with fewer people voting for their class party. This is because the distinctions between social classes have been eroded by greater affluence, improved access to higher education and changes in the labour market (e.g. the increase in women and part-time workers). The 'old working class' of manual workers who were employed in heavy industry and belonged to trade unions has shrunk. A 'new working class' of people working in the private sector, with better qualifications and owning their own home, emerged in the 1980s. New sectoral divisions have emerged, notably between those employed in the public and private sectors.

➤ **Partisan dealignment.** The number of voters who strongly identify with either Labour or the Conservatives has declined. In 1964, 43% of voters were 'very strong' supporters of one of the main parties, but by 2005 only 13% were. The **core vote** for the two main parties is therefore smaller — parties have to work harder to win over **floating voters** who do not have strong allegiances and may switch their vote from election to election. Partisan dealignment is also seen in the decline in party membership and the two-party system. Whereas more than 90% of voters in the 1950s voted for either Labour or the Conservatives, only 65% did so in 2010.

> **Key terms**
> ➤ **Class dealignment** The decline in the relationship between social class and voting.
> ➤ **Core vote** Voters who feel a strong attachment to a political party and vote for it in election after election.
> ➤ **Floating voters** Voters without a strong attachment to a particular party, who may switch their vote from election to election.
> ➤ **Partisan dealignment**. The decline in strong voter identification with political parties.
> ➤ **Socialisation**. The process by which individuals acquire their values and beliefs.

Class voting has been less pronounced in recent general elections. The Conservatives gained support from the working class in the 1980s, while Labour made significant gains among middle-class voters in 1997. New Labour was a 'catch-all' party with a cross-class appeal. It made further gains among middle-class voters in 2001 and 2005, but its working-class support fell (see Table 2.11). The Conservatives have made only small gains among middle-class voters since their 1997 defeat, making steadier progress in their levels of working-class support.

Despite the decline of class voting, it is important to recognise that Labour remains the most popular party among working-class voters and the Conservatives still perform best among middle-class voters.

Weblinks

www.politicsresources.net — click on 'Elections' and then scroll down to 'United Kingdom'.

Table 2.11 Class voting since 1974

Party	Middle class (ABC1)	Skilled working class (C2)	Unskilled working class (DE)
Conservative			
1974 (Oct.)	56	26	22
1979	59	41	34
1983	55	40	33
1987	54	40	30
1992	54	39	31
1997	39	27	21
2001	38	29	24
2005	37	33	25
2010	39	37	31
Labour			
1974 (Oct.)	19	49	57
1979	24	41	49
1983	16	32	41
1987	18	36	48
1992	22	40	49
1997	34	50	59
2001	34	49	55
2005	31	40	48
2010	27	29	40

Source: Ipsos MORI, www.ipsos-mori.com.

Other social factors

A number of other social characteristics have an impact on voting behaviour:

➤ **Gender.** For much of the postwar period, women were more likely to vote Conservative than men. This perhaps reflected social attitudes of the time and the fact that relatively few women went out to work. Labour made significant gains among women voters in the 1990s, drawing level with the Conservatives. The Conservatives overtook Labour in 2010, but Labour did better among women aged under 35.

➤ **Age.** Labour outperformed the Conservatives among younger voters in the 1990s. The Conservatives have long scored best among older voters.

➤ **Ethnicity.** A clear majority of ethnic minority electors vote Labour. Ethnic minority voters are not, though, a homogeneous group and tend to vote along class lines. The Iraq war contributed to a sharp fall in support for Labour in 2005 in constituencies with large Muslim populations, but Labour regained some of this support in 2010.

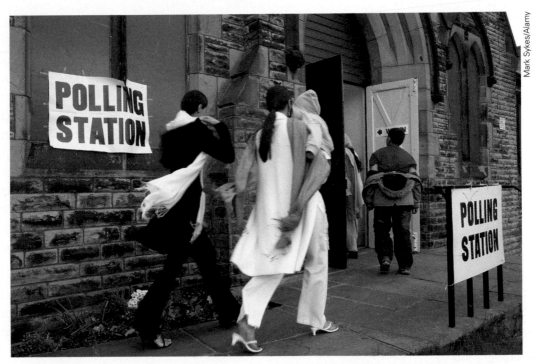

British Asian voters entering a polling station in Dewsbury, West Yorkshire

> **Region.** There are important regional variations in voting in Britain. A 'north–south divide' is evident, with Conservative support highest in southern England, the suburbs and rural areas, while Labour does best in the north of England, Scotland and Wales, in large urban areas and on council estates. Regional patterns of support are explained partly by the distribution of social classes (e.g. manual workers are concentrated in urban areas), but also by local political factors. The 2010 general election saw Labour–Conservative contests in London, the Midlands, the northwest and Yorkshire. But the main electoral battles in the southwest were between the Conservatives and Liberal Democrats, while some northern cities saw Labour–Liberal Democrat rivalry. Nationalist parties came second in Scotland and Wales. Northern Ireland has a distinctive party system and pattern of voting.

Rational choice approaches

The **rational choice model** of voting behaviour focuses on the choices made by individual voters. There are four main variants.

Issue voting

The issue voting model claims that people compare party policies and vote for the party whose position is closest to their own. To be significant, issue voting must favour one party over another. Electors must feel an issue is important, must identify the

Key term

> **Rational choice model** An approach to the study of politics that focuses on the actions of rational individuals who pursue their own interests.

61

Concepts explained

Valence issue

A valence issue is a policy issue on which the main parties are in broad agreement. When parties adopt a similar position, voters make judgements about their relative competence and ability to deliver the desired outcomes. A party will campaign on those valence issues on which voters believe it is the most competent.

same party as having the best policy, and then must vote for it. However, many voters see little difference between the main parties on key issues. Issues on which there is broad agreement between the parties (e.g. the economy, health) are **valence issues**. The valence model claims that voter judgements on trust and competence are crucial on these issues. At the 1997, 2001 and 2005 elections, Labour enjoyed strong leads over the Conservatives on key issues such as health and education. Voters believed that Labour was more likely to deliver a sound economy and good-quality public services than the Conservatives.

Economic voting

The economic voting model claims that voters are more likely to support the governing party if it has delivered a healthy economy. By looking at economic data (e.g. interest rates) and voters' personal economic expectations (i.e. whether they will be better or worse off), the model predicted the results of recent elections with a good degree of accuracy. A decline in economic pessimism as the UK emerged from recession saw support for Labour increase in 2010, helping to deny the Conservatives a parliamentary majority at the general election.

Party leaders

Party leaders have become more important in shaping electoral outcomes because of partisan dealignment and the personalisation of politics. Leaders are the public face of their party and carry much of the responsibility for communicating party policy. This was especially true in the 2010 election campaign when the Conservative, Labour and Liberal Democrat leaders took part in three televised debates. Voters use their judgements about the character and competence of leaders as short-cuts to reach verdicts about political parties as a whole. Tony Blair enjoyed high approval ratings in 1997, and even when his popularity waned after the invasion of Iraq, he was regarded as a more capable prime minister than his Conservative rivals. Gordon Brown was unpopular but David Cameron did not enjoy the high poll ratings that Blair had when in opposition.

Governing competence

This perspective suggests that voters make a judgement about the overall performance of the government. David Denver refers to this as 'judgemental voting'. If the governing party is widely perceived to have performed well in office, it will be rewarded. Attributes of governing competence might include policy success (particularly a sound economy), strong leadership, a clear agenda and party unity. Conversely, governments that are judged to have failed to achieve a modicum of governing competence can expect to be punished at the polls. Policy failures (especially in economic policy), weak leadership, a lack of direction and obvious disunity undermine a governing party's electoral chances. In 1997, voters reached a negative verdict on the Conservatives' performance in government and believed Labour would prove more effective. Voter satisfaction with Labour had declined by 2005, but perceptions of the Conservatives were even more negative. Although these had improved by 2010, many voters were not convinced that the Conservatives were ready for government.

Weblinks

www.ipsos-mori.com — a leading opinion pollster whose website includes detailed information on political trends.

Campaigns and the media

Political parties spend a great deal of time and money (more than £40 million in 2005) on their nationwide general election campaigns. They aim to set the agenda by promoting the issues on which they are favoured by voters. Parties also engage in negative campaigning by rubbishing the policies and leaders of their rivals in the hope of persuading voters to switch, or at least making supporters of other parties consider whether to vote at all.

Evidence on the significance of these national campaigns is patchy. Most voters have already made their mind up before the campaign gets under way. There is likely to be some movement in the opinion polls during a campaign, but much of it is 'churning' in which voters switch between parties rather than moving uniformly towards one party. The 2010 campaign saw an unusually high number of voters make up their minds late (one in four decided in the final week) or change their minds (particularly those considering voting Liberal Democrat).

Local campaigning can be significant. Parties focus much of their effort on marginal seats, in which small swings in support can change the outcome of the contest. Local campaigns are coordinated from the centre to a much greater extent, but an active local party can play an important role in canvassing voters.

Voters get much of their information on politics from the media. Television is a crucial medium, particularly with the advent of leaders' debates in 2010. One in four voters said that they changed their mind on how to vote after the first debate. Studies of the impact of newspapers on voting behaviour have not produced a definitive verdict. Rather, there are three broad perspectives:

➢ **Influence.** This perspective suggests that newspapers have a direct influence over the voting behaviour of their readers. Evidence suggests that, allowing for class and existing attitudes, readers of Labour-supporting newspapers are more likely to vote for Labour than are readers of pro-Conservative newspapers. The *Sun* claimed to

The 2010 leaders' debates were the first to be broadcast live in the run-up to a UK election

have influenced the outcome of the 1992 election and that in 1997, when it switched support to Labour. It backed the Conservatives in 2010.

➤ **Reinforcement.** This view suggests that newspapers reinforce the views already held by their readers. Most people read a newspaper that reflects their political views. But they often rely on television rather than newspapers for non-partisan coverage of politics.

➤ **Agenda shaping.** This perspective claims that the press is unlikely to have a direct influence on voting, but that newspaper coverage does help shape the political agenda. Newspaper coverage of, say, immigration or crime helps to frame the way in which these issues are perceived by voters.

Turnout

Turnout of around 60% in the 2001 and 2005 general elections was significantly lower than the postwar average of 78%. Turnout increased in 2010, but only to 65%. Studies of low turnout have focused on three main areas:

➤ **Rational choice.** Rational choice theory suggests that voters will not vote if the costs outweigh the potential benefits. Many non-voters cite practical reasons (e.g. inconvenience) for their abstention. People are more likely to vote in a close contest because their vote is more likely to make a difference to the outcome. Most people believe that voting is a civic duty, but the number is declining and is particularly low among young people.

➤ **Disillusion and apathy.** Dissatisfaction with Westminster politics and the main political parties has contributed to low turnout. The proportion of people who trust politicians or feel a strong attachment to a political party has declined. Some of the anger felt by voters about the MPs' expenses scandal had dissipated by the 2010 election, but it still depressed turnout. Recent general election campaigns have failed to motivate potential voters.

➤ **Social groups.** Turnout varies across social groups. Turnout is highest among elderly, middle-class and university-educated people. People aged over 65 were almost twice as likely to vote in 2005 as those aged 18 to 24. Turnout is higher in rural than urban areas.

The 2010 general election

The 2010 general election was the first to produce a hung parliament since February 1974. The Conservatives won a total of 307 seats, but fell short of the 326 needed for an overall majority in the House of Commons. The result was a disappointment for the Conservatives, given the unpopularity of the Labour government and the healthy lead they had in the opinion polls in 2009. But the Conservatives made a net gain of 97 seats and the Labour to Conservative swing of 5% was their largest since 1979.

Labour suffered a net loss of 91 seats and its 29% share of the UK vote was only marginally better than the party's postwar low in 1983. But it could have been worse: Labour had done enough to prevent a Conservative majority and had seen off a brief surge in support for the Liberal Democrats that had threatened to consign Labour to third in the popular vote.

The Conservatives and Labour together polled fewer than two-thirds of the vote for the first time in postwar politics. The Liberal Democrats' opinion poll ratings surged after Nick Clegg's performance in the first televised prime ministerial debate, but the election delivered only a small rise in their share of the vote and a net loss of five seats. A hung parliament saw them enter government as a junior partner in a Conservative–Liberal Democrat coalition.

Caroline Lucas became the first Green MP, but the party's nationwide vote share fell. UKIP polled more than 900,000 votes and the BNP more than 500,000, their highest general election totals, but they managed only six third-placed finishes between them. The two independents elected in 2005 were defeated, as was former Respect MP George Galloway.

Social characteristics of voting

Table 2.12 shows the social characteristics of voting at the 2010 general election. The most significant developments were:

➤ **Social class.** The Conservatives remained the favoured party of middle-class voters and Labour of working-class voters, but there was a slump in support for Labour among C2 (manual) and DE (semi-skilled and unskilled) voters. People employed in the public sector were less likely to vote Conservative than those working in the private sector.

- > **Gender and age.** Labour again had more support from women than men, although the Conservatives overtook Labour in terms of overall support from women voters. All parties had identified young mothers as a critical sub-set of the electorate. The Conservatives and Liberal Democrats made significant gains among women under 35, but Labour lost ground. Young voters were more likely to vote for the Liberal Democrats, while the Conservatives had strong leads among voters aged 55 and over.
- > **Region.** There was no uniform nationwide swing. A north–south divide in party support resurfaced. The Conservatives again did best in southern England and overtook Labour in the Midlands. Labour came top in northern England despite large swings to the Conservatives in Yorkshire and the northeast. Labour's best performance was in Scotland where it increased its share of the vote, while the Conservatives remained fourth and have only a single seat. The Conservatives gained five seats in Wales but a new electoral alliance with the Ulster Unionist Party flopped.

The swing to the Conservatives was slightly higher in Labour–Conservative marginals than elsewhere. But the swing to the Conservatives in Liberal Democrat–Conservative marginals was only 1%, allowing the Liberal Democrats to retain seats in southwest England. Labour topped the poll in London and the Conservatives failed to win seats in other large cities. They also underperformed in seats with a high proportion of black and minority ethnic voters, suggesting that Labour won back those voters who had deserted it in 2005 because of the Iraq war. Finally, incumbent Labour MPs tended to suffer smaller swings to the Conservatives than new candidates.

Rational choice voting

To understand fully why the Conservatives made gains but did not win a majority, it is necessary to examine rational choice accounts of the 2010 general election. They focus on the following:

- > **The economy and other issues.** Management of the economy was the issue ranked most important by voters. Some 29% of voters felt that the Conservatives had the best policy, a 3% lead over Labour, but 36% of voters believed that no party had the best economic policy. The Conservatives had failed to convince voters despite the economic problems of the Brown government. They did enjoy large leads over Labour on immigration, crime and defence, but Labour led the Tories on health and unemployment. However, a plurality of voters had little faith in the policies of any of the established parties on these issues.
- > **Party leaders.** Opinion poll evidence suggested that voters' opinions of the party leaders were as important as party policies in determining how people voted. David Cameron was preferred to Gordon Brown as the 'most capable prime minister', but only by a narrow margin. Brown was unpopular but Cameron was not particularly popular. High approval ratings for Nick Clegg did not bring a sizeable increase in the Liberal Democrat vote.

Table 2.12 The 2010 general election

	Conservative	Labour	Liberal Democrat
Share of the vote (%)	36.1 (+3.8)	29.0 (−6.2)	23.0 (+1.0)
Seats	307 (+97)	258 (−91)	57 (−5)
Social class			
AB	39 (+2)	26 (−2)	29 (0)
C1	39 (+2)	28 (−4)	24 (+1)
C2	37 (+6)	29 (−11)	22 (+3)
DE	31 (+6)	40 (−8)	17 (−1)
Gender			
Men	38 (+4)	28 (−6)	22 (0)
Women	36 (+4)	31 (−7)	26 (+3)
Age			
18–24	30 (+2)	31 (−7)	30 (+4)
25–34	35 (+10)	30 (−8)	29 (+2)
35–44	34 (+7)	31 (−10)	26 (+3)
45–54	34 (+3)	28 (−7)	26 (+1)
55–64	38 (−1)	28 (−3)	23 (+1)
65+	44 (+3)	31 (−4)	16 (−2)
Region			
North East	24 (+4)	44 (−9)	24 (+0)
Yorkshire and the Humber	33 (+4)	35 (−9)	23 (+2)
North West	32 (+3)	40 (−6)	22 (+0)
West Midlands	40 (+5)	31 (−8)	21 (+2)
East Midlands	41 (+4)	30 (−9)	21 (+2)
Eastern	47 (+4)	20 (−10)	24 (+2)
London	35 (+3)	37 (−2)	22 (+0)
South East	50 (+5)	16 (−8)	26 (+1)
South West	43 (+4)	15 (−7)	35 (+2)
Scotland	18 (+1)	42 (+3)	19 (−4)
Wales	26 (+5)	36 (−7)	20 (+2)

Note: Figures in brackets refer to change since 2005.

Sources: BBC election website, http://news.bbc.co.uk/1/shared/election2010/results/; Ipsos MORI, www.ipsos-mori.com/researchspecialisms/socialresearch/specareas/politics/trends.aspx.

> **Governing competence.** A majority of voters agreed that it was time for change, but most did not think that the Conservatives had a clear message and four in ten voters did not believe that they were ready for government. The Conservatives had failed to 'seal the deal'. Cameron had neutralised the negative image that his party had in earlier elections, but he had failed to build convincing opinion poll leads on key issues, on competence and on his own capability as a potential prime minister.

❯ What you should know

❯ Elections are a central feature of politics in a liberal democracy. Their main functions include determining and legitimising the government, holding politicians to account, and ensuring the participation and representation of the people in the democratic process.

❯ A representative should act in the interests of their constituents but is also free to exercise their own judgement. If a representative body should resemble society, then more women, ethnic minority and young MPs ought to sit in the House of Commons than do at present.

❯ The first-past-the-post system is used for general elections. The winning candidate in a single-member constituency needs only a plurality (i.e. one more vote than their nearest rival). Supporters of FPTP claim that it produces strong, stable and responsible government. Critics argue that it is disproportional, produces wasted votes and denies voters real choice.

❯ Four other electoral systems are used for elections beyond Westminster: the majoritarian supplementary vote, two proportional representation systems (the regional list system and the single transferable vote) and the mixed additional member system.

❯ The new electoral systems have produced more proportional outcomes than FPTP, although smaller parties may still be under-represented. They have also led to minority and coalition governments, reflecting the development of multi-party systems in the UK. Large numbers of spoiled ballot papers indicate that some voters find the new systems complex.

❯ The impetus for electoral reform for Westminster stalled when the Blair government broke its pledge to hold a referendum on a new voting system. But the Conservative–Liberal Democrat coalition pledged a referendum on the alternative vote system in 2010.

❯ Class and party identity played a crucial role in voting behaviour in the period 1945–70, but their importance has declined. However, the Conservatives still perform best among middle-class voters and Labour among working-class voters. Voter perceptions of the relative competence of the main parties and their leaders have been highly significant in recent general elections.

UK/US comparison

Electoral systems

➤ There are separate elections for the president and for Congress in the USA. Elections take place at fixed terms. Presidential elections take place every 4 years. Members of the House of Representatives are elected every 2 years. Senators serve a 6-year term, but there are rolling elections with one-third of the Senate elected every 2 years. Hundreds of thousands of other positions (from judges to local officials) are also subject to election. In the UK, the head of government (the prime minister) is not directly elected. General elections are not held at fixed-term intervals, but must be held at least every 5 years.

> Members of the House of Representatives are elected in single-member constituencies known as districts. Each of the 50 US states sends two representatives to the Senate. MPs in the UK represent single-member constituencies, but members of the House of Lords are unelected.

> The simple plurality system is used for elections to Congress. The winning candidate needs to secure a plurality rather than an absolute majority of votes. In presidential elections, the candidate who secures a plurality of votes in a state receives all the electoral college votes for that state. As in the UK, simple plurality can deliver a 'winner's bonus' and may produce the wrong result — Republican George W. Bush won the presidential election in 2000 even though Democrat Al Gore polled more votes nationwide.

> The USA retains a classic two-party system, whereas that in the UK is in decline. The Republicans and Democrats win most votes and seats in Congress, and have shared the presidency in modern times. Third-party candidates rarely have an impact.

> Social factors are less important in voting behaviour in the USA than in the UK, although the Democrats do better among poorer voters and the Republicans perform better among the well-off. Black and women voters are more likely to support the Democrats. Election campaigns have a greater impact than in the UK, and the character of the presidential candidates is often crucial.

Further reading

Denver, D. (2007) *Elections and Voters in Britain*, 2nd edition, Palgrave.

Kavanagh, D. and Cowley, P. (2010) *The British General Election of 2010*, Palgrave.

Lundberg, T. (2008) 'A decade of electoral reform in the UK', *Politics Review*, Vol. 18, No. 1, pp. 27–29.

Rallings, C. and Thrasher, M. (2009) 'First-past-the-post revisited', *Politics Review*, Vol. 19, No. 4, pp. 30–32.

Rallings, C. and Thrasher, M. (2010) 'The 2010 general election', *Politics Review*, Vol. 20, No. 1, pp. 2–5.

Smith, N. (2006) *UK Elections and Electoral Reform*, Philip Allan Updates.

Exam focus

Short-answer questions (around 5 minutes each)

Explain, using examples, the meaning of each of the following terms:

1 Proportionality
2 Wasted votes
3 Mandate
4 Class dealignment

Mid-length questions (around 10 minutes each)

Outline two arguments 'for' and two arguments 'against' each of the following:

1 FPTP
2 AV
3 AMS
4 STV

Mini-essays (around 25–30 minutes each)

Write a mini-essay in response to each of the following questions:

1 Evaluate the arguments in favour of adopting a proportional electoral system in elections to the Westminster Parliament.
2 'Elections play a vital role within the UK's democratic system.' Discuss.
3 'The rational choice voting model provides the most convincing explanation of voting behaviour in the UK.' Discuss.
4 'Experiments in the use of alternative electoral systems in various elections around the UK since 1997 have proven a failure.' Discuss.

Chapter 3

Political parties: structure

Key questions answered in this chapter
- ➤ What is a political party?
- ➤ What role do parties perform in the UK system?
- ➤ How are the main UK parties organised?
- ➤ How internally democratic are the main UK parties?
- ➤ How are the main UK parties funded and why is party funding so controversial?

What is a political party?

Political parties are groups of like-minded individuals who seek to realise their shared goals by fielding candidates at elections and thereby securing election to public office.

Most conventional UK parties would ultimately aim to emerge victorious at a general election, and thereby earn the right to form a government at Westminster. In this respect, parties differ significantly from **pressure groups**, for while some pressure groups employ electoral candidacy as a means of raising public awareness of their chosen cause, they generally have little interest in, or prospect of, being returned to office.

The origins of modern UK parties

Before the Great Reform Act of 1832, UK parties existed not as mass-membership organisations with formal structures outside of parliament, but as groups of like-minded individuals within the legislature, bound together by shared ideals, friendship or family ties. With electoral reform came the need to organise in order to mobilise the growing electorate. It was at this point that UK political parties as we know them today began to emerge.

Political parties and pressure groups

Distinguish between

Political parties

➤ Political parties tend to offer a broad portfolio of policies informed by a guiding ideology.

➤ The main UK political parties have open membership structures and are therefore inclusive.

➤ Political parties contest elections with a view to securing control of governmental power.

➤ The main UK parties are highly organised and offer their members an input into key decisions through formalised rules and procedures.

Pressure groups

➤ Pressure groups generally pursue a narrower cause or sectional interest.

➤ Many pressure groups — particularly sectional groups — are more exclusive in their membership.

➤ Those pressure groups that field candidates in elections are generally doing so simply as a means of raising their profile.

➤ Even the larger, more established pressure groups are often dominated by a small leading clique and few pressure groups display high levels of internal democracy.

Different types of political party

Mainstream parties

UK politics is dominated by three main political parties: the Conservative Party, which emerged from the Tory group within parliament in the mid-nineteenth century; the Labour Party, formed by trade unions and socialist organisations at the start of the twentieth century; and the Liberal Democrats (Lib Dems), which came into being as a result of the merger between the Liberal Party and the Social Democratic Party (SDP) in 1988.

Nationalist parties

Nationalist parties look to nurture the shared cultural identity and language of those indigenous to a given geographical area — whether a 'nation', as in the case of the Scottish National Party (SNP), or a region, as in the case of Mebyon Kernow ('Sons of Cornwall'). While some nationalist parties campaign for full independence for their region or nation (e.g. the SNP in Scotland), others do not (e.g. Plaid Cymru in Wales). The British National Party is different from most other nationalist parties in that it campaigns in support of the way of life and values that it claims are common to all indigenous UK peoples.

Single-issue parties

Recent years have seen a rise in the number of single-issue parties contesting elections in the UK. In some cases these parties offer a wide-ranging programme of policies rooted in a particular ideological perspective (e.g. the Green Party). In other cases, these smaller parties campaign on a particular issue (e.g. UKIP on the UK's role in the European Union), or even a specific policy (e.g. the Pro-Life Alliance on abortion and embryology). Recent elections have also seen the rise of local single-issue parties such as the Independent Kidderminster Hospital and Health Concern Party, whose candidate Dr Richard Taylor won the Wyre Forest constituency at both the 2001 and 2005 general elections.

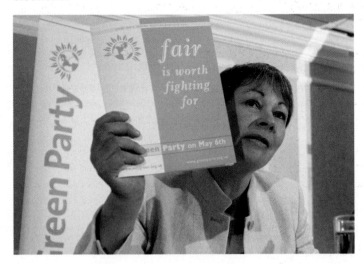

Caroline Lucas became the Green Party's first MP at the May 2010 general election

In many cases, such single-issue or ideological parties blur the boundary between political parties and pressure groups, as their primary goal is to raise awareness of a particular issue as opposed to winning an election and/or securing power (see Box 3.1).

Box 3.1 The Green Party: political party or attitude cause group?

It is possible for one or more pressure groups to evolve into a political party. A good case in point is the Green Party. Known prior to 1985 as the Ecology Party, the Green Party's origins can be found in a pressure group called 'People' that was formed in 1973. Although the Green Party itself initially appeared to be little more than a glorified single-issue group, it has developed a broader range of policies in recent years in an effort to improve its electoral prospects.

The growing appeal of minority parties

It is significant that the membership of many nationalist and single-issue parties has risen at the same time that mainstream parties have continued to haemorrhage members (see Table 3.1). Some argue that this is a function of the way in which the main UK parties have moved towards the centre of the political spectrum in recent years, thereby leaving some voters feeling unrepresented. Support for such minority parties at the ballot box may also reflect the fact that

Table 3.1 Individual party membership for the BNP, Green Party, SNP and UKIP (000s)

Year	BNP	Green	SNP	UKIP
2002	3.1	5.9	16.1	10.0
2003	5.5	5.3	9.5	16.0
2004	7.9	6.3	10.9	26.0
2005	6.5	7.1	11.0	19.0
2006	6.3	7.0	12.6	16.0
2007	9.8	7.4	13.9	15.9
2008	11.8	8.0	15.1	14.6

Source: John Marshall, *Membership of UK Political Parties*, House of Commons Library, 2009.

they provide an obvious vehicle for those looking to send a message to government or the main opposition parties by casting a protest vote.

Weblinks

www.parliament.uk/commons/lib/research/briefings/snsg-05125.pdf – the relevant Standard Note from the House of Commons Library.

The UK party system

Despite the rise of the Liberal Democrats and other smaller parties in recent years, most commentators still characterise Britain as a **two-party system**.

However, not all nations operate under a two-party system.

Key term

> **Two-party system** Where two fairly equally matched parties compete for power at elections and others have little realistic chance of breaking their duopoly.

Single-party systems

In a single-party system, one party dominates, bans other parties and exercises total control over candidacy at elections — where elections occur at all (e.g. in Nazi Germany or the Democratic People's Republic of Korea (North Korea)).

Dominant-party systems

In a dominant-party system, a number of parties exist but only one holds government power (e.g. Japan under the Liberal Democratic Party between 1955 and 1993).

Multi-party systems

In a multi-party system, many parties compete for power and the government consists of a series of coalitions formed by different combinations of parties (e.g. Italy between 1945 and 1993).

Viewpoint Is Britain a two-party system?

YES

- The Labour and Conservative parties are the only parties that have a realistic chance of forming a government in the near future, or at least of being the senior partner in a coalition.
- Even in 2010, the Labour and Conservative parties secured 65.1% of the popular vote and 86.8% of the 650 seats contested.
- The Liberal Democrats (in third) are still a long way behind the second-placed party.

NO

- 34.9% of voters backed parties other than the 'big two' in 2010.
- Although the Liberal Democrats are a third party, they are often second to Labour in the north and west and to the Conservatives in the south and east.
- In reality, different parts of the UK operate under different party systems. For example, in some parts of Scotland there is genuine four-way competition.
- Any party that could mobilise non-voters — 34.9% of registered voters at the 2010 general election — could win the election.

The roles performed by UK political parties

It is said that political parties perform five main roles: providing representation; facilitating political participation; engaging in political recruitment; formulating policy; and providing stable government.

Representation

Traditionally, parties were said to represent the views of their members. This was certainly true in an age of mass-membership parties when parties and voters were clearly divided along class lines. Partisan and class dealignment, accompanied by the rise of centrist 'catch-all parties', could be said to have undermined this primary role.

Participation

Parties encourage political participation by encouraging citizens to engage with the democratic process and giving them the opportunity to exercise power within their chosen party. The quality of participation afforded to members is shaped largely by the extent to which political parties are themselves internally democratic. This is one of the key issues that we will be addressing in the second half of this chapter.

Political recruitment

Parties play a central role in assessing the qualities of those who seek election to public office and casting aside those who are, for whatever reason, considered unsuitable. Parties also give those who will ultimately become the nation's leaders an opportunity to serve a political apprenticeship at a local level before 'graduating' to high office.

Policy formulation

Parties engage in detailed internal discussion and debate before drawing their proposals together and presenting them to voters in a single coherent programme (i.e. their manifesto). It is argued that this process is likely to result in a more considered, 'joined-up' style of government than that which might emerge in the absence of political parties.

Providing stable government

Without parties, it is argued, the Commons would simply be a gathering of around 650 individuals driven by their own goals and political ambitions. Parties present the voters with a clear choice at the ballot box and generally provide order following a general election by allowing a single party to form a government and secure the safe passage of its legislative proposals through the Commons.

The organisation of the main UK parties

Local and national level

Labour Party

Those who join the Labour Party are assigned to a local branch on the basis of their home postal address. These local branches are the lowest level of the party organisation.

They have a role in selecting candidates for local elections as well as sending delegates to the General Committee of the Constituency Labour Party (CLP). The CLP has a key role in organising the party at constituency level. It takes the lead in local and national election campaigns and plays a part in selecting candidates for parliamentary elections, although the extension of one member, one vote (OMOV) has diminished the role of constituency party leaders in favour of regular members.

The National Executive Committee (NEC) is the main national organ of the Labour Party. It enforces party discipline, ensures the smooth running of the party, oversees the preparation of policy proposals, and has the final say on the selection of parliamentary candidates. The party's annual conference was once the sovereign policy-making body within the Labour Party, although its role was diminished somewhat in the 1990s as we will see.

Conservative Party

The Conservative Party has a similar structure to the Labour Party at the local level. Branches corresponding to local council wards operate at the lowest level. Above the local branches are the constituency-level Conservative Associations. These bodies play a key role in organising the party at the grassroots level, planning election campaigns, and selecting parliamentary candidates. As with the Labour Party, however, these constituency associations no longer have a free rein in selecting parliamentary candidates.

The national party is organised around the Conservative Campaign Headquarters (CCHQ) at Millbank, Westminster. The party's headquarters were previously referred to as Conservative Central Office.

UK parties sitting in the European Parliament

UK members of the European Parliament (MEPs) traditionally sit in a number of transnational groups as opposed to a single UK block within the chamber. Following the UK elections to the European Parliament in 2009, the 25 Conservative MEPs elected sat with the newly formed European Conservative and Reformists (ECR) group, the 13 Labour MEPs sat with the Progressive Alliance of Socialists and Democrats (PASD), and the 11 Lib Dem MEPs sat with the Alliance of Liberals and Democrats for Europe (ALDE).

Internal party democracy

Political parties seek to exercise control over our democratic institutions and it is therefore not surprising that considerable attention focuses on the extent to which parties are themselves internally democratic.

Choosing and removing party leaders

One significant indicator of internal party democracy is the extent to which regular members are given an input into the process by which the party leader is chosen.

Concepts explained

Internal party democracy A measure of the extent to which rank-and-file members have genuine power within a given political party. Three processes are commonly considered when assessing how internally democratic a political party is: the way in which leaders are chosen; the way in which candidates for parliamentary elections are selected; and the way in which party policy is formulated.

Conservative Party

The current system for electing Conservative leaders was introduced in 1998 under William Hague, the Conservative Party leader at that time. Hague's successor, Iain Duncan Smith, became the first Conservative Party leader to be elected under the new system in 2001. Under the rules established by Hague, prospective candidates must be sitting Conservative MPs who take the party whip. They must also be nominated and seconded by fellow Conservative MPs. Once nominations close, a series of ballots is held among Conservative MPs, with the lowest-placed candidate in each ballot being eliminated, until only two candidates remain. Individual party members are then invited to choose between these two candidates in a run-off election by postal ballot.

The problem with the current system is that those in the parliamentary party can manipulate the final choice presented to rank-and-file members by voting tactically in the ballots of MPs. In 2001, for example, those on the right of the party deliberately switched their votes in the final ballot of MPs, with the effect of eliminating the early favourite Michael Portillo and presenting the rank-and-file members with a choice between their chosen candidate, the Eurosceptic Iain Duncan Smith, and the moderate Kenneth Clarke, a candidate whom Duncan Smith's supporters knew would not be able to defeat 'their man' in the ballot of individual party members.

Source: John Marshall, **Membership of UK Political Parties**, House of Commons Library, 2009.

Figure 3.1 Membership of the main UK parties as a percentage of the electorate, 1964–2005

Although it might appear sensible to offer individual party members the final say in such contests, doing so can prove problematic when the membership of all three main parties as a percentage of the electorate has contracted significantly in recent years (see Figure 3.1) and the members are themselves increasingly unrepresentative of the broader population. While Iain Duncan Smith was the clear favourite among Conservative Party members back in 2001, he proved singularly unable to capture the imagination of the broader electorate and was ultimately forced to resign by his own parliamentary party after just 2 years as leader. It was telling that individual members were effectively excluded from the process of electing Duncan-Smith's successor as a result of Michael Howard's unopposed 'coronation' as leader in 2003.

Weblinks

www.parliament.uk/commons/lib/research/briefings/snsg-05125.pdf — membership of UK political parties from a House of Commons Standard Note.

Labour Party

In the Labour Party, the party leader was once chosen by the Parliamentary Labour Party (PLP) alone, but since the 1980s leadership elections have operated under an electoral college system. In its present incarnation this electoral college is divided into three distinct sections, with one-third of the votes held by the Parliamentary Labour Party and the party's MEPs, one-third in the hands of **affiliated organisations** such as trade unions, and the final third being cast by **ordinary party members**. Since 1993 such contests have operated on a one member, one vote (OMOV) basis.

Concepts explained

Affiliated organisations

Groups that are formally linked to the Labour Party without their members holding regular membership of the party. Most trade unions are affiliated to the Labour Party, as are many socialist societies such as the Fabian Society and the Cooperative Society. Their affiliate status means that they retain a degree of input into the development of party policy and the election of party officials such as the party leader.

Those seeking to run for the post of leader must be nominated by at least 12.5% of the party's MPs where there is a vacancy and 20% of MPs where they seek to challenge the incumbent. If no candidate secures more than half of the votes cast on the first ballot, the rules state that further ballots must be held on an elimination basis until a clear winner emerges.

Although the system is obviously far more democratic than what went before it, rank-and-file members still have a fairly limited influence relative to individual MPs and the affiliated organisations. Indeed, individual members only have a say in the event that more than one candidate is able to secure the support necessary to validate their nomination. When Tony Blair stood down as party leader in 2007, Gordon Brown was

Ordinary party members and ordinary Members of Parliament

Ordinary party members

➤ The term 'ordinary party members' refers to individual members of a party or the 'rank-and-file' membership — those paid-up party members who do not hold senior positions within their chosen party at national level.

Ordinary Members of Parliament

➤ These are Members of Parliament (also known as backbenchers) who do not hold front-bench responsibilities as a government minister, shadow minister or party spokesperson.
➤ Although every MP will be a paid-up member of his or her chosen party, a question on ordinary party members will normally be expecting you to focus on the issue of internal party democracy — rather than the influence of backbenchers in relation to those on the front benches and their party leader.

elected unopposed. In addition, it is now far harder than it once was to remove a Labour Party leader while the party is in government. This is because such a challenge can only proceed following a majority vote at the annual party conference.

Liberal Democrats

The system by which the Lib Dems elect their leader is generally regarded as being the most democratic of the three main UK parties. Those wishing to stand must have the support of at least 10% of the parliamentary party and be nominated by no fewer than 200 members from at least 20 different local parties. The election itself then operates on an OMOV basis under a preferential, single transferable vote (STV) system — with losing candidates being eliminated and their votes transferred until one candidate commands the support of more than 50% of those members casting a ballot.

Candidate selection

As we have already noted, a key role commonly attributed to political parties is political recruitment. It is argued that parties play a role in training potential candidates through their involvement in grassroots party activity. Potential candidates thus serve a kind of political apprenticeship within the party.

Separating 'the wheat from the chaff'

The number of individuals wanting to be elected to parliament far exceeds the number of seats available in the Commons. Even within a given political party, one would expect to see a handful of willing candidates for every seat contested, hence the need for short-listing. Parties play a key role in separating the genuine contenders from the 'no-hopers'.

All three major parties have traditionally employed a similar three-stage process in selecting parliamentary candidates: first, hopefuls must get their names on to a centrally vetted and approved list of prospective candidates; secondly, the local party draws up a shortlist from those approved candidates who have expressed an interest; and thirdly, constituency members vote for their preferred candidate, whether in person at a meeting or by postal ballot.

Conservative Party

Traditionally, those seeking to represent the Conservative Party in parliamentary elections were subject to a tortuous and largely 'closed' process:

➤ First, prospective candidates had to get their names on to an 'approved' list of candidates by attending a formal interview before a panel.

➤ Secondly, they would have to apply to a constituency Conservative Association and succeed in getting their name on to a shortlist.

➤ Thirdly, they would need to garner the support of those party activists attending a constituency general meeting.

Even those candidates who were successful in securing the nomination of their constituency association by such means could still find their nominations vetoed by the national party's Ethics and Integrity Committee, established in the 1990s by the party leader William Hague. However, under the leadership of David Cameron the party looked to democratise the process of candidate selection further, first by introducing the so-called A-lists and later by trialling hustings and primaries.

A-lists

Cameron's first initiative was the introduction of so-called 'A-lists': the requirement that Conservative Associations included women and those from ethnic minorities in their shortlists. This move was seen by many as an echo of the policy of women-only shortlists first employed by the Labour Party. The Conservatives' A-List scheme did not go as far as requiring local associations to select candidates from certain backgrounds; it merely forced them to draw up more socially diverse shortlists — in reality, many of those candidates ultimately selected still fitted the Conservative stereotype of white, middle-aged men.

Hustings

Cameron's second innovation was the greater use of open hustings: events where local voters as well as paid-up, card-carrying local party activists were permitted to attend a meeting at which the assembled audience would be able to listen to and the pass their verdict on the prospective parliamentary candidates presented before them. Such hustings, sometimes referred to as primaries, had been used in around 100 contests by August 2009.

Open primaries

Cameron's third innovation was by far the most dramatic, for August 2009 saw the Conservative Party select its official parliamentary candidate in the parliamentary constituency of Totnes by means of an open primary — a popular ballot in which all registered voters (i.e. not just party members) have a hand in selecting the candidate who will run in the election proper. This was the first time that a major UK party had employed such a device in selecting a parliamentary candidate. Where the Totnes primary differed from the hustings used elsewhere was that participation was widened not simply by inviting non-members to attend a one-off meeting, but by the party sending out postal ballot papers to every one of the 68,000 registered voters in the constituency, at an estimated cost to the party of £38,000.

Labour Party

Those wishing to become prospective parliamentary candidates for the Labour Party must first get their names on to the National Executive Committee's approved list. This list is forwarded to Constituency Labour Parties, which draw up a shortlist from those approved candidates who have applied. Constituency party members then select their preferred candidate under one member, one vote. The NEC can impose its own choice of candidate, even where the CLP has already made a selection. The choice of members has also been limited by the introduction of **women-only shortlists** in many of Labour's safer seats.

Key term

> **Women-only shortlists** Where a constituency party is required to draw up an entirely female shortlist from which their parliamentary candidate will be chosen. The practice existed in its original form between 1993 and 1996, before being briefly outlawed in 1996 in a ruling under the Sex Discrimination Act. The government subsequently amended the legislation, thus allowing all-women shortlists again. The use of such shortlists in many safe Labour seats was largely responsible for the significant increase in the number of women MPs returned to parliament at the 1997 general election.

At the 2005 general election, the independent candidate Peter Law was elected to represent the constituency of Blaenau Gwent, having been prevented from seeking selection as the official Labour Party candidate by the party's imposition of an all-women shortlist.

Liberal Democrats

Because the Lib Dems operate under a federal structure, those wishing to become prospective parliamentary candidates for the party must first apply to their national party (England, Scotland or Wales). Those who pass this vetting procedure and become approved candidates can then apply to individual constituencies for selection. Those candidates short-listed by the constituency party go forward to a ballot of all party members in the constituency in question.

The deselection and imposition of candidates

Although the constituency-level party in all three major parties is normally allowed the final say in selecting parliamentary candidates from the nationally approved lists, the national parties do retain the ultimate power to deselect and impose candidates where they see fit. In 1986, for example, the Labour Party under Neil Kinnock deselected MPs Dave Nellist and Terry Fields for being part of the banned Militant Tendency. The Labour Party has also imposed candidates on constituencies from time to time: for example, parachuting the former Conservative MP Shaun Woodward in as the Labour candidate for the safe seat of St Helens South ahead of the 2001 general election. More recently, the scandal over MPs' expenses saw both the Conservative Party and the Labour Party moving to bar certain MPs from defending their seats at the 2010 general election.

Policy making
Conservative Party
Until the late 1990s, Conservative Party policy was largely determined by the leader of the day. Although the party leader was expected to take on board the views of senior colleagues on the front benches, the 1922 Committee, party elders and the grassroots membership, it was an unashamedly top-down process. As John Major famously said of the party's 1992 general election manifesto, 'it was all me'.

In 1998 the system appeared to have been democratised somewhat as part of the then party leader William Hague's 'Fresh Future' initiative. This programme saw the creation of a national party Policy Forum alongside a number of other initiatives aimed at enhancing participation within the party. However, critics argue that these changes were more in appearance than in substance, for while the party's 2001 manifesto appeared to have been the product of greater consultation, the Policy Forum was downgraded under Iain Duncan-Smith and the 2005 manifesto was largely decided by party leader Michael Howard and advisers such as the party's Australian campaign consultant Lynton Crosby.

Labour Party
The Labour Party conferences of the past were genuine policy-making events. From 1997, however, the party adopted a 2-year policy-making cycle (see Figure 3.2). The National Policy Forum appointed policy commissions to make proposals which were then to be formalised in the National Executive Committee before passing to the party conference for approval. This afforded the party leader more control and helped the party to avoid the kinds of nasty surprises and public shows of disunity common at earlier party conferences. However, critics have argued that the reforms have seen the conference transformed from being a sovereign policy-making body, to little more than a rubber stamp for policies agreed elsewhere.

Liberal Democrats
The party is federal in structure, comprising English, Scottish and Welsh state parties with a number of organisational tiers below each national party. What this means in

practice is that policy that will only affect Scotland, for example, will be developed by the Scottish party and confirmed at the conference of that party. Policies affecting England and the whole of the UK are dealt with at the main national conference — the Federal Conference — which meets twice-yearly. This conference is the supreme policy-making body of the party, but it spends most of its time considering proposals from the Federal Policy Committee, state parties, regional parties and local parties. The party leadership's influence over the Federal Policy Committee allows them to steer policy, at least to a degree.

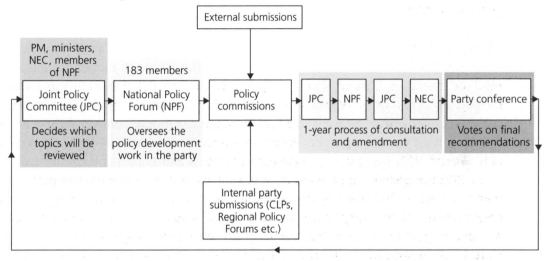

Source: Webb, P. (2000) 'Political parties: adapting to the electoral market' in P. Dunleavy et al., *Developments in British Politics 6*, Macmillan Press.

Figure 3.2 Labour's 2-year rolling policy-making cycle

Striking the right balance on policy

Although many political parties are keen to involve their ordinary members in the formation of party policy, they are painfully conscious of the fact that they need to have policies that appeal beyond their immediate rank-and-file if they are to have any chance of being returned to office. In an age of mass-membership parties, the views of members might have been a fair indication of how the broader public would react to a given policy. In the modern era, however, party membership is falling and those who do join are increasingly unrepresentative of the broader population. In this context, allowing regular members to determine policy could amount to electoral suicide.

While the Liberal Democrats are widely seen as having the most democratic method for determining party policy, some argue that some of the policies adopted in the past — for example, on cannabis possession, asylum seekers and the local income tax — were rather too easily picked off by Labour and Conservative activists during general election campaigns.

Bernie Ecclestone

Party funding

The changing basis of party funding

Most political parties receive income in the form of membership subscriptions. Until the 1990s, however, the lion's share of Labour Party funding came from fees paid by trade unions and other affiliated organisations, while the Conservative Party was said to be bank-rolled by wealthy business interests.

The decline of UK political parties as mass-member organisations has adversely impacted on party finances. The efforts to reduce the influence of trade unions within the Labour Party, under Neil Kinnock, John Smith and Tony Blair, also resulted in falling revenues. Such developments led parties to court donations from wealthy individuals such as Bernie Ecclestone and Lord Sainsbury for Labour, and Sir Paul Getty and Stuart Wheeler for the Conservatives.

Why has party funding provoked controversy?

The rise of large individual donations to political parties since the 1990s has led to the perception that one might be able to buy access or political influence — in much the same way that Mohamed Al Fayed claimed to have done with individual Conservative MPs such as Neil Hamilton in the closing years of John Major's time in office. For example, some felt that Bernie Ecclestone's £1 million donation to the Labour Party in 1997 may have resulted in the subsequent delay in the introduction of the ban on tobacco advertising in Formula 1 motor racing. Such controversy inevitably led to calls for regulation.

Political Parties, Elections and Referendum Act (2000)

The PPERA (2000) placed an overall limit on party spending in general election campaigns (£30,000 per constituency), established additional spending limits in respect of elections to devolved bodies and the European Parliament, and required that, nationally, parties had to declare all donations over £5,000 to the Electoral Commission. In so doing, the Act sought to make parties less reliant on wealthy individual backers, challenging the perception that politics was 'for sale'.

Political Parties and Elections Act (2009)

The PPEA (2009) built upon the regulations established under the PPERA:

➤ It allowed for the appointment of commissioners with more recent experience, by reducing the waiting period applying to those leaving an active career in politics to join the Electoral Commission from 10 to 5 years.

➤ It imposed tighter regulations on spending by candidates in the run-up to an election, with restrictions set to cover a longer period.

➤ It allowed the Electoral Commission to investigate cases under the regulations and impose civil sanctions (e.g. fines) as opposed to having to refer cases for criminal prosecution.

➤ It raised some of the thresholds in respect of receiving and reporting donations. For example, parties were required to report donations over £7,500 as opposed to the £5,000 set under the PPERA (2000).

➤ It limited donations over £7,500 to those who could prove that they were UK residents for tax purposes.

Weblinks

www.electoralcommission.org.uk/__data/assets/pdf_file/0005/82076/PPE-Act-Factsheet-v2.pdf — an Electoral Commission factsheet on the PPEA (2009).

The Phillips report

Two significant reports were published between these two Acts. The first, *Party Funding* (2006), was produced by the Constitutional Affairs Select Committee. The second, *Strengthening Democracy: Fair and Sustainable Funding of Political Parties* (2007) — the 'Phillips report' in shorthand — came at the end of a government-initiated review conducted under the chairmanship of Sir Hayden Phillips. Crucially, both reports concluded that one way forward might be greater state funding for UK political parties, with the Phillips report offering the prospect of some form of 'pence-per-voter' or 'pence-per-member' funding formula.

Although the case in favour of the comprehensive funding of UK political parties is still not universally accepted, it is worth remembering that 'public funds' are already in place in the form of the Policy Development Grants (PDGs) established under Section 12 of the PPERA (2000): **short money** and **Cranborne money**. The PDGs are particularly significant as they are available not only to the main opposition parties but as a share of a £2 million annual pot to any party that has two or more sitting MPs taking the

Concepts explained

Short money

Short money comprises those moneys paid to opposition parties in order to help them cover their administrative costs and thereby provide for proper scrutiny of the government. It is named after Edward Short, the leader of the House of Commons when the scheme was introduced in 1974, and is available to all opposition parties that win at least two seats or receive over 150,000 votes at a general election.

Cranborne money

In the House of Lords, such payments to opposition parties are known as Cranborne money after Lord Cranborne, the leader of the Lords when the scheme was introduced in 1996.

oath of allegiance (see Table 3.2) — there being seven such parties in 2010. Parties also receive subsidies in respect of their television broadcasts and help with their postage costs during election campaigns. Scottish parties receive assistance from the Scottish Parliament under the Assistance to Registered Parties scheme.

Table 3.2 Policy development grant allocations, 2005–09

Party	2005–06	2006–07	2007–08	2008–09
Conservative Party	£440,394	£457,997	£458,736	£457,387
Democratic Unionist Party	£132,866	£155,786	£154,754	£155,203
Labour Party	£440,394	£457,997	£458,736	£457,387
Liberal Democrats	£440,394	£457,997	£458,736	£457,387
Plaid Cymru	£134,393	£151,894	£151,845	£152,247
Scottish National Party	£145,828	£162,542	£162,438	£165,187
Social Democratic and Labour Party	£132,866	£155,786	£154,754	£155,203
Ulster Unionist Party*	£132,866	£0	£0	£0
Total	£2,000,000	£2,000,000	£2,000,000	£2,000,001

*The Ulster Unionist Party was removed from the scheme for 2006–07 because it no longer satisfied the eligibility requirement (of having two MPs who had taken the oath) contained in section 12 of the Political Parties, Elections and Referendums Act (2000).

Source: Electoral Commission

Weblinks

www.electoralcommission.org.uk — the official website of the Electoral Commission providing background on various pieces of legislation together with data on donations, both recent and historic.

Viewpoint Should political parties be state-funded?

- If parties are not funded by taxpayers, they will be funded by interest groups.
- State funding would allow politicians to focus on representing their constituents.
- Parties such as the Liberal Democrats could finally compete on an equal financial footing.

- Why should taxpayers bankroll parties that they may not support?
- Politicians could become isolated. It is good that interest groups are at the heart of government.
- Parties would always have unequal resources, even if state funding were to be introduced.

Has the reformed system worked?

Although the new system heralded by the passing of the PPERA (2000) has made party funding more transparent, there have been significant teething problems — not least the Labour Party's efforts to circumvent the PPERA's regulation of 'donations' by encouraging supporters to offer the party long-term, low-interest 'loans'. It was this tactic, and the inducements supposedly offered to secure such lines of credit (specifically, the alleged offer of ennoblement), that gave rise to the 'Loans for Peerages' scandal. Although the police investigation into the scandal ultimately ended without any prosecutions being brought, it is clear that the issue of party funding is still controversial. This can be seen, for example, in the efforts to address the status of donors not registered as taxpayers in the UK under the PPEA (2009) — a measure that many saw as being aimed squarely at individuals such as the long-term Conservative Party backer and party deputy chairman Lord Ashcroft, whose tax status continued to provoke debate and controversy well into 2010.

Table 3.3 Registered donations to British political parties, 2009

Party	Donations Value (£)	No.	Public funds Value (£)	No.	Total Value (£)	No.
Conservative Party	27,085,928	1,604	5,428,014	13	32,513,942	1,617
Labour Party	15,213,494	1,183	1,007,201	6	16,220,695	1,189
Liberal Democrats	3,886,634	1,020	2,326,175	15	6,212,809	1,035
UK Independence Party	1,403,987	184	0	0	1,403,987	184
Co-operative Party	924,916	59	0	0	924,916	59
Scottish National Party	160,879	20	260,142	18	421,021	38
Plaid Cymru — The Party of Wales	142,656	27	271,187	23	413,843	50
Green Party	352,163	143	0	0	352,163	143
Christian Party 'Proclaiming Christ's Lordship'	273,937	12	0	0	273,937	12
No2EU: Yes to Democracy	97,995	26	0	0	97,995	26
The New Party	72,500	11	0	0	72,500	11
Scottish Voice	70,000	2	0	0	70,000	2
Pro Democracy: Libertas.eu	69,491	11	0	0	69,491	11
Jury Team	50,000	3	0	0	50,000	3
British National Party	45,332	14	0	0	45,332	14
mums4justice	35,890	4	0	0	35,890	4
Mums' Army	26,918	3	0	0	26,918	3
United Kingdom First	25,441	8	0	0	25,441	8
East Hert People	22,048	2	0	0	22,048	2
Scottish Green Party	11,547	2	8,952	1	20,499	3
Fair Play Fair Trade	16,040	2	0	0	16,040	2
Christian People Alliance	13,630	24	0	0	13,630	24
Yes 2 Europe	12,000	4	0	0	12,000	4
Communist Party of Britain	10,084	2	0	0	10,084	2
Mebyon Kernow — The Party of Cornwall	9,411	4	0	0	9,411	4
Pirate Party UK	210	1	0	0	210	1
Grand total	50,033,130	4,375	9,301,670	76	59,334,800	4,451

Source: Electoral Commission.

It is also relevant that, while the PPERA (2000) places spending limits on parties and regulates donations, the moneys arriving into the coffers of the main UK political parties have still been significant. Even excluding public funds, the Labour Party, the Conservatives and the Liberal Democrats declared £9 million, £8 million and £4 million of donations respectively in 2005, and the main parties were all reporting significant donations in the run-up to the 2010 general election (see Table 3.3). In addition, it is clear that the wealthy individual backers that the PPERA (2000) sought to identify have not been put off by the prospect of losing their anonymity. For example, the Labour Party received two donations of around £1 million in the last quarter of 2009 alone — one from Lord Sainsbury (£1 million) and the other from Nigel Doughty (£1.01 million).

▶ What you should know

- ▶ A political party is a group of like-minded individuals who come together with the aim of realising their shared goals by fielding candidates at elections and thereby securing election to public office.

- ▶ Parties differ from pressure groups in that the latter would normally only contest elections as a mean of raising the profile of their chosen cause or sectional interest, as opposed to having a genuine desire to be returned to office.

- ▶ The main UK political parties are highly hierarchical organisations comprising a number of different organisational levels, from local and constituency parties to the national party level. The MEPs elected to represent the main UK parties in the European Parliament sit in transnational ideological groupings as opposed to a single national group.

- ▶ Although smaller minority parties of all types have made great strides in recent years, in terms of both votes won and candidates elected, the UK is still generally characterised as a two-party system, in which two fairly equally matched parties compete for power at elections and others have little realistic chance of breaking their duopoly.

- ▶ The study of party organisation often focuses on the issue of internal party democracy — the extent to which ordinary rank-and-file members are given a say in decision making within a given party. Analysis of internal party democracy commonly focuses on how parties select their leaders, how they choose candidates for parliamentary elections, and how they formulate party policy.

- ▶ Although the three main UK parties all allow ordinary members some say in choosing their party leader, the policy-making processes within the two main UK parties, the Conservative Party and Labour Party, leave a good deal of power and control in the hands of their party leaders.

- ▶ Party funding has proven a contentious issue in recent years, as the revenue generated from membership subscriptions has declined and the main parties have become increasingly reliant on donations from wealthy individuals.

- ▶ Attempts to reform party finance under the PPERA (2000) and the PPEA (2009) have addressed some of the main areas of concern, although many commentators still argue in favour of the introduction of a more comprehensive system of state funding of parties than exists at present.

UK/US comparison

Party structure and organisation in the USA

➤ The USA, like the UK, is generally characterised as a two-party system. All 435 members of the House of Representatives were either Democrats or Republicans in 2010, along with 98 of 100 US Senators. Every president since 1853 has been either a Democrat or a Republican.

➤ Whereas some UK minority parties are permanent, most minor parties (or 'third parties') in the USA are short-lived. Indeed, many might be seen as pressure groups employing electoral candidacy as a means of raising awareness of and support for their cause or sectional interest, as opposed to true political parties.

➤ US parties have traditionally been more decentralised in their organisation than their UK counterparts. The main US parties have no party leader as such, and the national parties have a far more limited role than their UK equivalents outside of elections.

➤ Whereas candidate selection in the UK remains largely controlled by political parties, the introduction of primaries in most US states has seen this power transferred to regular voters.

➤ The 1974 Federal Election Campaign Act (FECA) — as amended by subsequent legislation and moderated by rulings by the US Supreme Court — established a form of state funding of elections and regulated donations to candidates and parties. Despite this, campaign finance remains just as controversial an issue in the USA as it is in the UK.

Further reading

Durkin, M. and Lester, P. (2007) *Leadership Elections: Labour Party*, House of Commons Library Standard Note SN/PC/3938.

Fairclough, P., Kelly, R. and Magee, E. (2008) 'The funding of political parties: could Philips make a difference?' *UK Government and Politics Annual Survey 2008*, Chapter 10, Philip Allan Updates.

Kelly, R. (2005) 'The making of party policy', *Politics Review*, Vol. 15, No. 2.

Kelly, R. (2007) *Leadership Elections: Liberal Democrats*, House of Commons Library Standard Note SN/PC/3872.

Kelly, R. and Lester, P. (2005) *Leadership Elections: Conservative Party*, House of Commons Library Standard Note SN/PC/13665.

Lynch, P. (2009) 'Britain's multi-party systems', *Politics Review*, Vol. 18, No. 3.

Smith, N. (2007) *Advanced TopicMasters: UK Parties and Pressure Groups*, Philip Allan Updates.

Exam focus

Short-answer questions (around 5 minutes each)

Explain, using examples, the meaning of each of the following terms:

1 Party conference
2 Internal party democracy
3 One member, one vote
4 Constituency party

Mid-length questions (around 10 minutes each)

Outline two arguments 'for' and two arguments 'against' each of the following:

1 The UK as a 'two-party system'
2 Women-only shortlists
3 Primaries
4 State funding of political parties

Mini-essays (around 25–30 minutes each)

Write a mini-essay in response to each of the following questions:

1 Evaluate the view that the UK is now a 'multi-party system'.
2 How effectively do the main UK parties fulfil their core roles and functions?
3 'Individual party members have little real power within the main UK parties.' Discuss.
4 Critically assess the arguments in favour of the use of women-only shortlists and A-lists in selecting candidates for political office.

Chapter 4

Political parties: policies and ideas

Key questions answered in this chapter
➤ What do we mean by 'party ideology'?
➤ What is the 'political spectrum'?
➤ What ideological positions have the main British parties traditionally adopted and how has party ideology evolved in recent years?
➤ Have we entered a post-ideological age of 'catch-all' parties?

Party ideology

As we saw in Chapter 3, political parties are groups of like-minded individuals who seek to realise collectively held goals by fielding candidates at elections and thereby securing election to public office. The first British parties were loosely bound together by shared ideals, friendships or family ties. However, electoral reform in the nineteenth century brought the need to organise and present a clearer message to the growing electorate. It was at this time that political parties as we know them today began to emerge.

For most of the twentieth century, it was common to characterise the British parties in ideological terms because the members of such organisations were committed not simply to a raft of discrete policies, but to a coherent set of ideas and beliefs that underpinned such headline proposals. Thus the Conservative Party was said to favour conservatism; the Liberals, liberalism; and the Labour Party, socialism. However, by the late 1990s commentators on all sides were referring to the 'end of ideology' and the rise of so-called 'catch-all' parties, which were driven by a desire to win power at all costs, rather than campaigning on the basis of deeply held ideological convictions.

In this chapter we chart the changing character of the main British parties and assess the extent to which they remain distinctive, in terms both of their stated policies and of the ideas and values that underpin them.

Ideology and policy

Distinguish between

Ideology

➤ An ideology is a coherent set of beliefs or values that guide one's actions. Most mainstream British political parties traditionally subscribed to an ideology. The Labour Party, for example, was established along socialist lines.

Policy

➤ A policy is a proposed or actual strategy aimed at addressing a particular issue or area of government provision. Policies are often based upon a deeply held ideological position. For example, the Labour Party's desire to nationalise key industries after the Second World War was rooted in its commitment to socialism. However, policy may also serve purposes that are not essentially ideological in nature, such as the desire to appeal to wavering voters at an election or to bring a potential coalition partner on board in the wake of a 'hung' (or 'balanced') parliament.

The political spectrum

Party ideology in the UK has generally been discussed in terms of the simple left–right **political spectrum** (see Figure 4.1) that emerged in revolutionary France at the end of the eighteenth century. In modern usage, those on the extreme left of the political spectrum are said to favour some form of communal existence, with all property being held 'collectively' as opposed to 'individually', while moderate left-wingers accept capitalism but favour greater government intervention in the economy and a more comprehensive welfare state. In contrast, those on the right are said to favour private enterprise over state provision, resulting in a process that the former Conservative prime minister Margaret Thatcher described as 'rolling back the frontiers of the state'.

Figure 4.1 The left–right political spectrum

In the UK, where the extreme ideologies of communism (on the left) and fascism (on the right) have never really taken hold, the debate over the direction of government policy has generally centred on the battle between socialists and conservatives. However, all three of the main British parties are better seen as 'broad churches', each comprising members of various different political shades. This truth can be seen in the way in which the Conservative leader David Cameron (a moderate in his own party) was able to accommodate the Liberal Democrat leader Nick Clegg (seen as being on the right of his party) and form a coalition government in the wake of the 2010 general election. The extent to which all three of the main British parties have tended to occupy the centre of this simple political spectrum in recent years is a theme that we will return to at the end of this chapter.

Critics of the left–right spectrum argue that it ignores significant differences between some of the groups that occupy each wing, as well as the significant overlaps between some of the groups that are said to occupy the polar opposites on the spectrum. For example, some forms of socialism and many of those regimes that would have described themselves as communist (e.g. Soviet Russia) appear similar in some respects to some of those on the extreme right wing of the spectrum (for example, Nazi Germany). While such problems can be partly explained by a certain confusion regarding precisely what communism entails, similar issues arise if one studies some of the major philosophical works of the nineteenth century.

The German philosopher Max Stirner is a case in point. In his 1845 work *The Ego and Its Own*, Stirner championed the importance of the individual and attacked **authoritarian** forms of government. Yet Stirner is said to have inspired both anarchists (on the left) and those on the conservative right who rail against the state and champion the importance of individual liberty.

Such problems with the notion of a simple political spectrum have been addressed in a number of ways. Some commentators have argued that it is better to see the linear spectrum as a circle or 'horseshoe' with the extremes of 'left' and 'right' coming together (see Figure 4.2).

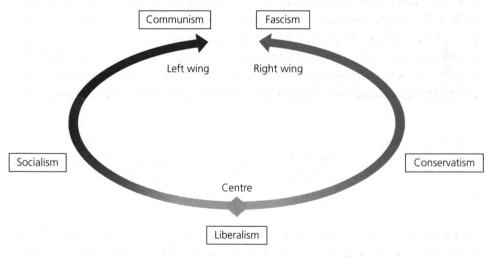

Figure 4.2 'Horseshoe' theory

Others argue that it makes more sense to move towards a four-pointed 'compass' as opposed to a traditional linear spectrum, because this allows us to make a distinction between those approaches to government which are more authoritarian and those which are more **libertarian** (see Figure 4.3).

Figure 4.3 The ideological compass

Key terms

> **Authoritarian** In the political sense, describing any approach that favours strict obedience to the authority of the state.

> **Libertarian** Any approach that favours civil liberties and the rights of the individual over the authority of the state. Libertarians generally believe that society as a whole is best served by allowing citizens to operate relatively free from state intervention.

> **Political spectrum** A device by which different political standpoints can be mapped across one axis or more as a way of demonstrating their ideological position in relation to one another.

Weblinks

www.politicalcompass.org — a site that allows you to position yourself on the political spectrum by answering a series of question relating to how you feel about different aspects of policy.

Ideology and policy in the Conservative Party

Conservative ideology

The Conservative Party emerged from the Tory Party in the 1830s, with many dating its birth to Robert Peel's Tamworth Manifesto (1834). In the twentieth century, the party was in office (either alone or in coalition) for 67 years and enjoyed two extended periods in office:

> 1951–64 under Churchill, Eden, Macmillan and Home

> 1979–97 under Thatcher and then Major

One-nation conservatism

For most of the twentieth century, the Conservative Party was truly conservative in ideology: that is, rooted in pragmatism and the belief in gradual improvements founded on experience and existing institutions. This was a form of collectivist or **paternalist** conservatism which favoured pluralism and social inclusion, and held that while authority should be centralised, the state should be benevolent, caring for the neediest.

The proponents of this form of conservatism, now commonly referred to as one-nation Tories, were committed to: a mixed economy (Keynesianism); more significant state intervention, where necessary; slow, gradual change (evolution not revolution); internationalism and increasing European integration; and support for a universal welfare state.

One-nation conservatism versus Thatcherism

The late 1970s and early 1980s saw the rise of a new form of liberal or libertarian conservatism on both sides of the Atlantic. Dubbed the 'New Right', this movement combined a belief in **monetarism**, free market economics and deregulation (an approach commonly referred to as **neo-liberalism**) with a more orthodox conservative approach in the sphere of social policy: for example, support for the traditional family unit and more traditional views on sexual orientation. The US president Ronald Reagan (1981–89) and UK prime minister Margaret Thatcher (1979–90) were key figures in this movement — the latter to the degree that this broad approach has become known simply as **Thatcherism** in the UK context. Thatcherism marked the death-knell of the **postwar consensus** and the emergence of **adversarial politics**.

Concepts explained

Conservatism

A loose ideology that favours a pragmatic approach to dealing with problems while seeking to preserve the status quo. Some argue that conservatism is in fact not an ideology at all, because it looks to work with and improve upon what exists already as opposed to building from the ground up from a more ideological standpoint.

Key term

Paternalism Where power and authority are held centrally but the state acts benevolently, caring for the neediest. Paternalism is said to be a key characteristic of traditional one-nation conservatism.

Ronald Reagan and Margaret Thatcher in 1988

Supporters of this approach, known as Thatcherites, favoured the importance of the individual over the needs of society as a whole, offering a radical agenda including policies such as:

> deregulation in the field of business
> privatisation of publicly owned industries
> statutory limits on the power of trade unions
> limited state intervention in the economy
> a smaller state ('rolling back the frontiers of the state')
> defence of national sovereignty
> more limited state welfare provision (a lower 'safety net')

Thatcher referred to those who were not prepared to sign up to this agenda, in many cases the old one-nation Tories, as 'wets'. Committed Thatcherites, in contrast, were referred to as 'dries' — with the then prime minister's most loyal acolytes dubbed 'ultra dry'.

Key terms

> **Adversarial politics** The instinctive antagonism between the two main Westminster parties, similar to so-called 'yah-boo' politics. The theory was used by Professor S. E. Finer and commonly applied to UK politics from the 1970s.
> **Monetarism** An economic theory that advocates controlling the money supply as a means of keeping inflation in check.
> **Postwar consensus** Characterising the broad agreement between the Labour and Conservative parties over domestic and foreign policy that emerged after the Second World War. The consensus saw the parties cooperating over the creation of the welfare state and the adoption of a Keynesian economic policy. The postwar consensus began to break down in the 1970s and was said to have ended with the more ideological, adversarial approach that accompanied Thatcherism.

Concepts explained

Thatcherism

An ideological approach combining a free-market, neo-liberal economic policy with a more orthodox conservative social policy in areas such as the family and law and order. Thatcherism was the dominant Conservative Party ideology of the 1980s and 1990s, and was closely associated with the ideas of Sir Keith Joseph and right-wing think-tanks such as the Adam Smith Institute.

Neo-liberalism

A political ideology closely related to classical liberalism. Neo-liberals stress the importance of the free market, individual rights and limited government. In the UK context, neo-liberalism is closely associated with Thatcherism.

Intra-party squabbles

The factional infighting that came to the fore as a result of this shift in direction under Margaret Thatcher led to formal challenges to her leadership of the party in 1989 (Anthony Meyer) and 1990 (Michael Heseltine). Though the latter led to Thatcher's resignation, in November 1990, the Conservative leaders who followed on from her — Major, Hague, Duncan Smith, Howard and Cameron — often struggled to command the full confidence of the entire parliamentary party due to internal party factions and personal rivalries.

Although Philip Norton identified seven broad and overlapping factions within the parliamentary Conservative Party in the 1990s, most commentators prefer to identify two more straightforward, if rather simplistic, ideological cleavages:

➢ One-nation Tories, 'wets', Europhiles (e.g. Tory Reform Group, founded 1975, president Kenneth Clarke)
➢ Thatcherites, 'dries', eurosceptics (e.g. Bruges Group, founded 1988, honorary president Margaret Thatcher)

One-nation conservatism and Thatcherism

Distinguish between

One-nation conservatism
➢ pragmatic
➢ incremental change
➢ paternalistic
➢ mixed economy

Thatcherism
➢ dogmatic
➢ radical change
➢ individualistic
➢ free-market economy

The Conservatives under Cameron

David Cameron's election as party leader in 2006, following three successive general election defeats for the Conservatives in 1997, 2001 and 2005, was widely seen as analogous to the kind of watershed or epiphany that the Labour Party had experienced a decade earlier under Tony Blair. Cameron's election was significant because it marked the point at which rank-and-file party members recognised the need to choose a leader who could appeal to those outside of the party — and thereby win an election.

Cameron sought to lead the Conservatives away from those areas of policy over which the party was deeply divided (e.g. Europe) and towards those where it could gain electoral advantage (e.g. the environment). He recognised the extent to which the party had come to be regarded as 'toxic' and set about 'detoxifying' the Conservative brand. This shift towards the centre saw the 'greening of conservatism', with the party attempting to lead the way on issues such as climate change. The desire to challenge the perception that the Conservatives were the 'nasty party' was also reflected in former Conservative leader Iain Duncan Smith's work with the Centre for Social Justice. The think-tank's early reports, *Breakdown Britain* and *Breakthrough Britain*, offered the prospect of the party becoming more receptive to strategies aimed at addressing poverty and social exclusion. Such thinking was at the heart of the Conservatives' pledge to fix 'broken Britain' in their 2010 general election campaign.

Such developments saw many commentators drawing parallels between the Cameron–Osborne double act and that of Blair–Brown in the early days of New Labour. As a result, many dubbed Cameron's Party the 'New Tories' or, as Cameron himself put it on at least one occasion, 'liberal conservatives'. It was significant also that Cameron was himself often referred to as 'the heir to Blair'.

Locating the 'Cameroons' on the political spectrum

Although electoral success can be based, to a degree at least, on negative sentiment — a reaction against a party too long in office — it is hard to establish anything of real worth unless one can articulate some kind of coherent vision as to where one wants to take the country.

In this respect it is probably fair to say that 'the jury was still out' on Cameron at the time of the 2010 general election. In a piece entitled 'Conservatism under Cameron' in *Politics Review*, vol. 17, no. 3 (2008), Richard Kelly offered three possible perspectives on Cameron's conservatism:

- first, that it represented a 'flagrant capitulation to New Labour'
- secondly, that it should be seen as a 'subtle continuation of Thatcherism'
- thirdly, that it amounted to little more than 'shameless opportunism'

In reality, there are elements of truth in all three judgements on the approach that Cameron has taken since becoming party leader; it was the latter that presented the biggest obstacle as he looked to move the Conservatives from the mentality of a party in opposition to that of a party in power.

The substance of policy

Although David Cameron's Conservative Party issued a swathe of policy proposals in the run-up to the 2010 general election, the leader was frequently accused of 'playing to the galleries' with carefully crafted rhetoric as opposed to coming forward with substantive detail on specific policies. This is a failing forgivable in a party in opposition but less so in one on the verge of taking up the reins of power. Talk of replacing the Human Rights Act (1998) with a new UK Bill of Rights, mooted early on in Cameron's stewardship of the party, appeared without further elaboration in the party's 2010 manifesto. The same criticism could be levelled at many of Cameron's other proposals in the area of democratic renewal.

The party's position on tax appeared similarly opaque. Back in 2007 the emphasis had been on bringing back the married person's allowance (even extending it to same-sex couples in civil partnerships) and raising the threshold for inheritance tax — an announcement that had wrong-footed Labour at the time and was said to have contributed to Brown's decision not to call a snap election in the autumn of 2007. By the time of the 2010 general election, however, the focus had switched to pensions and public sector pay cuts, with the party even giving up its inheritance tax pledge as part of the coalition deal brokered with the Liberal Democrats in the wake of the election.

While the unravelling global credit crisis clearly played a part in reordering the party's priorities, some criticised what they saw as a tendency to issue policy statements for short-term effect without really taking the time to consider the mid- to long-term consequences of what was being proposed.

Beyond the core support

Criticisms were also levelled at the party's efforts to court the 'green vote', not least the adoption of the party's new green tree logo in preference to the long-serving blue torch and the suggestion that voters should 'vote blue, go green'. Cameron's decision to side with the Liberal Democrats and the Ghurkhas in their fight with the incumbent Labour government over residency rights clearly also played well with many voters, as did the party's admission that Margaret Thatcher was wrong when she asserted that there is 'no such thing as society', with Cameron asserting that there was such a thing as 'society', but that it was not the same as 'the state'.

A new 'Third Way'?

Although David Cameron dropped references to 'progressive conservatism' in his 2009 address to the Conservative Party conference, it remains unclear, even in the wake of the 2010 general election, just how he is going to reconcile (or 'triangulate') his desire to adopt traditionally liberal positions on the environment and social welfare with his commitment to pursue the Thatcherite agenda of 'rolling back the frontiers of the state'. The kinds of change envisaged can surely not be brought about entirely by voluntary groups and charitable institutions — the 'little platoons' championed by many Cameroons.

It is probably too early to speak of New Tories or a new 'Third Way', while the overall shape of what Cameron is trying to create is still so unclear. We may well be witnessing the re-emergence of the more pragmatic one-nation conservatism of the 1950s and 1960s as opposed to something truly new. Moreover, the waters have been further muddied by Cameron's decision to enter into a formal coalition with the Liberal Democrats — a point we will revisit towards the end of this chapter.

Ideology and policy in the Labour Party

Labour Party ideology

The Labour Party was created at the start of the twentieth century. Although the Independent Labour Party, the Fabians and the Social Democratic Federation were involved in forming the Labour Representation Committee in 1900, it is important not to underestimate the role of the Trade Union Congress (TUC): 94% of the Labour

Representation Committee's affiliated membership in 1900 was from the unions, and in the 1990s they still controlled around 80% of the votes at party conference and provided a similar proportion of the party's annual income.

The Labour Party was formed to represent the working classes at a time when the franchise had not yet been extended to such groups. The decision to give all men over 21 the right to vote in 1918 provided the Labour Party with the potential base of support necessary to launch a serious electoral challenge.

The party's origins in the unions and socialist societies of the late nineteenth and early twentieth centuries meant that it originally pursued an agenda centred on **socialism**.

Concepts explained

Socialism

A political ideology advocating greater equality and the redistribution of wealth. Socialists are suspicious of capitalism. They favour greater government intervention, both in economic policy and in social policy.

In the nineteenth century, socialism was often seen as similar to communism. In the UK, socialism was closely associated with the Labour Party, from the party's creation at the start of the twentieth century through to the emergence of New Labour under Tony Blair in the 1990s.

Broadly speaking, socialism can be subdivided into two distinct strands:

➤ revisionist (or 'reformist') socialism, which looks to improve capitalism (e.g. **social democracy**).

➤ revolutionary (or 'fundamentalist') socialism, which aims to abolish capitalism and bring all property into common ownership (e.g. Marxist communism)

Social democracy

A political ideology that accepts the basic premise of capitalism while advocating a more equitable distribution of wealth along the lines favoured by all socialists.

Labour Party constitution (1918)

The extension of the franchise to all adult men coincided with the adoption of the new Labour Party constitution (1918). Clause Four of this constitution (see Box 4.1) provided a clear commitment to public ownership of key industries and the redistribution of wealth.

Box 4.1 Extract from the 'old' Clause Four (1918)

...to secure for the workers by hand or by brain the full fruits of their industry and the most equitable distribution thereof that may be possible upon the basis of the common ownership of the means of production...

Labour factions

Despite its left-wing origins, the party was the home to a number of ideological factions by the 1970s. For example, the Labour prime minister James Callaghan (1976–79) and those on the right of the party took the view that public sector pay demands had to be resisted, whereas those on the left (e.g. Michael Foot and Tony Benn) still favoured greater wealth redistribution.

Labour's defeat in the 1979 general election, which came in the wake of the period of industrial unrest known as the 'Winter of Discontent', saw those on the left gain control of the party under the leadership of Michael Foot. Foot led Labour into the 1983 general election with one of the most left-wing manifestos in the party's history. It included commitments to state control of all major industries, tighter regulation of business, enhanced workers' rights, support for unilateral nuclear disarmament and a withdrawal from NATO. Dubbed 'the longest suicide note in history' by the then Labour leading-light Gerald Kaufman, the manifesto was seen as a key factor in the Conservative Party's landslide victory. Indeed, so left-wing was the manifesto that the Conservatives ran a campaign with the tag-line 'nice manifesto comrade', drawing parallels between key clauses in Labour's programme and similar passages in *The Communist Manifesto* (1848), drafted by Karl Mark and Friedrich Engels.

Old Labour versus New Labour

Although the Labour Party was formed to represent the working classes, changes in the class and occupational structure of the nation since the 1960s, together with the general election defeats of 1979, 1983 and 1987, saw the party looking to broaden its appeal beyond this core support.

This process of 'outreach', started by leaders such as Neil Kinnock (leader 1983–92) and John Smith (1992–94), is most closely associated with the leadership of Tony Blair (1994–2007). Under Blair, the party was rebranded as **New Labour** and the iconic Clause Four was controversially reworded (see Box 4.2). Some critics accused Blair and other Labour modernisers of abandoning the socialist principles upon which the party was founded.

Key term

➤ **'Old Labour'** Characterising the Labour Party prior to the modernisation programme begun by Neil Kinnock in 1983 and completed by Tony Blair. It refers to the party's historic commitment to socialism and its links with socialist societies, trade unions and the old working class.

Box 4.2 **Extract from the 'new' Clause Four (1995)**

[We] work for a dynamic economy, serving the public interest in which the enterprise of the market and the rigour of competition are joined with the forces of partnership and cooperation to produce the wealth the nation needs and the opportunity for all to work and prosper, with a thriving private sector and high quality public services.

Concepts explained

New Labour

Characterising the party that emerged to fight the 1997 general election following a process of party modernisation completed by Tony Blair. Blair first used the phrase 'New Labour' when addressing the Labour conference as party leader in 1994.

Labour's modernisation programme began under Neil Kinnock, following the party's landslide defeat at the 1983 general election.

It involved a less powerful role for the trade unions and a rebranding exercise designed to make the party more appealing to middle-class voters.

In ideological terms, the New Labour project was characterised by the concept of **triangulation**.

Triangulation

The process of melding together core Labour Party principles and values, such as the party's commitment to greater social justice, with the lessons learnt from Thatcherism. It was closely associated with New Labour and the notion of a **Third Way**.

Third Way

An ideological position said to exist between conventional socialism and mainstream capitalism, closely associated with Tony Blair and New Labour, and also referred to as the 'middle way'.

Old Labour and New Labour

Distinguish between

Old Labour	New Labour
➤ dogmatic	➤ pragmatic
➤ working class	➤ catch-all
➤ interventionist	➤ market economy
➤ public sector provision	➤ public–private partnerships
➤ social justice	➤ social inclusion
➤ universal welfare	➤ targeted welfare

Labour policy under Brown

Gordon Brown's accession as Labour leader in June 2007 was greeted with optimism by those on the liberal left, who felt that he would offer a more progressive programme of change than that pursued by his predecessor Tony Blair. In particular, some felt that Brown's commitment to the concept of **social justice** was far greater than Blair's and, by implication, that the former chancellor had been prevented from doing all that he wanted to do during his time at the Treasury.

Crucially, Brown had also offered the prospect that his premiership might herald in a more orthodox Old Labour position with regard to public spending. Indeed, according to the *Guardian*, Brown made promises totalling £39 billion of new spending during his first 7 weeks in post, including:

➤ an extra £7.7 billion for defence, through to 2011
➤ £15 billion to improve the railways
➤ £4 billion extra on early years education over 3 years
➤ £8 billion on affordable housing

Key term

➤ **Social justice** The goal of greater equality of outcome, as opposed to equality of opportunity alone. It is achieved through progressive taxation and other forms of wealth redistribution. The idea is closely associated with the Labour Party and with other parties of the left and centre-left, such as the Greens.

In the area of constitutional reform, Brown was also expected to offer more than the outgoing regime. On 13 May 2007, the *Guardian*'s Mary Riddell offered 'Three cheers for this new bill of rights', reporting that 'one of the first plans of the Prime Minister-in-waiting is to create a written constitution', and that 'his real target may be the monarchy'. In the event, the *Governance of Britain* Green Paper (2007), the Constitutional Renewal Bill (2008) and the Constitutional Reform and Governance Act (2010) that followed largely failed to fulfil such high expectations.

The end of New Labour?

It is perhaps ironic that, while many had expected Brown to return to more traditional Labour policies, most of those who wrote mock obituaries marking the death of the New Labour project in 2009 saw its passing not as a result of anything Brown had initiated, but instead as a consequence of the global financial crisis that had engulfed the nation.

Whereas Chancellor Brown had once favoured deregulation and a 'light touch' approach to economic management, 2009 and 2010 saw Prime Minister Brown's administration nationalising a number of high street banks and offering the prospect of a return to tax and spend, with a higher top rate of income tax and a government commitment to maintain public spending during the recession. The party's hard-fought reputation for economic competence — a key factor in its election victories in 1997, 2001 and 2005 — was ultimately surrendered, along with much of the political capital that the former chancellor had accrued during his decade at the Treasury.

It is perhaps significant that in the wake of the party's election defeat in 2010, even the most ardent former Blairites, such as the then leadership candidate David Miliband, were distancing themselves from the New Labour tag; 'New Labour is not the future', the former foreign secretary acknowledged in an article in the *Observer* on 16 May 2010, 'I'm interested now in Next Labour.'

Ideology and policy of the Liberal Democrats

Liberal Democrat ideology

The Liberal Democrats were formed in 1988 with the merger of the Liberal Party and the Social Democratic Party (SDP). The Liberal Party had been the main party of government in the early twentieth century but was a distant third by the 1960s, rarely polling more than 10% of the vote. The SDP, in contrast, had been formed as a result of the decision of four leading Labour politicians to leave the party in 1981. Roy Jenkins, David Owen, Bill Rodgers and Shirley Williams felt that the Labour Party had come under the control of hard-line left-wingers following the defeat of James Callaghan's moderate Labour administration in 1979.

This **Gang of Four**, as they were known, launched the SDP with their 1981 Limehouse Declaration. With the Labour Party in disarray, the SDP formed an electoral alliance with the Liberals (the **SDP–Liberal Alliance**) in 1983, securing 26% of the popular vote, yet only gaining 23 seats in parliament. Following a similarly disappointing return for the Alliance in 1987, the parties merged in 1988 to form the Social and Liberal Democrats, with Paddy Ashdown being elected as party leader. The following year the party was renamed the Liberal Democratic Party (Liberal Democrats, or Lib Dems for short).

The launch of the SDP in 1981 by (left to right) Roy Jenkins, David Owen, Bill Rodgers and Shirley Williams: the 'Gang of Four'

Whereas Conservatives traditionally emphasise the role of society in shaping individuals, **liberalism** places a greater emphasis on the importance of the individual. Traditionally, liberals looked to a society formed of free, autonomous individuals of equal worth.

Key terms

➢ **Gang of Four** Refers in the UK context to the four former Labour cabinet ministers who left the party in 1981 to form the Social Democratic Party (SDP). The four were Bill Rodgers, Roy Jenkins, Shirley Williams and David Owen. The creation of the new party was announced in the Limehouse Declaration of 25 January 1981. The Gang of Four left Labour believing that the party had fallen under the control of left-wingers in the wake of Labour's defeat at the 1979 general election. They lacked confidence in the party's leader at the time, Michael Foot.

➢ **SDP–Liberal Alliance** The electoral alliance between the Liberal Party and the Social Democratic Party in place at the time of the 1983 (26.0% of the vote, 23 seats) and 1987 (23.1% of the vote, 22 seats) general elections. The two parties merged in 1988 to form the Liberal Democrats.

Concepts explained

Liberalism

A political ideology associated with notions of personal liberty, toleration and limited government. It is often subdivided into two separate strands:

Classical liberalism

An early form of liberalism favouring minimal state intervention, which emerged in the nineteenth century. Classical liberals stressed the importance of freedom, toleration and equality. They believed that self-reliance and self-improvement had a bigger part to play than the state in improving the lives of those from less privileged backgrounds. Some of the classical liberal agenda was adopted by the Thatcherite New Right from the later 1970s, resulting in their being referred to as neo-liberals.

Progressive (or 'new') liberalism

A more compassionate form of liberalism that saw the need for some regulation of the market as well as the provision of basic welfare. It was originally advanced by writers such as T. H. Green and L. T. Hobhouse. Progressive liberalism later developed into the mixed economy supported by John Maynard Keynes and William Beveridge.

This second, more progressive form of liberalism — with its emphasis on reform, individual rights and a mixed economy — provided the ideological foundation for all of the liberal centre parties of the second half of the twentieth century, and most recently the Liberal Democrats.

Liberal Democrat policy under Clegg

The 2008 Lib Dem party conference saw the drawing together of many of the threads of policy identified in the early months of Clegg's leadership of the party. The result was a provisional programme for government that challenged many of the tenets upon which the party had been based since its formation 20 years earlier. Moreover, this was a programme that was largely carried through into the party's 2010 manifesto, where such policies co-existed alongside more orthodox Lib Dem policies on issues such as constitutional reform and the protection of civil liberties.

Repositioning on Europe

Of the big three UK parties, the Lib Dems have traditionally been the most enthusiastic supporters of the European project. Clegg himself had served as a leading official at the European Commission in the 1990s and was also an MEP for a time before he was elected to the Commons in 2005. It was a surprise to many, therefore, that the 2008 conference saw the Lib Dems abandoning their orthodox Europhile stance in favour of something rather more circumspect. As the party's Treasury spokesman, Vince Cable, put it in the *Observer*, 'there are various things that we have learnt about Euroland, and about the Eurozone, which are clearly problems that need to be resolved...The Common Agricultural Policy is a complete disgrace...a lot of institutional reform is necessary.'

Although Clegg had already indicated a more direct approach to tackling the European issue with his call for a referendum on continued UK membership back in February 2008, the debate at conference took things a stage further — offering the possibility that 'Europe', an area of policy that had traditionally undermined the party's attempts to reach out to a wider audience, would be neutralised as an electoral issue. Moreover, the party's repositioning on Europe also served to remove one of the potential barriers to a coalition with the Conservatives in the event of a hung parliament.

Taxation and government spending

The Lib Dems have long been associated with a commitment to increase public spending and have not been afraid, in the past, to make public their plans to fund such programmes through an increase in the basic rate of income tax. As Chris Huhne noted at conference, however, there was a clear paradox in the fact that while government spending had increased by 46% in real terms over the course of New Labour's first decade in office, there was still widespread concern about both the range and the quality of services provided. Huhne's recognition that 'it might be time to try something different' saw the party 'thinking the unthinkable'. The result was a pledge to deliver around £20 billion of cuts in existing public spending in order to pay for improvements in areas such as education, and to offer voters a cut in income tax worth somewhere in the region of 4–6p in the pound.

Although many were stunned by the sheer scale of the Lib Dems' proposed tax cut — this at a time when even the Conservatives were unwilling to commit to a significant reduction in the basic rate of tax — Clegg defended the move, arguing in the *Guardian* that 'aspiring to hand back money to people from central government is impeccably liberal'.

A more realistic foreign policy

Conference called for a full review of long-term strategic defence planning with a view to developing a foreign policy more clearly linked to available resources. Although Clegg's commitment to the operation in Afghanistan remained, it was suggested that the conventional military resources needed in such theatres of war could be funded in large part by a 50% cut in the UK's nuclear arsenal and a further delay in the decision over the replacement of Trident.

The end of ideology?

Daniel Bell, in his 1960 book *The End of Ideology: On the Exhaustion of Political Ideas in the Fifties*, argued that the traditional ideological movements that had taken root in the nineteenth century and flourished in the early twentieth century had lost their power to inspire and mobilise the masses by the 1950s. Bell suggested that the postwar period had witnessed the rise of a new consensus around the social democratic model, and that in future political parties would be offering piecemeal, incremental changes as opposed to a more fundamental reordering of society along ideological lines.

In recent years, the phrase 'end of ideology' has been applied more specifically to characterise the changes that have taken place in the field of British party politics since the 1990s. As we have seen, British parties were once said to be ideologically based. In recent years, however, they are said to have moderated their traditional ideological positions as part of an effort to appeal to as wide a range of voters as possible. Although it is probably fair to say that British parties were always broad churches (or 'big tents'), these modern 'catch-all parties' are criticised as being little more than election-winning machines.

Viewpoint   **Have recent years witnessed 'the end of ideology'?**

- The three main parties are all essentially social democratic in nature. They are concerned with making piecemeal changes to the current arrangements as opposed to imposing an ideological model.
- The ideological wings of each of the three main parties have been marginalised.
- There are significant overlaps in the stated policies of the three main parties, as can be seen in their 2010 general election manifestos.
- Parties that once appeared fundamentally opposed to one another were able to enter into a coalition government in 2010.
- There is an increased emphasis on presentation and personality over substance.

- The three main UK parties still have distinct ideological traditions and a committed core support that strongly identifies with such traditions.
- The ideological dividing lines became more apparent in the wake of the global financial crisis.
- The rise of smaller ideological and single-issue parties and pressure groups suggests that ideology still matters to a significant proportion of the electorate.

Party policy at the 2010 general election

The prevailing economic climate meant that all three of the main UK political parties were forced to accept that there would need to be significant spending cuts and tax rises in the wake of the 2010 general election. While the Institute for Fiscal Studies criticised all three party leaders for failing to identify the full scale of cuts needed when drafting their election manifestos, few voters would have been under any illusion as to what was to come following the poll. The only significant cleavage between the parties appeared to be on the issue of not 'if' but 'when' the cuts would come, with the Conservatives promising an emergency budget and cuts of up to £6 billion in the first year, and Labour and the Lib Dems favouring maintaining spending in the first year as a means of avoiding a so-called 'double-dip' recession.

As can be seen from the summary provided in Table 4.1, there was also significant agreement among two parties (e.g. over the scrapping of ID cards) or all three parties (e.g. over giving voters the right to recall MPs) in many other areas of policy.

Party policy in an age of coalition government

Critics of coalition government commonly argue that it lacks legitimacy as a result of the horse-trading and compromise that inevitably follows in the wake of a hung (or 'balanced') parliament: where party ideology and principles are sacrificed upon the altar of political expediency. So it was that the Liberal Democrats were cast in the role of 'king-makers' in 2010, having to choose between returning Labour to office for a fourth consecutive term or, in effect, handing the baton on to David Cameron's Conservatives.

Table 4.1 2010 party manifestos digested

Policy area	Conservative Party	Labour Party	Liberal Democrats
Economic policy	Emergency budget within 50 days. Up to £6 billion in public spending cuts in first year. Cuts in corporation tax and National Insurance. Freeze on council tax. 'No' to the euro.	No major cuts in first year. Sale of nationalised banks. No increase in income tax. A referendum before any decision to join the euro.	No major cuts in first year. No income tax on first £10,000. 'Mansion tax' on properties over £2 million. Close tax loopholes. Break up banks. Favour joining the euro, but only after a referendum.
Home affairs	Scrap ID-cards scheme. 'Grounding orders' for anti-social behaviour. Annual cap on immigration. Prison sentences for those carrying knives.	Maintain police numbers. Successful police forces to take over failing ones. Points-based system to limit immigration. More prison places.	Scrap ID-cards scheme. 'Amnesty' for most long-term illegal immigrants. 30,000 more police officers. Stop building new prisons. Regional, points-based immigration system.
Education policy	Reduce state control over schools. Give headteachers more control over teachers' salaries and school discipline. Raise entry qualifications to the teaching profession.	Take over around 1,000 mediocre or failing schools. Free school meals for primary school children. Widen access to university.	Slim down curriculum. Phase out university tuition fees. Help poorest students going to university. Additional £2.5 billion to help struggling pupils.

Policy area	Conservative Party	Labour Party	Liberal Democrats
Health policy	Access to GPs at weekends. Keep accident and emergency and maternity wards open. Abandon waiting list targets.	Access to GPs in the evenings. Cancer tests within a week of referral. Enhance patient choice. High-achieving hospitals to take over weaker ones.	Prioritise preventative care. Limit managers' pay and restructure the Department of Health. Give patients the right to go private. Compulsory language and competence tests for doctors.
Other social policy	Tax breaks for married couples on low to middle incomes. Remove tax credits for households earning more than £50,000. Form of national service for 16-year-olds. Neighbourhood groups to take over badly performing public services.	Protect Sure Start centre budgets. 15 hours' free nursery provision for 3–5-year-olds. Enhanced paternity leave. Restore link between state pension and average earnings from 2012.	Time-off for fathers to attend antenatal appointments. Shared parental leave extended to 18 months. Access to 20 hours of free childcare from age of 18 months. Scrap compulsory retirement ages. Immediately restore link between state pension and average earnings.
Environment	Move towards a 'low carbon economy'. Incentives for recycling and loans to help energy-saving home improvements. Move towards renewable power generation, nuclear power and cleaner coal-fired power stations.	400 000 new 'green jobs'. 40% clean electricity. Ban on unnecessary landfill. Green investment bank. Help to insulate homes.	Replace road tax with national road-pricing scheme. 100% clean energy by 2050. Help with energy-saving home improvements. Push for strict international agreements on carbon emissions.
Foreign policy and security	Replace Trident missile system. Establish US-style National Security Council.	Maintain nuclear deterrent and build two new aircraft carriers. Give aid to failing states. Regulate arms trade.	No direct replacement for Trident. Regulate arms exports. Inquiry into UK involvement in torture.
Constitutional reform	Cut the number of MPs. Equalise the size of constituency electorates. Allow recall of MPs in cases of serious wrongdoing. Parliamentary debate for any public petition gaining 100,000 signatures. Prevent former ministers taking up lobbying posts within 2 years. Replace the Human Rights Act with a British Bill of Rights.	Recall of MPs Referendum on moving to the AV system for elections to the Westminster Parliament. Referendum on Lords reform. Greater power for local government. Fixed-term parliaments. Register of lobbyists. Votes for 16-year-olds.	Cut the number of MPs. Recall of MPs. Freedom Bill to regulate CCTV and protect Human Rights Act. Proportional system for elections to the Westminster Parliament. Fully elected second chamber. Greater power for local government. Fixed-term parliaments. Votes for 16-year-olds.

Yet the very fact that the Conservatives were able to reach an accommodation with the Liberal Democrats, forming a coalition that few on the left would previously have considered either likely or tenable, suggests that we might need to start thinking about the whole concept of party policy in an entirely different way.

David Cameron and Nick Clegg announce their coalition agreement at a press conference in the garden of No. 10 Downing Street

The terms of the Conservative–Lib Dem coalition — which saw the Conservatives giving up their pledge on inheritance tax and accepting the Lib Dem policy of moving towards a personal income tax allowance of £10 000, as well as guaranteeing a referendum on the introduction of the alternative vote (AV) system for elections to the Westminster Parliament — were indeed remarkable. Equally remarkable was the extent to which the parties were able to reach agreement on Europe (see Box 4.3) — in part a result of Cameron's desire to avoid reopening splits within his own party, but also a consequence of the shift in the Lib Dem approach towards Europe signalled 2 years earlier.

Should such coalitions become more of a 'norm' in the coming years, it may well be that party manifestos will come to be seen less as an agenda for action — as has been the case in the past — than as a starting point for negotiations. Such a shift in thinking will necessarily involve a reassessment of many of the fundamental principles that are common to any study of UK government and politics — not least the doctrine of the **mandate**.

Concepts explained

Mandate

The right of the governing party to pursue the policies it sets out in its general election manifesto. The doctrine of the mandate gives the governing party the authority to pursue its stated policies, but it does not require it to do so or prevent it from drafting proposals not included in its manifesto.

Box 4.3 The 2010 Conservative–Lib Dem coalition deal on the EU (extracts)

…We agree that there should be no further transfer of sovereignty or powers over the course of the next parliament. We will examine the balance of the EU's existing competences and will, in particular, work to limit the application of the working time directive in the UK…

…We agree that we will amend the 1972 European Communities Act so that any proposed future treaty that transferred areas of power…would be subject to a referendum…

…We will examine the case for a UK sovereignty bill to make it clear that ultimate authority remains with parliament…

…We agree that Britain will not join or prepare to join the euro in this parliament.

▶ What you should know

- ▶ We use the political spectrum as a means of distinguishing between different ideological traditions and locating individual parties in relation to one another.

- ▶ UK political parties were once regarded as ideological in character: the Labour Party being socialist; the Conservatives, conservative; and the Liberal Party and its successors, liberal.

- ▶ In reality, all three of the main UK parties were broadly social democratic in the postwar period, with competition between them centring on the 'detail' as opposed to the 'fundamentals' of policy. This was the postwar consensus.

- ▶ The emergence of New Right thinking in the 1970s and the Thatcherite revolution of the 1980s marked the end of consensus, with the two main UK parties once again adopting more ideologically coherent positions.

- ▶ The Conservatives under Margaret Thatcher pursued a neo-liberal agenda whereas the Labour Party under Michael Foot went into the 1983 general election on the basis of an orthodox left-wing manifesto that was later described as 'the longest suicide note in history'.

- ▶ Under the Leadership of Neil Kinnock, John Smith and Tony Blair, the Labour Party sought to reposition itself on the political spectrum and broaden its appeal beyond traditional Labour voters.

- ▶ This modernisation programme involved adopting a Third Way, arrived at by triangulating traditional Labour values and approaches with the lessons learnt from Thatcherism.

- ▶ This New Labour project saw the party elected to three consecutive terms in office on a platform which rejected the 'tax and spend' approach of previous Labour administrations in favour of establishing partnerships between the public and private sectors and creating internal markets within public services as a way of improving efficiency.

- ▶ While Labour accepted many of the lessons of Thatcherism, the Thatcherite emphasis on the individual and Thatcher's suspicion of 'big government' notions of 'society' saw the Conservatives characterised as the 'nasty party'.

❯ David Cameron sought to 'detoxify' the Conservative brand by campaigning on issues such as the environment and social inclusion, and thereby reaching out beyond his party's core support.

❯ Some argue that the convergence of the three main parties on the centre ground has led to the 'end of ideology'. There were more similarities in than differences between the manifestos published by the three main parties at the time of the 2010 general election.

❯ The fact that the Conservatives and the Lib Dems were able to reach agreement and form a joint administration suggests that we might be experiencing a new age of consensus.

UK/US comparison

Party policies and ideas in the USA

➤ The traditional 'left–right' political spectrum is less useful when discussing US politics because the two main parties are both regarded as right of centre. Instead, commentators tend to describe policies and parties as being 'more liberal' or 'more conservative'.

➤ Whereas UK parties were once seen as broadly ideological in character, the two main US parties have always been regarded as broad churches or 'big tents'.

➤ While one would expect a Conservative Association in Surrey to stand by the same broad programme of policies as one in Yorkshire, many commentators speak of the USA as having '50 party systems' or 100 distinctive parties (i.e. two per state).

➤ This is because the differences between Democrats (or between Republicans) in different states can be more significant than the differences between the official party platforms of the Democrats and Republicans nationally: in other words, there may be more differences within the parties than between them.

➤ While the UK is said to have undergone a period of ideological convergence in recent years, with the rise of catch-all parties, US parties became more ideologically coherent and distinctive in the first decade of the twenty-first century.

Further reading

Fairclough, P. and Magee, E. (2009) 'Nick Clegg: new beginning or more of the same?', in *UK Government and Politics Annual Survey 2009*, Chapter 5, Philip Allan Updates.

Fairclough, P. and Magee, E. (2010) 'David Cameron: ready for power?', in *UK Government and Politics Annual Survey 2010*, Chapter 2, Philip Allan Updates.

Fairclough, P., Kelly, R. and Magee, E. (2008) 'Blair to Brown: continuity or change?', in *UK Government and Politics Annual Survey 2008*, Chapter 1, Philip Allan Updates.

Fielding, S. (2009) 'Whatever happened to New Labour?', *Politics Review*, Vol. 19, No. 1, pp. 8–11.

Graham, P. (2009) 'Has conservatism moved beyond Thatcherism?', *Politics Review*, Vol. 19, No. 2, pp. 28–31.

Lynch, P., 'Conservative policy under Cameron', *Politics Review*, Vol. 19, No. 3, pp. 28–31.

Smith, N. (2007) 'Is this the era of post-ideological parties?' in *UK Parties and Pressure Groups*, Philip Allan Updates.

Exam focus

Short-answer questions (around 5 minutes each)

Explain, using examples, the meaning of each of the following terms:

1 Ideology
2 Consensus
3 Catch-all party
4 Social democracy

Mid-length questions (around 10 minutes each)

Outline two arguments 'for' and two arguments 'against' each of the following:

1 That all three main UK parties are social democratic in character.
2 The concept of a simple 'left–right' political spectrum.

Outline the main differences between:

3 One-nation conservatism and Thatcherism.
4 Old Labour and New Labour.

Mini-essays (around 25–30 minutes each)

Write a mini-essay in response to each of the following questions:

1 Assess the extent to which the Conservative Party has abandoned Thatcherism in recent years.
2 'New Labour was simply a capitulation to Thatcherism.' Discuss.
3 'The last two decades have witnessed the end of ideology.' Discuss.
4 'There was little to choose between the manifestos of the three main UK parties at the time of the 2010 general election.' Discuss.

Chapter 5

Pressure groups

Key questions answered in this chapter
- ➤ What are pressure groups and what roles do they perform in the British system?
- ➤ How are British pressure groups classified?
- ➤ What methods do pressure groups employ?
- ➤ How does membership of the EU affect pressure group activity in the UK?
- ➤ Why are some pressure groups more successful than others?
- ➤ Does pressure group activity threaten or enhance democracy in the UK?

What are pressure groups?

Pressure groups are groups of like-minded individuals who come together on the basis of shared interests or a commonly held cause in order to put pressure on policy-makers at Westminster and beyond. Pressure groups are significantly more numerous than political parties because whereas the parties tend to aggregate and accommodate

---

Pressure groups and social movements

Distinguish between

Pressure groups
- ➤ Pressure groups tend to benefit from some kind of formal organisation. Many have formal membership structures and identifiable leaders, and most have offices and an officially sanctioned internet presence.

Social movements
- ➤ Social movements are far looser in terms of organisational structure. They generally bring together individuals who are also members of more organised pressure groups, and they are generally seen as bringing together political parties and pressure groups that operate in a given area of policy. For example, the 'green movement' in the UK can be said to include numerous pressure groups, such as the Soil Association, Greenpeace and Plane Stupid, as well as the Green Party.

a wide range of views in an effort to see their candidates elected to public office, pressure groups have a tendency to fragment opinion. Recent years have seen the emergence of looser **social movements** and more focused **single-issue groups**, replacing the larger, more traditional groups common in the 1950s and 1960s. Many commentators see the rise of such groups as a fundamental change in the nature of political participation in the UK — as the emergence of a so-called **new pressure group politics**. It is even suggested that such changes threaten the very principles upon which democracy has traditionally operated in the UK.

Key terms

➢ **New pressure group politics** Characterising the rise of more loosely organised social movements, protest movements, direct action campaigns and grassroots activities. It is distinct from the more tightly organised and choreographed pressure group activity of earlier decades, where mass-membership groups with formal structures and procedures looked to bring their influence to bear.

➢ **Pressure group** A group of like-minded individuals who come together on the basis of shared interests or a commonly held cause in order to put pressure on policy-makers at Westminster and beyond. Pressure groups are a key feature of a pluralist democracy (see Chapter 1).

➢ **Single-issue group** A pressure group or protest movement that focuses on a single issue as opposed to a range of issues underpinned by a broader set of guiding principles or an ideology. Single-issue groups often disband once their central objective is achieved (e.g. the Snowdrop Campaign).

Weblinks

http://news.bbc.co.uk/onthisday/hi/dates/stories/october/16/newsid_3110000/3110949.stm — background from the BBC on the Dunblane Massacre and the Snowdrop Campaign.

Pressure group roles

Pressure groups are traditionally said to perform three main roles within the UK system.

Participation

Pressure groups provide citizens with an avenue for participation between elections. Although the representative model of democracy (or **trustee model**) suggests that MPs should be free to use their judgement once elected, democracy demands that the channels of communication remain open between elections, and pressure groups play a key role in this area.

By engaging citizens in a form of structured participation, pressure groups also serve to moderate the views of those who might otherwise adopt more extreme strategies in pursuit of their goals. Pressure group participation can also serve as a route into a career in politics, thereby serving a secondary function in the area of political recruitment.

Key term

> **Trustee model** The Burkean model of representation provided for in a representative democracy. Politicians are returned to office on the understanding that they are free to use their judgement in the interests of their constituents and the nation as a whole. This contrasts with the delegate model of representation, where those elected are expected to act in accordance with clear instructions or guidelines provided by those who elected them to office.

Representation

Pressure groups enhance representation by aggregating and articulating the common interests or concerns of a given group of individuals. Whereas contemporary political parties are often criticised for being little more than 'catch-all', election-winning machines (see Chapter 4), pressure groups are able to represent the specific interests or concerns of citizens. For example, groups such as Life and the Society for the Protection of Unborn Children (SPUC) serve to represent the interests of those who oppose abortion, at a time when the three main UK parties are broadly sympathetic to the availability of such practices and choose not to impose a party line on moral issues when votes are taken in the Commons.

Weblinks

www.spuc.org.uk — the SPUC website.
www.lifecharity.org.uk — the Life website.

Education

Pressure groups have an educative function in that they act as a source of specialist knowledge, helping the government to weigh up the merits and demerits of proposed policies. This benefits the broader public by helping the government to avoid costly mistakes and unnecessary conflict. Pressure groups also serve to educate the broader public, making them aware of areas of policy that they might otherwise be ignorant of, and thereby making it more likely that the government will be held to account.

Pressure group typologies

Pressure groups are commonly classified according to two broad typologies. The first, the sectional group–cause group typology, classifies pressure groups according to their core aims. The second, the insider–outsider typology, classifies pressure groups according to their status in relation to the government.

Classifying pressure groups by aims

First developed by writers such as J. D. Stewart in the 1950s, the sectional group–cause group typology seeks to classify pressure groups according to their core aims.

Sectional groups

Sometimes referred to as 'protectionist groups', 'private interest groups' or simply 'interest groups', sectional groups are those that aim to advance the shared interests of their members, as opposed to campaigning for a broader cause. Sectional groups are normally 'exclusive', in the sense that individuals must meet certain requirements in order to qualify for group membership. For example, those seeking to join the British Medical Association (BMA) must be qualified medical practitioners or students training to enter the profession.

Weblinks

www.bma.org.uk — the website of the British Medical Association.

Cause groups

Also referred to as 'promotional groups' or 'public interest groups', cause groups seek to promote approaches, issues or ideas that are not of direct benefit to group members. Cause groups tend to be 'inclusive', in that they generally look to establish a wide membership base and do not put in place as many barriers to entry. The Royal Society for the Protection of Birds (RSPB), for example, has become one of the largest and most visible UK cause groups in recent years with somewhere in excess of 1.2 million members in 2010. The cause group category is commonly subdivided into three further categories: **attitude cause groups**, **political cause groups** and **sectional cause groups**.

Weblinks

www.rspb.org.uk — the website of the Royal Society for the Protection of Birds.

Distinguish between

Sectional and cause groups

Sectional groups

- Sectional groups serve the interests of their members.
- Sectional groups tend to be more 'closed' (i.e. 'exclusive') in terms of their membership: for example, requiring members to be serving in a particular profession.

Cause groups

- Cause groups campaign on those policies that they believe will benefit others or the interests of society as a whole.
- Cause groups generally seek a wider membership and are open to all.

Weblinks

www.greenpeace.org.uk — the website of Greenpeace.

www.unlockdemocracy.org.uk — the website of Unlock Democracy.

www.nspcc.org.uk — the website of the National Society for the Prevention of Cruelty to Children.

Key terms

➢ **Attitude cause group** A group that seeks to change people's attitude on a particular issue (e.g. Greenpeace).

➢ **Political cause group** A group that campaigns in pursuit of a cause that is essentially political in nature (e.g. Charter 88, now part of Unlock Democracy).

➢ **Sectional cause group** A group that represents a specific section of society that is distinct from its own membership (i.e. not simply a sectional group). For example, the National Society for the Prevention of Cruelty to Children (NSPCC) is a sectional cause group because it seeks to represent the interests of children but is not organised or run by children.

Problems with the aims typology

Critics of the sectional group–cause group typology argue that it is more helpful to look at group status (see 'Classification by group status', below) than the nature of a group's aims when assessing its chances of success. A further criticism of the typology is that some groups do not fit neatly into any of the 'boxes' identified. For example, a teaching union such as the National Association of Schoolmasters and Union of Women Teachers (NASUWT) clearly campaigns for the sectional interests of its members (a sectional group) but would also claim to raise awareness and promote reform in the field of primary and secondary education (an attitude cause group) and thereby bring immediate benefits to school pupils (a sectional cause group).

Classification by group status

The problems associated with classifying pressure groups according to their core aims has led writers such as Wyn Grant to suggest that it is more helpful to subdivide groups according to their status in relation to the government. The resulting insider–outsider typology largely sees group success as a function of the extent to which any given group is able to develop secure, positive relationships with politicians and officials.

Insider and outsider groups

Distinguish between

Insider groups

➢ Insider groups have regular contact with decision-makers.

➢ Insiders generally work behind the scenes rather than engaging in high-profile publicity stunts that could embarrass the government and threaten the group's privileged status.

➢ Insider groups tend to have mainstream goals.

Outsider groups

➢ Outsider groups do not have regular contact with decision-makers.

➢ Outsiders are often forced to engage in publicity stunts as a means of moving their cause or interest up the political agenda.

➢ Many outsider pressure groups are campaigning on issues that provoke considerable controversy.

Insider groups

Those groups that enjoy closer and more positive relationships with those in government are referred to as insider groups. Those that have particularly strong two-way relationships with policy-makers across a broad range of issues (e.g. the BMA) are described as **core insiders**. Those granted such status within a more narrow area of expertise (e.g. the Worldwide Fund for Nature, WWF) are known as **specialist insiders**. A third group, **peripheral insiders**, are those who have access to, but are only rarely needed by, the government due to the narrow nature of their interest or cause (e.g. the Dogs Trust, formerly the National Canine Defence League).

Key term

➤ **Core insiders** An insider pressure group that works closely with government and is consulted regularly across a broad range of policy areas.

➤ **Peripheral insiders** An insider group whose area of expertise or interest is so narrow that government would only rarely consult its members.

➤ **Specialist insiders** An insider group with which the government consults across only a narrow range of policies.

Weblinks

www.wwf.org.uk — the website of the Worldwide Fund for Nature.

www.dogstrust.org.uk — the website of the Dogs Trust.

Outsider groups

Groups that work outside of the 'political loop' are referred to as outsider groups. Those which might one day gain insider status, but have not yet established good working relationships with those in government, are referred to as **potential insiders. Outsiders by necessity** are those groups that are forced to operate as outsiders because they are

Key terms

➤ **Ideological outsiders** Those outsider groups that look to avoid establishing close working relationships with government for ideological reasons. Groups such as Amnesty International, for example, must avoid becoming too closely associated with any national government if they are to preserve their reputation for impartiality. Other pressure groups, such as those campaigning against globalisation, may well see government as part of the problem, rather than part of the solution.

➤ **Outsiders by necessity** Pressure groups that are forced to operate as outsider groups as a result of there being no realistic prospect of regular consultation with government — whether because of the group's core aims or its chosen methods (e.g. Fathers4Justice).

➤ **Potential insiders** Outsider groups that might ultimately achieve insider status but are currently lacking in terms of support and/or experience. Governments may be reluctant to grant such groups insider status because they regard them as lacking legitimacy.

unlikely ever to achieve insider status — perhaps due to the nature of their cause or as a consequence of their preferred methodology. The term **ideological outsiders** refers to those groups that prefer to distance themselves from the government for reasons of ideology.

Weblinks

www.amnesty.org.uk — the website of Amnesty International.

Problems with the insider–outsider typology

Classifying different groups by group status (insider–outsider) addresses some of the problems inherent in categorising pressure groups according to their core aims. It may also be more useful in terms of assessing the likelihood of a group achieving its central aims. However, such labels tend to ignore the fact that many groups can operate both as 'insiders' and 'outsiders' to some extent, and that groups can move surprisingly quickly from 'outside' to 'inside' and vice versa. For example, the political cause group Charter 88 was clearly outside of the political loop before the 1997 general election, but assumed more influence following Labour's victory in that year. In contrast, the National Farmers' Union's long-held core insider status came under threat as a result of growing EU control over agricultural policy and a period of 13 years when the Conservative Party was out of office.

Consequently, Wyn Grant has argued that it might be more appropriate to divide insider groups into 'high-profile' insider groups (which court the media as well as working with government behind the scenes), 'low-profile' insider groups (which focus largely on establishing relationships behind the scenes) and so-called **'captive' or 'prisoner' groups**.

> **Key term**
>
> **'Captive' or 'prisoner' groups** Pressure groups which are dependent on government, either because they rely largely or entirely upon government funding or because the government played a part in their creation. For example, the Equality and Human Rights Commission (EHRC) was established under the Equality Act (2006).

Weblinks

www.equalityhumanrights.com — the website of the Equality and Human Rights Commission.

Pressure group methods

The nature of pressure group activity is greatly dependent upon the scope and extent of group aims and objectives. Pressure groups can make use of a range of access points (see Box 5.1). Those groups whose aims are local and limited in scale may be able to achieve their goals without ever needing to engage with government at Westminster.

Box 5.1 Access points

Access points (or 'points of leverage') are the points within the political system at which pressure groups and other interested parties can exert pressure on those who hold political power. In a unitary system, where sovereign power is held at the centre, access points tend to be less numerous and less meaningful than in a federal system, where the ultimate power over different areas of policy is held at different levels of government. Systems that incorporate a clear separation of powers and an entrenched system of checks and balances (e.g. the USA) are also likely to offer pressure groups a greater range of meaningful access points than those where the three main elements of state power (executive, legislative and judicial) are fused and the checks on the executive are weak (e.g. the UK).

However, a number of factors have served to increase the range of access points available to British pressure groups in recent years: for example, the establishment of a Scottish Parliament with wide-ranging primary legislative powers, the creation of assemblies and executives in Wales, Northern Ireland and London, and the creation of a more independent UK Supreme Court, separate from the House of Lords.

Broader-based environmental groups will, in contrast, need to work at local, national and supranational levels in order to achieve their core aims.

Traditional pressure group methods

Many groups still favour traditional methods, such as letter writing campaigns, petitions, public demonstrations and conventional lobbying (see Box 5.2).

The anti-abortion organisation Life compiled a petition of more than 2 million names in the mid-1980s and employed postcard campaigns in 1989 and 1990 in opposition to the bill which ultimately became the Human Fertilisation and Embryology Act (1990).

Marches and demonstrations organised by the Anti-Poll Tax Federation in 1990 were said to have contributed both to Margaret Thatcher's downfall (in November of that year) and to the subsequent replacement of the community charge with the council tax in 1993.

Over 400,000 supporters of the Countryside Alliance were said to have taken part in the group's Liberty and Livelihood march in September 2002. An estimated 1 million took to the streets in

The Countryside Alliance 'Liberty and Livelihood' march in central London, September 2002

February 2003 as part of the Stop the War Coalition's efforts to persuade the government not to deploy UK forces in Iraq.

Weblinks

www.countryside-alliance.org.uk — the website of the Countryside Alliance.

www.stopwar.org.uk — the website of the Stop the War Coalition.

Box 5.2 Lobbying

In its broadest sense, lobbying is, as John Kingdom put it, the 'act of seeking the ear of a member of government'. At a simple level, individuals or members of pressure groups may write to a government minister or visit the Palace of Westminster to lobby in person those who have influence over the group's area of interest or expertise. However, in the modern era it has become more common for groups to work through professional lobbying firms. For a fee these organisations will direct professional lobbyists to use their contacts on behalf of the pressure group in question. For example, the lobbying group Ian Greer Associates arranged the initial contact between Mohamed Al Fayed and the then Conservative MP and junior trade minister Neil Hamilton — an association that was at the heart of the 'cash for questions scandal'.

Influencing the legislative process directly

As we have seen, some groups have regular contact with government over a broad range of related issues. These core insider groups have the ability to influence the formation of policy at an early stage through consultation with ministers, civil servants and government-appointed bodies working on legislative proposals. Many larger groups employ lobbyists to pursue their legislative goals and some maintain permanent Westminster offices.

Embarking on legal action

Litigation can be an effective, if expensive, pressure group tactic. Such action can work on four levels:

➤ where a court finds that the government has acted in a manner beyond the authority granted it (ultra vires)
➤ where the rules in place appear to violate EU law
➤ where an Act of Parliament or action of a public official is deemed to be incompatible with the Human Rights Act (1998)
➤ where, 'win' or 'lose', litigation raises public awareness of a particular issue — as in the case of the Pro-Life Alliance's challenges over the application of the Human Fertilisation and Embryology Act (1990).

Note that the extent of judicial power is dealt with more comprehensively in Chapter 9.

Working through a political party

Pressure groups routinely seek to cultivate links with political parties, with a view to influencing the formation of policy once the party in question secures power. Such relationships are far harder to develop when a party is in government, as the government is likely to be subject to far greater demands on its time and the policy-making process is necessarily more 'top-down'. The easiest time for pressure groups to gain a foothold within parties is when they are in opposition. Examples are the way in which anti-fox hunting groups and those favouring wholesale constitutional reform established links with the Labour Party between 1979 and 1997.

Direct action

Direct action is an increasingly popular form of pressure group action. It starts from the premise that conventional methods of influencing policy are flawed and that more visible and direct protests, perhaps even involving **civil disobedience**, illegal methods or violence, may offer the best opportunity of success because they attract media attention, raise public awareness and force politicians to sit up and listen.

Concepts explained

Direct action

Direct action includes those forms of political protest that move beyond traditional pressure group methods and may involve a degree of civil disobedience, illegality or even violence. Those engaged in direct action generally aim to raise the profile of their chosen cause by attracting local or national media coverage. Direct action is said to have gained in popularity as groups adopting more conventional methods have failed to achieve their goals.

Civil disobedience

Civil disobedience is the act of refusing certain orders given by the state, without resorting to physical violence. It is closely associated with the approach of non-violence adopted by political leaders such as Mahatma Gandhi in India and Martin Luther King Jr in the USA. The campaign against the poll tax saw widespread civil disobedience. Many thousands refused to register for the tax; others refused to pay and then failed to attend court when issued with a summons. Many local Anti-Poll Tax Unions used non-violent protest as a way of preventing their local councils from setting the level at which the tax would be charged. The scale of civil disobedience made it impossible for the courts to process all the cases arising.

Although many feel that direct action techniques provide the most immediate way of articulating their views and achieving tangible results, critics argue that the rise in single-issue, direct action politics undermines our system of representative democracy. This is because such campaigns prevent governments from implementing their programmes and from pursuing policies that address the 'bigger picture'.

The scope and scale of direct action campaigns has increased significantly since the 1990s. The anti-roads protests of recent years, the campaign against live animal exports, the campaigns against fox hunting and vivisection, the fuel protests and the campaigns by groups such as Fathers4Justice and environmental groups such as Greenpeace and Plane Stupid (see Box 5.3) have all been seen to have had some effect on policy or opinion.

Box 5.3 Case study: Plane Stupid

The environmental **umbrella group** Plane Stupid was founded in 2005 by university graduates Richard George, Graham Thompson and Joss Garman. It employs direct action tactics in an effort to limit further airport expansion.

In February 2008 one of the group's activists, Tamsin Omond, took to the roof of the Palace of Westminster in order to launch paper aeroplanes made from documents condemning the government's plans for a third runway at Heathrow. She also unfurled two massive banners — one demanding 'No third runway', the other labelling parliament as 'British Airports Authority HQ'.

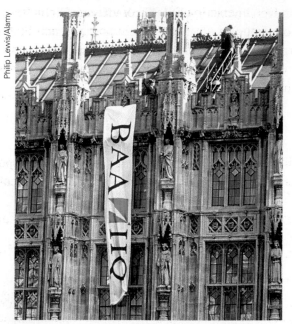

Activists from the umbrella group Plane Stupid on the roof of the Palace of Westminster in February 2008

Key term

> **Umbrella group (or 'peak group')**
A pressure group that brings together or speaks on behalf of a number of pressure groups that share a common interest or campaign in favour of associated causes. The Trades Union Congress (TUC), for example, is a peak group speaking on behalf of a large number of individual trade unions. The Confederation of British Industry (CBI) represents a range of UK businesses and employers. The Make Poverty History campaign and the Stop the War Coalition could also be seen as peak groups.

In recent years, direct action groups have increasingly sought to target suppliers, investors and those working in the transport industry as a way of curtailing the operations of those businesses they oppose.

'Pressure groups' or 'terrorist groups'?

In some cases, the methods adopted by those engaging in direct action causes groups to cross that imperceptible line between 'pressure group' and 'terrorist group'. Direct action groups such as the Animal Liberation Front have been banned on both sides of the Atlantic and other groups have also courted controversy. For example, the anti-vivisection group Save the Newchurch Guinea Pigs (1999–2005) exhumed the body of one of the dead relatives of the owners of a farm supplying animals for experimentation, in an ultimately successful effort to force the closure of the business. The campaign against Huntingdon Life Sciences by the group Stop Huntingdon Animal Cruelty (SHAC) also proved controversial. In both of these cases, group activists have been given lengthy prison sentences as a result of the methods they employed in pursuit of their cause.

Managing the media

Groups increasingly employ sophisticated media techniques to advance their cause or sectional interests. They may use paid media, taking out whole-page adverts in the national press, using direct mail or producing and airing TV adverts. Established caring charities have also made widespread use of such tactics. For example, Barnardo's ran a series of hard-hitting magazine adverts depicting the fate of vulnerable children. The NSPCC also made extensive use of television advertising in support of their Full-Stop campaign, which sought to address violence against children. Groups can also use unpaid media, eliciting news coverage by organising stunts, planning marches or employing other direct action techniques.

Pressure groups and the European Union

Pressure groups in the UK increasingly look to organise and lobby at EU level as opposed to focusing their attention solely on British institutions. Pressure groups are particularly likely to turn to the EU where:
- they are faced with a national government that is unsympathetic to their cause, and/or
- their sectional interest or cause is supranational (i.e. Europe-wide)

The growing power of the EU

Under the terms of the European Communities Act (1972), European law takes precedence over British law where the two are in conflict. Pressure groups can therefore lobby in an effort to force change on their national governments by, in effect, going 'over their heads' to the EU.

Since 1986, decisions in the Council of the European Union (formerly known as the Council of Ministers) have increasingly been taken under a system of qualified majority voting (QMV) rather than on the basis of unanimity. This means that groups must work to build up a broader European support, rather than simply lobbying their own national governments to block measures using their national veto. Though QMV makes life more complicated, it also presents opportunities for pressure groups (see Box 5.4). A UK-based group can, for example, campaign in favour of a measure affecting the UK in the knowledge that the British government alone cannot prevent it from happening. As the process of EU integration sees the Union move beyond the economic sphere into many aspects of social, foreign and security policy, a wider range of British pressure groups are likely to turn to Europe.

Box 5.4 Case study: environmental pressure groups and the EU

Environmental pressure groups have two good reasons to lobby at the EU level:

➤ Many environmental issues, by definition, do not respect territorial borders. It therefore makes more sense to deal with environmental issues at a European or international level, rather than simply at a national level.

➤ The EU is already committed to environmental protection and is, therefore, more sympathetic towards the core aims of many environmental pressure groups than are the national governments of most of the 27 EU member states.

In the broad areas of economic and environmental policy, the proliferation of Europe-wide regulation provides an opportunity for real influence not often afforded to pressure groups at a national level.

On issues such as the improvement of water quality, for example, environmental groups in the UK have made great progress by working through the European Union.

➤ Many beaches in England, previously categorised as unfit for bathing due to sewage pollution, have been improved under pressure from the EU.

➤ The policy of awarding blue flags for clean beaches has also had the effect of raising the public profile of the EU.

➤ Groups such as Surfers Against Sewage (SAS) have played a part in bringing about such changes.

Weblinks

www.sas.org.uk — the website of Surfers Against Sewage.

The emergence of Eurogroups

If pressure groups in each member state conducted their activities independently of one another, their voices might easily be lost. In fact, like-minded pressure groups from different EU member states often aggregate their efforts, establishing Eurogroups which simply by virtue of their size and coverage possess the resources and legitimacy needed to have their views heard.

The scale and structural complexity of the EU provides numerous access points. The European Commission, for example, has a massive appetite for information and recognises Eurogroups as a legitimate source of information. Clearly, the most successful Eurogroups will be those which possess the material resources needed to take advantage of such opportunities. While an EU office is the ideal, not all groups can afford a permanent office in Brussels.

Weblinks

www.copa-cogeca.be — the website of COPA–COGECA (see Box 5.5).

Box 5.5 **Case study: the National Farmers' Union and COPA–COGECA**

The National Farmers' Union (NFU) has a permanent office in Brussels, but it is also a member of the Eurogroup COPA–COGECA.

COPA is the umbrella organisation representing the main agricultural organisations in the EU.

COGECA is the equivalent organisation for agricultural cooperatives.

In 2010, COPA–COGECA had a total of 95 member organisations from EU states and many other affiliated organisations from beyond the EU's borders. In total, the group represented in excess of 12 million farmers.

Factors affecting pressure group success

Precisely how effective individual pressure groups are is often hard to gauge — not least because many core insider groups prefer not to publicise the extent of their influence, for fear of alienating the government and losing their privileged status. Similarly, while high-profile protests and stunts might appear impressive, they rarely affect the course of government policy. Indeed, even at the time of the nationwide 'fuel protests' in 2000, the government chose to speak to the Road Hauliers' Association, rather than to those blockading refineries and bringing motorways to a standstill.

At a simple level, we can measure the extent to which a pressure group is deemed 'a success' in terms of the degree to which it is able to achieve its central aims and objectives. If we are prepared to accept this narrow definition of success, a pressure group's chances of success will depend upon four key variables: group aims, group resources, group status and group methods.

However, the dividing lines between these four factors are not as hard-and-fast as they might first appear to be. For example, while it is true that groups adopting extreme methods are unlikely to achieve success, such groups may only be adopting such tactics because their aims have failed to garner sufficient support among the public at large, and they have been unsuccessful in establishing a relationship with government. Similarly, those groups with large memberships (resources) are also likely to be seen by the government as more legitimate (affecting status).

Group aims

Group aims are vital to understanding why some groups are more successful than others. Central to this theme are the twin concepts of practical achievability and public receptivity.

Practical achievability means the extent to which a group's main goals are achievable in practice. For example, while the Snowdrop Campaign's aim of banning handguns in the UK was clearly an achievable goal in practical terms, the core aim of most anti-globalisation protesters is probably not. We might also regard small, local pressure group campaigns with limited goals as being more practically achievable than campaigns that require statutory changes at UK or EU level.

Public receptivity points to the extent to which the general public are sympathetic to group aims. Those groups which have aims that are diametrically opposed to the prevailing popular mood are unlikely to achieve success in the short term. In contrast, those groups whose aims are broadly in tune with the prevailing public mood are likely to find that they are, in effect, 'pushing at an open door'. This can be seen in the differing fortunes of those campaigning for better conditions in prisons (e.g. the Howard League for Penal Reform) and those seeking to help the victims of crime (e.g. Victim Support).

Crucially, however, while the practical achievability of group aims may remain fairly constant, the public mood — and with it the extent to which that group will be well received — will change over time. For example, while the Snowdrop Campaign's central aim was always achievable in practical terms, it was the public reaction to the Dunblane High School Massacre in 1996 that eased the passage of the Firearms (Amendment) (No. 2) Act (1997), banning private ownership of handguns.

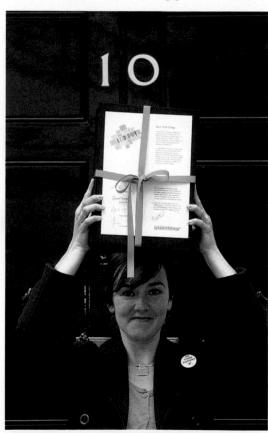

Anna Jones from Greenpeace delivers a message of thanks to No. 10 Downing Street, 2010, after the new coalition government scrapped plans for a third runway at Heathrow airport

Group resources

The extent to which a given group is able to campaign as it wishes will inevitably be shaped to a large degree by its resources. In simple terms, we can divide group resources into human resources (size and quality of membership, availability of technical skills, etc.) and material resources (money, equipment, offices, etc.). While it is certainly true that some groups are able to raise their profile without access to great material resources, such groups inevitably rely heavily on the skills of group members (i.e. human resources). For example, while the material resources available to the group Fathers4Justice were clearly limited, it benefited both from the presence of members who were prepared to risk personal injury in pursuit of their cause, and from a leader, Matt O'Connor, who was articulate, presentable and familiar with the world of public relations.

Group status

We have already discussed at some length the supposed advantages of insider status. Although outsider groups have enjoyed greater media coverage in recent years and could even be said to have contributed to some changes in policy (e.g. the work of groups such as Greenpeace and Plane Stupid in opposing the proposed third runway at Heathrow), it is generally accepted that groups which have at least some contact with government behind the scenes are more likely to achieve some or all of their objectives than those which do not.

Group methods

The methods adopted by a particular group will inevitably have an effect on its chances of success. While an inability to achieve insider status might force some groups into adopting more high-risk strategies as a means of attracting attention, groups that employ extreme methods involving high levels of violence and/or illegality are rarely successful. In truth, successful groups are often characterised by the wide range of tactics they employ in pursuit of their cause, although the ability to plan and resource pressure group campaigns on many fronts using different strategies may just as easily be a product of groups' success as a cause of it.

Pressure groups and democracy

Are pressure groups a threat to democracy?

In Chapter 1 we explored the meaning of the term 'democracy' and considered the concepts of **representative democracy**, **liberal democracy** and **pluralist democracy**.

Concepts explained

Liberal democracy

Liberal democracy is a style of democracy incorporating free and fair elections, and a belief in the importance of certain key rights and responsibilities.

Pluralist democracy

Pluralist democracy is a system of government that encourages participation and allows for free and fair competition between competing interests.

Representative democracy

Representative democracy is where citizens elect representatives who enact laws on their behalf — but there is no obligation on the part of those elected to defer to or seek further approval from citizens before they introduce new policies.

While the concept of representative democracy might lead one to believe that those returned to the Commons should be left largely to their own devices in the wake of a general election, it is clear that pressure groups have a central role in both the liberal and pluralist models of democracy. In the case of liberal democracies, the protection afforded to fundamental rights such as the freedom of speech, the right of assembly and the right to petition the government for redress of grievances would all appear to point towards the likelihood of widespread pressure group activity. The pluralist model, with its emphasis on the open interplay of competing — or 'countervailing' — interests would also appear to necessitate the existence of pressure groups.

However, while all three models of democracy clearly 'allow' for the existence of pressure groups, it is often argued that the way in which certain groups operate does more to undermine than to enhance the political process as a whole. Such criticisms of pressure groups can be crystallised into three main arguments.

Pressure groups reinforce inequalities

When commenting on pluralism at work in some aspects of the US system of government, Ernest S. Griffiths remarked that the unwritten belief underpinning such democratic arrangements is that 'truth customarily emerges from a battle of protagonists'. However, the battle between those groups 'for' and 'against' a particular issue or policy proposal is rarely an even one, bringing into question the idea of countervailing interests (where opposing groups in effect serve to cancel one another out).

Groups representing business interests clearly have an advantage in open competition. First, while they often have considerable material resources and a significant financial incentive to lobby, such groups are generally free from the problems associated with organising mass-membership cause groups. Secondly, as Wyn Grant has noted, the government has a vested interest in listening to such groups, as its re-election will be based in part on delivering economic success.

In more general terms, it is commonly observed that the most successful groups tend to be those that benefit from both a highly skilled and articulate membership, and a sound financial base. As a result, it could be said that pressure groups representing middle-class interests are in a better position to compete — and that pressure group competition thus serves to reinforce as opposed to break down social inequalities. All of this suggests that, far from contributing to pluralism, pressure groups may in fact be a feature of **elitism**.

> **Concepts explained**
>
> **Elite theory**
>
> Elite theory is the belief that modern societies are dominated by an elite that uses its privileged position to benefit its own members while at the same time excluding others from the key decision-making processes. It is closely associated with the work of American sociologist Charles Wright Mills and his seminal book *The Power Elite* (1956).

Pressure groups 'strangle efficient government'

It was the former Conservative cabinet minister Douglas Hurd who famously described pressure groups as 'serpents that strangle efficient government'. Hurd's criticism can be interpreted in two broad ways.

First, the way in which many insider groups have been able to become an established element in the machinery of government adds a further 'level' to the policy-making process. Groups such as the RSPB work closely with government and are consulted across a range of policy areas at the drafting stage. While some might argue that this is helpful, as it serves to reduce the likelihood of unforeseen problems emerging further down the legislative road, it is clear that the existence of such insider groups must by definition result in other groups being excluded from the process, thus undermining pluralism. The existence of such privileged groups also acts as an internal check on the ability of government to pursue its legislative agenda.

Secondly, while governments must weigh up the merits and demerits of different policies and, ultimately, seek to 'balance the books', pressure groups are generally concerned only with a specific area or at best a limited range of policies. Thus governments seeking to deliver 'joined-up' government are all too often forced to take a reactive stance when facing single-issue outsider campaigns, as opposed to being proactive in seeking to deliver on their manifesto pledges. In forcing the government to 'fire-fight' in this way, pressure groups distort the decision-making process and make it far harder for those in office to make the difficult decisions. This is particularly true in the broad area of central government finance, where the activities of pressure groups, campaigning publicly and privately for increased government expenditure in their area of interest, apply a relentless upward pressure on public sector spending and — particularly in times of economic downturn — public sector borrowing.

Pressure groups can be internally undemocratic

Although pressure groups are said to play a vital role within a liberal democracy, by providing avenues for representation and participation, many membership groups are themselves not internally democratic, affording little real power to individual members or supporters.

The growth of passive, 'cheque-book' group membership in recent years clearly has implications for the quality of participation provided for by pressure groups. More important, however, is the extent to which the level of internal democracy present in a group may have a bearing on its legitimacy. As Wyn Grant notes, 'we need [to be able] to ask questions about whom [groups] represent and how their policies are arrived at'. While some groups are clearly engaged in intense internal debate (e.g. the RSPCA over fox hunting), others (e.g. Greenpeace — see Box 5.6) have tended to be more centralised, despite having large individual memberships.

How are pressure group officers chosen?

In many cases, pressure group officers are appointed, as opposed to being elected by the group's members on a one member, one vote (OMOV) basis. This means that those leading pressure groups are often not directly accountable to members.

How do pressure groups make decisions?

In many pressure groups, key decisions are taken not by members, but by a central committee or board which is itself unelected. Neil McNaughton suggests that groups such as the British Medical Association and the Automobile Association are particularly poor at consulting their members over questions of policy and direction: in short, that the organisation of many groups reflects elitism rather than pluralism.

Some sectional groups, such as trade unions, have been forced to become more internally democratic as a result of employment and union legislation passed in the 1980s (e.g. the requirement to hold ballots before national strike action). Other sectional groups (e.g. non-membership business groups) may display little or no internal democracy. Many cause groups start as a small group of committed individuals and control often remains with these individuals, or their chosen successors, even when the group's membership expands significantly.

Box 5.6 Is Greenpeace internally democratic?

According to Wyn Grant, Greenpeace is a hierarchical organisation that allows little democratic control over the direction of campaigns.

➤ It has a strictly bureaucratic, if not authoritarian, internal structure.

➤ A small group of people has control over the organisation both at the international level and within national chapters.

➤ Local action groups, which exist in some countries, are totally dependent on the central body.

➤ The rank and file is excluded from all decisions.

Viewpoint Are pressure groups good for democracy?

YES

● Pressure groups occur naturally under any system of government. People have a natural desire to unite in protection of their own interests or in advancing a particular cause.

● Pressure groups allow people to organise and articulate their views between elections.

● Groups provide an additional avenue for participation, at a time when some other more traditional forms (e.g. party membership and voting) are waning.

● Pressure groups allow a wider range of opinions to be represented than is possible through political parties, particularly in a post-ideological age of catch-all parties.

● Groups play an essential role in moderating the views of their more extreme members. Without such groups, individuals with extreme views might never have their views challenged and changed.

● Pressure groups allow the strength (i.e. intensity) of opinions to be expressed, as opposed to simply counting the number of people supporting a view — as happens at elections.

● Pressure groups play a role in educating the public and providing the government with specialist information and expertise.

NO

● The quality of participation offered by pressure groups is often very low, even where membership is high. Many members do little more than pay their annual membership fee. This is referred to as 'passive membership' or 'cheque-book membership'.

● Many pressure groups lack legitimacy because they exhibit low levels of internal democracy.

- Many non-membership groups are simply fronts for wealthy and influential business interests which may have little interest in the greater public good. This is true of many core insider groups.

- Pressure groups do not compete on an equal financial footing. Less wealthy groups find it far harder to access the policy-making process.

- Groups tend to be more successful where they have articulate, educated leading members. This tends to favour groups run by the middle classes: in other words, pressure group activity is more 'elitism in action' than 'pluralism in action'.

- Groups often have an effect on government that is disproportionate to their size or to the merit of their cause, often by employing direct action tactics.

- Pressure group activity gets in the way of joined-up government.

- The information produced by some groups is unreliable. Far from 'educating', many groups are in fact misleading or indoctrinating.

▶ **What you should know**

- ❯ Pressure groups are groups of like-minded individuals who come together on the basis of shared interests or a commonly held cause in order to put pressure on policy-makers at Westminster and beyond.

- ❯ Recent years have seen the rise of less formally structured social movements and direct action campaigns.

- ❯ Pressure groups perform three main functions: a participatory function, a representative function and an educative function.

- ❯ The right to engage in pressure group activity is protected under the style of liberal democracy practised in the UK. This is because freedom of speech, freedom of association and the right to petition the government for redress of grievances are protected.

- ❯ Pressure groups are also an essential feature of pluralist democracy, where competing interests (so-called countervailing groups) fight it out in support of their interests or cause.

- ❯ Pressure groups are normally classified either according to their core aims (under the sectional group–cause group typology) or in terms of their status in relation to government (under the insider–outsider typology).

- ❯ The UK's unitary system and the absence of a formal separation of powers has traditionally limited the number and range of meaningful access points open to groups, but new avenues have been opened up as a result of devolution and the ongoing process of European integration.

- ❯ Pressure groups seek to advance their interests or cause by a variety of means: traditional methods (such as letter writing, public demonstrations and lobbying); cultivating links with political parties; direct action; accessing the mass media; and the use of legal action.

- ❯ A pressure group's chances of success will be shaped largely by the nature and appeal of its core aims, its resources, its status and its methods.

- ❯ Some commentators argue that pressure groups threaten to undermine democracy in the UK because they give undue influence to wealthy, well-educated groups (favouring elitism over pluralism), because they hinder the government's efforts to deliver joined-up government, and because many groups lack legitimacy as a result of their not being internally democratic.

UK/US comparison

Pressure groups in the USA

➢ While both the USA and the UK are said to be liberal democracies, the USA is generally seen as being further along the road towards pluralism.

➢ This is due both to the sheer diversity present in US society and to the numerous access points created as a result of power being fragmented both vertically and horizontally, through federalism and the system of checks and balances.

➢ US pressure groups play a far more significant role at election time than their British counterparts, not least due to the continued influence of so-called Political Action Committees (PACS) and the moneys they provide to candidates who are sympathetic to their interests or cause.

➢ The financial cost of running an election campaign in the USA makes elected politicians far more receptive to those pressure groups that backed their campaign. Senator Barbara Mikulski went as far as to describe the US legislature as a 'coin-operated Congress'.

➢ Single-issue groups have a far greater role in US politics than has traditionally been the case in the UK. Many of these groups campaign on issues of great political or moral controversy: for example, on 'gun rights' or 'abortion rights'. Candidates who take positions that run contrary to group aims often become a target for group-funded negative campaigns or 'attack-ads'.

➢ The presence of a codified constitution in the USA means that the use of legal action as a pressure group tactic is far more prevalent there than in the UK, with groups often sponsoring test cases in an effort to establish a legal precedent in their favour. As Alexis de Tocqueville once noted, 'scarcely any political question arises in the US that is not resolved sooner or later into a judicial question'.

Further reading

Fairclough, P. and Magee, E. (2009) 'Pressure groups: the return of the big beasts?', in *UK Government and Politics Annual Survey 2009*, Chapter 6, Philip Allan Updates.

Grant, W. (2009) 'Pressure groups in the UK: good or bad for democracy?', *Politics Review*, Vol. 19, No. 1, pp. 12–15.

Jordan, G. (2008) 'Pressure groups: identifying the target for study', *Politics Review*, Vol. 18, No. 1, pp. 17–19.

Smith, N. (2007) *Advanced TopicMaster: UK Parties and Pressure Groups*, Philip Allan Updates.

Exam focus

Short-answer questions (around 5 minutes each)

Explain, using examples, the meaning of each of the following terms:

1 Access points
2 'New pressure group politics'
3 Internal pressure group democracy
4 Eurogroups

Mid-length questions (around 10 minutes each)

Outline two arguments 'for' and two arguments 'against' each of the following:

1 Single-issue groups
2 Direct action

Outline the main differences between:

3 Sectional (interest) and cause groups
4 Insider and outsider groups

Mini-essays (around 25–30 minutes each)

Write a mini-essay in response to each of the following questions:

1 'Pressure groups rarely have any effect on the course of government policy.' Discuss.
2 Why are some pressure groups more successful than others?
3 Are pressure groups 'good' or 'bad' for democracy in the UK?
4 'Serpents that strangle efficient government.' Assess this view of pressure groups in the UK context.

Chapter 6

The constitution

Key questions answered in this chapter

➤ What are the key sources and principles of the British constitution?

➤ What are the main strengths and weaknesses of the traditional constitution?

➤ Is parliament sovereign?

➤ How significant were the constitutional reforms introduced by the Labour governments of 1997–2010?

➤ Should the UK adopt a codified constitution?

What is a constitution?

A **constitution** sets out the laws, rules and practices by which a state is governed, specifying the powers of the governing institutions and the formal relationships between them, and the relationship between citizens and the state. It provides the framework for the political system, establishing the main institutions of government and determining where decision-making authority resides. The relationship between the state and its citizens should also be spelled out (e.g. in a **Bill of Rights**) and the basic rights of citizens guaranteed.

In liberal democracies, the constitution provides an important defence against the abuse of power by the state and its institutions. It upholds a system of **limited government** in which a system of checks and balances prevents over-mighty government, and the rights of the citizen are protected from arbitrary state power. Reference to the constitution can determine when state action is lawful and legitimate (i.e. is constitutional) and when it is not (i.e. is unconstitutional).

Key terms

➤ **Bill of Rights** An authoritative statement of the rights of citizens, often entrenched as part of a codified constitution.

➤ **Limited government.** A system in which the powers of government are subject to legal constraints, and checks and balances within the political system.

Constitutions should not be seen as existing outside normal political activity. Instead, they impact upon day-to-day politics and are inherently political. A constitution is not static: the rules and practices it sets out have to be interpreted and sometimes adapted to meet changing circumstances. Nor are constitutions neutral: the framework they provide (e.g. the electoral system) may favour some actors, while others may seek to change it.

Concepts explained

Constitution

The House of Lords Select Committee on the Constitution (2001) defined a constitution as 'the set of laws, rules and practices that create the basic institutions of the state and its component and related parts, and stipulate the powers of those institutions and the relationship between the different institutions, and between those institutions and the individual'.

Constitutionalism

The theory and practice of government according to the rules and principles of a constitution. A constitutional democracy is one which operates within the framework of a constitution that sets limits on the powers of government institutions and provides protection for the rights of citizens. A government or public authority acts in an unconstitutional manner when its actions are not in accord with the principles and practices set out in the constitution.

Codified and uncodified constitutions

A key distinction is that between codified and uncodified constitutions. A **codified constitution** is one in which the major principles underpinning the political system are collected in a single authoritative document. This is a constitution with a capital 'C', such as the US Constitution. An **uncodified constitution** has no single source for

Concepts explained

Codified constitution

A codified constitution is a single document that sets out the laws, rules and principles on how a state is to be governed, and the rights of citizens. The key provisions governing the political system are collected in one authoritative document, often called 'the Constitution'.

Uncodified constitution

An uncodified constitution is one in which the laws, rules and principles specifying how a state is to be governed are not gathered in a single document. Instead they are found in a variety of sources, some written (e.g. statute laws) and some unwritten (e.g. conventions).

The distinction between codified and uncodified constitutions is significant, but it should be remembered that no constitution is either entirely written or unwritten, and that codified constitutions often have some flexibility.

these principles; rather, they are found in a number of places. The UK constitution is the prime example. It is frequently described as 'unwritten', but this is misleading. While it is true that constitutional principles are not gathered in a single document, most are written down, notably in the form of statute law (Acts of Parliament) and decisions of the higher courts. But others take the form of unwritten conventions that lack the clarity of a codified constitution.

The distinction between codified and uncodified constitutions is not as sharp as it might appear. No constitution ever spells out each and every practice. All constitutions contain a mixture of written and unwritten rules. Students of American politics will, for example, learn little about the formal powers of the Supreme Court or the informal powers of the president from reading the US Constitution. The US Constitution has been periodically reinterpreted by the Supreme Court so that its eighteenth-century principles make sense in the modern world. A codified constitution is, then, not a detailed blueprint but a reference point for an evolving political system.

Features of codified constitutions

There are nevertheless significant differences between codified and uncodified constitutions. Codified constitutions are often produced at a critical juncture in a nation's history: for example, after independence (the US Constitution in 1787), authoritarian rule or war (West Germany's Basic Law in 1949). In this situation, institutions derive their authority from the constitution. By contrast, the UK constitution has evolved over time and is not based upon a definitive statement of abstract principles. Some of its practices (e.g. prerogative powers) are centuries old, whereas others (e.g. the Scottish Parliament) are recent additions.

A codified constitution has the status of **fundamental law** or higher law, placing it above ordinary law made by the legislature. There is a two-tier legal system with the constitution having a higher status than all other law. A constitutional (or supreme) court determines whether its provisions have been violated. The provisions of a codified constitution are also **entrenched**: that is, there are special procedures for its amendment which make it more difficult to change than ordinary legislation. For the constitution to be amended, a super-majority (a higher fraction than a half) in the legislature or approval in a referendum may be required. Codified constitutions are characterised as rigid and uncodified constitutions as flexible. But degrees of flexibility are also evident in codified constitutions — only 17 amendments have been added to the US Constitution since the 1791 Bill of Rights (which consists of the first ten amendments), but the 1958 constitution of the French Fifth Republic was amended 17 times in 50 years.

Key terms
➤ **Entrenched** Secured; difficult to change.
➤ **Fundamental law** Law derived from decisions in court cases and from general customs.

The UK's uncodified constitution

There are no special legal mechanisms for amending the British constitution — the uncodified constitution can be amended by a simple Act of Parliament. The British constitution is, in a sense then, reducible to what parliament enacts. Nor, in a single-tier legal system, is there fundamental law. There are no constitutional 'no go areas' into which parliament cannot step. As we will see below, the doctrine of parliamentary sovereignty endows parliament with legislative supremacy, enabling it to legislate on any matter of its choosing and to overturn any existing law. Parliament can change the constitution in the same way that it can amend any other legislation.

Parliamentary sovereignty and an uncodified constitution mean that **judicial review** is limited in the UK. Judicial review is the power of the courts to determine whether the government and public authorities have acted within the bounds of their authority when making decisions. Without a codified constitution, there is no definitive criterion for determining what is unconstitutional. However, as Chapter 9 will examine, judicial review of legislation and of ministerial decisions has increased significantly over the last 30 years.

> ### Key term
> **Judicial review** The power of senior judges to review the actions of government and public authorities, declaring them unlawful if they have exceeded their authority.

Weblinks

www.psr.keele.ac.uk/const.htm — Dr Richard Kimber's Political Science Resources site, which includes the texts of many national constitutions.

Codified and uncodified constitution

Distinguish between

Codified constitution

- The rules and principles governing the state are collected in a single authoritative document, 'the Constitution'.
- It has the status of fundamental law, above all other law.
- It is entrenched, with special procedures for its amendment that make it difficult to change.
- The courts, particularly a constitutional court, use it to determine if actions are constitutional.

Uncodified constitution

- There is no single authoritative document; rather the rules and principles governing the state are found in a number of sources, both written and unwritten.
- It has the status of ordinary law; there is no hierarchy of laws.
- It is not entrenched, but can be amended in the same way as ordinary law.
- Judicial review is limited; there is no single authoritative document that senior judges can use to determine if an action is unconstitutional.

Sources of the British constitution

In the absence of a codified document, we must look for the key rules and practices of the UK's political system in different places. There are five principal sources of the British constitution:

➤ statute law
➤ common law
➤ conventions
➤ authoritative works
➤ European Union law

Statute law

Statute law is law created by parliament. In the legislative process, Acts of Parliament have to be approved by the House of Commons, the House of Lords and the monarch before they are placed on the statute book (i.e. gain the force of law). They are then implemented by the executive and enforced by the courts. Statute law is the most important source of the principles and rules making up the British constitution because parliament is the sovereign body.

Not all Acts are of constitutional significance: legislation on funding for schools will have an important effect on policy but not on the constitution. Examples of statute law that have been of historical constitutional importance include:

➤ the Great Reform Act (1832), which extended the franchise
➤ the Parliament Act (1911), which established the House of Commons as the dominant chamber of parliament
➤ the European Communities Act (1972), by which the UK joined the European Economic Community (EEC)

More recent examples are:

➤ the Scotland Act (1998), creating a Scottish Parliament
➤ the Human Rights Act (1998), which enshrined key rights in UK law

Common law

The **common law** includes legal principles that have been developed and applied by UK courts. The courts interpret and clarify the law where there is no clear statute law. Common law is thus legal precedent made by judges concerning, for example, the rights of homeowners to tackle intruders who enter their property. Judicial decisions have clarified the rights of citizens *vis-à-vis* the state. Such rulings become part of the body of the common law and serve as a guide to future lawmakers. In the last decade, however, judges have been more likely to look to the Human Rights Act (1998) than to precedents in British common law. Government ministers may clarify or amend common law through Acts of Parliament.

The common law also includes customs and precedents that have become accepted practice. They relate to the role of the monarchy, parliament and the executive. Particularly important is the **royal prerogative** — the powers exercised in the name of the Crown. The Crown retains a number of formal powers that date back to the period before the UK became a constitutional monarchy in the late seventeenth century. The Crown's prerogative powers include the right to:

➤ declare war and negotiate treaties
➤ dissolve parliament
➤ appoint government ministers
➤ appoint judges

Government ministers exercise prerogative powers in the name of the Crown. It is the prime minister who declares war, decides the date of a general election and appoints government ministers and judges. The prime minister will inform the monarch of his or her decision, but the monarch has no real power to veto prime ministers' actions or dissuade them from their chosen course. The 2007 'Governance of Britain' Green Paper included proposals to give parliament a greater say over how ministers exercise prerogative powers.

Conventions

Conventions are rules or norms that are considered to be binding. They are neither codified nor enforced by courts of law; it is long usage that gives conventions their authority. The British constitution is regarded as flexible because some of its key elements are based on convention. By convention, the monarch must assent to Acts of Parliament: if the queen were to refuse, a constitutional crisis would ensue. But conventions are an imprecise guide to what should be considered constitutional. Three examples illustrate this ambiguity.

Key term

➤ **Common law** Law derived from decisions in court cases and from general customs.
➤ **Conventions** Established norms of political behaviour rooted in past experience rather than the law.
➤ **Royal prerogative** Discretionary powers of the Crown that are exercised in the monarch's name by government ministers.
➤ **Statute law** Law derived from Acts of Parliament and subordinate legislation.

Appointing the prime minister

It is the monarch who appoints the prime minister. Convention dictates that the leader of the largest party in the House of Commons will be invited to Buckingham Palace after a general election and invited to form a government. The last member of the House of Lords to become prime minister was Alec Douglas-Home in 1963. It had become a convention by then that the prime minister should be a member of the Commons, so he resigned from the Lords and successfully fought a by-election to take a seat as an MP. The first-past-the-post (FPTP) electoral system usually produces a clear outcome, rendering the monarch's decision on which party will form the next government a formality.

However, should a general election produce a hung parliament — one in which no single party has an overall majority — the monarch could face a difficult decision. When the February 1974 general election produced no clear winner, the defeated prime minister, Edward Heath, did not resign until the possibility of forming a coalition government with the Liberals had been exhausted. Only then was Harold Wilson, the leader of the largest party in the Commons, invited to form a minority Labour government.

Ministerial responsibility

The circumstances under which government ministers ought to resign are also governed by convention. The convention of collective ministerial responsibility suggests that ministers who cannot accept a policy position agreed by the cabinet should leave the government. That of individual ministerial responsibility holds that ministers should resign if they, or their department, are guilty of serious political mistakes. As we will see in Chapter 8, neither convention is clear cut or holds fast for all cases.

Salisbury Convention

The Salisbury Convention (also known as the Salisbury–Addison Convention) states that the House of Lords should not vote down or wreck bills that seek to enact a manifesto commitment of the governing party. It marked an acceptance in the 1940s that an unelected upper house with an inbuilt Conservative majority should not frustrate the will of the Commons and the electorate. But Liberal Democrat and Conservative peers voted against government legislation on identity cards even though it had featured in Labour's manifesto at the 2005 general election. They argued that Labour did not have a sufficient mandate (it won just 35% of the vote on a low turnout) and that no party now had a majority in a reformed House of Lords stripped of most hereditary peers.

Authoritative works

A number of established legal and political texts have become accepted as works of authority on the British constitution. These texts have no formal legal authority but prove helpful in interpreting the core values that underpin the constitution, and shed light on the more obscure areas of constitutional practice. They act as a guide to the workings of institutions and the political system in general.

There are only a handful of examples:

➤ Erskine May's *Treatise on the Law, Privileges, Proceedings and Usage of Parliament* (1844) is regarded as the 'Bible' of parliamentary practice, providing a detailed guide to its rules and practices.

➤ Walter Bagehot's *The English Constitution* (1867) set out the role of the cabinet and the prime minister, describing the latter as 'first among equals'.

➤ A. V. Dicey's *An Introduction to the Study of the Law of the Constitution* (1884) examined the relationship between the law and the nineteenth-century constitution, focusing on parliamentary sovereignty and the rule of law. It described a system of responsible cabinet government in a parliamentary democracy with a constitutional monarchy, where parliament was legally sovereign and the people politically sovereign.

European Union law

On 1 January 1973, the UK became a member of the European Economic Community. This was subsequently renamed the European Community (EC) and, after the Maastricht Treaty came into force in 1993, the European Union (EU). The treaties establishing the European Union, legislation emanating from the EU and judgments of the European Court of Justice have all become a part of the British constitution. (See p.150 for more detail.)

Basic principles of the British constitution

Four core principles formed the building blocks of the traditional British constitution:
➢ parliamentary sovereignty
➢ the rule of law
➢ the unitary state
➢ parliamentary government in a constitutional monarchy

Membership of the European Union has added a fifth main characteristic. Here it is discussed in the context of parliamentary sovereignty, with the nature of the EU and the UK's membership examined in greater depth in Chapter 11.

Parliamentary sovereignty

Parliamentary sovereignty is the cornerstone of the UK constitution. It states that the Westminster Parliament is the supreme law-making body. **Sovereignty** means legal supremacy: parliament has ultimate law-making authority. This legislative supremacy is constructed around three propositions:
➢ Parliament can legislate on any subject of its choosing.
➢ Legislation cannot be overturned by any higher authority.
➢ No parliament can bind its successors.

Fotolia

Parliamentary sovereignty states that the Westminster parliament is the supreme law-making body

The nature of parliamentary sovereignty and the constraints upon it are examined in detail in the next section of this chapter.

Concepts explained

Parliamentary sovereignty

The doctrine that parliament has absolute legal authority within the state. It enjoys legislative supremacy: parliament may make law on any matter it chooses, its decisions may not be overturned by any higher authority and it may not bind its successors. Parliamentary sovereignty is a legal theory concerning the location of law-making authority. EU membership, devolution, the judicial review of legislation and the use of referendums raise questions about how meaningful it is. There is also a gap between legal theory and political reality, for no institution has absolute power to do as it wishes.

Key terms

➤ **Civil liberties** Fundamental individual rights and freedoms that ought to be protected from interference by the state.

➤ **Rule of law** A system of rule where the relationship between the state and the individual is governed by law, protecting the individual from arbitrary state action.

➤ **Sovereignty** Legal supremacy; absolute law-making authority that is not subject to a higher authority.

The rule of law

The **rule of law** concerns the relationship between the state and its citizens, ensuring that state action is limited and responsible. All UK citizens must obey the law and are equal under it. The courts can hold government ministers, police officers and public officials accountable for their actions if they have acted outside the law or been negligent in their duties.

Laws passed by parliament must be interpreted and applied by an independent judiciary, free from political interference. The rights of citizens are thus protected from arbitrary executive action. Aggrieved citizens can take the government or a local authority to court if they feel they have been treated improperly. Individuals charged under the law are also entitled to a fair trial and should not be imprisoned without due regard for the legal process.

The rule of law is an essential feature of a liberal democracy. Parliamentary sovereignty theoretically enables parliament to abolish these rights. However, a sustained effort to overturn the key elements of the rule of law would be widely regarded as illegitimate and anti-democratic, making it untenable. As we will see below, the Human Rights Act (1998) gives greater protection to basic **civil liberties**. Yet governments of both main parties have restricted the rights of citizens (and of third-country nationals, such as asylum seekers) to have full recourse to the legal process. The Criminal Justice Act (2003) restricted the right to trial by jury, allowing complex fraud cases and those where 'jury nobbling' is feared to be heard by judges alone, and enabled judges to decide if juries should hear details of previous offences. It also (from 2005) overturned the double jeopardy principle — that individuals acquitted of a serious crime should not be tried again for the same offence — for cases where new and compelling evidence was available.

www.liberty-human-rights.org.uk — the website of Liberty, a civil liberties pressure group.

A unitary state

Constitutions may be classified according to whether they concentrate political power at the centre, or divide it between central and regional tiers of government. An important distinction is that between **unitary constitutions** and **federal constitutions**. The traditional British constitution is a unitary constitution. Although the United Kingdom consists of four component nations — England, Scotland, Wales and Northern Ireland — it has been a highly centralised state in which sovereignty is located at Westminster. In a unitary constitution, subnational institutions do not have autonomous powers that are constitutionally safeguarded. Local government has had little power and regional government has historically been weak or non-existent.

In a federal constitution, such as in Germany or the United States, power is shared between national (i.e. federal) and regional (i.e. state) governments. Each tier of government is given specific powers and granted significant autonomy; one tier of government cannot abolish the other.

Concepts explained

Unitary constitution

A unitary constitution is one in which sovereignty is located at the centre. Central government has supremacy over other tiers of government, which it can reform or abolish. A unitary state is a centralised and homogeneous state: political power is concentrated in central government and all parts of the state are governed in the same way.

Federal constitution

A federal constitution divides sovereignty between (normally) two tiers of government. Power is shared between national government (the federal government) and regional government (the states). Regional government is protected by the constitution: it cannot be abolished or reformed significantly against its will.

The UK has traditionally been described as a unitary state, but the label does not reflect fully its multinational character. An alternative is to see the UK as a union state. A **unitary state** exhibits a high degree of both centralisation and standardisation: all parts of the state are governed in the same way and share a common political culture. In a **union state**, by contrast, important political and cultural differences remain. These asymmetries reflect the different ways in which parts of the state were united.

The component nations of the UK came together in different ways: Wales was invaded by England, Scotland joined the union through an international treaty, while Northern Ireland remained part of the UK after the establishment of the Irish Free State. Political and cultural differences survived. Scotland retained its own legal system, Wales its own language and Northern Ireland separate institutions and political parties. By the second half of the twentieth century, the interests of each nation were represented in London by a government department headed by a cabinet minister. But these departments were relatively weak and political power was concentrated at the centre.

Key terms

➢ **Union state** A state in which there are cultural differences and where, despite a strong centre, different parts of the state are governed in slightly different ways.

➢ **Unitary state** A homogeneous state in which power is concentrated at the political centre and all parts of the state are governed in the same way.

As we will see below, the devolution of some policy responsibilities from central government to new institutions in Scotland, Wales and Northern Ireland has raised further questions about the classification of the UK state and its constitution. Oxford professor Vernon Bogdanor claims that the constitution is now 'quasi-federal'. In practice, but not in legal theory, Westminster no longer has the power to make domestic policy in many areas for Scotland. The Supreme Court can rule on which body has constitutional authority where disputes about competence arise, and other institutions have been created to manage relations between the UK government and the devolved bodies.

Parliamentary government in a constitutional monarchy

Under the UK constitution, government takes place through parliament under a **constitutional monarchy**. Government ministers are politically accountable to parliament and legally accountable to the Crown, and must face the verdict of the electorate at least every 5 years. Between general elections, a government relies upon its majority in the House of Commons to survive and enact its legislative programme.

The balance of power between the different institutions of the state has, of course, altered over time. The Glorious Revolution of 1689 established the supremacy of parliament over the monarchy. The key conventions of the constitutional monarchy gradually fell into place: the monarch retained formal powers (e.g. to assent to legislation) but their usage was constrained. The extension of the franchise enhanced the position of the House of Commons; it had overtaken the House of Lords as the predominant legislative chamber by the early twentieth century. Political parties emerged as key actors in the conduct of government. The FPTP electoral system and two-party system tended to produce single-party government. The majority party thus controlled the cabinet and exercised considerable discipline over its members in the House of Commons.

By the mid-nineteenth century, the UK political system was one of **cabinet government**. Cabinet was then the key policy-making body, but a century later considerable power was vested in the office of prime minister. This led some commentators to argue that **prime ministerial government** had replaced cabinet government (see Chapter 8).

Key terms

➤ **Cabinet government** A system of government in which executive power is vested in a cabinet, whose members exercise collective responsibility, rather than a single office.

➤ **Constitutional monarchy** A political system in which the monarch is the formal head of state but the monarch's legal powers are exercised by government ministers.

➤ **Parliamentary government** A political system in which government takes place through parliament, and in which the executive and legislative branches are fused.

➤ **Prime ministerial government** A system of government in which the prime minister is the dominant actor and is able to bypass the cabinet.

Sovereignty and the constitution

Characteristics of parliamentary sovereignty

The doctrine of parliamentary sovereignty establishes the Westminster Parliament as the supreme law-making body in the UK. According to legal theory:

➤ Parliament can legislate on any subject of its choosing.
➤ Legislation cannot be overturned by any higher authority.
➤ No parliament can bind its successors.

Law on any matter

There are no constitutional restrictions on the scope of parliament's legislative authority. Parliament's right to make retrospective laws and to reform itself provide useful examples. Concerning the former, the War Crimes Act (1991) gave the British courts the right to try people who became British citizens after 1990 for crimes they had committed in Nazi-occupied Europe in the Second World War (1939–45). Critics of the Act cautioned that evidence relating to events from over half a century ago could not be robust. Only one person has been convicted under the Act.

The Parliament Act (1911) is a prime example of parliament's right to reform itself. It stipulated that the House of Lords could no longer block bills approved by the House of Commons, but only delay them from entering into force for 2 years. This was reduced to 1 year in 1949. Parliamentary sovereignty effectively meant the sovereignty of the Commons. This was challenged by opponents of the ban on fox hunting, who claimed that the Hunting Act (2004) was invalid because it was passed under the Parliament Act. But the Law Lords upheld the ban in the Jackson case (2005). One possible implication of the Parliament Act is that the Commons could vote to reform or abolish the House of Lords without requiring the consent of the upper house.

Legislative supremacy

The second element of parliamentary sovereignty is legislative supremacy. In many liberal democracies, a constitutional court (e.g. the Supreme Court in the United States) has the power to declare legislation unconstitutional and to annul it. But this is not the case in the UK. As parliament enjoys legislative supremacy, the courts cannot strike down statute law on the grounds that it is unconstitutional or that it conflicts with the common law.

Equality of legislation

Constitutional law has a higher status than other forms of law in many liberal democracies: it cannot be amended or repealed by simple majority votes in the legislature. This is not the case in the UK. Major changes to the constitution (e.g. devolution, reform of the House of Lords) have been enacted by simple majority votes in parliament. As no parliament may bind its successors, all legislation is of equal status. Legislation that brings about major constitutional change has the same status as, say, animal welfare law. It is not entrenched: one piece of legislation can be amended in the same way as any other.

Some constitutional experts, such as Vernon Bogdanor, argue that legislation of such constitutional significance should be considered *de facto* fundamental law. Although parliament retains the legal right to repeal the Scotland Act (1998), it is politically unthinkable that it would do so against the wishes of the Scottish Parliament and people. A similar view followed from the *Thoburn* v *Sunderland City Council* (2002) case. The case concerned a campaign by market traders to use imperial rather than metric measures, but its main significance was the Law Lords' view that there was a hierarchy of Acts of Parliament: 'ordinary' statutes and 'constitutional' statutes, which had special status. Constitutional statutes — for example, the European Communities Act (1972), Human Rights Act (1998) and Scotland Act (1998) — should only be repealed when parliament does so by express provisions, rather than as an unintended consequence of a new law.

Fusion rather than separation of powers

Parliamentary sovereignty has contributed to the centralisation of power in the UK. In the USA, the three branches of government — the **legislature**, **executive** and **judiciary** — have different powers and different personnel. This is known as the **separation of powers**. But in the British legislature and executive there is a **fusion of powers**: members of the government are also Members of Parliament, and the executive dominates

Key terms

➤ **Executive** The branch of government responsible for the implementation of policy.

➤ **Fusion of powers** The intermingling of personnel in the executive and legislative branches found in parliamentary systems.

➤ **Judiciary** The branch of government responsible for interpreting the law and deciding upon legal disputes.

➤ **Legislature** The branch of government responsible for making law.

the legislature. It controls the parliamentary timetable and can normally use its parliamentary majority to push through its legislative programme.

Lord Hailsham, a Conservative who served three terms as Lord Chancellor, coined the term **elective dictatorship** in 1976 to describe the concentration of power in the executive branch. It implies that government can do whatever it wants because of parliamentary sovereignty, the FPTP electoral system that invariably gives one party a majority in the Commons, and executive dominance of the House of Commons. A government without a majority of the popular vote could change the constitution and introduce major policy change.

Lord Hailsham, who coined the term 'elective dictatorship'

Weblinks

www.parliament.uk/works/notes_on_parliament_and_constitution.cfm — guides to parliament and the constitution from the official parliament site.

Concepts explained

Separation of powers

The separation of powers is the principle that the legislative, executive and judicial branches of government should be independent of each other. They should have different functions and distinctive memberships which should not overlap. The idea emerged in liberal thought as a means of preventing tyranny and the concentration of absolute power in one body (e.g. the Crown). The French philosopher Montesquieu (1689–1755) developed a theory of the separation of powers which influenced the American Founding Fathers. The US Constitution provides a rigid separation of powers. It also includes other checks and balances, such as a Bill of Rights, a bicameral legislature (i.e. one with two houses) and federalism.

Elective dictatorship

The excessive concentration of power in the executive branch. It implies that the only check on the power of government is the need to hold (and win) general elections at regular intervals. Beyond this, the government is regarded as free to do as it wishes because the constitution concentrates power in the executive branch and does not provide effective checks and balances.

Constraints on parliamentary sovereignty

The doctrine of parliamentary sovereignty means that, in legal theory, parliament can make or unmake any law of its choosing. In practice, however, a series of constraints limit the range of issues on which parliament can hope to legislate successfully. Some areas of life lie outside the reach of parliamentary power. No parliament can, for example, change the laws of physics or ensure that England will win the World Cup. The most significant political constraints on parliamentary sovereignty are:

- executive power
- membership of the European Union
- the Human Rights Act (1998)
- devolution
- referendums

Executive power

For students of politics, a major criticism of the doctrine of parliamentary sovereignty is that political reality is very different from legal theory. There are numerous informal and formal constraints on what parliament can do. Parliament is legally sovereign, but its authority derives from the electorate: were parliament systematically to ignore the wishes of the people, its legitimacy would be undermined. The doctrine of the mandate allows governments to claim that they have popular support for measures that featured in their election manifestos, but it also suggests that the right of governments to make law is less clear if their proposals have not received popular endorsement.

Parliamentary sovereignty concerns formal legal authority, whereas **political sovereignty** suggests absolute political power. The fusion of the legislative and executive branches means that parliamentary sovereignty gives the executive great power. As we have seen, this creates the potential for elective dictatorship. But government power is far from absolute. Government defeats in parliament are more numerous today than 40 years ago, although parliament still finds it difficult to impose its own will. The House of Lords has also become more assertive in the last decade. Defeat or the threat of defeat in the Lords forced the Blair government to amend bills on civil liberties issues such as the treatment of terrorist suspects, trial by jury and the introduction of the offence of incitement of racial hatred. Conventions and traditional modes of behaviour may also shape opinion on what is practicable and desirable. It is expected, for example, that proposals for significant constitutional reform should be put before the electorate before they are enacted.

Key terms

- **Political sovereignty**
  Absolute political power.

European Union

The UK's membership of the EU provides the most significant challenge to the traditional view of parliamentary sovereignty. The legal basis for British membership of the then EEC was provided for by the European Communities Act (1972). Its provisions on Community (now EU) law in the UK have important constitutional implications:

- The Act gave legal force to existing and all future EU law. EU regulations do not need to receive the explicit assent of parliament before they become binding.
- The British courts apply EU law directly. Where questions of interpretation of EU law arise, they are referred to the European Court of Justice for a ruling.

> EU law has precedence over domestic British law. In the event of a conflict between the two, EU law must be applied. This may mean that British law has to be amended. The key example was provided in the 1990 Factortame case, which resulted in the Merchant Shipping Act (1988) being disapplied as its provisions restricting non-British citizens from registering fishing boats as British were contrary to Community law.

Recognition by British courts of the primacy of EU law fits uneasily with the legislative supremacy of parliament. But parliament retains sovereignty as it has the right to repeal the European Communities Act (1972), although the terms of British withdrawal from the EU would have to be negotiated.

Membership of the European Union also impacts upon sovereignty in other ways:

> The range of policy areas in which the EU has competence (i.e. responsibility) has increased significantly since the Single European Act (1986). The EU has exclusive competence in trade, agriculture and fisheries policy. Policy responsibility for issues such as regional policy, working conditions and environmental policy is shared between the EU and its member states. In recent decades, the EU has gained competences in areas such as defence, immigration and monetary policy (although the UK has not adopted the euro) that have traditionally been the preserve of nation states.

> The Council of Ministers, in which ministers from national governments negotiate EU policy, increasingly takes decisions by qualified majority voting. This means that a member state opposing a policy decision cannot veto it. But unanimity remains the norm for particularly sensitive issues such as taxation and treaty change.

> The EU's supranational institutions have gained powers: the European Parliament acts as the EU's co-legislature with the Council of Ministers, and decisions of the European Court of Justice have furthered European integration.

Eurosceptics often speak of sovereignty in absolute terms: legislative supremacy cannot be diluted, for parliament either has ultimate authority or it does not. But they also focus on the democratic deficit within the EU — parliament and the electorate have little opportunity to hold EU decision-makers accountable. Eurosceptics would like to see policy competences restored to the nation state. David Cameron is likely to seek fresh British opt-outs from areas such as EU social and employment policy. Many Eurosceptic Conservatives would also like to see an Act reasserting the supremacy of parliament and requiring the British courts to comply with Westminster legislation even if it is incompatible with EU law. Were parliament expressly to approve such legislation, the courts would have to deal with conflicting claims of primacy. For some Eurosceptics, withdrawal from the EU is the optimal means of restoring sovereignty.

Pro-Europeans argue that EU membership has had positive consequences. Instead of viewing sovereignty as a legal concept concerned with ultimate law-making authority, they define sovereignty in terms of effective influence and a practical capacity to act. The UK has **pooled sovereignty** rather than lost it. EU member states each delegate some of their sovereign authority to the EU and gain a greater capacity to achieve their policy objectives. By pooling sovereignty, the UK has achieved policy objectives such as the single European market which it could not have done alone, and more influence on the world stage.

Globalisation also means that no state can act fully independently on issues such as the environment, economic policy and terrorism. States exercise, and cede some of, their sovereignty by signing international treaties and joining international organisations.

Concepts explained

Pooled sovereignty

The decision-making authority of the member states of an international organisation is combined. This is said to enhance the collective power and achieve the joint interests of the member states, producing outcomes that could not be reached by individual state action or in a system in which member states could veto outcomes. The whole is greater than the sum of its parts.

Key terms

➤ **Globalisation** The widening and deepening interconnectedness between peoples and societies across the world in economic, political, social and cultural activities.

Human Rights Act

The Human Rights Act (1998) incorporated the rights set out in the European Convention on Human Rights (ECHR) into UK statute law. All new legislation must be compatible with these rights and the British courts decide cases brought under the ECHR. Strictly speaking, parliamentary sovereignty is preserved by the Act because the courts cannot automatically strike down laws. If legislation is found to be incompatible with the ECHR, it is for parliament (in effect, ministers) to decide whether to either amend the law or launch an appeal. In practice, a law deemed contrary to human rights will lack moral authority and will be subject to further legal challenge. There had been 20 declarations of incompatibility by 2006, six of which were overturned on appeal.

Devolution

Devolution means that, in many policy areas, Westminster no longer makes laws that apply across the entire territory of the UK. The Scottish Parliament and Northern Ireland Assembly have primary legislative authority on devolved matters such as education and health. Westminster continues to make primary legislation for Wales, but the Welsh Assembly executes it and makes secondary legislation.

Westminster no longer makes law on devolved matters, but it retains legislative supremacy. It has sole authority over 'reserved matters' such as the UK economy, social security and the constitution. The UK Parliament can also decide to legislate on Scottish, Welsh and Northern Irish matters, and abolish the devolved assemblies, but it would be politically difficult to do so in the face of elite and public opposition.

Concepts explained

Devolution

Devolution is the transfer of political power from central government to regional or subnational government(s) with limited territorial jurisdiction. Sovereign authority is not divided but remains at the centre. The regional tier of government is subordinate to central government and can be changed or removed by it. This contrasts with federalism, where the autonomy of regional government is protected in a codified constitution. Legislative devolution is the most significant form of devolution because it involves the creation of separate parliaments with law-making powers.

The Scottish Parliament in session in Edinburgh, August 2009

Many Scottish political commentators view parliamentary sovereignty as an English doctrine and regard **popular sovereignty** as an important element of Scottish political culture. This distinction could be significant if the Scottish National Party (SNP) government in Edinburgh fulfils its pledge to hold a referendum on opening negotiations on Scottish independence. The Scottish Parliament does not have the authority to change the UK's constitution, but a referendum 'yes' vote might be difficult for politicians at Westminster to ignore.

Weblinks

www.devolution.ac.uk — key findings of academic research projects on devolution.

Referendums

Referendums have been proposed by UK governments on a number of constitutional issues. Only one UK-wide referendum has been held: the 1975 vote in favour of continued membership of the European Community. But devolution for Scotland, Wales and Northern Ireland was approved in referendums in these nations. The Blair governments proposed referendums on the European single currency and the EU Constitution but abandoned them when, first, they decided against joining the euro and, secondly, 'no' votes in referendums on the constitution in France and the Netherlands led to the shelving of the referendum in the UK.

Key terms

➤ **Popular sovereignty**
Supreme authority resides with the people.

➤ **Referendum** A vote in which the electorate is asked to express its view on a specific issue of public policy.

Adherents to the traditional view of parliamentary sovereignty oppose referendums because they place decision making in the hands of the electorate rather than MPs and peers. The increased use of referendums suggests a shift towards popular sovereignty, but parliament retains ultimate authority: although parliament risks damaging its legitimacy if it ignores the outcome, referendums are still advisory rather than binding.

The main parties appear to have accepted that, because devolution was supported in referendums in the late 1990s, further major changes to the powers of the devolved bodies should also be put to a popular vote. But governments are not obliged by the constitution to do this. The refusal of the Labour government to hold a referendum on the Lisbon Treaty, having earlier promised one on the EU Constitution, confirmed that it is up to the government to decide if an issue warrants a referendum — and governments are loath to hold referendums that they might lose.

Strengths and weaknesses of the traditional constitution

Strengths

The UK's traditional constitution is known as the **Westminster model**. This not only provides a description of the workings of the British political system but also claims (or assumes) that this is how a political system ought to operate. Supporters of the traditional constitutional settlement argue that it has a number of enduring strengths. While they recognise that improvements are required, they believe that reform should be limited and pragmatic. Changes should work with the grain of the existing constitution rather than overhaul it.

Key terms

➤ **Westminster model**
A form of government exemplified by the British political system, in which parliament is sovereign, the executive and legislature are fused and political power is centralised.

Adaptability

One perceived strength of the traditional constitution is its proven worth. The constitution has proved its value by operating effectively over many years. Pragmatic reforms, introduced where there is a clear case for change, have enabled the constitution to adapt to changed circumstances. This flexibility is another positive feature, as the mechanics of the constitution can be adapted smoothly and speedily.

Evolution

Conservatives view the constitution as an organic body of rules rather than an artificial creation. It has evolved over time and reflects the history and enduring values of the British people. The rules and practices that make up the constitution form a coherent and intelligible whole.

Strong government

The traditional constitution provides for strong and effective government. The doctrine of parliamentary sovereignty establishes supreme authority within the political system. But it is the government, particularly the core executive, rather than Parliament that is at the heart of the policy-making process. The process of government is conducted by political parties: the cabinet is party-based and the governing party exercises significant control over the legislative process in the House of Commons. Power is thus concentrated at the centre, enabling the government of the day to implement most of its political objectives. Ministers, not judges or bureaucrats (or the people), make crucial political decisions.

Accountability

Strong government is also responsible government. The government is accountable to parliament, which scrutinises its activities, and responsive to the electorate. In a general election in a two-party system, voters effectively choose between alternative governments. The FPTP electoral system usually gives the winning party a parliamentary majority, allowing it to fulfil its mandate. An unpopular government will pay the price at the polls. Government is also responsible, as the rule of law protects citizens against arbitrary power.

Viewpoint Was the traditional British constitution effective?

YES
- It was tried and tested, evolving in response to genuine needs.
- Its rules and principles added up to a coherent whole: the Westminster model.
- It provided a clear centre of authority, ensuring strong government.
- It provided for responsible government that is accountable to the electorate.
- The rule of law protected the rights of citizens against the state.
- It was sufficiently flexible to accommodate political and social change.

NO
- It was outdated, with pre-democratic elements unsuitable for a modern liberal democracy.
- It produced an excessive centralisation of power, with few checks and balances.
- It provided few opportunities for citizens to get involved in decision making.
- The rights afforded to individuals were weak and not adequately protected.
- It was prone to manipulation by single-party governments.

Weaknesses

Critics of the traditional constitution argue that it had a number of serious weaknesses that could only be rectified by a significant reform programme.

Lack of clarity

The uncodified nature of the constitution creates problems of clarity and interpretation. It is not always clear when a government has acted unconstitutionally: conventions on ministerial responsibility, for example, are unclear. Parliament, which is controlled by the government of the day, is the final arbiter of the constitution. There is no constitutional court to check the power of the state and defend civil liberties.

Concentration of power

Power is concentrated dangerously at the centre. There are few safeguards against the arbitrary exercise of state power. Parliamentary sovereignty and the absence of a codified constitution mean that even the key tenets of the rule of law are not fully protected. A government with a strong majority can force through legislation undermining civil liberties and weakening other institutions. It can overturn traditional principles and practices in response to populist sentiment. There are insufficient checks and balances, and there is no formal separation of powers. The executive exercises considerable control over the legislative process. Neither local nor subnational government has constitutionally protected status.

Outdated and undemocratic

Critics of the traditional constitution depict it as outdated, inefficient and undemocratic. Conventions are unclear and key elements of the common law, notably the royal prerogative, date back to a pre-modern era. The House of Lords is also a throwback to a pre-democratic era: the hereditary principle cannot be justified in a liberal democratic state.

The constitution under pressure

For much of the twentieth century, there was a broad political consensus supportive of the constitution and the key institutions of the UK state. The Westminster model was held up as a paragon of constitutional theory and practice. The constitution evolved in a largely peaceful and pragmatic fashion. Governments of different political persuasions were happy to work within the existing constitutional framework. Political elites and the electorate regarded the constitution as legitimate and effective.

Early twentieth century

At times, however, the constitution was the focus of serious political dispute. The 'Irish Question' came close to provoking civil war before a solution of sorts was reached in 1921–22 with the creation of the Irish Free State (which became the Republic of Ireland in 1949) and a six-county Northern Ireland that remained part of the UK. A constitutional crisis also arose when the House of Lords refused to support the Liberal government's budget of 1909. It was resolved when the Parliament Act (1911) reduced the powers of the House of Lords.

The 1970s

The 1970s brought further challenges to the traditional constitution, including the decline of the two-party system, the 'Troubles' in Northern Ireland and EEC membership.

Conservative politician Lord Hailsham warned that executive dominance of the legislature created an elective dictatorship and proposed a codified constitution. Political scientist S. E. Finer believed that the FPTP electoral system produced adversarial politics in which parties entering government systematically overturned the policies of their predecessors, creating instability. He advocated proportional representation (PR) as a remedy.

Thatcher and Major

The Conservative governments of Margaret Thatcher (1979–90) and John Major (1990–97) had important constitutional consequences. There was a further centralisation of political power, evident in the abolition of the Greater London Council. In areas where the Conservatives maintained the constitutional status quo — by refusing demands for Scottish devolution, for example — they were criticised for undermining the legitimacy and efficiency of the traditional constitution. The FPTP electoral system came under further pressure, for it enabled the Conservatives to carry out radical reforms having won four successive elections without securing a majority of the popular vote.

In the 1990s, traditional methods of government gave way to new forms of **governance**. Formal institutions such as government departments and local authorities had been responsible for allocating public funds and implementing policy decisions, but many of these functions were now transferred to quangos. Nationalised industries were privatised and new regulatory agencies established. Public trust in parliament and politicians waned as **sleaze** cases hit the headlines. Not even the monarchy was immune from this loss of faith in the traditional constitution.

The case for reform

In response, a coherent case for constitutional reform was developed by bodies such as the pressure group Charter 88 (now Unlock Democracy). It was taken up by the Liberal Democrats and, most significantly, the Labour Party. For much of its history, Labour

Key terms

➤ **Governance** A form of decision making in which a wide range of institutions, networks and relationships are involved.

➤ **Sleaze** In politics, behaviour characterised by low standards of honesty or morality.

Members of the pressure group Charter 88 show their support for political reform

had viewed constitutional reform as an unwelcome distraction from its main goal of improving conditions for the working class. Now it embraced a liberal perspective on reform which focused on a number of key themes:

> **Modernisation.** Institutions such as parliament, the executive and the civil service were using outdated and inefficient procedures that were in need of reform.
> **Democratisation.** Participation in the political process would be encouraged through electoral reform and greater use of referendums.
> **Decentralisation.** Decision-making powers would be devolved to new institutions in Scotland and Wales, and the role of local government enhanced.
> **Rights.** The rights of citizens would be strengthened and safeguarded.

Labour advocated policies such as devolution, a Bill of Rights and reform of the House of Lords, but it did not support electoral reform for Westminster or a written constitution. Labour and the Liberal Democrats worked together to develop proposals for Scottish devolution, and after Labour's 1997 general election victory, senior Liberal Democrats sat on a cabinet subcommittee examining constitutional reform.

Reforming the constitution: the Blair governments, 1997–2007

The constitutional reforms introduced by the Labour governments (1997–2010) are discussed in detail in other chapters. Here, the main reforms are outlined and their significance assessed (see Table 6.1).

Human rights

The Human Rights Act (HRA, 1998) enshrined most of the provisions of the European Convention on Human Rights (ECHR) in UK law. The rights protected by the convention include:

> the right to life
> the right to liberty and security of person
> the right to a fair trial
> respect for private and family life
> freedom of thought and expression
> freedom of peaceful assembly and association
> the right to marry and found a family
> freedom from torture and degrading treatment
> freedom from discrimination

The HRA requires the British government to ensure that legislation is compatible with the convention. All bills introduced at Westminster (and in the devolved assemblies) must receive a declaration of compatibility with the ECHR from lawyers. UK courts and tribunals now decide cases brought under the convention — before the HRA, cases had

Table 6.1 Labour governments' constitutional reforms, 1997–2010

Area	Reforms	Frustrated or incomplete reforms
Rights	Human Rights Act (1998) incorporates European Convention on Human Rights into UK law. Freedom of Information Act (2000) gives greater access to information held by public bodies.	Derogation from Article 5 of Human Rights Act (2001–05) overturned. New Bill of Rights and Duties was proposed but no legislation was introduced.
Devolution	Scottish Parliament with primary legislative and tax-raising powers. Welsh Assembly with secondary legislative powers. Northern Ireland Assembly with primary legislative powers.	Proposal for regional assemblies in England dropped after 2004 'no' vote in referendum in northeast England.
Decentralisation	Elected mayor of London and London Assembly. Elected mayors in some English authorities.	Only 12 local authorities adopted the elected mayor model.
Electoral reform	New electoral systems for devolved assemblies, European Parliament and elected mayors.	No action on 1998 Jenkins report on electoral reform for Westminster.
Parliament	All but 92 hereditary peers removed from the House of Lords. Limited reforms to business of House of Commons.	Unable to forge consensus on next stage of House of Lords reform. MPs' expenses scandal damaged trust in parliament. Some *Governance of Britain* proposals not enacted.
Judiciary	Supreme Court started work in 2009. New judicial appointments system. Changes to role of Lord Chancellor.	Reforms of office of Lord Chancellor were diluted.
Participation	Referendums on devolution in Scotland, Wales and Northern Ireland. Referendums on mayor of London and regional assembly for northeast England. Political Parties, Elections and Referendums Act (2000) regulates conduct of parties and elections.	Proposed referendums on electoral reform, European single currency and EU Constitution were shelved. Trials of alternative voting methods produced mixed results.

to be heard by the European Court of Human Rights in Strasbourg. The UK courts can declare legislation incompatible with the ECHR and overturn executive decisions. But the courts cannot automatically overturn legislation that is declared incompatible: it is up to ministers to decide whether to amend it through a fast-track process in parliament or appeal against the court's decision.

The Anti-terrorism, Crime and Security Act (2001) introduced a derogation (i.e. a temporary exemption) from Article 5 of the ECHR, the right to liberty and security, to allow the indefinite detention without charge of those foreign nationals suspected of terrorist activity who could not be deported to a safe country. But in 2004 the House of Lords ruled that this was unlawful as it discriminated against foreign nationals. The legislation was then replaced with the Prevention of Terrorism Act (2005), which introduced control orders (e.g. house arrest and surveillance) for UK citizens and foreign nationals suspected of terrorist activity. The House of Lords ruled in June 2009 that the government had violated Article 6 of the ECHR, the right to fair trial, by not allowing those under control orders to see the evidence against them.

The HRA has the potential to clarify and redefine the relationship between the individual and the state. It helped several celebrities to win cases in which they claimed that their privacy had been breached. In 2008 Max Mosley, the president of the body which governs motor sport worldwide, was awarded damages after the *News of the World* published allegations about his private life. Critics claim that the HRA is being used to create a law on privacy, even though parliament has avoided passing specific legislation on this matter. Verdicts allowing prisoners to claim damages, and nine Afghans who hijacked a plane to remain in the UK also provoked controversy. Labour proposed a new Bill of Rights and Duties to build on the HRA, while the Conservatives planned to scrap it and replace it with a less extensive Bill of Rights.

Weblinks

www.justice.gov.uk — website of the Ministry of Justice, responsible for rights, the legal system, reform of the House of Lords and electoral administration.

Devolution

Devolution involves the transfer of powers — legislative, executive and tax-raising — from central government to subnational institutions. In 1999 power was devolved to new institutions in Scotland, Wales and Northern Ireland, following 'yes' votes in referendums in each nation. The new system was one of asymmetric devolution — rather than following a standardised blueprint, the devolved bodies have different powers and distinctive features.

The Scottish Parliament has primary legislative and tax-varying powers. It and the Scottish Executive have sole responsibility for policy on issues such as education, health and local government. The Parliament can also vary the rate of income tax by 3% (i.e. 3p in the pound). The National Assembly for Wales, commonly referred to as the Welsh Assembly, is weaker. It has secondary legislative and executive powers, but does not have primary legislative authority. This means that it can only fill in the details of, and implement, legislation passed by Westminster in policy areas such as education and health. The Northern Ireland Assembly has legislative powers over a similar range of policy areas to the Scottish Parliament, but does not have tax-raising powers. Special procedures exist in the Assembly to ensure cross-community support.

Constitutional implications of devolution

Devolution has had a significant impact on the traditional constitutional settlement. The UK no longer fits the classic definition of a unitary state — although even the pre-devolution UK was more like a union state. Nor does the UK fit the standard definition of a federal state: that is, a state in which power is shared between different tiers of government, with autonomous subnational institutions enjoying significant authority.

The new constitutional settlement has **quasi-federal** features: central government does not make some domestic policy for parts of the UK and disputes over competences are decided by senior judges. New bodies were created to handle relations between the UK government and the devolved bodies (i.e. intergovernmental relations). The legislation creating the devolved institutions, however, sought to safeguard parliamentary sovereignty and place limits on the powers of the new bodies. Westminster remains sovereign and retains the right to overrule or abolish the devolved institutions. The legislation also identified 'reserved powers' that remain exclusive to Westminster. These include crucial areas such as economic policy, foreign and defence policy, and constitutional affairs.

Concepts explained
Quasi-federalism

Quasi-federalism occurs when the central government of a unitary state devolves some of its powers to subnational governments. It exhibits some of the features of a unitary state and some of a federal state. In legal theory there is one supreme legal authority located at the centre, as in a unitary state. But in practice the centre no longer makes domestic policy for some parts of the state and it would be difficult politically for the centre to abolish the subnational tier of government. Different policy frameworks operate within the state. Senior judges rule on questions concerning the division of competences.

As Chapter 10 examines, devolution has produced differential policy across the UK. Prescription charges have, for example, been abolished in Wales but not England, and Scotland provides free personal care for the elderly. Devolution is a process, not an event. Further changes are likely in the medium term. The Government of Wales Act (2006) allows the Welsh Assembly to request that further executive powers be transferred from Westminster and opens up the prospect of the Assembly getting primary legislative powers. In Scotland, the SNP government has pledged to hold a referendum on opening negotiations on independence. The other parties oppose this but do support the further extension of the Scottish Parliament's powers: for example, on taxation and public spending.

Devolution has also raised questions about how England should be governed. There is, for example, no simple answer to the 'West Lothian Question', which asks why Scottish MPs at Westminster should be able to vote on purely English matters when English MPs can no longer vote on matters devolved to the Scottish Parliament. The Blair governments' policy of creating (weak) assemblies in the English regions was abandoned after a 'no' vote in a referendum in northeast England in 2004.

Decentralisation

The Blair governments also made changes to local government in England, notably in London. Here an executive mayor has powers in areas such as the environment and transport, the latter leading to the creation of a congestion charge for motorists entering central London. The directly elected London Assembly scrutinises the mayor's actions. All local authorities were obliged to reform their political management, but by 2009 only 12 had adopted the government's preferred option of a directly elected mayor.

Electoral reform

The Blair governments' record on electoral reform was a mixed one. Proportional representation was introduced for elections to the Scottish Parliament, Welsh Assembly, Northern Ireland Assembly and European Parliament, and for directly elected mayors in a number of towns and cities. However, no action has been taken to change the FPTP system used in general elections. The government set up an Independent Commission on the Voting System chaired by Roy Jenkins to examine the case for using proportional representation in general elections. The Jenkins report (1998) recommended a mixed electoral system called 'AV plus' in which most MPs would be elected by FPTP and a minority by the alternative vote system. The government did not endorse the report and a promised referendum on electoral reform was never held.

In London, the mayor has powers in areas such as transport, which in 2003 led to the introduction of the congestion charge

The new electoral systems introduced in the UK are not uniform (see Chapter 2). The additional member system is used in elections for the Scottish Parliament and Welsh Assembly. This is a mixed electoral system in which a majority of representatives are elected by FPTP in single-member constituencies, with the remainder elected by a regional list system of proportional representation in multi-member constituencies. The latter are 'top-up seats' allocated to political parties on a corrective basis. A closed list system of proportional representation is used in Great Britain for elections to the European Parliament. Electors cast one vote for their favoured party in multi-member regions, but they cannot choose between candidates on the party's list.

Directly elected mayors, such as in London, are elected by the supplementary vote in which electors indicate their first and second preferences. All but the top two candidates are eliminated and second preferences cast for them are added to their total. The single transferable vote system is used to elect the Northern Ireland Assembly and, following a decision by the Scottish Parliament, Scottish local authorities. Electors rank their preferred candidates in multi-member constituencies. To win, a candidate must achieve a fixed quota of votes; votes are redistributed until all seats are filled.

Weblinks

www.electoral-reform.org.uk — the website of the Electoral Reform Society, a pressure group that supports electoral reform.

Parliamentary reform

The House of Lords Act (1999) abolished the right of all but 92 hereditary peers (i.e. those who inherited their titles) to sit and vote in the upper house. This was intended as the first stage of the reform process. The Lords now comprised mainly life peers, and no political party had an overall majority. But the Blair governments made little progress with stage two of the reforms, when the final composition and powers of the reformed House of Lords would be settled. MPs and peers rejected a series of options for reform, including an all-appointed Lords and a hybrid house containing both elected and appointed peers. In 2007 MPs voted for a 100% elected or 80% elected House of Lords, but no legislation followed in the short term. Lords reform is examined in more detail in Chapter 7.

Blair's initiatives on reform of the House of Commons were less spectacular. Changes to Prime Minister's Question Time and the working hours of the Commons, plus additional sittings in Westminster Hall have modernised proceedings. Parliament has greater opportunity to scrutinise the government's legislative proposals. Devolution has affected procedures in the Commons too: matters devolved to the Scottish Parliament cannot, for example, be dealt with at Westminster. Overall, these measures did not alter the balance of power and executive dominance of the legislature continued.

The judiciary

The Constitutional Reform Act (2005) focused on judicial reform. A Supreme Court, which started work in 2009, became the UK's highest court and removed the judicial role of the House of Lords. This enhances the separation of powers, but the Supreme Court does not have the authority to strike down legislation. The government has intended to abolish the office of Lord Chancellor and so bring about the separation of the legislative, executive and judicial functions of the office. The Lord Chancellor was a member of the cabinet (with responsibility for the law and rights), the legislature (as speaker of the House of Lords) and head of the judiciary. But it proved difficult to disentangle these roles and the office was retained, but shorn of some of its some judicial responsibilities, such as the appointment of judges. A Judicial Appointments Commission is now responsible for the latter. These issues are explored in greater depth in Chapter 9.

Weblinks

www.judiciary.gov.uk — official site of the judiciary of England and Wales.

Freedom of information

The Freedom of Information Act (2000) gave individuals a general right of access to personal information held on them by public bodies. But there are a number of crucial exemptions. Information can be withheld on the grounds of national security or public safety, while citizens do not have an automatic right to see the policy advice provided to ministers. In 2009 the government exercised its right to veto a decision by the Information Tribunal that the minutes of cabinet meetings concerning the legality of the 2003 invasion of Iraq should be released. Politicians, journalists and citizens have used the Act to gain access to information on matters such as government policy, the activities of local authorities and police forces, school inspections and the performance records of hospital surgeons.

Weblinks

www.ico.gov.uk — website of the Information Commissioner's Office.

Elections, referendums and parties

The Political Parties, Elections and Referendum Act (2000) established an independent Electoral Commission to administer elections and referendums, set an upper limit on national campaign expenditure by political parties, required parties to disclose donors and donations, and banned foreign donations. But discussions on a new system of state funding for political parties failed to produce agreement. The Blair governments also encouraged alternative methods of voting (e.g. all-postal ballots) to increase turnout, although they also led to concerns about electoral fraud.

The Blair governments used referendums more frequently than any of their predecessors. Devolution referendums were held in Scotland, Wales and Northern Ireland, while a number of English towns and cities held local referendums on creating a directly elected mayor. But proposed referendums on electoral reform for Westminster, British membership of the European single currency and the EU Constitution did not take place. Some local authorities have made use of legislation that allows them to hold referendums on local issues. A referendum in Manchester in 2008, for example, voted against a proposed congestion charge for the city.

Weblinks

www.ucl.ac.uk/constitution-unit — website of the Constitution Unit, an academic research centre that provides authoritative analysis of constitutional issues. The 'Monitor' newsletter provides regular updates.

Reforming the constitution: the Brown government, 2007–10

Constitutional reform is a major part of Blair's legacy, but he took little personal interest in the details of reform and did not develop an overarching vision of where the reforms should lead. Gordon Brown, by contrast, had long been interested in constitutional reform and it became a key theme of the first months of his period as prime minister. It was the subject of his government's first major publication, 'The Governance of Britain' (CM 7170, 2007). The reforms proposed in this Green Paper were built around four main objectives:

> limiting the powers of the executive
> making the executive more accountable
> reinvigorating democracy
> improving the relationship between the citizen and the state

The first two objectives would rebalance the relationship between the legislature and the executive by enhancing the role of parliament. Parliament would, it was proposed, be given more say over the exercise of prerogative powers by the government. The prime minister would have to seek parliament's approval before committing forces to armed conflict abroad, and would present a report on the objectives and legality of the proposed deployment. There would be some exceptions concerning emergencies, operational secrecy and the use of special forces. Proposals for the dissolution of parliament could also be subject to a vote in the House of Commons, although this would be little more than a formality.

Consultation on the plethora of proposals, a White Paper and a government bill followed, but concrete action in the areas mentioned above was limited. The executive's role in appointing bishops and judges was, though, reduced and the House of Commons began to stage hearings on some public appointments. The Constitutional Reform Act (2010) created a statutory basis for the civil service and enshrined in law its core values — impartiality, integrity, honesty and objectivity. It also created a statutory basis for parliamentary scrutiny of treaties.

The third objective, reinvigorating democracy, also produced little in practice. A 2008 White Paper on reform of the House of Lords made suggestions on what a 100% or 80% elected upper house might look like. The government's official review of the new electoral systems was finally issued in 2008 but was generally supportive of the status quo for Westminster elections. In its 2010 election manifesto, Labour promised to hold same-day referendums on a fully elected House of Lords and the alternative vote system for the House of Commons.

The fourth objective was potentially the most far-reaching, but legislation was not forthcoming before the general election. 'The Governance of Britain' anticipated a national debate on British values that would lead to a British Bill of Rights and Duties to replace the HRA. But the 2009 'Rights and Responsibilities' Green Paper (CM 7577) was a low-key document that suggested a declaratory statement on duties (e.g. jury service) and further rights (e.g. welfare entitlements), but which did not propose that these should be directly legally enforceable.

MPs' expenses

Brown's constitutional reform programme was blown off the agenda by the economic crisis that began in 2008. However, it returned to centre stage as the scandal over MPs' expenses claims raged in 2009. Public trust in politicians and parliament fell still further as the claims made by some MPs for second homes and subsistence were revealed. Action to restore the reputation of parliament followed swiftly. An independent Parliamentary Standards Authority was created to manage MPs' expenses, and many (but not all) of the recommendations made by Sir Christopher Kelly's report on expenses and allowances were accepted. The expenses scandal and its implications for parliament are considered in more detail in Chapter 7.

The 'Governance of Britain' proposals to revitalise the House of Commons were revisited. A Select Committee on Reform of the House of Commons, chaired by eminent parliamentarian Tony Wright, was established in 2009. It recommended that:

➤ chairs of select committees should be elected by backbenchers
➤ a backbench business committee should determine the business of the House of Commons for 1 day a week
➤ a procedure petitions committee should select issues for debate that had been suggested by the public via an e-petition system

The proposals did not make the statute book before the 2010 general election was called. A variant of the third proposal did, however, feature in the manifestos of the main parties. So did the right for constituents to recall an MP found guilty of misconduct. Gordon Brown also announced his support for moving to the alternative vote system for general elections.

Weblinks

http://governance.justice.gov.uk — The 'Governance of Britain' site details the Brown government's constitutional reform proposals.

A new constitutional settlement

Tony Blair and Gordon Brown introduced the most important package of constitutional reform in modern British history. Commentators talked of a 'new constitutional settlement' replacing the traditional constitution. Many of the rules, procedures and principles of the traditional constitution were affected. Few key institutions remained untouched. Devolution, new electoral systems, the Human Rights Act and reform of the House of Lords changed the constitutional landscape. Overall, the reforms brought about a rebalancing of the relationship between state institutions and between the citizen and the state. More checks and balances were introduced: the Human Rights Act increased judicial review of legislation, the reformed House of Lords proved more willing to amend or block government legislation, electoral reform produced coalition government in the devolved assemblies and they departed from central government policy frameworks.

Impact of the reforms

These reforms enhanced British democracy, although falling turnout in general elections and low levels of public trust in the political system were causes for concern. However, the reforms were evolutionary rather than revolutionary. Change was introduced in a piecemeal rather than 'big bang' fashion. The Labour governments did not produce a written constitution or a tailor-made UK Bill of Rights. Significantly, the underlying principles of the British constitution were adapted rather than overturned. Labour was careful to avoid too many direct challenges to the core principles of the constitution. The impact of the reforms on four principal features of the constitution was as follows:

- **Uncodified constitution.** The reforms did not introduce a codified constitution, but they did establish key principles and procedures (e.g. human rights, devolution) in statute law.
- **Parliamentary sovereignty.** The legislative supremacy of parliament has been preserved, but parliament has ceded significant powers. The Scotland Act (1998) states that the Westminster Parliament remains sovereign and retains the power to make laws for Scotland. It can also repeal the Act itself. However, Westminster will not legislate on matters devolved to the Scottish Parliament, so parliamentary sovereignty no longer means a real power to make law across the UK. The Human Rights Act (1998) also preserved the sovereignty of parliament. If the courts find legislation incompatible with the ECHR, that legislation is not automatically struck down. It is up to parliament to decide on amendments. Similarly, the Constitutional Reform Act (2005) states that the Supreme Court cannot overturn legislation. These important statutes have, in practice if not in theory, the status of fundamental law because they are unlikely to be overturned without the express approval of parliament and the electorate.
- **The rule of law.** The power of the state was restricted and the rights of citizens were strengthened by the Human Rights Act (1998) and the Freedom of Information Act (2000), although these did not go as far as some reformers had hoped for.
- **The unitary state.** Asymmetric devolution means that the component parts of the UK are governed in different ways. Policy differences have also emerged, so elements of the welfare state are no longer uniform across the UK.

Appraisal of the reforms

When judged in relation to the themes of modernisation, democratisation, decentralisation and rights, the verdict on Labour's reforms is mixed:

- **Modernisation.** Most hereditary peers were removed from the House of Lords, but 92 remained and reform was incomplete. Some of the proposals for reform of prerogative powers were not put into action. The constitution remained uncodified.
- **Democratisation.** New electoral systems were introduced for the devolved assemblies, European elections and mayoral elections. But FPTP remained in place for Westminster elections and continues to produce disproportional outcomes.

Elections and political parties are better regulated, but turnout fell and public faith in politicians was low.

➤ **Decentralisation.** Power was devolved to new institutions in Scotland, Wales and Northern Ireland, bringing government closer to the people. But local government remains weak and questions about how England should be governed had not been addressed effectively. In other respects, political power became still more concentrated in Downing Street and the executive continued to dominate the legislature.

➤ **Rights.** The Human Rights Act (1998) put the rights of citizens on a stronger statutory footing and has been used by the courts to put limits on state power. But other measures restricted civil liberties (e.g. the right to trial by jury).

The influential Dutch political scientist Arend Lijphart located liberal democracies on a spectrum with majoritarian democracy at one extreme and consensual democracy at the other. In a majoritarian democracy, political power is concentrated at the centre and there are few limits to its exercise. Common features include a flexible constitution, a FPTP electoral system, a two-party system, a dominant executive and a unitary state. In a consensual democracy, political power is diffused. Typical features are a rigid constitution, proportional representation, multiparty politics, the separation of powers and a federal system. There are also important differences in political culture. Politics is adversarial in a majoritarian democracy, whereas power sharing is the norm in a consensual democracy.

The British Westminster model is the archetypal case of majoritarian democracy, while Switzerland is a leading example of consensual democracy. The constitutional reforms of the Blair and Brown governments introduced elements of consensual democracy, notably devolution and the Human Rights Act. But the UK is still close to the majoritarian extreme. Parliamentary sovereignty remains the guiding constitutional principle, the fusion of the legislature and executive has not been disturbed greatly, and the FPTP system is still used for Westminster elections.

Majoritarian and consensual democracy

Distinguish between

Majoritarian democracy

➤ Uncodified constitution which can be amended by a simple legislative majority.
➤ Dominant executive controls the legislative branch.
➤ Legislature determines the constitutionality of its laws.
➤ Unitary state with power concentrated at the centre.
➤ FPTP.
➤ Adversarial two-party system.

Consensual democracy

➤ Codified constitution which can be amended only by weighted majority.
➤ Balance of power between the executive and legislative branches.
➤ Laws can be struck down by a constitutional court.
➤ Federal system with power divided between tiers of government.
➤ Proportional representation.
➤ Cooperative multiparty system.

Weblinks

www.democraticaudit.com — the Democratic Audit, an independent research unit, analyses the state of British democracy.

Viewpoint | **Did Labour's reforms (1997–2010) produce a new constitutional settlement?**

YES

- They were the most extensive package of reforms in modern times, with few institutions untouched.
- Reform is an ongoing process whose effects will continue to be felt for years to come.
- The balance of power between institutions changed, with further checks and balances introduced.
- The rights of citizens were strengthened and given greater protection.
- Key legislation has *de facto* status as fundamental law and is likely to endure.

NO

- They were evolutionary rather than revolutionary, developing rather than dismantling the key principles of the constitution.
- They did not add up to a coherent whole and lacked an overarching vision.
- They were unfinished and raised new problems (e.g. the government of England).
- More radical changes were rejected or not attempted, notably electoral reform for Westminster and a codified constitution.
- Parliament remains sovereign and power is still concentrated in the executive.

Criticisms of Labour's reforms

Labour's reforms were subject to criticism from two broad perspectives: a liberal perspective which argued that the reforms did not go far enough, and a conservative perspective which held that Labour had damaged the traditional British constitution. Both accused the Blair and Brown governments of incoherence: changes were introduced without an overarching philosophy or sufficient thought on their impact. So, little consideration was given to how devolution might impact upon the role of the House of Lords. In addition, some reforms were incomplete. Labour did not deliver on its early promises on an elected House of Lords, devolution in England and a referendum on electoral reform for Westminster. The Blair governments' reform programme largely ran out of steam after 2001. Brown tried to pick up the pace on some issues that had not been addressed (e.g. prerogative powers) but delivered little as the economic situation worsened. Only after the expenses scandal did Labour offer new solutions to reform of the House of Commons, House of Lords and electoral system.

Liberal critique
Labour's reforms grew out of a liberal agenda for constitutional change. But proponents of the liberal model of constitutional reform were critical of both the details and vision of Labour's reforms. They questioned the coherence and comprehensiveness of the new

constitutional settlement. Although much changed, liberal reformers argued that Blair and Brown had adopted a minimalist rather than a maximalist reform agenda. They were also concerned by perceived infringements of civil liberties, particularly after the 11 September 2001 terrorist attacks on New York and Washington and those in London on 7 July 2005.

An alternative maximalist reform package might include:

➢ a written constitution
➢ a Bill of Rights
➢ a federal state with regional assemblies in the English regions and a federal parliament at Westminster
➢ an elected upper chamber of parliament
➢ proportional representation for general elections
➢ state funding of political parties
➢ a transfer of power from quangos to elected local authorities
➢ reform of the monarchy (or its abolition)

This liberal perspective is associated with the Liberal Democrats, who support many of the demands listed above. Having worked with Labour on constitutional reform in the 1990s, they became more critical after the 2001 election.

Weblinks

www.unlockdemocracy.org.uk — website of Unlock Democracy, the most influential advocate of liberal constitutional reform.

Conservative critique

The conservative perspective supports the traditional constitution, believing that it required only limited reform. Its critique argues that Labour's reforms damaged the fabric of the constitution so that its component parts no longer form a coherent and effective whole. The reforms also brought new problems in their wake. Devolution raised questions about the government of England; the Human Rights Act increased the political role of the judiciary and opened up a can of worms on the nature of rights such as privacy. The academic and Conservative peer Lord (Philip) Norton is a leading advocate of this conservative critique.

Before the 1997 general election, the conservative critique was most associated with the Conservative Party. It opposed Labour's proposals for reform of the House of Lords, electoral reform and the incorporation of the European Convention of Human Rights into domestic law. The Conservatives claimed that legislative devolution would bring about the break-up of the Union. But the Conservatives adopted a more pragmatic position on many areas of constitutional reform following their election defeat in 1997. After the 'yes' results in the Scottish and Welsh referendums, the Conservatives accepted devolution and pledged to work constructively with the new institutions.

The conservative perspective on the constitution has often been a defensive one. But with much of the traditional constitution changed by the Labour governments, some conservatives (e.g. the journalist Simon Heffer) argue that radical reforms are needed to restore parliamentary sovereignty. These include the return from the EU to Westminster of substantial policy responsibilities, or withdrawal from the EU. Some conservatives also support an English Parliament, or even English independence.

The Conservative–Lib Dem coalition

The Conservatives and Liberal Democrats formed a coalition government after the 2010 general election. There was some common ground on constitutional reforms in their election manifestos but important differences on electoral reform and the Human Rights Act (see Table 6.2).

Both parties made compromises in the coalition agreement. The Conservatives had opposed electoral reform for Westminster while the Liberal Democrats supported the single transferable vote system. They agreed to hold a referendum on introducing the alternative vote system, but that the two parties would be free to campaign on different sides.

In other areas of disagreement, the coalition established commissions to examine reform. But it was agreed that the commission on a British Bill of Rights would ensure that ECHR rights remained enshrined in UK law, and the commission on the House of Lords would propose an upper house wholly elected or mainly elected by proportional representation. Firmer commitments were made on fixed-term parliaments, the recall of MPs, implementation of the Calman Commission recommendations on the further devolution of powers to the Scottish Parliament, and a referendum on further devolution in Wales.

Weblinks

www.nortonview.wordpress.com — a blog by Conservative peer and constitutional expert Lord Norton.

A codified constitution for the UK?

Labour's reforms brought about a greater codification of the British constitution. The Human Rights Act (1998) and the Scotland Act (1998), for example, wrote important constitutional principles into statute law. As we have seen, some scholars and judges claim that such Acts have *de facto* status as fundamental law or as 'constitutional statutes'. But Labour did not take its constitutional reforms to what the liberal perspective viewed as their logical conclusion — a codified constitution.

Labour's 'Governance of Britain' Green Paper proposed a national debate on a British statement of values which would be fed into a Bill of Rights and Duties. The Green Paper suggested that, in time, this could lead to a concordat (i.e. an official agreement

Table 6.2 Constitutional reform proposals at the 2010 general election

Area	Labour	Conservative	Liberal Democrat
Rights and liberties	Will not repeal the Human Rights Act.	Replace the Human Rights Act with a Bill of Rights.	Protect the Human Rights Act. Freedom Bill to protect rights.
Devolution	Implement Calman Commission recommendations: new tax-raising powers for Scottish Parliament. Support referendum on new powers for Welsh Assembly.	Support Calman Commission: more fiscal powers for Scottish Parliament. Will not stand in the way of referendum on new powers for Welsh Assembly. New parliamentary rules to address West Lothian Question.	Implement Calman Commission recommendations: new tax-raising powers for Scottish Parliament. Support referendum on new powers for Welsh Assembly. Codified constitution to address England's status in a federal UK.
House of Lords	Remove hereditary peers. Creation of fully elected second chamber over three elections. Referendum on elected second chamber by October 2011.	Build consensus for mainly elected House of Lords.	Fully elected House of Lords.
House of Commons	Right of recall of MPs guilty of financial misconduct. Fixed-term parliaments. Right to petition House of Commons to trigger debate.	Right of recall of MPs guilty of financial misconduct. Cut number of MPs. Right to petition House of Commons to trigger debate.	Right of recall of MPs guilty of financial misconduct. Fixed-term parliaments. Cut number of MPs by 150. Some House of Commons debates chosen by public.
Electoral reform	Referendum on alternative vote for general elections by October 2011.	Support FPTP. Equalise constituency sizes.	Referendum on single transferable vote for general elections.
Participation	Free vote in parliament on reducing voting age to 16. Local referendums to be triggered for directly electing a mayor.	Local referendums to be triggered for local issues, elected mayors and freeze on council tax. Directly elected police chiefs.	Reduce voting age to 16. Elected health and police boards.
Codified constitution	All-party commission to chart a course to a written constitution.		Codified constitution, determined in a citizens' convention and subject to approval in a referendum.
European Union		Referendum lock to ensure future treaties transferring power to EU are subject to a referendum. UK Sovereignty Bill to make it clear that parliament has ultimate authority.	In/out referendum when UK next agrees fundamental change in relationship with EU.

between institutions) on the relationship between the legislative and executive, or a codified constitution. Labour's 2010 manifesto proposed that an all-party committee should 'chart a course' to a codified constitution.

Arguments for a codified constitution

Supporters of a codified constitution claim that it would provide greater clarity on what is, and what is not, constitutional. The rules governing the British political system would be set out in an authoritative document, reducing the ambiguities that exist in the current uncodified constitution and its myriad conventions. The rights of citizens would also be given further constitutional protection. A codified constitution would also tackle the centralisation of power (and the potential for elective dictatorship) by setting limits on the power of the executive and introducing more effective institutional checks and balances. Local and subnational governments would enjoy constitutional protection.

In drawing up a codified constitution, politicians and the public would have to give greater thought to the core principles of the British constitution than was evident during Labour's reform programme. The process of drawing up the new constitution would also educate citizens and, proponents hope, provide the people with a greater sense of shared values and citizenship, while bestowing additional legitimacy on the political system.

Arguments against a codified constitution

Opponents argue that codification would remove the flexibility and adaptability that is often seen as a key strength of the existing uncodified constitution. The British constitution has endured because it has developed organically and been adapted when the case for change has been proven. A codified constitution may reflect the mood of the time when it was produced — although this too may be doubtful, given the difficulty of forging consensus — but values change and constitutional legislation often requires amendment within a few years because of unintended consequences or the emergence of new issues. Codified constitutions are rigid and not easy to change. Codification, critics argue, will place too much power in the hands of judges because they will be called upon to determine whether laws and political processes are constitutional. A government acting on a popular mandate to introduce, say, stricter measures on law and order could find its legislation overturned by the courts. Judges would become more overtly political and this might reduce faith in the legal system.

A move to a codified constitution would bring about a fundamental change in the British political system and in the country's political culture. The traditional view is that a codified constitution would be incompatible with parliamentary sovereignty. Whereas codified constitutions set limits on the powers of the legislature and executive, the doctrine of parliamentary sovereignty gives Westminster supreme authority. A codified constitution could not be entrenched or have the status of fundamental law for so long as parliament retains the power to alter it at will.

An extensive national debate that produces elite and popular consensus on the guiding principles of the political system and authorising their codification might offer a way out of this conundrum. In such circumstances, parliament would be reluctant to counter the express will of the people. But disputes over the treatment of England in the post-devolution UK, reform of the House of Lords and the future of the Human Rights Act suggest that elite (and popular) consensus on the constitution is some way off.

View**point** Should the UK have a codified constitution?

YES
- It is the logical conclusion of recent constitutional reforms.
- It would provide greater clarity on what is constitutional.
- It would be an authoritative reference point for the courts.
- It would set limits on the powers of the state and its institutions.
- It would provide greater protection for the rights of citizens.
- It would better inform citizens about the values and workings of the political system.

NO
- Pragmatic adaptation has worked well and is preferable.
- There is no agreed process for establishing a codified constitution.
- There is no elite consensus on what a codified constitution should include.
- It would be rigid and difficult to amend.
- It would give judges, who are unaccountable, greater political power.
- There is no great popular demand and other issues are more important.

▶ What you should know

▷ The British constitution is uncodified. The most important provisions are not gathered in one document, but are found in a variety of sources: Acts of Parliament, the common law, conventions, works of authority, and the treaties and law of the European Union. The uncodified nature of the British constitution means that it can be adapted to meet new political realities, but also that there is no definitive view of what is unconstitutional and that protection of individual rights is limited.

▷ Parliamentary sovereignty is the core principle of the British constitution. It establishes parliament as the supreme law-making body. But this legal theory has come under pressure given EU membership, the Human Rights Act, devolution and the use of referendums. Political practice also differs significantly from legal theory. No institution has absolute power; all are subject to significant internal and external constraints. The UK, however, has been a highly centralised state.

▷ The British constitution was changed significantly by the Labour governments of 1997–2010. Devolution, the Human Rights Act, new electoral systems and reform of the House of Lords changed the constitutional landscape. They provided greater protection for the rights of citizens and introduced more effective checks and balances and more democratic elements into the political system. The reforms have important implications for parliamentary sovereignty. Critics claim that the reform programme was incomplete and lacked a unifying vision.

○ Further reform is likely as the new constitutional settlement continues to evolve. The Scottish Parliament and Welsh Assembly will get more powers, and changes to the Human Rights Act are expected. Labour's reform programme also left some questions unanswered. Debates continue on the composition of the House of Lords, electoral reform, the government of England and codification of the constitution. The constitution is not above politics, but is an important political issue in its own right.

UK/US comparison

The US and UK constitutions

➤ The US Constitution is codified. It was produced by the Founding Fathers in 1787 following the Declaration of Independence. The constitution has just seven articles setting out the role and powers of the legislature, executive and judiciary. Some important features of the US political system (e.g. the Supreme Court's power of judicial review) are not described in the constitution but have evolved as conventions. The British constitution is not codified.

➤ The US Constitution is entrenched. The constitution establishes special procedures for its amendment. Amendments must be approved by two-thirds of members in both houses of Congress and ratified by three-quarters of state legislatures in the 50 states. Since the first ten amendments, which form the Bill of Rights, were approved in 1791, only 17 other amendments have come into force. The British constitution is not entrenched: there are no special procedures for its amendment.

➤ The US Constitution is subject to extensive judicial review. The Supreme Court can declare Acts of Congress and the actions of the executive, and those of state legislatures and executives, to be unconstitutional and strike them down. Some Supreme Court decisions (e.g. *Roe* v *Wade* 1973 on abortion) have provided crucial contemporary interpretations of the eighteenth-century constitution. Parliamentary sovereignty and the uncodified constitution mean that judicial review is limited in the UK.

➤ The US Constitution is a federal constitution. The Tenth Amendment states that all powers apart from those assigned to the federal government by the constitution are reserved to the states and to the people. Sovereignty is divided rather than located in a single authority. The UK has traditionally been a highly centralised state but has developed quasi-federal features since devolution.

➤ The US Constitution is inspired by liberal and republican principles. It establishes a strict separation of powers, reflecting the Founding Fathers' fear of despotism. The executive, legislature and judiciary have different powers and personnel. There is also an extensive system of checks and balances to prevent one branch of government becoming pre-eminent. In the UK, there is a fusion rather than separation of powers. The executive dominates the legislature.

➤ The Bill of Rights sets out the rights of individual American citizens and protects them from state encroachment. The Human Rights Act (1998) incorporated ECHR rights into statute law.

➤ The US Constitution establishes a presidential system of government in which the head of the executive branch is directly elected, the executive and legislative branches have distinct membership and functions, and neither branch can dismiss the other. The UK has a parliamentary system in which the prime minister is the leader of the largest party in the House of Commons, the executive and legislative branches are fused, and the House of Commons can dismiss the government.

Further reading

Bogdanor, V. (2008) 'A codified constitution for Britain?', *Politics Review*, Vol. 18, No. 1, pp. 2–4.

Bogdanor, V. (2009) *The New British Constitution*, Hart.

Lynch, P. (2007) 'Is parliament still sovereign?', *Politics Review*, Vol. 17, No. 1, pp. 30–33.

Norton, P. (2006) 'The unsettled British constitution', *Politics Review*, Vol. 16, No. 1, pp. 6–9.

Norton, P. (2008) 'The constitution under Gordon Brown', *Politics Review*, Vol. 17, No. 3, pp. 26–29.

Norton, P. (2009) 'Constitutional reform: why has it stalled under Gordon Brown?', *Politics Review*, Vol. 19, No. 2, pp. 17–19.

Exam focus

Short-answer questions (around 5 minutes each)

Explain, using examples, the meaning of each of the following terms:

1 Constitution
2 Uncodified
3 Parliamentary sovereignty
4 Statute law

Mid-length questions (around 10 minutes each)

Outline two arguments 'for' and two arguments 'against' each of the following:

1 An uncodified constitution.
2 The view that parliament is still sovereign.
3 A fusion of powers.
4 Entrenched rights.

Mini-essays (around 25–30 minutes each)

Write a mini-essay in response to each of the following questions:

1 Critically assess the arguments in favour of introducing a codified constitution for the UK.

2 'Far from being flexible, the UK constitution has in fact proven remarkably rigid.' Discuss.

3 To what extent have the core constitutional principles of parliamentary sovereignty, the rule of law and the unitary state been eroded in recent years?

4 Does the UK constitution present a sufficient check on the growth of executive power?

Chapter 7

Parliament

Key questions answered in this chapter
➢ What are the main features of parliamentary government?
➢ What are the powers and composition of the House of Commons and House of Lords?
➢ What are the functions of parliament, and how well does it perform them?
➢ How has the House of Commons been reformed?
➢ How has the House of Lords been reformed? Are these reforms sufficient?

The Houses of Parliament, located in the Palace of Westminster on the banks of the River Thames, are the most familiar symbols of British democracy. The UK Parliament is one of the oldest in the world and is sometimes called the 'mother of parliaments'. The importance of **parliament** is also reflected in the description of the UK political system as the 'Westminster model'.

Parliamentary government

The UK has a parliamentary system of government. The key features of a parliamentary system are as follows:

➢ **The executive and legislative branches are fused.** There is overlap between the membership of the two branches, with the government consisting of members of the **legislature**.
➢ **The legislature can dismiss the executive.** The government is accountable to parliament, which can remove the government through a vote of confidence. The government can dissolve parliament by calling a general election.
➢ **Parliamentary elections decide the government.** Governments are formed according to their strength in parliament. The person who commands a majority in parliament, usually the leader of the largest party, becomes prime minister.
➢ **Collective government.** The executive branch is led by a prime minister who, in theory at least, is 'first among equals' in a cabinet of senior ministers (see Chapter 8).

> **Separate head of state.** The head of the executive branch (the prime minister) is not the **head of state**. The latter is often a ceremonial role with little political power, as in the case of the UK monarchy.

Presidential government is the main alternative system. In a presidential system, there is a clear separation of powers between the executive and legislative branches, and the executive is dominated by a single individual (the president) who is directly elected.

Key terms

> **Head of state** The chief public representative of a country, such as a monarch or president.
> **Legislature** The branch of government responsible for passing laws.
> **Parliament** An assembly that has the power to debate and make laws.

Parliamentary and presidential government

Parliamentary government

> The executive and legislative branches are fused — government ministers must be members of the legislature, and are responsible to it.
> Parliament can dismiss the government through a vote of confidence; the government can dissolve parliament by calling a general election.
> Power is exercised collectively within the executive branch — the prime minister is the head of a cabinet.
> The prime minister is the person who can command a majority in the parliament following a general election.
> The head of the executive is not the head of state.

Presidential government

> There is a clear separation of powers between the executive and legislative branches — members of the executive cannot be members of the legislature.
> The legislature cannot dismiss the president, except in special circumstances, and the executive cannot dissolve the legislature.
> Power in the executive is concentrated in the office of president.
> The president is directly elected by the people.
> The president is also head of state.

The Westminster model

The **Westminster model** is the traditional way of understanding British politics. As the name suggests, it puts parliament at the heart of the British political system — the guiding principle of the constitution is that parliament has supreme law-making authority.

The Westminster model not only describes the British political system, it also claims or assumes that the British case is the best example of how a political system should operate. Two of the main virtues of the Westminster model are said to be:

> **Representative government.** Government takes place through parliament, where decisions are taken by elected representatives of the people. The people do not make decisions on public policy directly, but elect MPs to do so on their behalf.
> **Responsible government.** The government is accountable to parliament for its actions, and is ultimately accountable to the people through elections. Collective

responsibility means that the government can be forced to resign by parliament. Individual ministerial responsibility means that ministers must account for their actions in parliament (see Chapter 8). The people can remove the government at a general election.

The usefulness of the Westminster model as a description of how the British political system works is disputed. There is a significant disparity between the ideal presented by the model and the reality. In particular, there is a clear imbalance in the relationship between the executive and legislature. A parliamentary majority, party discipline in the House of Commons and government control of the parliamentary timetable all enable the executive to dominate parliament.

Concepts explained

The Westminster model

The traditional way of understanding the British political system, which focuses on the constitution and major institutions. It both describes the British system and claims that it is the ideal. The key features of the Westminster model are parliamentary sovereignty, an uncodified constitution, cabinet government, the first-past-the-post electoral system, a two-party system and a unitary state (see Chapter 5). All of these face significant challenges which raise important questions about the future of the Westminster model.

Structure of Parliament

The UK has a **bicameral** legislature — that is, parliament has two chambers. Formally, the UK Parliament actually has three component institutions:
- the House of Commons
- the House of Lords
- the 'Crown in Parliament', i.e. the monarchy

Concepts explained

Bicameralism

A political system in which there are two chambers in the legislature. The lower house is usually elected in a general election and tends to be the dominant chamber. The composition of upper houses varies: they may be directly elected or indirectly elected (e.g. appointed by ministers), or be a hybrid of both. Bicameralism has a number of benefits: the upper house provides checks and balances, provides for greater scrutiny and revision of legislation, and may represent different interests (e.g. states in a federal system). Problems associated with bicameralism include, first, that institutional conflict between the two houses may emerge, producing legislative gridlock, and second, that an indirectly elected upper house may frustrate the will of the democratically elected lower house.

Weblinks

www.parliament.uk — the home page of the UK Parliament, with information on its composition and functions, as well as parliamentary publications.

House of Commons

MPs gather in the House of Commons for the first time since the general election, May 2010

The House of Commons is the lower house of the UK Parliament. It has been the dominant chamber for over a century. The role and functions of the House of Commons will be examined in detail later in this chapter, but it is important to note at this stage two key powers of parliament that are, in effect, exercised by the Commons:

> **Parliamentary sovereignty.** A central principle of the British constitution, this gives parliament legislative supremacy. Parliament has ultimate law-making authority within the UK. In theory, this means that parliament can legislate on any matter of its choosing and these laws cannot be overturned by any higher authority. The legal theory and practical limitations of parliamentary sovereignty were explored in depth in Chapter 5.

Key term

> **Motion of no confidence**
A parliamentary motion which, if passed, requires the resignation of the government and dissolution of parliament.

> **Motion of no confidence.** The House of Commons can remove the government by defeating it in a motion of no confidence (also known as a vote of confidence). The convention of collective ministerial responsibility states that the entire government must resign if this happens and parliament is dissolved. There have only been four government defeats on confidence motions since 1895. The most recent was in 1979

when James Callaghan's Labour government, which did not have a parliamentary majority, was defeated in a motion of no confidence initiated by the opposition. A government can initiate a vote of confidence to pressurise its MPs to support key legislation, as John Major did over the Maastricht Treaty in 1993.

Composition

The House of Commons is a democratically elected chamber consisting of 650 Members of Parliament (MPs). Each MP is elected in a single-member constituency by the first-past-the-post electoral system (see Chapter 2). The number of MPs is not fixed, but can change following reviews of parliamentary constituencies.

In the chamber, the governing party (or parties) sit on the benches to the right of the Speaker's chair, and members of opposition parties on the benches to its left. More than 100 MPs hold ministerial positions in the government — the figure rose to 140 in 2009. The main opposition party appoints 'shadow ministers' to confront their rivals. Ministers and shadow ministers are known as **frontbenchers** because they occupy the benches closest to the floor of the chamber. The majority of MPs have no ministerial or shadow ministerial posts and are known as **backbenchers**.

Almost all MPs are elected as a representative of a political party. Two independent MPs were elected in 2005, but a further 13 resigned from, or were expelled by, their party during the 2005–10 parliament. Only one independent, Lady Sylvia Hermon in Down North, was elected in 2010. The party system in the House of Commons has traditionally been strong. Each party appoints a number of MPs to act as **whips**. They have three main roles:

➤ To ensure that MPs attend parliamentary **divisions** (votes), or approve the absence of MPs when their vote will not be required.
➤ To issue instructions to MPs on how to vote. Each week, MPs receive instructions on their attendance — also known as a **whip**. Debates where there will be a vote are underlined on this letter. A 'three-line whip' is a strict instruction that an MP must attend and vote according to the party line, or face disciplinary action. It is usually issued on only the most important divisions.
➤ To enforce discipline within the parliamentary party. The whips seek to persuade wavering MPs to vote with their party by providing assurances, making offers and issuing threats. They can expel rebel MPs from the parliamentary party by 'withdrawing the whip'.

Key terms

➤ **Backbencher** An MP who does not hold a ministerial or shadow ministerial position.
➤ **Division** A vote in parliament.
➤ **Frontbencher** An MP who holds a ministerial or shadow ministerial position.
➤ **Whip** (a) A party official responsible for ensuring that MPs turn up to parliamentary votes and follow party instructions on how to vote. (b) An instruction to vote that is issued to MPs by political parties.

Weblinks

www.parliament.uk — click on 'House of Commons' for the Commons website, with detailed information on the business of the house.

Box 7.1 The speaker

The speaker of the House of Commons presides over debates in the chamber, selecting speakers and maintaining order. He or she may temporarily suspend MPs who break parliamentary rules. The speaker is a senior MP who is elected by his or her fellow MPs by secret ballot. He or she must stand down when a general election is called, but is normally re-elected at the start of the next parliament. Once chosen, the speaker must give up his or her party affiliation and be non-partisan. The speaker does not vote unless there is a tie, in which case he or she has the casting vote — but uses it to provide further debate rather than a final decision. Three deputies assist the speaker by chairing some sessions (e.g. the budget debate).

Former Labour MP Michael Martin became the first speaker to be forced from office in 174 years when he resigned in 2009. Martin had been criticised for his handling of the MPs' expenses scandal (see below) and was viewed as an obstacle to reform. When the leaders of the main parties indicated that they no longer supported him, Martin stepped down before a formal motion of no confidence could be heard. Conservative MP John Bercow was then chosen as speaker ahead of nine other candidates, having won an absolute majority on a third ballot of MPs.

The Lord Speaker chairs proceedings in the House of Lords. The holder of the post is elected by his or her fellow **peers** and is politically neutral. The Lord Chancellor, a cabinet minister, had overseen debates in the Lords until stripped of this role by the Constitutional Reform Act (2005). Baroness Hayman became the first Lord Speaker in 2006.

Concepts explained

Parliamentary sovereignty

The doctrine that parliament has absolute legal authority within the state. Parliament can make law on any matter it chooses, its decisions may not be overturned by any higher authority and it may not bind its successors. Parliamentary sovereignty is a legal theory concerning the location of law-making authority. But EU membership and devolution, for example, raise questions about how meaningful it is in practice (see Chapter 5).

Key term

Peer A member of the House of Lords.

House of Lords

The House of Lords is the upper house of the UK Parliament. It is an unelected chamber and is subordinate to the House of Commons. The House of Lords can delay most bills passed by the House of Commons for up to 1 year. Prior to 1911, the Lords could block bills passed by the Commons indefinitely. The Parliament Act (1911) restricted this veto power to two parliamentary sessions (i.e. 2 years), which was subsequently reduced to 1 year by the Parliament Act (1949). The 1911 Act also prevented the Lords from delaying 'money bills': that is, bills that include significant provisions on taxation or expenditure (e.g. relating to the budget).

These measures transformed the House of Lords into a revising chamber. The Lords can propose amendments to bills passed by the Commons (except money bills). The Commons can then either accept these amendments, reject them or introduce new amendments of its own. The Lords cannot force the Commons to accept its amendments. If the Commons refuses to accept the wishes of the Lords, the upper house is faced with the choice of backing down or blocking the bill from becoming law for 1 year. If it chooses the latter, the bill can be passed unchanged in the following session of parliament without the consent of the Lords using the Parliament Act (1949). This has been invoked on only four occasions:

➢ the War Crimes Act (1991)
➢ the European Parliamentary Elections Act (1999)
➢ the Sexual Offences (Amendment) Act (2000)
➢ the Hunting Act (2004)

The Salisbury–Addison convention states that the House of Lords should not reject or wreck bills that seek to enact a manifesto commitment of the governing party. As a convention, it does not have the force of law. It arose in the 1940s as an acceptance that the unelected Lords should not frustrate the will of the elected Commons. The convention came under strain when Liberal Democrat and Conservative peers voted against an identity cards bill, even though it had featured in Labour's 2005 manifesto. They argued that Labour had not won sufficient support at the election to have a valid mandate, and that the Salisbury–Addison convention applied to a time when the upper house had a Conservative majority. The application of the convention to the Conservative–Liberal Democrat coalition agreement is also questionable because many of its provisions are diluted versions of manifesto commitments and the document was not put before voters directly.

Until 2009, the House of Lords also had a judicial role. The Law Lords — senior judges who sat in the Lords — acted as the UK's highest court of appeal. The Supreme Court took over this role in 2009.

The House of Lords consists of:

➢ hereditary peers
➢ life peers
➢ Lords Spiritual
➢ Lords of Appeal

Hereditary peers

The House of Lords Act (1999) ended the right of all but 92 hereditary peers to sit and vote in the Lords. Before the Act came into force, the House of Lords contained more than 750 hereditary peers who had inherited their title and a place in the upper house. Some hereditary peerages dated back centuries, but most were created in the nineteenth and early twentieth centuries when the power of the aristocracy was in decline.

The Peerages Act (1963) allowed hereditary peers to renounce their titles and membership of the Lords. It enabled Alec Douglas Home, the 14th Earl of Home, to leave the Lords and win a by-election to the House of Commons when he became Conservative Party leader and prime minister in 1963. Tony Benn renounced his hereditary title (Viscount Stansgate) to become a long-serving Labour MP. The Act also allowed women hereditary peers to sit in the Lords. The right of primogeniture, under which aristocratic titles are transferred to the eldest son, meant that the vast majority of hereditary peers were men.

The House of Lords Act (1999) transformed the hereditary element of the Lords into a new category of 'elected hereditary peers'. The 15 hereditary peers who became deputy speakers were chosen in a ballot of the whole House. Two others hold royal appointments. The remaining 75 were elected by ballots of hereditary peers from their party and crossbench groups. When an elected hereditary peer dies, a by-election is held in which peers from the same group as the deceased member choose a replacement from the register of hereditary peers. Ten such by-elections had been held by 2010.

Life peers

The Life Peerages Act (1958) gave the prime minister the right to appoint members of the upper house for life. Their title and right to sit in the Lords cannot be inherited. With the removal of most hereditary peers, life peers now form the largest category of members of the upper house (see Table 7.1). An independent House of Lords Appointments Commission recommends individuals for appointment as non-party peers, and vets those nominated by political parties.

Lords Spiritual

Two archbishops and 24 senior bishops of the Church of England sit in the House of Lords.

Lords of Appeal

These are senior judges or retired judges who sit in the House of Lords. It is important to distinguish them from the Law Lords (properly known as Lords of Appeal in Ordinary) who are no longer members of the upper house. The Law Lords in office became the first justices of the Supreme Court in 2009, and were disqualified from sitting and voting in the Lords. They may return to the Lords on retirement, but future appointments to the Supreme Court will not be members.

The Life Peerages Act (1958) and the House of Lords Act (1999) brought about significant changes to the composition and day-to-day working of the upper house. The creation of life peers increased the diversity and professionalism of the House of Lords. The body of life peers includes former ministers and MPs, as well as leading figures from business, education and the arts. Some 20% of life peers are women. Life peers have also proved more likely to play an active role in the house. Many hereditary peers, known as 'backwoodsmen', did not attend the House of Lords regularly.

The House of Lords Act (1999) also ended the historical predominance of the Conservative Party in the upper house. Many hereditary peers had taken the Conservative whip. Following the removal of all but 92 hereditary peers, no party had a majority (see Table 7.2). Crossbench members of the upper house have no formal party allegiance; nor do the Lords Spiritual and Lords of Appeal. The removal of hereditary peers also increased the proportion of women in the House of Lords. In April 2010, there were 147 women peers — 21% of the house compared to 9% before the 1999 reform.

Table 7.1 Composition of the House of Lords by type, April 2010

Type	Men	Women	Total
Hereditary peers under the House of Lords Act (1999)	89	2	91
Life peers under the Life Peerages Act (1958)	452	144	596
Life peers under the Appellate Jurisdiction Act (1876)	22	1	23
Archbishops and bishops	26	0	26

Note: Excludes 12 peers on leave of absence, 16 disqualified as senior members of the judiciary, and 1 disqualified as an MEP.

Table 7.2 The House of Lords by party, October 1999 and April 2010

Party	October 1999			April 2010		
	Life peers	Hereditary	Total	Life peers	Hereditary	Total
Conservative	172	299	471	139	47	186
Labour	160	19	179	207	4	211
Lib Dem	49	23	72	67	5	72
Crossbench	128	225	353	153	33	186
Bishops	0	0	26	0	0	26
Other	32	80	229	24	2	26
Total	571	759	1,330	590	91	707

Note: Figures for October 1999 exclude 113 hereditary peers and 4 life peers on leave of absence; figures for April 2010 exclude 12 peers on leave of absence, 16 disqualified as senior members of the judiciary and 1 disqualified as an MEP.

Weblinks

www.parliament.uk — click on 'House of Lords' for the Lords website, with information on its composition and business.

The monarchy

The monarchy retains a formal and ceremonial role in parliament. The monarch is head of state, but many of the powers associated with the Crown, such as the power to declare war, are exercised by ministers (see Chapter 8). The monarch's role in parliament entails:

> **The royal assent.** Approval by the monarch is the final stage in the legislative process. Only when a bill has been signed by the monarch can it become law. Constitutional convention dictates that the monarch must always grant the royal assent.

> **Appointing the prime minister.** The monarch appoints the prime minister. This is usually a formality, with the leader of the largest party in the House of Commons

The State Opening of Parliament, May 2010

invited to form a government. When no single party has a majority — a hung parliament — the convention is that the incumbent prime minister is given the first opportunity to form a government. If he or she fails, the leader of the main rival party will get their turn. The monarch will only invite a party leader to form a government once negotiations between parties have produced a definitive outcome, thereby avoiding personal involvement in the process.

➤ **Dissolving parliament.** The prime minister must ask the monarch for permission to dissolve parliament and call a general election. Once again, this is usually a formality. But the monarch may be placed in a difficult position if there is a hung parliament and a party leader requests a speedy second election.

➤ **The Queen's Speech.** At the State Opening of Parliament, the monarch opens the new parliamentary session and delivers the Queen's Speech. It sets out the main bills that the government intends to introduce that year. The speech is written by the prime minister and his or her officials in Downing Street, not by the monarch.

Weblinks

www.royal.gov.uk — official site of the British monarchy, including information on the role of the queen.

Functions of parliament

Parliament performs a number of functions in the British political system. The most significant are:

➤ legislation
➤ scrutiny and accountability
➤ representation

➤ recruitment of ministers
➤ legitimacy

This section outlines the main parliamentary procedures for dealing with these functions, with a particular focus on the House of Commons because of its status as the dominant chamber. It also assesses how effective parliament is in performing these roles.

Legislation

Parliament is the legislative branch (the 'legislature') of a political system. The term reflects parliament's primary function — making law.

Key terms

➤ **Act** A legislative proposal that has completed the legislative process and entered into law.

➤ **Bill** A legislative proposal that has yet to complete the parliamentary legislative process.

➤ **Green Paper.** A government document setting out various options for legislation and inviting comment.

➤ **Public bill** A bill concerning a general issue of public policy, introduced by a government minister.

➤ **White Paper** A government document setting out a detailed proposal for legislation.

The legislative process

A **bill** is a draft legislative proposal that is debated in parliament. When a bill has completed the legislative process and enters into law, it is known as an **Act** of Parliament. The most significant bills are **public bills**. These are promoted by a government minister and concern general issues of public policy. Public bills are also the most common because the executive exercises significant control over the parliamentary timetable.

The government sets out its legislative programme in the Queen's Speech at the beginning of a parliamentary session. For a minority government, the votes at the end of this debate may determine its chances of survival. The government may produce a consultative **Green Paper** that sets out various options for legislation, and/or a **White Paper** which explains the objectives of government policy.

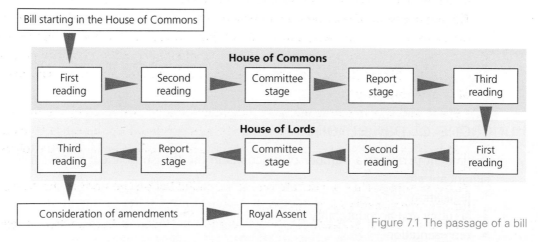

Figure 7.1 The passage of a bill

Legislation follows an established process of debate, scrutiny and amendment (see Figure 7.1). Most legislation originates in the House of Commons, but some bills on non-controversial or complex matters of law are introduced in the House of Lords. The main stages in the legislative process for a bill introduced in the House of Commons (except a money bill) are as follows:

➤ **Pre-legislative scrutiny.** The Blair government introduced measures to improve pre-legislative scrutiny before the formal legislative process. Many bills are now published in draft form and considered by a departmental select committee, allowing recommendations to be heard at an earlier stage. This may prove inadequate if the government is determined to pursue a particular course, allows insufficient time for consultation, and is not prepared to listen to constructive objections.

➤ **First reading.** This is the formal presentation of the title of the bill on the floor of the house by a minister from the responsible department. There is no debate or vote at this stage.

➤ **Second reading.** The main debate on the principle of the bill. The government minister explains and justifies the objectives of the bill, the shadow minister responds and backbenchers contribute to the debate. If the bill is contested, a vote is taken. Government defeats at second reading stage are extremely rare, occurring only twice in postwar British politics. The last occasion was in 1986 when the Sunday Trading Bill, which would allow more shops to open on Sundays, was defeated by 14 votes even though the government had a majority of 140.

➤ **Committee stage.** Bills are sent to a public bill committee — known as a standing committee until 2006 — where detailed scrutiny of each clause occurs and amendments can be made. A new public bill committee is established for each bill, and is named after it. Once the bill has completed this stage, that committee is dissolved. In 2008–09, there were 22 public bill committees.

Key terms

➤ **Committee of the Whole House** A meeting held in the chamber in which the full House of Commons considers the committee stage of a public bill.

The membership of the committee, which ranges from 16 to 50, reflects that of the House as a whole, and whips instruct MPs how to vote. Public bill committees may take evidence from outside experts. The annual Finance Bill and bills of particular constitutional significance are scrutinised on the floor of the house, in a **Committee of the Whole House**.

➤ **Report stage.** Amendments made in committee are considered by the full house. It may accept, reject or alter them. The Major government lost a crucial vote on the Maastricht Treaty in 1993, but made the issue a matter of confidence on the following day and won by 40 votes.

➤ **Third reading.** This is a debate on the amended bill on the floor of the house. No further amendments are permitted.

➤ **House of Lords stages.** The bill is sent to the House of Lords, where it follows the same procedure. If amendments to the bill are made in the Lords, the Commons may agree them, reject them or amend them further. A bill may go back and forth between the two houses in a process known as 'parliamentary ping pong'. Common ground is normally found, but if not, the government must decide whether to accept changes made by the Lords, drop the bill or invoke the Parliament Act.

Other bills

In addition to public bills, two other types of legislative proposal are noteworthy: private members' bills and secondary legislation.

Legislative proposals initiated by backbench MPs rather than by the government are known as **private members' bills**. Early in each parliamentary session, 20 names of MPs who wish to introduce a bill are drawn in a ballot. Some will already have a cause they wish to pursue; others will take soundings from lobbyists or their party. MPs can also introduce Ten Minute Rule bills, which offer a brief slot to introduce a legislative proposal, but few get beyond this first hurdle.

Key terms

> **Private member's bill**
A bill sponsored by a backbench MP.

> **Secondary legislation**
Law made by ministers, who have been granted this authority by an Act of parliament, rather than by parliament.

Only a small number of private members' bills become law. Those that do tend to enjoy the support, or at least the benevolent neutrality, of the government. Time constraints and the difficulty of persuading other MPs to back a proposal mean that most fall at an early stage. Two landmark laws to originate as private members' bills were the Murder (Abolition of Death Penalty) Act (1965) and the Abortion Act (1967). Crucially, both had the support of the government. More recent examples include the Autism Act (2009) and the Sustainable Communities Act (2006), which were promoted by lobbying organisations and supported by the government.

The authority to issue **secondary legislation** in specific policy areas is delegated by parliament to government ministers. Some 2,500 pieces of secondary legislation, known as statutory instruments, are issued each year on matters such as immigration, taxation and education. Parliamentary scrutiny is limited to examination by the statutory instruments committee.

Effectiveness of legislation

In theory, the UK parliament can make, amend or repeal any laws it chooses. In practice, the situation is very different. The government is responsible for most of the laws passed by parliament. Professor Philip Norton, an academic expert on parliament and a member of the House of Lords, has developed a threefold classification of legislatures:

> **Policy-making legislatures.** These amend or reject legislative proposals made by the executive, and can put forward alternative bills.
> **Policy-influencing legislatures.** These can modify or reject legislative proposals from the executive but are unable to develop extensive legislative proposals of their own.

> **Legislatures with little or no policy influence.** These are unable to modify or veto legislative proposals from the executive, and cannot formulate meaningful alternative policy proposals of their own.

The UK parliament is a policy-influencing legislature. Law making occurs through, not by, parliament. It has only modest influence over policy and reacts to government proposals rather than taking the lead in formulating policy. Parliament can vote against government bills and pass amendments. But parliament's effectiveness in making and scrutinising law is limited by the dominance of the executive. This is evidenced by:

> **Government bills.** Most bills that come before parliament originate from the government. Private members' bills have little chance of success unless they have government backing.

> **Parliamentary timetable.** The executive controls much of the legislative timetable and can use 'guillotine motions' to curtail debate.

> **Party discipline.** The whip system ensures that government proposals are rarely defeated and that most amendments are acceptable to it.

> **House of Lords.** The upper house scrutinises and revises legislation, but does not alter the key features of most bills.

Weblinks

www.parliament.uk — select 'Parliamentary business' and then 'Bills & legislation' for information on bills before parliament, and the legislative process.

Scrutiny and accountability

In addition to scrutinising a government's legislative proposals, parliament also exercises a general scrutiny and oversight role. It scrutinises the actions of the executive and ensures government **accountability** by requiring ministers to explain and justify their actions. The convention of individual ministerial responsibility states that ministers are accountable to parliament; they must explain and justify their policies and actions — and those of their department — in parliament. Ministers who mislead parliament may be required to resign. The convention is examined in detail in Chapter 8.

Concepts explained
Accountability

In politics, the principle that an office holder or institution must account for their actions. In a system of parliamentary government, ministers are accountable to parliament and to the electorate. They have a duty to explain their policies and actions to parliament. Ministers may also be held responsible for policy failures (see Chapter 8). MPs face the electorate at a general election, where their constituents may take their record in office into account when deciding whether to vote for them.

A number of routes for scrutinising the executive are available to MPs in the chamber.

Question Time

Government ministers face questions from MPs on the floor of the house. The parliamentary timetable includes question sessions for ministers from each government department. The most high-profile event is Prime Minister's Questions, which takes place each Wednesday at noon for half an hour. This provides an opportunity for the leader of the opposition, the leader of the third largest party and backbenchers selected by the speaker to question the prime minister on a matter of their choosing. A backbencher might raise a constituency matter, but most ask questions provided for them by the whips. The leader of the opposition will often try to embarrass the prime minister by highlighting a policy failure. Prime Minister's Questions tends, then, to produce more heat than light — it provides parliamentary theatre rather than effective scrutiny.

Away from the floor of the House, MPs send written questions to ministers asking for information on issues of public policy (e.g. data on crime or carbon emissions).

The opposition

The largest party not included in the government is the official opposition. The very architecture of the House of Commons is confrontational, with the government and opposition facing each other across the chamber. The party in opposition is expected to perform two major tasks that do not always sit easily together. First, it will oppose many of the government's legislative proposals, and harry the government throughout the legislative process by tabling amendments and forcing votes. The leader of the opposition will also confront the prime minister at Question Time. But the opposition will also try to appear as an alternative government-in-waiting. It will need to develop its own policies and might consider supporting government measures that it agrees with. When the government has a comfortable majority, a period in opposition can prove frustrating and fruitless. But when it has only a small majority or none at all, the opposition may be able to force government u-turns or inflict defeats.

The government enjoys significant institutional advantages in parliament. It can draw upon the expertise of the civil service, while the opposition relies on limited state funding ('Short money') to fund parliamentary researchers. Government control over the parliamentary timetable also means that the opposition has few opportunities to set the agenda. The opposition is permitted to choose the topic for debate on 20 days in the parliamentary year ('opposition days'). On 3 further days, the leader of the third largest party determines the debate. The government suffered a rare defeat on an opposition motion in 2010 when the Liberal Democrats initiated a debate on the Brown government's refusal to grant citizenship to Gurkhas who had served in the UK armed forces.

Debates

MPs can also express their views and try to influence policy in debates on current events and government actions. The half-hour adjournment debates at the end of each day give MPs a chance to raise a particular issue. Ministers also make statements to parliament on major issues, and these are followed by debate.

Many debates are poorly attended, but those at times of crisis can provide moments of high drama. Prime minister Neville Chamberlain resigned after losing the support of a significant number of MPs, even within his own party, as a credible war leader following a debate on the German invasion of Norway. The debate that followed the invasion of the Falkland Islands by Argentina in 1982, and that which preceded the invasion of Iraq in 2003, saw high-quality contributions from both sides of the argument, and reflected the difference of opinion within the nation as a whole.

Weblinks

www.parliament.uk — select 'Parliamentary business' and then click on 'Hansard' in the 'Publications and records' section for the official verbatim report of proceedings in the Commons and Lords.

Select committees

Select committees have proved more effective than debates at scrutinising the actions of the executive and holding it to account. Departmental select committees were created in 1979 to scrutinise the policy, administration and expenditure of government departments. There were 19 departmental select committees in 2010 (see Table 7.3).

The membership of select committees, which varies from 11 to 14 backbench MPs, reflects the party balance in the Commons. The chairs of the committees are shared between the parties according to the overall composition of the house. Committee chairs often have a reputation for independence. This can cause government unease. The Major government removed Conservative MP Nicholas Winterton as chair of the Health Select Committee in 1992, but the Blair government failed in its attempt to remove Labour MP Gwyneth Dunwoody as chair of the Transport Select Committee in 2001 after a rebellion within its own ranks.

A desire for independence extends to select committees as a whole. The atmosphere is one of constructive engagement rather than confrontation. Since a unanimous report is likely to carry maximum weight, members have a vested interest in striking compromises across party lines, to the displeasure of their whips. Over time, committee members can become more expert in their chosen field than the relevant ministers, who usually have short tenures in a specific office.

Table 7.3 Departmental select committees, 2010

Business, Innovation and Skills
Communities and Local Government
Culture, Olympics, Media and Sport
Defence
Education
Energy and Climate Change
Environment, Food and Rural Affairs
Foreign Affairs
Health
Home Affairs
International Development
Justice
Northern Ireland Affairs
Science and Technology
Scottish Affairs
Transport
Treasury
Welsh Affairs
Work and Pensions

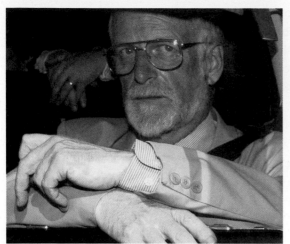

Dr David Kelly leaving the House of Commons after giving evidence to the Foreign Affairs Select Committee in 2003

Select committees decide the issues that they are going to examine. They have wide powers to summon witnesses and to examine restricted documents. The committees spend much of their time questioning ministers, officials and outside experts. The former bosses of HBOS and RBS appeared before the Treasury Select Committee during its investigation on the banking sector in 2009. Jamie Oliver appeared before the Health Select Committee in 2008. Certain witnesses, particularly civil servants, have been notably unhelpful, only appearing if their ministers approve and then saying little of interest. Weapons expert Dr David Kelly was subject to stern questioning on weapons of mass destruction when he appeared before the Foreign Affairs Committee in July 2003. He committed suicide days later.

Governments are not obliged to accept recommendations made in select committee reports. They may issue a formal response that merely notes the recommendations, before quietly rejecting them. Reports may be debated in Westminster Hall sessions.

Other important (non-departmental) select committees in the House of Commons include:

➤ **Public Accounts Committee.** The oldest committee in parliament, this examines government expenditure to check that value for money is being achieved. It does not consider the merits of government policy. It is chaired by a senior opposition MP.

➤ **Standards and Privileges Committee.** This examines the conduct of MPs, overseeing the Register of Interests and dealing with disciplinary cases against MPs.

➤ **Modernisation Committee.** Established in 2005, this examines how the practices and procedures of the House of Commons might be reformed. Unusually, it is chaired by a government minister, the leader of the House of Commons.

➤ **Liaison Committee.** This includes the chairs of all select committees. Its most significant meetings are the twice-yearly sessions in which the prime minister is questioned on public policy.

➤ **European Scrutiny Committee.** This assesses the significance of European Union documents, reporting in detail on about 475 of the 1,000 or more it receives each year.

In the House of Lords, a smaller number of committees conduct in-depth inquiries on topical issues. The European Union Committee, which has seven subcommittees, and the Constitution Committee have developed impressive bodies of work.

Effectiveness of scrutiny and accountability

The select committee system has improved and extended parliament's scrutiny of the executive. It has deepened the accountability of government to parliament, and debate on major policy issues has been enhanced. The remit of select committees has been widened in recent years. Select committees are beginning to scrutinise legislation that has come into force, and hold hearings on some public appointments.

However, select committees still lack resources, witnesses may prove unhelpful, and the government can ignore their recommendations. In 2010, MPs approved proposals that select committee chairpersons should be elected by the house and that other members should be chosen by their parties in a secret ballot. The Cameron government is expected to put these proposals into effect, thereby limiting the power of the whips to control membership and enhancing further the independence of select committees.

Weblinks

www.parliament.uk — select 'Parliamentary business' and 'Bills and legislation' for information on, and documents from, parliamentary committees.

Viewpoint Are select committees effective in scrutinising the executive?

- Select committees have a high degree of expertise in their field, and carry out detailed inquiries into the policies and actions of government departments.
- They decide which issues to examine, and often look into controversial matters.
- They can question ministers, civil servants and outside experts, and can request access to government papers.
- They have established a reputation for independence, working in a consensual rather than an adversarial manner.
- The government is required to issue a formal response to their reports, which may also be debated in Westminster Hall.

- Select committee membership reflects that in the House of Commons — a government with a majority in the house will also have a majority in committees.
- Their membership is influenced by the whips, who try to place loyal MPs on key committees and have tried to remove independent-minded committee chairs.
- Ministers and civil servants might not provide much information when questioned, and access to documents may be denied.
- They have no power to propose policy — governments can ignore the recommendations made by select committees.

Representation

The House of Commons consists of 650 MPs, elected from single-member constituencies on the basis of universal suffrage among adults over 18. The geographical nature of representation is supposed to ensure that individual MPs can be identified as the exclusive representatives of their constituents, as opposed to the multi-member constituencies produced by proportional representation systems (see Chapter 2).

Constituency work takes up a greater proportion of an MP's time than in the recent past — almost half of it, according to a 2005 Hansard Society study. MPs hold regular surgeries in which constituents can discuss problems. They may then take up grievances that individual constituents have against a public authority: for example, by contacting the relevant body, writing to a minister or raising the issue in the Commons. MPs also defend the interests of the constituency as a whole. They might, for example, campaign to maintain jobs or improve local services.

Some MPs can win enviable local reputations for their constituency work, and reap a sizeable personal vote in a general election. The Electoral Commission's 2007 *Audit of Political Engagement* showed that 41% of people were satisfied with the way their local MP was doing his or her job, and 12% dissatisfied. When asked how MPs in general were doing their job, only 30% were satisfied and 37% dissatisfied.

Weblinks

www.theyworkforyou.com — here you can find your MP, read their speeches in parliament and discover how they have voted.

Descriptive representation

Descriptive representation occurs when a legislature mirrors the society it represents. In this perspective, parliament should be a microcosm of society with all major social groups included in numbers proportional to their size in the electorate. In the UK, attention has focused on the under-representation of women in the House of Commons. The number of women MPs has risen in recent decades, reaching 143 at the 2010 general election. But women make up only 22% of the Commons compared to 51% of the UK population (see Table 7.4).

The two key methods that parties have used to increase the number of women candidates have been:

Table 7.4 Women candidates and MPs, 1983–2010

	Conservative		Labour		Liberal Democrat		Total women MPs
	Candidates	MPs	Candidates	MPs	Candidates	MPs	
1983	40	13	78	10	75	0	23
1987	46	17	92	21	106	2	41
1992	63	20	138	37	143	2	60
1997	69	13	157	101	140	3	120
2001	92	14	146	95	135	5	118
2005	118	17	166	98	142	10	128
2010	151	49	189	81	137	7	143

Note: 'Total women MPs' includes MPs from other parties.

Most of the Labour Party's female MPs gather outside the Members' Entrance to the House of Commons for the first sitting of the House following the 2010 general election

➤ **All-women shortlists.** These were used by Labour for the 1997, 2005 and 2010 general elections. Some constituency Labour parties are required to select their parliamentary candidate from a list consisting only of women. This boosted significantly the number of female Labour MPs elected at the 1997 general election. The Sex Discrimination (Election Candidates) Act (2002) permits political parties to use positive measures to reduce inequality in the number of women elected to parliament. All-women shortlists are 'equality guarantees': they ensure that a woman candidate will be selected in a constituency.

➤ **Priority lists.** David Cameron introduced a priority list (the 'A list') in 2005 for the top 100 Conservative target seats. This was an 'equality promotion' initiative that set a general target of more women MPs, but did not guarantee that women would be selected in winnable seats. Constituency associations chose from a priority list of aspirant candidates, half of whom were women. From 2006 constituency associations were required to draw up shortlists, on which at least half the aspirant candidates were women. In 2010, 36 new women Conservative MPs were elected, taking the party's total to 49, although only 19 of them had been on the 'A list'.

These 'demand-side' initiatives have helped to increase the number of women MPs, but 'supply-side' obstacles remain. Career choices, family issues, money and a lack of political connections may prevent women from putting themselves forward as candidates.

The 2010 speaker's conference on parliamentary representation recommended that if the number of women MPs did not increase significantly at that year's election (the proportion rose from 20% to 22%), then equality guarantees should be considered.

Other areas of under-representation in the House of Commons include:

- **Ethnic diversity.** In 2010, 26 black and minority ethnic (BME) MPs were elected, an increase of 11. This is only 4% of the house, compared to 8% of the population. The speaker's conference on parliamentary representation recommended all-BME shortlists.
- **Age.** The average age of MPs fell to 50 in 2010 because of the high number of MPs who stood down or were defeated in the election. Young and older people are under-represented in the Commons, with most MPs being in the 35 to 55 age range.
- **Sexual orientation.** There are 20 openly gay MPs in the 2010 parliament.
- **Education.** More than a third of MPs elected in 2010 attended a fee-paying school, but fewer than 10% of voters did. Nine out of ten MPs have been to university, with over a quarter going to either Oxford or Cambridge.
- **Social class.** The number of MPs who used to be manual workers has declined. Only 10% of Labour's MPs in 2005 had been manual workers. Occupations such as the law, financial services and public relations are well represented in the Commons. MPs who worked in business are more likely to be found on the Conservative benches, and those who worked in the public sector (e.g. teachers) on the Labour benches.

Recruitment of ministers

Government ministers must be members of either the House of Commons or the House of Lords. Parliament is, therefore, a recruiting ground for government. By law, the number of paid ministerial jobs — the so-called 'payroll vote' — is fixed at 109. There were more than 140 government posts (some unpaid) in the last year of the Brown government.

Traditionally, future ministers have learned about the political process and carved out their reputations in the House of Commons. However, parliament's effectiveness in this area is questionable:

- **Communications skills.** Being an effective communicator is important for the career prospects of an MP. But parliament is no longer the key arena in which politicians display their oratorical skills. Ambitious MPs must excel on television if they are to reach the highest echelons of their profession.
- **Experience.** A total of 227 new MPs entered the Commons in 2010. Government needs individuals with managerial, leadership and organisational skills, rather than just communications skills. The proportion of MPs who worked in politics before entering parliament (e.g. as researchers or advisers) reached 20% in 2010. They have little experience of life beyond politics. The proliferation of career politicians also widens the gap between the 'political class' and ordinary voters.
- **Conformity.** Unswerving loyalty is important for an MP's career prospects. Reliable MPs have a better chance of rising through the ranks than troublemakers, who may

be offered junior posts to keep them quiet. For most backbenchers the legislative routine allows little opportunity for independent thought or action.

Legitimacy

Parliament helps to maintain the legitimacy of the British political system. Government policies are scrutinised and discussed by elected MPs who represent the people. MPs also hold the executive accountable and represent the interests of their constituents. Parliamentary debates provide some assurance that major issues are being considered.

However, there are limits to the legitimacy of parliament. The House of Lords plays an important role in revising legislation and constraining the executive. But its legitimacy is limited because it is unelected.

In the House of Commons, the partisan point-scoring of Prime Minister's Question Time fosters negative perceptions of parliament. Parliament's reputation has also been damaged by sleaze. Public trust in parliament declined after the 'cash for questions' scandal of the 1990s when some MPs accepted money to table parliamentary questions. The Committee on Standards in Public Life and a code of standards were established. But allegations that individuals were offered peerages for making donations to political parties, and concerns about former ministers taking lobbying roles, emerged under the Blair and Brown governments.

Most damaging were revelations made by the *Daily Telegraph* in May 2009 about the expenses claimed by MPs. Notorious claims included those by Conservative MPs Anthony Steen and Douglas Hogg for a 'duck island' and the clearing of a moat respectively, and by Labour home secretary Jacqui Smith for adult movies. More serious were tax avoidance and the 'flipping' of second homes — changing the property designated as a second home so that expenses could be claimed on different properties. Four Labour MPs faced criminal charges.

Many of the claims actually fell within the rules of the Additional Costs Allowance (ACA). It covered costs that MPs from constituencies outside London incurred attending parliament, including mortgage interest payments, fixtures and fittings, and utility bills. In 2009, up to £24,222 could be claimed. MPs had been reluctant to vote themselves higher salaries, even when they had been recommended by the independent Senior Salaries Review Body, for fear of negative publicity. So the ACA was treated as a salary top-up to which MPs felt entitled. As the scandal broke, many MPs announced that they would step down at the 2010 election and some of the worst offenders lost their party whip. Speaker Michael Martin was forced to resign because he was seen as an obstacle to change. An independent audit by Sir Thomas Legg required 373 MPs to pay back claims that were deemed excessive.

The main changes to the expenses and allowances system that followed were:

> The Parliamentary Standards Act (2009) created an Independent Parliamentary Standards Authority to run the expenses system. But only the Commons Standards and Privileges Committee will be able to instruct MPs to repay money.

> The Kelly report (2009), produced by the chair of the Committee on Standards in Public Life, recommended that MPs should not be able to claim towards buying a second home. The Independent Parliamentary Standards Authority agreed and MPs will now only be able to claim rent up to the value of a one-bedroom flat. Kelly's proposed ban on MPs employing family members was not accepted — they will be permitted to employ one close family member on strict terms.

Weblinks

www.hansardsociety.org.uk — the website of the Hansard Society, an independent research body promoting the strengthening of parliamentary democracy.

Parliament and government

The relationship between parliament and government is an unequal one, with the executive the dominant actor. This does not mean, however, that parliament is impotent. The power to dismiss the government is an important weapon in the parliamentary armoury, albeit one of last resort. Select committees have enhanced parliament's ability to scrutinise the government and hold it to account.

The relationship between parliament and government is not determined simply by the institutional resources that each possesses, but is also shaped by the political context. Three contextual factors are of particular significance:

> the government's parliamentary majority
> the level of party unity
> the assertiveness of the House of Lords

Government majority

The size, or absence, of a majority for the governing party in the House of Commons is an important factor in the relationship between the legislature and executive. The first-past-the-post electoral system often, but not always, delivers a working majority for the party that wins most votes in a general election. A government with a large majority is in a commanding position, able to push its legislation through parliament by utilising the whip system and controlling the parliamentary timetable.

The larger a government's majority, the less likely it is that the other parties in the Commons will be able to defeat or amend government bills. The ability of backbenchers to influence policy is also limited because a government with a substantial majority will be able to absorb dissent from within its own ranks. With a majority of 167 at the 2001 election, the Blair government survived large rebellions from Labour backbenchers on Iraq, tuition fees and foundation hospitals. Within months of its majority being cut to 65 at the 2005 election, the government suffered its first Commons defeat.

A governing party that has a slender majority, or none at all, can find itself in a precarious position A hung parliament occurs when no single party commands an absolute majority of seats in the House of Commons. One of two types of government is likely to emerge:

> **A coalition government.** Two or more parties form the government, having reached a formal agreement on a legislative programme and the distribution of cabinet posts. When the 2010 election failed to deliver an outright majority for the Conservatives, they formed a coalition government with the Liberal Democrats. The two parties agreed a programme covering the major areas of public policy, and five Liberal Democrats took seats in David Cameron's cabinet. This was the first coalition in Britain since that led by Winston Churchill (1940–45) during the Second World War, and the first in peacetime since the National Government of the 1930s.

> **A minority government.** The party with the largest number of seats governs alone. It may be able to persuade a smaller party not to vote against it on key measures such as the budget or Queen's Speech – a 'confidence and supply' deal. But it has to find parliamentary majorities on a bill-by-bill basis. A minority government may be relatively stable in the short term, particularly if other parties do not want another general election, and may be able to implement some policy changes. But it is difficult to sustain a minority government for long.

There are three postwar examples of minority governments:

> **Wilson government, 1974.** Harold Wilson's Labour government had no majority after the February 1974 election. It called another election that October and secured a majority of 3 seats.

> **Callaghan government, 1976–79.** James Callaghan succeeded Wilson as Labour prime minister in 1976, but his majority disappeared after by-election defeats. The 1977–78 'Lib–Lab pact' saw the Liberals support the government on key decisions in the Commons.

> **Conservative government, 1996–97.** John Major's government had lost its majority by 1996 after a series of by-election defeats and defections. It was supported by Ulster Unionist MPs on some divisions, but there was no formal deal.

Party unity

It is a common perception that MPs slavishly follow the party whips without exercising their own judgement. It is true that MPs vote with their party on the overwhelming majority of divisions in the House of Commons. When a **parliamentary rebellion** does occur, it is usually small and can be easily absorbed by a government with a working majority. But rebellions have become more frequent in recent decades, and some have been highly dramatic.

Key terms

> **Parliamentary rebellion** A division in which MPs vote against their party whip.

In the 1950s and 1960s, the Conservative governments of Eden, Macmillan and Douglas-Home suffered no defeats in the Commons. Things began to change in the 1970s when ideological divisions within both the Labour and Conservative parties became more pronounced.

> **Heath government, 1970–74.** A rebellion by 39 Conservatives meant that European Communities Act (1972) was passed only because 69 Labour MPs had defied a three-line whip.
> **Wilson (1974–76) and Callaghan (1976–79) governments.** Labour operated with either a slender parliamentary majority or none at all. Some 45% of Labour MPs rebelled and the government suffered 59 defeats in the Commons, the final one on a motion of no confidence.
> **Major government (1992–97).** John Major's government suffered a serious rebellion during the passage of the Maastricht Treaty (1992–93). After a defeat on a Labour motion on the social chapter, Major called a confidence motion to force the treaty through the Commons. Further rebellions followed on gun control and VAT on domestic fuel.

Research by Professor Philip Cowley has demonstrated that the 2001–05 parliament was the most rebellious since the Second World War — but was subsequently overtaken by the 2005–10 parliament. Examples of disunity included:

> **2001–05 parliament.** There were rebellions by Labour MPs on 21% of divisions. There were sizeable rebellions on votes on legislation concerning foundation hospitals (65 Labour rebels) in 2003 and university tuition fees (72 rebels) in 2005, but Labour's majority was sufficient for the bills to be passed. On the March 2003 vote on the invasion of Iraq, 139 Labour MPs defied the whip and supported a motion stating that the case for war had not been established. This was the largest rebellion of MPs from a governing party in modern British politics.
> **2005–10 parliament.** There were rebellions by Labour MPs on 28% of divisions, and a total of 174 Labour MPs voted against the party line at least once. In November 2005, the Blair government was defeated by 322 votes to 291 on its proposal to allow terrorist subjects to be detained for up to 90 days without charge. It also lost two votes on House of Lords amendments to the Racial and Religious Hatred Bill in 2006. The Brown government lost a 2009 vote on a Liberal Democrat motion on the right of Gurkhas to live in the UK. Labour needed Conservative support to win votes on the 2006 Education Bill and the renewal of the Trident nuclear weapons system, and the support of the Democratic Unionist Party on a 2008 vote on the Counter Terrorism Bill's provisions on the detention of terrorist suspects for 42 days.

Rebellions are a visible sign of the limits of party unity and the ability of backbench MPs to exert influence. More subtle methods may also be productive. If the whips expect a high level of opposition to a measure, the government may withdraw or revise it rather than risk defeat or cause ill-will by exerting pressure on MPs. In April 2008, ministers made important concessions to backbench opponents of the budget proposals to abolish the 10% income tax band.

Weblinks

www.revolts.co.uk — data on, and analysis of, parliamentary rebellions under the Blair and Brown governments from Professor Philip Cowley.

An assertive House of Lords

The 1999 reform of the House of Lords strengthened the upper house and helped it become more assertive in the legislative process. The Lords blocked the Sexual Offences (Amendment) Act (2000) and the Hunting Act (2004), forcing the government to employ the Parliament Act (1949) so that the legislation could come into force without the Lords' consent after a 1-year delay.

In the first decade since the removal of all but 92 hereditary peers, the House of Lords inflicted more than 400 defeats on the government — compared to seven defeats in the Commons. Many of these defeats occurred on judicial and constitutional matters, which are of particular interest to the Lords. Liberal Democrat, Conservative and crossbench peers worked together to defeat Labour's proposals.

Notable examples included:

➤ **Counter-terrorism.** There were several disputes between the Lords and the government over the treatment of terrorist suspects. In 2005, the Lords amended proposals on control orders and only accepted the bill when the government introduced a clause requiring that the Act be replaced a year later.

➤ **Religious hatred.** Government proposals to introduce a new offence of incitement to religious hatred were amended or blocked by the Lords in 2001 and 2005.

➤ **Trial by jury.** The Lords blocked attempts to restrict the right to trial by jury in 2000 and 2007.

The increased effectiveness of the House of Lords in checking the powers of the executive and forcing changes to legislative proposals is a result of a number of factors:

➤ **Party balance.** No party has a majority in the House of Lords, so the government must win cross-party support for its legislation. The votes of Liberal Democrat and crossbench peers were crucial to the fortunes of government proposals under the Blair and Brown governments.

➤ **Enhanced legitimacy.** Since the 1999 reform, the Lords is more confident of its legitimacy and more willing to flex its muscles on legal and constitutional issues.

➤ **Government mandate.** Liberal Democrat and crossbench peers argued that the Blair and Brown governments did not have a mandate to introduce legislation restricting the rights of citizens because they were elected with the support of fewer than a third of the electorate. The Conservative–Liberal Democrat coalition agreement reflects compromises on manifesto commitments made by both parties and was not put before voters directly.

➤ **Support from MPs.** The Lords has been most effective in forcing the government to amend its proposals when MPs have accepted amendments made in the upper house. Backbench support for Lords' amendments limits the prospects of the government overturning the changes. It is then more likely to compromise during the 'parliamentary pingpong' in which bills are passed between the two houses, rather than risk defeat in the Commons or resort to the Parliament Act. Four out of every ten defeats in the Lords were substantially accepted by the Blair and Brown governments.

Weblinks

www.lordsoftheblog.net — a blog on the work of the House of Lords, to which Lord Norton contributes.

Reform of the House of Commons

Extensive reform of the House of Commons was not part of the constitutional reform agenda of the Blair government when it entered power in 1997. The changes it introduced aimed to modernise the Commons' archaic procedures rather than shift power from the executive to the legislature. In opposition, politicians complain about executive dominance of the Commons, but once they win office, this can appear more attractive. The changes made to the Commons included:

➤ **Pre-legislative scrutiny.** Greater scrutiny of draft bills was introduced, before the formal legislative process gets under way.

➤ **Carry-over of legislation.** Bills that fail to get through the legislative process in one parliamentary session can complete the process in the next, provided they pass in one calendar year.

➤ **Modernisation Committee.** This was set up to consider reforms of the Commons' procedures. It recommended changes to working hours to limit late-night sittings. A proposal to create a backbench committee to nominate MPs for select committees was defeated in 2002.

➤ **Liaison Committee.** From 2002, the prime minister faced questions from this committee twice a year. This allows for greater scrutiny than occurs in the more partisan atmosphere of the chamber.

➤ **Prime Minister's Questions.** A single 30-minute slot at noon on Wednesday replaced the two 15-minute slots on Tuesday and Thursday.

➤ **Westminster Hall sittings.** Additional sessions of the House of Commons in Westminster Hall to deal with non-controversial issues and select committee reports.

The devolution of primary legislative powers to the Scottish Parliament and Northern Ireland Assembly — the Welsh Assembly has only secondary legislative powers (see Chapter 10) — has changed procedures of the House of Commons. For example:

➤ Westminster no longer makes law on policies that have been devolved.

➤ Questions on devolved matters can no longer be addressed to UK government ministers at Westminster.

➤ Westminster can make law for Scotland on devolved areas when the Scottish parliament requests that it does so through the 'Sewell motion' procedure.

Reform under Gordon Brown

Gordon Brown proposed further reform of the House of Commons when he became prime minister in 2007. The 'Governance of Britain' Green Paper proposed that parliament be given more say over the exercise of prerogative powers by the executive. Parliament would have the right to vote before the UK went to war, would have a decisive say in the ratification of international treaties, and would vote on a proposal for the dissolution of parliament. The Commons would also hold hearings ahead of key public appointments. Concrete action was limited, but the House of Commons did stage hearings on some public appointments and the Constitutional Reform Act (2010) created a statutory basis for parliamentary scrutiny of treaties. An independent Parliamentary Standards Authority was created in response to the expenses scandal.

Conservative–Liberal Democrat coalition

The 2010 coalition agreement between the Conservatives and Liberal Democrats included provisions for reform of the House of Commons. The key proposals were:

➤ **Fixed-term parliaments.** Parliament will have a fixed 5-year term. The prime minister will no longer be able to decide the date of the general election. The government will still be required to resign if it loses a motion of no confidence, but 55% of MPs must agree to dissolution. This proposal is controversial — it would prevent one of the coalition partners from forcing the government to step down, but would allow it to stay in office if it could not command a bare majority.

➤ **Implementation of the Wright proposals.** A Select Committee on Reform of the House of Commons, chaired by Tony Wright, had recommended in 2009 that: chairs of select committees should be elected by backbenchers; a backbench business committee should determine the business of the Commons for 1 day a week; and a petitions committee should select issues for debate that had been suggested by the public.

➤ **Public reading stage for bills.** Members of the public will be able to comment online on draft bills, with comments discussed on a public reading day at the committee stage of a bill.

➤ **Recall of MPs.** Constituents will have the right to dismiss an MP who has been found guilty of misconduct and force a by-election (see Chapter 1).

➤ **West Lothian Question.** A committee will be established to consider this issue.

➤ **Referendum on AV.** Voters will be offered a choice between the first-past-the-post electoral system and the alternative vote system (see Chapter 2).

Weblinks

www.parliament.uk — select 'Topics' and 'Parliament, government & politics' for current parliamentary material on reform of the Commons.

Reform of the House of Lords

Reform under Blair

Major reform of the House of Lords occurred under the Blair governments. In its 1997 manifesto, Labour proposed that all hereditary peers be removed as a first stage in the reform process. But the government accepted an amendment from the House of Lords that 92 hereditary peers, elected by their fellow peers, would remain until the second stage of the reform process. When the House of Lords Act (1999) entered into force, 655 hereditary peers lost their right to attend and vote. There were no significant changes to the powers of the upper house.

The intention was that this 'transitional house' would not remain in place for long. However, a search for consensus on the composition of the Lords proved fruitless and the second stage of the reform process was not completed. Supporters of a wholly elected or mainly elected upper house claimed that it would have greater legitimacy and be better placed to challenge executive powers. Those who favoured an appointed house argued that an elected upper house would clash with the Commons and would be dominated by party whips.

Viewpoint   Should the House of Lords be wholly elected?

YES

- A fully elected House of Lords would have the legitimacy that can only be derived from democratic elections.
- It would be better placed to scrutinise and amend government bills, improving the quality of legislation.
- If no party has a majority, as would be likely under proportional representation, it would be able to challenge the executive.
- If elected by proportional representation, it would be more representative of the electorate.

NO

- It would come into conflict with the House of Commons, as both would claim democratic legitimacy.
- Institutional conflict between two elected chambers with similar powers would produce legislative gridlock.
- An appointed house would retain the expertise and independence of crossbench peers.
- The shortcomings of party control found in the House of Commons would be duplicated in an elected upper house.

Further proposals for reform

A series of proposals for Lords reform have been made since 1999, but none has garnered sufficient support within the cabinet or parliament. The main proposals have been:

> **Report of the Royal Commission on Reform of the House of Lords, 2000.** Headed by former Conservative minister Lord Wakeham, the commission recommended that the majority of peers be appointed, with 20% recommended by

an independent appointments body. Between 12% and 35% would be elected by proportional representation. The remaining hereditary peers would be removed.

➤ **White Paper, 2001.** This proposed that 20% of peers be elected, but the figure was criticised for being too low and was dropped. MPs were given a free vote in February 2003 on seven options proposed by a parliamentary joint committee. None attracted majority support. Blair's favoured option, an all-appointed house, proved the least popular. An 80% elected house was defeated by just three votes. In the Lords, peers voted for a fully appointed house.

➤ **White Paper, 2003.** This proposed a wholly appointed house, but was widely criticised. In its 2005 manifesto, Labour proposed to set a limit of 60 sitting days for the consideration of most bills in the Lords.

➤ **White Paper, 2007.** This proposed a hybrid house: 50% appointed and 50% elected. A series of votes on reform options were held in parliament. A wholly elected house was approved, as was the 80% elected option (see Table 7.5). But some MPs who backed the former were trying to wreck the process, knowing that ministers had doubts about it. The Lords again voted for a wholly appointed house.

➤ **White Paper, 2008.** This explored how a wholly elected or 80% elected house might function, with members chosen over three elections.

Table 7.5 Votes on House of Lords reform, March 2007

Option	House of Commons			House of Lords		
	For	**Against**	**Majority**	**For**	**Against**	**Majority**
100% appointed	196	375	−179	361	121	+240
50% elected	155	418	−263	46	410	−364
60% elected	178	392	−214	45	393	−348
80% elected	305	267	+38	114	336	−222
100% elected	337	224	+113	122	326	−204
Abolish upper house	163	416	−253	–	–	–
Remove hereditary peers	391	111	+280	–	–	–

More than a decade after stage one of Lords reform took effect, the transitional house remained in place. There is wide agreement on removing the remaining hereditaries, strengthening the Appointments Commission and reducing the size of the house. The Conservative–Lib Dem coalition that took office in 2010 agreed to establish a committee to bring forward proposals for a wholly or mainly elected upper house, elected by proportional representation. Meanwhile, appointments would be made with the objective of creating a chamber that reflected the share of the vote won by parties in 2010.

Weblinks

www.guardian.co.uk/politics/lordreform — coverage of Lords reform from the *Guardian* newspaper.

⏵ **What you should know**

⏵ The UK has a system of parliamentary government in which government takes place through parliament. There is a fusion rather than separation of powers. The executive is the dominant actor, but its ability to control proceedings in parliament is affected by the size of its majority, the extent of party unity and the assertiveness of the House of Lords.

⏵ Parliament comprises the monarchy, the House of Lords and the House of Commons. The House of Commons is the dominant chamber. It consists of 650 MPs who are directly elected. Almost all are members of a political party. The House of Lords is a revising chamber and can delay legislation for a year. It is unelected. Since the 1999 reform that removed all but 92 hereditary peers, life peers make up the largest category of members. The judicial role of the House of Lords ended in 2009.

⏵ Parliament is the supreme legislative body in the UK. But parliament is a policy-influencing rather than policy-making institution. Most successful bills originate from the government. Party discipline and government control of the parliamentary timetable ensure that most government proposals are accepted by the House of Commons.

⏵ Parliament debates important issues, scrutinises government actions and holds it to account. Select committees carry out detailed examinations of the activities of government departments, but the government is not required to accept their recommendations.

⏵ Reforms of the House of Commons under Labour did not strengthen parliament significantly. The MPs' expenses scandal weakened public trust in parliament. The under-representation of women and rise of career politicians also damages the image of parliament.

⏵ Reform of the House of Lords stalled after the completion of the first stage in 1999. Support has grown for a wholly elected or mainly elected upper house. This would enhance the legitimacy of the second chamber, but might create tensions between the Lords and Commons.

UK/US comparison

US Congress and UK Parliament

➤ The US Congress is a bicameral legislature. The lower chamber is the House of Representatives, which consists of 435 elected members. The Senate, which consists of 100 elected members, is the upper chamber. The two chambers have broadly equal powers. In the UK, only the House of Commons is elected. The unelected House of Lords is politically and legally subordinate.

➤ Congress is a policy-making legislature. It can reject or amend proposals from the president, and puts forward legislative proposals of its own. Most proposals come from the president, who has the power of veto — although this can be overridden by Congress. The UK parliament is a policy-influencing legislature that modifies government proposals, but does not propose extensive bills of its own.

➤ There is a strict separation of powers in the USA. Members of the executive branch cannot be members of the legislature. The president cannot dismiss Congress, but Congress can impeach the president. The US Constitution also gives Congress the power to declare war, and Senate the power to veto appointments made by the president.

➤ Party discipline has grown stronger in the USA, but it is still weaker than in the UK. A president cannot rely on the support of members of his own party in Congress. Members of Congress are more likely than MPs to place the interests of their constituents above those of party.

➤ Standing committees in Congress have significant influence over US government departments. Committee chairs are powerful figures in Congress. Departmental select committees in the UK are much less powerful.

Further reading

Childs, S. and Campbell, R. (2009) 'Women's representation in parliament', *Politics Review*, Vol. 18, No. 3, pp. 8–10.

Cowley, P. (2005) *The Rebels: How Blair Mislaid His Majority*, Methuen.

Cowley, P. (2008) 'The House of Commons: unimportant, unreformable, unrepresentative and unloved?', *Politics Review*, Vol. 18, No. 2, pp. 2–5.

Fairclough, P. and Magee, E. (2009) 'MPs' expenses: an end to the gravy train?', *Politics Review*, Vol. 19, No. 4, pp. 5–7.

Grant, M. (2009) *The UK Parliament*, Edinburgh University Press, 2009.

Norton, P. (2005) *Parliament in British Politics*, Palgrave.

Russell, M. (2007) 'The House of Lords: reform past and future', *Politics Review*, Vol. 17, No. 1, pp. 2–5.

Exam focus

Short-answer questions (around 5 minutes each)

Explain, using examples, the meaning of each of the following terms:

1 Parliament
2 The Westminster model
3 Bicameralism
4 Scrutiny

Mid-length questions (around 10 minutes each)

Outline two arguments 'for' and two arguments 'against' each of the following:

1 Unelected peers
2 Commons reform

Outline the main differences between:

3 MPs and peers
4 Public Bill (or 'standing') committees and departmental select committees

Mini-essays (around 25–30 minutes each)

Write a mini-essay in response to each of the following questions:

1 'Departmental select committees are toothless watchdogs.' Discuss.
2 'Parliament does not perform any of its functions particularly well.' Discuss.
3 Critically assess the arguments in favour of a fully elected second chamber.
4 Discuss the view that the UK Parliament has been reduced to the status of a 'rubber stamp'.

Chapter 8

The prime minister and the core executive

Key questions answered in this chapter

➢ What powers does the prime minister have?

➢ What are the constraints on the prime minister's power?

➢ What role does the cabinet play?

➢ In what circumstances do government ministers resign?

➢ Where does power lie within the executive?

The **executive** is the branch of government concerned with the formulation and implementation of policy. In the UK system of parliamentary government, all ministers are drawn from parliament and are accountable to it. The **prime minister** and **cabinet** are the main institutions within the executive.

Key terms

➢ **Cabinet** The committee of senior cabinet ministers that is the main collective decision-making body of the government.

➢ **Executive** The branch of government responsible for policy making and policy implementation.

➢ **Prime minister** The head of government and of the executive branch. The prime minister chairs the cabinet.

The prime minister

The prime minister is the head of the government. He or she provides political leadership within the cabinet system and the country at large, chairs the cabinet, appoints ministers and is leader of the largest party in the House of Commons. The office of prime minister emerged in the early eighteenth century and gradually became the accepted title for the person who is still officially the First Lord of the Treasury. Robert Walpole (1721–42) is generally recognised as the first prime minister because he commanded majority support in the Commons and cabinet, stamping his imprint on government. King George II gave 10 Downing Street to the office of First Lord of the Treasury. From the start of the twentieth century, prime ministers have used it as their official residence and home. Details of UK prime ministers since the Second World War are given in Table 8.1.

Table 8.1 Postwar British prime ministers

Prime minister	Period in office	Governing party
Clement Attlee	1945–51	Labour
Winston Churchill	1951–55	Conservative
Anthony Eden	1955–57	Conservative
Harold Macmillan	1957–63	Conservative
Alec Douglas-Home	1963–64	Conservative
Harold Wilson	1964–70	Labour
Edward Heath	1970–74	Conservative
Harold Wilson	1974–76	Labour
James Callaghan	1976–79	Labour
Margaret Thatcher	1979–90	Conservative
John Major	1990–97	Conservative
Tony Blair	1997–2007	Labour
Gordon Brown	2007–10	Labour
David Cameron	2010–	Conservative–Liberal Democrat

Requirements of a prime minister

Three requirements must be fulfilled for a person to become prime minister. First, he or she must be a member of the Westminster Parliament. Until the late nineteenth century, the prime minister was usually a member of the House of Lords. As the House of Commons then emerged as the dominant chamber, it became a constitutional convention that the prime minister should be an MP in the Commons. When Harold Macmillan resigned as prime minister in 1963, the Earl of Home replaced him. He renounced his hereditary peerage to be known as Alec Douglas-Home, and stood successfully in a by-election for the Commons.

Secondly, he or she must be leader of a political party. The prime minister must command the support of his or her party. If they are forced to step down as leader of their party, they also relinquish the office of prime minister, as happened when Margaret Thatcher failed to achieve victory in the Conservative Party leadership election in 1990. Five postwar prime ministers took office having become party leader when the incumbent stood down. The most recent were John Major, who succeeded Thatcher in 1990, and Gordon Brown, who took over from Tony Blair in 2007. The prime minister is not required to call an immediate general election in these circumstances.

Thirdly, the political party that he or she leads should normally be the majority party in the House of Commons. Winning a general election is the most common route to becoming prime minister. The monarch invites the leader of the party that has won a majority of seats to form a government. Thatcher and Blair became prime minister as a result of their election victories (each won three). Prime ministers defeated in a general election (e.g. Major in 1997) are required to resign. **Majority governments** are the norm at Westminster. A 'hung parliament' occurs when no party has an absolute majority of seats. In such circumstances, the incumbent prime minister is not required to resign immediately but is given the chance to negotiate with other parties to form either a **minority government** or a **coalition government**. The 2010 general election produced a hung parliament and a Conservative–Liberal Democrat coalition government was formed (see Box 8.1).

The 2010 general election resulted in a coalition government

Majority, minority and coalition government

Distinguish between

Majority government

➤ One political party has an absolute majority of seats in the House of Commons and forms the government.

➤ Government ministers are members of this one party.

Minority government

➤ No political party has an absolute majority of seats in the House of Commons.

➤ A party without a majority (often, but not necessarily, the largest party) forms a government but must try to secure support from other parties for key measures.

➤ Government ministers are members of this one party.

Coalition government

➤ No political party has an absolute majority of seats in the House of Commons.

➤ Two or more parties agree a deal to form a government, following negotiations and a formal agreement on policy.

➤ Ministerial positions in the government are shared between two or more parties.

Weblinks

www.number10.gov.uk — includes details of the office of prime minister and its holders.

Box 8.1 Hung parliament

If a general election produces a hung parliament in which no party has an absolute majority of seats, a minority government or a coalition government may emerge. A second general election may also be called within a short period of time.

The February 1974 and 2010 general elections produced hung parliaments. In the former, Labour won 301 seats and the Conservatives 297, although the Conservatives polled more votes. Defeated Conservative prime minister Edward Heath exercised his constitutional right as incumbent to try to form a government, but negotiations with the Liberals and Ulster Unionists failed. Heath resigned and the Queen invited Labour leader Harold Wilson to form a minority government. Wilson called another general election in October 1974 and won a slender three-seat majority.

In 2010 the Conservative Party won 307 seats, falling 19 short of an absolute majority. Prime minister Gordon Brown stayed in office but Liberal Democrat leader Nick Clegg negotiated with the Conservatives first because they had won more seats and votes. They initially discussed a 'confidence and supply' deal in which the Liberal Democrats would support a Conservative minority government on key votes in the House of Commons (e.g. the Queen's Speech and budget).

When talks with the Conservatives entered a fourth day, Clegg also opened formal negotiations with Labour. Brown had announced that he would stand down as Labour leader by the autumn. Many Liberal Democrat MPs were ideologically closer to Labour than to the Conservatives, but a Labour–Liberal Democrat coalition would not have had a parliamentary majority and would have needed the support of several smaller parties. The vocal opposition of some Labour MPs raised further doubts about a deal. Five days after the election, the Conservatives and Liberal Democrats agreed to form a coalition government with a detailed policy programme. (The average duration of coalition negotiations in the EU is 40 days.) Both parties made compromises, dropping manifesto commitments on taxation, immigration, electoral reform and Europe. Brown resigned and David Cameron became prime minister. Five Liberal Democrats joined the coalition cabinet, with Clegg as deputy prime minister.

Role of the prime minister

The role of the prime minister is not set out in statute law. Tony Blair claimed that 'it is not possible to precisely define' the role. The key functions of the post have become accepted as constitutional conventions. They are:

➤ **Political leadership.** The prime minister decides the political direction taken by the government, setting its priorities and broad strategy. He or she will determine (or at least shape) policy, particularly on high-profile issues.

➤ **National leadership.** The prime minister is the predominant political figure in the UK and provides national leadership at times of crisis such as war or terrorist attack. The heightened media focus on the prime minister has furthered their role as communicator-in-chief for the government.

➤ **Appointing the government.** The prime minister determines the membership of his or her cabinet and government, appointing and dismissing ministers.

- **Chairing the cabinet.** The prime minister chairs meetings of the cabinet, sets its agenda and steers its decisions. He or she also creates and makes appointments to cabinet committees, and holds bilateral meetings with ministers.
- **Managing the executive.** The prime minister is responsible for the overall organisation of the government and is head of the civil service. He or she can create or merge government departments, and reform the civil service.
- **Managing relations with parliament.** The prime minister makes statements to, and answers questions in, the House of Commons. He or she also shapes the government's legislative programme.
- **Representing the UK in international affairs.** As head of government, the prime minister represents the UK in the European Union, international organisations and meetings with other leaders.

Powers of the prime minister

The significance of these roles gives the prime minister greater resources than other cabinet ministers. However, these roles do not automatically produce prime ministerial power. The resources available to the prime minister are subject to important constraints and will vary according to circumstances.

The main resources available to the prime minister are:

- patronage
- authority within the cabinet system
- party leadership
- public standing
- policy-making role
- the Prime Minister's Office

Patronage

The prime minister has important powers of **patronage** that are not available to other cabinet ministers. The most significant is the power to appoint government ministers (see below). Other elements of the prime minister's patronage powers include:

> **Key terms**
> **Patronage** The power of an individual to appoint someone to an important position.

- **Judicial and ecclesiastical appointments.** Until recently, the prime minister was responsible for appointing judges, senior members of the Church of England and the heads of numerous public bodies. But the prime minister's direct role has been greatly reduced since the 2007 'Governance of Britain' Green Paper (Cm 7170). He or she now plays no role in judicial appointments, and is given only one name to approve for ecclesiastical appointments.
- **The honours system.** The prime minister's role in the honours system has also been reduced. A police inquiry into allegations of 'cash for honours' — that wealthy donors to the Labour Party were rewarded (or enticed) with peerages — ended in

2007 without any criminal charges being brought. Blair subsequently announced that the prime minister would not add or remove names from the final list presented by the independent Honours Committee.

➤ **Life peers.** The prime minister can appoint people to the House of Lords in order to give them ministerial positions. In 2007 Gordon Brown gave government portfolios and life peerages to five prominent public figures who were not politicians, including former CBI head Sir Digby Jones and former navy chief Sir Alan West. Most of the so-called 'goats' — Brown spoke of a 'government of all talents' — made little impact and left office within 2 years. Brown also gave Peter Mandelson a seat in the Lords on his return to government. The power to nominate life peers also enables prime ministers to alter the party balance within the Lords. Blair appointed a large number of Labour peers before embarking on reform of the upper house. An independent Appointments Commission now makes recommendations on non-party appointments to the Lords, but the prime minister still makes political nominations.

Appointing cabinet ministers

The prime minister's power to appoint and dismiss government ministers, particularly at cabinet level, gives him or her a crucial advantage over colleagues. The Conservative Party gives its leader a free hand in appointing cabinet ministers. But since 1981, a Labour prime minister forming his or her first cabinet after a spell in opposition must select it from those MPs who had been elected to the shadow cabinet. This tied Blair's hands in 1997 but not in 2001 or 2005.

In theory, prime ministers can create a cabinet in their own image, rewarding supporters and penalising disloyal MPs. In practice, however, the prime minister does not have a free hand.

A prime minister is unlikely to overlook senior party figures, some of whom may be rivals for their job. John Major's opponents in the 1990 Conservative Party leadership election, Michael Heseltine and Douglas Hurd, were given cabinet posts. John Prescott and Margaret Beckett lost out to Blair in the 1995 Labour leadership contest but were included in his cabinet. Senior politicians may have claims to office because of their high profile or standing within the party. Some might have sufficient clout to demand a post of their own choosing. Gordon Brown was a striking example. Brown agreed not to stand in the 1995 Labour leadership election in order to improve Blair's chances of victory. In return, Brown gained assurances that he would become chancellor of the exchequer in a future Labour government and would exercise significant influence over other areas of government policy. David Cameron had to include senior Conservatives and Liberal Democrats in his coalition cabinet in 2010. Liberal Democrat leader Nick Clegg became deputy prime minister.

Ideological considerations are also important when constructing a government. A cabinet that contains politicians from only one wing of a party may not have the full support of that party. Before she established a strong grip on the levers of power,

Margaret Thatcher included both economic 'dries' (Thatcherites) and 'wets' (one-nation Conservatives) in her cabinet, but gave her allies the key positions. In the 1990s, Major ensured that both the pro-European and Eurosceptic wings of his party were represented in cabinet, but he sought to prevent either from garnering enough strength to challenge his authority directly. Blair's cabinets contained mainly 'New' Labour politicians, although traditional 'Old' Labour was appeased by the appointment of John Prescott as deputy prime minister. When Gordon Brown was facing unrest within the Labour Party in 2008, he strengthened his position by bringing the prominent Blairite Lord (Peter) Mandelson back into the cabinet. Five Liberal Democrats sat in the 2010 coalition cabinet, alongside Conservatives from the left and right of the party.

The prime minister's choice of ministers is constrained by the talent available in the party. Rising stars should be promoted to give them experience of government. A party that has had a long spell in power, such as the Conservatives in the 1990s, may become stale.

Cabinet reshuffles

Prime ministers can also reshuffle cabinet portfolios. Some ministers might be moved to another post and others dismissed entirely. This allows the prime minister to promote successful ministers, demote those who have underachieved and freshen up the team. Ministers whose continued presence might damage the standing of the government can be axed. The prime minister decides the timing of a **cabinet reshuffle**, but a sudden resignation may force an unwanted reshuffle.

Key terms

➤ **Cabinet reshuffle** A series of changes to the personnel of the cabinet and the positions they occupy, instigated by the prime minister.

The power to dismiss cabinet ministers is a blunt weapon that can blow up in the prime minister's face. A botched reshuffle may raise questions about the prime minister's judgement, reveal cabinet divisions and highlight policy failings. This was true of Harold Macmillan's 1962 reshuffle, dubbed the 'night of the long knives', in which he sacked seven cabinet ministers. Thatcher's demotion of foreign secretary Sir Geoffrey Howe in 1989 also had damaging consequences. Howe's anger eventually boiled over in 1990, when he resigned from the cabinet and launched a withering attack on the prime minister that helped bring about her downfall. John Major was accused of not being ruthless enough with troubled ministers. Norman Lamont survived as chancellor for 9 months after sterling's exit from the exchange rate mechanism (ERM) in 1992. Major also seemed reluctant to sack ministers embroiled in personal scandal, such as David Mellor. Blair speedily dismissed ministers whose behaviour was questioned, notably his close ally Peter Mandelson who was twice forced to leave the cabinet.

After the 2005 election, Blair was forced to negotiate the distribution of some cabinet positions with his heir apparent, Gordon Brown. Having announced that he would not serve a full term, Blair found that ministers were already considering how they might

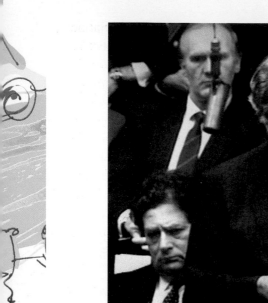

After Sir Geoffrey Howe's resignation in 1990 he launched a withering attack on the prime minister that helped bring about her downfall

curry favour with Brown. The refusal of ministers to change posts may also thwart a prime minister's plans. Brown intended to make Ed Balls chancellor of the exchequer in a 2009 reshuffle, but the incumbent, Alastair Darling, let it be known that he would refuse to accept another post. Fearing the political damage that the resignation of his chancellor would cause, Brown relented. David Cameron was obliged to discuss appointments to his cabinet with Nick Clegg, with Liberal Democrats appointed to ministerial positions in most major government departments.

Authority in the cabinet system

With the post of prime minister comes specific authority within the core executive. The prime minister thus:

> chairs cabinet meetings
> manages the agenda of cabinet meetings, and determines their frequency and length
> directs and sums up cabinet discussions
> creates cabinet committees and appoints their members
> holds bilateral meetings with ministers
> appoints senior civil servants
> organises the structure of government

This authority gives the prime minister a significant advantage over other cabinet ministers. As chair of the cabinet, the prime minister steers discussions and sums up. Skilful prime ministers can use this role to ensure that their favoured position prevails. However, if a group of senior ministers promote an alternative viewpoint, the prime minister may not get his or her way so easily. Poor management of the cabinet by a prime minister who is too domineering or too indecisive will ultimately weaken his or her authority. An effective prime minister will direct much government policy but act as coordinator or broker on disputed issues. It is the prime minister's role to direct the government's general strategy, giving a sense of purpose, cohesion and direction.

Agenda setting

The prime minister can determine the agenda of cabinet meetings by:

- controlling the information presented to ministers by determining which issues and papers should be brought before cabinet
- keeping potentially difficult issues off the agenda of the full cabinet and dealing with them in a cabinet committee or in **bilateral** discussions with the relevant minister instead
- deciding the chair, membership and remit of cabinet committees, where much detailed policy work occurs

> **Key terms**
> - **Bilateral** A meeting between the prime minister and a departmental minister in which policy is agreed.

The prime minister can also establish committees to examine issues that he or she wants to promote. But the prime minister is unlikely to take a direct role in proceedings and cannot control all aspects of decision making at this level.

While in office, a prime minister can significantly reshape the structure and top personnel of central government. Government departments might be restructured. Harold Wilson created a short-lived Ministry of Economic Affairs to rival the Treasury in the late 1960s. Blair merged responsibility for the environment and agriculture in a new Department for the Environment, Food and Rural Affairs in 2001. Cameron was advised against making significant changes to the machinery of government by senior civil servants. The prime minister also makes appointments to the top posts in the civil service and can reform the role and organisation of the civil service as a whole.

Party leadership

The prime minister is the leader of the largest party in the House of Commons. A working majority in parliament strengthens the position of the prime minister, as it means that he or she is more likely to enjoy the confidence of the Commons and be able to enact the government's policy programme. The executive exerts significant control over the legislative process through, for example, party discipline and the parliamentary timetable. However, the increased incidence of rebellion by backbench MPs unwilling to follow the party whip on controversial issues suggests that a prime minister cannot regard MPs in his or her party as 'lobby fodder' who will vote for the government come what may. Blair suffered sizeable rebellions on the war in Iraq, university tuition fees and foundation hospitals in his second term. In his first year in office, Brown made concessions to rebel Labour MPs on the abolition of the 10p income tax band.

Party leadership strengthens the authority of the prime minister. Labour and Conservative leaders are elected by their MPs and party members. This legitimises their position and policy programme. A prime minister is unlikely to face a leadership challenge if he or she won strong support from across the party in a leadership election. The length, cost and complexity of the leadership election process also make the sudden removal of a prime minister by his or her party less likely.

A party's support for its leader is not unconditional. Thatcher was forced out of Downing Street when she failed to muster sufficient support from Conservative MPs to win the 1990 leadership contest. The party leadership rules at that time dictated that the leader could face an annual leadership challenge even if he or she were also prime minister. Major resigned as leader of the Conservative Party — but not as prime minister — in 1995, calling a leadership contest in the hope that this would reassert his authority. Major secured a 218 to 89 vote victory over the Eurosceptic John Redwood, who had resigned from the cabinet to stand against him, but one-third of the party failed to support him.

Blair enjoyed great authority within his party in his first years in office, having secured two landslide election victories and reformed Labour's organisation so as to enhance the position of the leader. But support for Blair within the Labour Party waned after the launch of the war in Iraq in 2003. Ahead of the 2005 general election, Blair announced that he would not serve another full term as prime minister. But this did not satisfy some supporters of Gordon Brown, who launched failed attempts to oust Blair during his third term. A junior minister and six ministerial aides resigned in an attempt to force a change of leadership in 2006, but the rebellion petered out. Blair finally stepped down in June 2007, before he had originally intended, because support for him in the Labour Party was ebbing away.

Brown became prime minister having being elected as Labour leader unopposed. But he too had to survive efforts by Labour MPs to force him out. In 2009, James Purnell resigned from the cabinet and called for Brown to step down, while an attempt by former cabinet ministers Geoff Hoon and Patricia Hewitt to force a secret ballot on Brown's leadership failed in early 2010. There was unease among right-wing Conservative MPs about the policy compromises that David Cameron had made when forming a coalition with the Liberal Democrats in 2010.

Public standing

The prime minister enjoys a high public profile. He or she provides political leadership at home and represents the UK in international affairs. The prime minister has regular discussions with other world leaders and attends formal meetings of heads of government, such as European Union summits. Thatcher and Blair made a significant impact on the world stage, in part because they both forged a strong relationship with the president of the United States.

The media spotlight has focused more on the prime minister in recent years. The prime minister has taken on the role of communicator-in-chief for the government, articulating its policy programme and objectives. The prime minister's monthly press conferences and twice-yearly appearances before the House of Commons Liaison

Committee are a formal expression of this. Opinion polls record far higher levels of public recognition of the prime minister than other ministers. High ratings in the polls strengthen the prime minister's position: a prime minister who is regarded as a strong and effective leader by a majority of people has much greater authority and room for manoeuvre than one who is perceived as weak or out of touch.

Thatcher polarised public opinion during her period in office, but she was widely regarded as a determined leader with a clear agenda. This image was a profitable one for much of her premiership, but towards the end she became associated with unpopular policies (e.g. the poll tax) and was regarded as autocratic. Major enjoyed record poll ratings in the 1991 Gulf War, but his popularity fell sharply when his government ran into a series of problems. Blair enjoyed high poll ratings during his first term, but the war in Iraq damaged his standing, after which he was trusted by fewer voters. Brown was seen as competent and experienced when he first became prime minister, but his personal standing plummeted to a record low in the polls in 2009.

Policy-making input

The prime minister's policy-making role is not confined to a specific field. Instead, he or she has licence to get involved in issues across the political spectrum. A prime minister with a strong interest in an issue can give it a central place in the government's programme.

The prime minister is the most important actor when political crises occur. Prime ministers will also take an active interest in economic and foreign policy. The chancellor of the exchequer and foreign secretary are powerful actors in their own right, but the prime minister is likely to play an active role in setting objectives, and directing and coordinating policy in these crucial areas. The prime minister needs the backing of senior figures on controversial matters. Chancellor Nigel Lawson and foreign secretary Geoffrey Howe forced Thatcher to shift government policy on the ERM in 1989 by threatening to resign if she continued to rule out British entry.

Thatcher was a hands-on politician who played an active role in many policy fields. Instances of policy success (e.g. the 1982 Falklands War) strengthened her position. But in the case of the poll tax, policy failure undermined her authority. Both Major and Blair chose to play an active role in the Northern Ireland peace process. Blair sidelined secretary of state for Northern Ireland Mo Mowlam in the final stages of talks on the 1998 Good Friday Agreement, taking charge of the negotiations himself. Despite the rapid removal of Saddam Hussein, the 2003 invasion of Iraq undermined Blair's position. Blair's support for the American-led invasion and doubts about the government's case for war raised questions about his judgement and trustworthiness.

Neither Major nor Blair enjoyed the success they hoped for in some domestic policy areas on which they focused their energies. Major's Citizen's Charter changed the nature of governance in the UK, but it did not bring great political reward. Blair's efforts to improve health and education bore fruit slowly: public spending increased by 40%

between 1997 and 2002, but productivity rose by only 14%. During his 10 years as chancellor, Brown forged a strong reputation for economic competence, but the credit crunch and recession undermined his economic credibility when he was prime minister. David Cameron's room for manoeuvre was limited by the formal agreement on policy reached by the Conservative–Liberal Democrat coalition.

The Prime Minister's Office

The prime minister does not head a government department, nor is there a formal prime minister's department. Within **10 Downing Street**, however, lies the **Prime Minister's Office** and this has grown in importance in the last 20 years. Its staff of some 190 people contains a mix of career civil servants and special advisers, the latter being political appointees from outside government.

Key terms

➤ **10 Downing Street** The residence and office of the prime minister. 'Number 10' and 'Downing Street' are sometimes used to refer to the Prime Minister's Office.

➤ **Prime Minister's Office** The group of senior civil servants and special advisers, based at 10 Downing Street, who provide advice and support for the prime minister, particularly on policy and communications with government, parliament and the media.

The Prime Minister's Office has a number of different roles, which are carried out by individual directorates and units. A reorganisation in 2001 bolstered two important aspects of the work of the Prime Minister's Office:

➤ **Policy advice.** The Prime Minister's Office provides the prime minister with policy advice, and may offer alternative views to those that he or she receives from cabinet ministers. Prime ministers appoint their own senior advisers on Europe and foreign affairs, for example. The Prime Minister's Office also engages in strategic thinking, helping the prime minister to forge the future direction of government policy. In recent years, it has also had an important role coordinating policy making and policy implementation across government.

➤ **Communications.** The Prime Minister's Office is also responsible for the presentation of government policy and for relations with the media. This role has grown in importance as the media focus on the prime minister has intensified. Thatcher's press officer, Bernard Ingham, was one of her most important advisers. Alasdair Campbell, as press officer and then communications director, was an influential member of Blair's inner circle. But overall responsibility for government communications was transferred to a senior civil servant in 2004 following criticism of the politicisation of communications.

In the 1980s and 1990s, some commentators argued that a prime minister's department was needed to better direct and coordinate government activity. The strengthening of the Prime Minister's Office that took place under Blair, and the changes that saw the

Cabinet Office serve the prime minister more directly, meant that something akin to a prime minister's department now existed in practice if not in name. Blair's reforms established a template for the Prime Minister's Office that was accepted by both Brown (although it did not function as effectively in his premiership) and Conservative leader David Cameron.

Viewpoint — Do the resources the prime minister has bring him or her significant power?

	YES	NO
Patronage	Appoints ministers.	Senior colleagues have claims to posts.
	Can place allies in key roles.	Desirability of ideological balance.
	Dismisses ministers.	Botched reshuffles create rivals.
	Can appoint outsiders to government.	Availability of talent.
Authority in the cabinet system	Chairs and manages cabinet meetings.	Problems arise if senior ministers feel ignored.
	Steers, and sums up cabinet discussions.	Senior ministers may challenge prime minister's policy preference.
	Creates cabinet committees and appoints their members.	Not involved in detailed policy making in cabinet committees.
	Uses bilateral meetings with ministers to steer policy.	Ministers represent departmental interests.
Party leadership	Authority as party leader.	Support of party is not unconditional.
	Elected as leader by MPs and party members.	Party rules allow for a leadership challenge.
	Party normally has majority in the House of Commons.	Backbench rebellions have become more frequent.
Public standing	Has higher public profile than other ministers.	Unpopularity with voters undermines authority.
	Communicator-in-chief for the government.	Blamed for government's failings.
	National leader in times of crisis.	Expected to represent the public mood.
Policy-making role	Directs government policy and sets agenda.	Expected to be able to articulate a vision.
	Can direct policy in areas of their choosing.	Lacks time and expertise.
	Represents UK in international affairs.	Globalisation has reduced scope for action.
Prime Minister's Office	Provides advice and support.	Has limited resources.

Prime ministerial leadership style

The structural advantages that the office of prime minister brings its incumbent are important but not sufficient for an understanding of the location of power within the

Concepts explained

Leadership

Political leadership is the exercise of power over public policy making by an individual or institution. The study of political leadership has focused on institutional structures (e.g. the offices of president and prime minister), relations between leaders and followers, the personality traits of leaders (e.g. their charisma) and styles of leadership. On the latter, James Macgregor Burns' book *Leadership* (1978) identified three styles of leader:

➤ laissez-faire leaders, who adopt a hands-off approach to issues and delegate decision-making responsibility

➤ transactional leaders, who favour collective decision making and broker compromise deals

➤ transformational leaders, who are conviction politicians and seek to impose their own strong views

John Major is an example of a transactional leader, while Margaret Thatcher and Tony Blair were transformational leaders.

executive. Power is not static, but dynamic. The context in which a prime minister operates is significant. Policy success and a large parliamentary majority, for example, can strengthen a prime minister's position considerably. But policy failure, divisions within their political party and unforeseen crises can weaken them. For Harold Macmillan, it was 'events, dear boy, events' that a prime minister feared.

A prime minister's style of **leadership** is vital. Vision and political will are important here, as are the prime minister's relationship with the cabinet and senior ministers.

Thatcher as prime minister

Margaret Thatcher made less use of cabinet than her predecessors. Detailed policy work was done in cabinet committees or in bilateral meetings with ministers. Thatcher often began cabinet discussions by announcing the government's policy and kept some issues away from the cabinet. Senior ministers like Nigel Lawson accused her of paying greater attention to her advisers than to cabinet ministers.

Early in her premiership, Thatcher's skilful management of the cabinet enabled her to cement her authority at a time when many ministers doubted her policies. Her refusal to bow to pressure to tone down the monetarist budget of 1981 — and her colleagues' unwillingness to flex their muscles — proved decisive. Thatcher was then able to construct a cabinet of ideological allies.

By 1990, Thatcher had few loyal allies left in the cabinet. Chancellor John Major exploited her relative weakness to persuade Thatcher to agree entry into the exchange rate mechanism (ERM) — a policy she had previously opposed. Within weeks, Thatcher had failed to win on the first ballot of the Conservative leadership election. She then met her cabinet ministers one by one, but few offered their full support and Thatcher resigned. Economic problems, unpopular policies, cabinet divisions and low opinion poll ratings were factors in her downfall. However, Thatcher was in part the author of her own misfortune. By ignoring the concerns of ministers and bypassing cabinet, she had not strengthened her position but weakened it, alienating colleagues whose support she needed. When Thatcher was vulnerable, ministers struck back.

Weblinks

www.margaretthatcher.org — website of the Margaret Thatcher Foundation, with an archive of the former prime minister's speeches.

Major as prime minister

John Major adopted a more collegiate style. Cabinet once again discussed government policy and exercised greater influence over policy direction. Major has been portrayed as a weak prime minister. He failed to put across a clear vision, was unable to set the political agenda and appeared overwhelmed by events. But Major recognised the limitations of his authority, managing his cabinet in a way that ensured he stayed in office for over 6 years despite never appearing totally secure. Although he undoubtedly made mistakes, Major could be tactically astute. He used cabinet meetings to bind both pro-European and Eurosceptic ministers to government policy on Europe. By working closely with senior figures such as Michael Heseltine and Kenneth Clarke, he lessened the chances of a serious rival for his job emerging.

Blair as prime minister

In Blair's first years in office, seasoned observers of prime ministerial power such as Peter Hennessy, Dennis Kavanagh and Michael Foley depicted him as a more dominant prime minister than Major and even Thatcher. For Hennessy, Blair's was a 'command premiership', while Kavanagh described Blair's leadership style as 'Napoleonic'. As we will see, Foley argued that the Blair era offered confirmation of the 'presidentialisation' of the office of prime minister. Blair took key decisions and acted as communicator-in-chief for the government.

Blair had little time for cabinet government, preferring to conduct government business through bilateral meetings in which he agreed policy objectives with individual ministers. Key decisions were reached in informal meetings of Blair's inner circle of advisers. This style of government was dubbed 'sofa government'. This informality and neglect of the cabinet system was criticised by the former head of the home civil service, Lord Butler, in his 2004 report on the use of intelligence on Iraq's weapons of mass destruction. Butler was 'concerned that the informality and circumscribed character of the government's procedures which we saw in the context of policy-making towards Iraq risks reducing the scope for informed collective political judgement'.

Blair also strengthened the Prime Minister's Office and brought parts of the Cabinet Office within the prime minister's remit. He sought to command swathes of government policy from Downing Street and improve policy coordination and delivery. Numerous taskforces and special units were created to do this, and the number of special advisers doubled. But devolution, European integration and the decision to grant the Bank of England the power to set interest rates removed some policies from the remit of the executive.

In his first two terms in office, Blair enjoyed a number of advantages that had eluded Major: big parliamentary majorities, a strong position within his party and a largely loyal cabinet. But he faced large-scale rebellions by Labour MPs on Iraq, foundation hospitals and tuition fees in his second term, and his opinion poll ratings fell. Labour won a third election in 2005, but its reduced majority limited Blair's room for manoeuvre. Blair's announcement that he would step down during this third term also weakened his authority and he had to fend off attempts from within his own party to hasten his departure. By stepping down in June 2007, Blair may well have jumped before he was pushed. But it would be too simplistic to write Blair off as a lame duck after 2005 because he extended his public sector reform agenda and brokered the return of devolution in Northern Ireland.

Despite the prime minister's 'command leadership', the Blair government was unusual for the extent of chancellor of the exchequer Gordon Brown's influence. Commentators talked of a 'dual monarchy' in which Blair and Brown had their own spheres of influence and 'courts' (i.e. teams of loyal ministers and advisers). They met regularly to bargain about policy. Blair allowed Brown unparalleled influence in policy areas such as pensions, enterprise and welfare-to-work that stretched beyond a chancellor's usual domain. Comprehensive spending reviews allowed Brown to shape government priorities in these areas.

The relationship was often fraught. In Labour's second term, it came under severe strain on issues such as foundation hospitals and tuition fees. A dispute over policy 'ownership' also arose over the European single currency. Brown's determination that the Treasury should be the ultimate judge of whether the five economic tests for membership of the euro had been passed was a crucial factor in the June 2003 decision that Britain was not yet ready to adopt the single currency. Brown supporters were prominent figures in the failed attempts to force Blair out of office in his third term. Although often bitter and damaging to the smooth operation of the government, the relationship between Blair and Brown was also one of mutual dependence: one could not maintain his position without the support of the other.

Weblinks

http://news.bbc.co.uk/1/hi/in_depth/uk_politics/2007/blair_years/default.stm —BBC News analysis of Blair's period as prime minister.

Brown as prime minister

Gordon Brown enjoyed a strong start to his period as prime minister. He secured the Labour leadership without a challenge, responded steadfastly to terrorist attacks, and gave the impression that his was a government with new ideas (notably on democratic renewal), but without the 'spin' of the Blair period. Brown allowed speculation about an early election to intensify in autumn 2007, only to rule it out. The tide turned. Brown was thereafter perceived as indecisive and his hard-earned reputation for economic competence was dented by the credit crunch and recession. He appeared vulnerable.

Brown had promised a return to a more collegiate style of decision making, but he soon reverted to reliance on an inner circle. The Prime Minister's Office did not function as effectively as it had under Blair, as senior advisers departed and Brown struggled to articulate a vision. He faced dissent within the Labour Party and the cabinet. James Purnell resigned as the 2009 European election polls closed, calling for Brown to make way for a new leader. With no other cabinet ministers willing to force him out, the prime minister clung to office, but his authority had been damaged and he was not able to impose his will. Brown enjoyed few obvious policy successes as the recession and record levels of government debt forced other issues off the agenda, but by propping up the banking system he may well have staved off an even greater economic crisis.

The cabinet

The traditional constitutional view is that executive power in the UK is vested in a **cabinet** whose members exercise collective responsibility. But the importance of the cabinet waned in the modern era. It now plays only a limited role in decision making, as many key policy decisions are made elsewhere in the executive. Suggestions that the cabinet has joined the ranks of Walter Bagehot's 'dignified institutions' — those that retain a symbolic role but have no real influence — may be premature. As Thatcher's resignation illustrated dramatically, a prime minister who fails to recognise his or her dependence on senior cabinet colleagues risks losing office.

Key terms
> **Cabinet** The meeting of senior ministers and heads of government departments. It is formally the key decision-making body in British government.

Cabinet ministers

The cabinet consists of the senior ministers in the government. Membership averaged just over 20 in the twentieth century. The number who can receive a cabinet minister's salary is currently limited to 22. Cameron's cabinet in 2010 also included an additional cabinet minister who did not receive the full salary, and a further six ministers who attend despite not being cabinet ministers (see Figure 8.1). Only four cabinet ministers were women, compared with eight in 2006.

Most cabinet ministers are heads of government departments. Departments such as the Treasury, Foreign Office and Home Office have long been represented in cabinet. The lead ministers in spending departments such as health, education and social security have also been fixtures in the cabinet in the postwar period. Other cabinet posts are more recent creations, reflecting organisational change in Whitehall (e.g. international development, created in 1997).

Patrick McLoughlin, 52
Chief whip, parliamentary secretary to the treasury*

David Willetts, 54
Minister of state, minister for universities and science*

Oliver Letwin, 53
Minister of state in the cabinet office*

Francis Maude, 56
Minister for the cabinet office, paymaster general*

Sir George Young, 68
Leader of the House of Commons, Lord Privy Seal*

Baroness Warsi, 39
Minister without portfolio (unpaid)

David Cameron, 43
Prime minister, First Lord of the Treasury and minister for the civil service

Lord Strathclyde, 50
Leader of the House of Lords, chancellor of the Duchy of Lancaster

Cheryl Gillan, 58
Secretary of state for Wales

Michael Moore, 38
Secretary of state for Scotland

Owen Paterson, 53
Secretary of state for Northern Ireland

Danny Alexander, 44
Chief secretary to the treasury

Jeremy Hunt, 43
Secretary of state for culture, media and sport

Dominic Grieve, 53
Attorney general†

William Hague, 49
First secretary of state, foreign secretary

George Osborne, 38
Chancellor of the exchequer

Kenneth Clarke, 69
Lord chancellor, secretary of state for justice

Theresa May, 53
Home secretary, minister for women and equalities

Liam Fox, 48
Secretary of state for defence

Vince Cable, 67
Secretary of state for business, innovation and skills; president of the Board of Trade

Nick Clegg, 43
Deputy prime minister, Lord President of the Council

Iain Duncan Smith, 56
Secretary of state for work and pensions

Chris Huhne, 55
Secretary of state for energy and climate change

Andrew Lansley, 53
Secretary of state for health

Michael Gove, 42
Secretary of state for education

Eric Pickles, 58
Secretary of state for communities and local government

Philip Hammond, 54
Secretary of state for transport

Caroline Spelman, 52
Secretary of state for environment, food and rural affairs

* Attends cabinet, but not a cabinet minister
† Attends cabinet when ministerial responsibilities are on the agenda

Andrew Mitchell, 54
Secretary of state for international development

Figure 8.1 The cabinet, May 2010

The first cabinet meeting of Britain's new coalition government after the May 2010 general election

Cabinet ministers must be Members of Parliament, to which they are politically accountable. Most are drawn from the House of Commons. It is now rare for members of the Lords to hold senior cabinet posts. A recent exception is Lord Mandelson, who was secretary of state for business, innovation and skills, and first secretary (in effect, the deputy prime minister) in the Brown government.

Cabinet meetings

The frequency and length of cabinet meetings have fallen steadily since the 1950s. Then it tended to meet twice per week, whereas under Blair and Brown the cabinet met only once a week when parliament was in session. Cabinet meetings under Blair tended to last about an hour, although some were over in barely half that time. Brown held some cabinet meetings outside London for the first time since 1921.

Cabinet meetings are rather formal affairs: there is a fixed seating arrangement; the agenda is settled in advance; and items are introduced by departmental ministers, with interventions from senior ministers and relevant departmental ministers given priority.

Weblinks

www.cabinetoffice.gov.uk — the Cabinet Office website, which includes information on ministerial responsibilities and the machinery of government.

The role of the cabinet

The functions of the cabinet are as follows:

➤ registering and ratifying decisions taken elsewhere in the cabinet system
➤ discussing and deciding on major issues

> receiving reports on key developments and determining government business in parliament
> settling disputes between government departments

Registering decisions

The *Ministerial Code*, an official handbook on the conduct of the **cabinet system**, states that the main business of the cabinet and cabinet committees is:

> questions that engage the collective responsibility of government because they raise major policy issues or are of critical public importance
> matters on which there is an unresolved dispute between government departments

Key terms

> **Cabinet system**
The cabinet and its associated bodies, including cabinet committees and the Cabinet Office.

Many issues are decided at lower level in ministerial standing committees, in bilateral meetings between the prime minister and a minister, or in correspondence between departments. Decisions are taken in committee and reported to the cabinet as 'done deals'. The cabinet thus acts as a clearing house for policy, registering or ratifying decisions taken elsewhere. If the prime minister and the cabinet minister responsible for the policy in question are agreed, other ministers will have little chance of changing a decision. Ministers are discouraged from reopening issues where a decision has already been reached.

The ability of cabinet to decide policy is constrained by the infrequency of meetings, its size and the detailed nature of much policy. It is impractical for ministers to engage in detailed discussions across a range of issues. Most cabinet ministers are primarily concerned with policy in their department. They have little time to study policy in other departments, lack expertise and may not see the relevant papers. This need not stop ministers offering their opinion on an issue outside their brief, but it curbs their influence. The frequent turnover of ministers may also limit their impact.

The cabinet takes fewer decisions than it used to. Diaries produced by cabinet ministers from the 1960s and 1970s reveal that on issues such as UK membership of the European Economic Community (the predecessor of the EU) and economic policy, the cabinet held lengthy discussions over several sessions, in which most ministers expressed their views. But Thatcher and Blair were notable for their distaste of lengthy cabinet discussions. One of the fullest cabinet discussions to feature in Alastair Campbell's diaries was on the Millennium Dome, when some of the meeting was chaired by John Prescott because Blair had another engagement.

Discussing or deciding major issues

Formally, the cabinet remains the supreme decision-making body in UK government. Yet for most areas of government activity, the cabinet is not an important actor in the decision-making process. It may play a more active role in some circumstances, for example when:

> issues are especially important or sensitive
> major or unexpected developments require a rapid decision
> government departments and ministerial committees have been unable to reach agreement

Even when the cabinet does consider major issues, however, its role is largely advisory. In June 2003, a special cabinet meeting was devoted to the Treasury's verdict on the UK and the euro. Ministers were able to air their views, but in reality the cabinet was merely endorsing a decision — that the UK was not yet ready to adopt the single currency — which had already been taken in bilateral meetings between the prime minister and chancellor. The Butler report of 2004 noted that the cabinet was briefed on Iraq by the prime minister, foreign secretary or defence secretary on 24 occasions in the year before the invasion. But ministers did not have access to key papers. Without these, the report concluded, ministers would not have been able to 'bring their political judgement and experience to bear'.

Ministers can advise and warn, but it is the prime minister who takes the final decision. The prime minister sums up the discussions and announces a verdict. Votes are very rarely taken, as they would reveal divisions.

Government policy on important issues is, then, often settled with little or no discussion in the full cabinet. The final decision on the poll tax was taken by a ministerial committee and discussed only briefly in cabinet. The prime minister may also want to keep a sensitive issue away from cabinet to minimise the possibility of his or her views being challenged. Thatcher did not want open discussion on membership of the ERM. Similarly, only a handful of senior ministers were consulted about the decision to give operational independence to the Bank of England in 1997.

Reports and discussions

The cabinet hears reports on current developments, allowing ministers to keep abreast of events and policy change. It also allows ministers to discuss policy and the government's priorities.

Cabinet meetings have a formal agenda which includes the following items as standard:
> a report on parliamentary business
> a report on economic and home affairs
> a report on foreign affairs

In the parliamentary report, the leaders of the House of Commons and House of Lords outline the following week's business. This reflects the cabinet's formal role in timetabling government bills and ministerial statements. Blair's cabinets were also presented with a plan showing ministerial engagements and announcements.

On domestic and foreign affairs, ministers may wish to clarify or question policy. They may offer their personal view, or that of a department or a section of their party. But the cabinet is not a debating society and time for discussion is limited. Only a small number of interventions, usually by senior ministers, will be taken. Blocking discussion of sensitive issues may prove counterproductive for a prime minister, as it allows discontent to fester. It will be better to gauge the views of colleagues, assure them that they are being considered and persuade them of the worth of the chosen policy and of cabinet unity.

Settling disputes

It is a key working principle of the cabinet system that decisions should, where possible, be reached in ministerial standing committees or bilateral agreements. If an issue cannot be settled at committee level, it will be referred up to the cabinet. Some appeals are relatively straightforward matters of arbitration between the competing claims of departments. Examples include disputes between departments and the Treasury over spending allocations or where more than one department is striving to be the lead policy actor. The cabinet judges the strength of the cases presented before it and reaches a binding decision.

Appeals to the cabinet are only permitted in special circumstances. Government could not work efficiently if ministers were continually required to wade through complex policy papers and force reluctant departments to give ground. This role as a court of appeal does not always proceed smoothly. In the 1985 Westland affair, secretary of state for defence Michael Heseltine resigned because he was unhappy with Thatcher's ruling that cabinet would not hear his appeal against a cabinet committee decision on the award of a defence contract. Secretary of state for trade and industry Leon Brittan was then forced to resign after instructing a civil servant to leak information on the case.

Cabinet committees

A considerable proportion of decision making occurs within **cabinet committees**. These include:

➤ ministerial standing committees, which are permanent for the prime minister's term of office
➤ ministerial subcommittees, which report to a standing committee
➤ ad hoc committees — temporary committees set up to deal with a particular issue
➤ official committees of civil servants, which shadow ministerial committees

Key terms

➤ **Cabinet committees**
Committees appointed by the prime minister to consider aspects of government business. They include standing committees and ad hoc committees.

Policy decisions are also reached in bilateral meetings between the prime minister and a departmental minister. Blair conducted much government business in this manner.

Ministerial standing committees have considerable autonomy to determine the direction and detail of policy. Only where a final verdict has not been reached will the full cabinet concern itself with the deliberations of a ministerial committee. The prime minister is responsible for the creation, membership, chairmanship and terms of reference of cabinet committees. Following criticism in the Hutton report of Blair's preference for informal meetings, cabinet committees were given greater priority, with the prime minister chairing 15 of the then 44 committees and subcommittees. In 2010, Cameron chaired or co-chaired five committees.

The list of cabinet committees was first made public in 1992. The Cabinet Office website now lists the committees together with their membership and terms of reference (see Table 8.2). The most important tend to be those working on the following areas:

➢ domestic affairs

➢ economic affairs

➢ public services and expenditure

➢ overseas and defence policy

➢ national security

➢ the government's legislative programme

Table 8.2 Cabinet committees and subcommittes, 2010

Cabinet committee	Members	Chair
Coalition Committee	10	Prime minister and deputy prime minister
National Security Council (NSC)	11	Prime minister
NSC (Threats, Hazards, Resilience and Contingencies)	18	Prime minister
NSC (Nuclear Deterrence and Security)	7	Prime minister
European Affairs Committee	14	Foreign secretary
Social Justice Committee	10	Secretary of state for work and pensions
Home Affairs Committee	19	Deputy prime minister
Public Health Subcommittee	–	–
Olympics Subcommittee	–	–
Economic Affairs Committee	13	Chancellor of the exchequer
Banking Reform Committee	7	Chancellor of the exchequer
Parliamentary Business and Legislation Committee	13	Leader of the House of Commons

Weblinks

www.cabinetoffice.gov.uk — click on 'Government business', then 'Cabinet Secretariat and Cabinet Committees', then 'Cabinet Secretariat' for details on the cabinet and its committees.

Standing committees working in these areas often delegate work to ministerial subcommittees. The number of subcommittees and ad hoc committees has increased since 1997, although some meet infrequently. Ad hoc committees (known as MISC groups) are temporary bodies examining particular issues. Some have a short lifetime; others sit for most of the life of the government. Those meeting under the Brown government included one planning for a swine flu pandemic. Whereas the members of cabinet committees are primarily cabinet ministers, subcommittees and ad hoc committees include junior ministers. The Joint Consultative Committee with the Liberal Democrats (set up in 1997 to discuss constitutional reform) was unusual as it included members of a non-government party. David Cameron established a Coalition Committee, co-chaired by himself and Nick Clegg, to resolve disputes between Conservative and Liberal Democrat ministers. Each committee also had a chair from one party and a deputy chair from the other.

The detailed content of material entering the cabinet system is largely determined in government departments. Legislative and policy proposals to be considered in cabinet committees must receive prior approval from the Treasury and government law officers. If a proposal impacts upon the work of another department, the lead minister should seek its views.

'Kitchen cabinet'

Prime ministers periodically hold meetings with small groups of ministers, advisers and officials. In times of crisis, a select group of senior ministers may meet regularly to discuss developments and formulate policy. When this occurs, the group is often dubbed a **kitchen cabinet** or 'inner cabinet'. No such institution exists officially, although Harold Wilson did create a short-lived 'inner cabinet' in 1968–69 to deal with the sterling crisis. 'War cabinets' of senior ministers and defence chiefs were in place during the Falklands War (1982), military action in Kosovo (1999) and the war in Iraq (2003). On Black Wednesday, 16 September 1992, John Major held a series of meetings with senior colleagues to decide sterling's fate in the ERM.

The Cabinet Office

The **Cabinet Office** was created in 1916 to provide support for the cabinet system. Its key unit is the Cabinet Secretariat, which regulates and coordinates cabinet business. It calls meetings, circulates papers, prepares the agenda and writes the minutes of meetings. The secretariat also coordinates policy work on issues that bridge the interests of several departments, and acts as a neutral facilitator in case of disputes between departments. It is responsible to the prime minister and to committee chairs. The secretary of the cabinet is the head of the secretariat and of the home civil service. He or she attends cabinet meetings.

Key terms

➤ **Cabinet Office** A government department responsible for supporting the cabinet system and the prime minister, and managing the civil service.

➤ **Kitchen cabinet** An informal grouping of the prime minister's senior ministerial colleagues.

Located within the secretariat are further individual secretariats. The Economic and Domestic Secretariat, the Foreign and Defence Policy Secretariat, and the European and Global Issues Secretariat coordinate work on matters that cross department boundaries. Others deal with security issues. The Civil Contingencies Secretariat draws up contingency plans for dealing with domestic threats such as disease or terrorism. The Security and Intelligence Secretariat oversees the intelligence work of the Secret Intelligence Service (MI6) and the Security Service (MI5) on, respectively, international and domestic threats to the security of the UK. David Cameron established a National Security Council to oversee UK security, and appointed a national security adviser based in the Cabinet Office.

Under Blair, and to a lesser extent Brown, the Cabinet Office took a leading role in policy delivery and public service reform. Units such as the Social Exclusion Task Force and the Office of the Third Sector also coordinated policy on issues that cut across departmental lines of responsibility. They reported directly to the prime minister. The Cabinet Office was, in effect, brought within the remit of 10 Downing Street.

Weblinks

www.cabinetoffice.gov.uk — click on 'About the Cabinet Office', then 'Cabinet Secretariat and Cabinet Committees' for details of the role and organisation of the Cabinet Office.

Government ministers

There are more than 100 ministers in the UK government. Ministers are allocated positions in government departments. Senior ministers hold the rank of secretary of state, sit in the cabinet and head government departments. Below them in the hierarchy come the posts of minister of state and parliamentary under-secretary. These junior ministers are given specific policy roles in a department. In the Brown government, the Home Office had one secretary of state, two ministers of state (responsible for crime reduction and policing; and borders and immigration) and three parliamentary under-secretaries. Finally, parliamentary private secretaries are unpaid assistants to ministers, but do not have ministerial status.

Ministerial roles

The main roles performed by ministers are as follows:

➤ **Policy leadership.** A minister does not have the time or knowledge to play a hands-on role in all detailed policy, but plays an important role in policy initiation and selection. Only a small number of ministers, such as former home secretaries Michael Howard and David Blunkett, have changed their department's policy framework dramatically.

➤ **Representing departmental interests.** Ministers represent the interests of their department in the cabinet and negotiate for funding increases. They represent both the government and their department in meetings of the Council of Ministers of the European Union.

➤ **Departmental management.** Ministers play a strategic role in managing the work of their department, setting objectives and shaping the internal distribution of resources.

> **Relations with parliament.** Ministers perform two main roles in parliament. First, they steer their department's bills through parliament. Secondly, they are accountable to parliament for decisions taken in their department, answering questions in the House and appearing before select committees.

Collective responsibility

The cabinet is theoretically a united body. Ministers are usually members of the same party who stood on an agreed manifesto at the general election. However, the sense of unity is undermined by departmental and personal rivalries. As well as being members of the government, ministers are also heads of government departments, whose interests they fight for in cabinet. Money and influence are scarce resources for which ministers must bargain. Departments provide ministers with authority, policy advice and technical information, so they may be tempted to act primarily as departmental chiefs rather than as members of a collegiate body.

Collective responsibility is a core principle of collective government. It has three main elements:

> **Secrecy.** Ministers must keep the details of discussions in the cabinet system secret. This ensures that sensitive information does not enter the public domain and prevents differences of opinion from being revealed.
> **Binding decisions.** Once a decision is reached in the cabinet system, it becomes binding on all cabinet and junior ministers regardless of whether they had opposed it or were not directly involved in the decision-making process. Those unable to accept this should resign or expect to be dismissed. Senior ministers who have resigned because of their disagreement with government policy include Nigel Lawson (1989), Sir Geoffrey Howe (1990) and Robin Cook (2003) (see Table 8.3). The Blair and Brown governments saw instances of ministers resigning in an attempt to force a change of party leader. Junior minister Tom Watson resigned in 2006, having signed a letter urging Blair to resign. Secretary of state for work and pensions James Purnell resigned in 2009, calling on Brown to stand aside.
> **Confidence vote.** The entire government must resign if it is defeated in a vote of confidence (i.e. one explicitly concerning the life of the government), and call a general election. This last happened in 1979 when James Callaghan's Labour government lost a vote of confidence after its bill on Scottish devolution was defeated in the House of Commons.

The convention under strain

The convention of collective responsibility has, however, been steadily eroded. Four main factors account for this:

> **Temporary suspension.** On rare occasions, prime ministers have suspended collective responsibility temporarily to prevent ministerial resignations. Harold Wilson allowed ministers to campaign for either a 'yes' or a 'no' vote during the 1975 referendum on the European Economic Community, despite the government

Table 8.3 Ministerial resignations over collective responsibility: examples

Date	Minister	Post	Reason for resignation
1986	Michael Heseltine	Secretary of state for defence	Opposed defence procurement policy (Westland affair)
1989	Nigel Lawson	Chancellor of the exchequer	Opposed prime minister's conduct of economic policy
1990	Sir Geoffrey Howe	Leader of the House of Commons	Opposed policy on Europe
1995	John Redwood	Secretary of state for Wales	Launched leadership challenge
1998	Frank Field	Minister of state for social security and welfare reform	Opposed welfare policy
2003	Robin Cook (and two junior ministers)	President of the Council and leader of the House of Commons	Opposed invasion of Iraq
2003	Clare Short	Secretary of state for international development	Opposed policy on Iraq
2006	Tom Watson	Under-secretary of state for defence	Signed letter calling on Blair to resign
2008	David Cairns	Minister of state, Scotland Office	Critical of Brown's leadership
2009	James Purnell	Secretary of state for work and pensions	Called on Brown to stand down
2009	Caroline Flint	Minister of state (Europe), Foreign Office	Critical of Brown's leadership style

supporting a 'yes' vote. This allowed a government that was divided on Europe to function in a more united fashion on other issues. Gordon Brown granted ministers a 'free vote' on three specific areas of the 2008 Human Fertilisation and Embryology Bill, but they were required to support it in its entirety at second and third reading. Three cabinet ministers — Des Browne, Ruth Kelly and Paul Murphy — backed an unsuccessful attempt to ban research on 'hybrid' embryos. Browne and Murphy fell back in line and voted for the legislation at second and third reading, but Kelly was absent from the second reading vote and opposed the bill at third reading, by which time she had left the government.

The 2010 Conservative–Liberal Democrat coalition agreement stated that ministers from the two parties would be free to campaign on different sides in a proposed referendum on the alternative vote. Liberal Democrat MPs will also be allowed to abstain on the construction of new nuclear power stations, tax allowances for married couples and higher education funding, and be able to make the case against the renewal of the Trident nuclear deterrent.

➤ **Leaks.** Disgruntled ministers and their advisers sometimes leak information on cabinet discussions to the media. Coded signals and unattributed briefings are the preferred routes for ministers who want dissatisfaction about the policy or conduct of government to be aired, but who do not want to put their heads above the parapet. In the 1990s, the press published details of divisions on Europe in Major's cabinet and purportedly verbatim accounts of discussions in the Blair cabinet. Cabinet discussions have also been made public in diaries written by cabinet ministers such as Tony Benn and Robin Cook. Alasdair Campbell told the Chilcot inquiry into the Iraq war that secretary of state for international development Clare Short had been excluded from some discussions because of fears that she would leak sensitive material.

- **Dissent and non-resignation.** Cabinet ministers who oppose important aspects of government policy have survived in office even when their concerns have been public knowledge. 'Wets' in Thatcher's first cabinet scarcely concealed their opposition to her economic policy. None resigned and Thatcher dismissed them only when her position had been secured. Eurosceptic ministers like Michael Portillo retained their posts in Major's cabinet despite their sympathy for the stance taken by backbench Eurosceptic rebels. Clare Short remained in the cabinet for 2 months after publicly expressing concerns about the 2003 invasion of Iraq, before finally resigning.

- **Prime ministerial dominance.** Some cabinet ministers who served in the Thatcher and Blair governments believed that the prime minister had undermined the convention of collective responsibility by ignoring the cabinet. Heseltine, Lawson and Howe all cited Thatcher's contempt for collegiality as a reason for their resignation. Mo Mowlam and Clare Short complained that Blair did not consult cabinet sufficiently. Caroline Flint resigned from Brown's cabinet in 2009, accusing him of running a two-tier government with an inner circle that included few women.

Individual ministerial responsibility

The convention of **individual ministerial responsibility** states that ministers are accountable to parliament for their own personal conduct, the general conduct of their department and the policies they pursue. The convention is not a rigid one, however, and confusion exists as to when a minister should be obliged to resign.

Governments have long drawn a distinction between ministerial accountability (i.e. a minister's duty to give an account to parliament) and their individual responsibility. Home secretary Sir David Maxwell-Fyfe stated in 1954 that ministers cannot be held responsible for decisions taken by civil servants which they had no knowledge of, or which they disagreed with. Ministers are not obliged to resign if failings are traceable to the actions (or inaction) of civil servants. But they are constitutionally responsible for informing parliament of the actions of their department.

The 1996 Scott report on the sale of arms to Iraq stated that ministers had a duty to be as open as possible, withholding information only when disclosure would not be in the public interest, but ministers were culpable only if they misled parliament 'knowingly'. The report chronicled a number of occasions on which ministers misled parliament about changes in government policy, but none resigned because they denied culpability. The *Ministerial Code* states that ministers must give 'accurate and truthful information to Parliament'; those who 'knowingly mislead Parliament will be expected to offer their resignation'. Immigration minister Beverley Hughes resigned in 2004 after admitting that she had unwittingly given a 'misleading impression' to MPs on checks on migrants from eastern Europe.

A further distinction is that between policy and operations. Ministers are responsible for policy, but officials are responsible for day-to-day operational matters. In a number of cases, home secretaries argued that prison escapes were the result of operational rather than policy failure. Michael Howard sacked Derek Lewis, the chief executive of the Prison Service in 1995, blaming him for the escapes. But Lewis claimed that Howard had actively intervened in operational decisions. When the SATS exam results for some pupils were delayed in 2008, the company responsible for administering the exams lost its contract and the head of the Qualifications and Curriculum Agency resigned. Secretary of state for children, schools and families Ed Balls stayed in office because, he claimed, the problems resulted from operational not policy decisions.

These two cases illustrate how the transfer of policy implementation functions from government departments to executive agencies, which operate at arm's length from government, has added to the complexity surrounding ministerial responsibility.

Grounds for resignation

Four main categories of resignation on the grounds of individual ministerial responsibility can be identified, but in practice they may overlap (see Table 8.4).

> **Mistakes made within departments.** A clear example of a minister carrying the can for mistakes made by his civil servants was the 1954 resignation of the agriculture minister, Sir Thomas Dugdale. He resigned when mistakes made by civil servants in the Crichel Down case came to light — although he had come under pressure to resign. Such cases are rare. It is much easier to find cases (e.g. on 'arms to Iraq' and BSE) where ministers survived despite mistakes in their departments being brought to light.

> **Policy failure.** Ministerial resignations following policy failure include that of chancellor of the exchequer James Callaghan after the 1967 devaluation of sterling, although he became home secretary in the ensuing cabinet reshuffle. Foreign secretary Lord Carrington and two of his junior ministers resigned after Argentina invaded the Falkland Islands in 1982. This is often cited as an example of ministers standing down because of policy failure. But Carrington stated that he did not believe that the situation had been mishandled, and that he had resigned to ensure national unity in the build-up to war. Defence secretary John Nott remained in office. Another minister who survived policy failure was Norman Lamont, who did not resign as chancellor when sterling left the ERM in 1992.

> **Political pressure.** This category is looser than the others because it covers resignations that are not attributable to a single policy problem or scandal. Instead, they result from a period of sustained pressure from parliament, the party or the press about a minister's performance. In 2002, secretary of state for transport Stephen

Byers resigned after an accumulation of problems including policy failure, disputes between civil servants and special advisers in his department, press criticism and Byers' admission that he had given inaccurate information to parliament.

➤ **Personal misconduct.** Ministers are expected to follow the 'seven principles of public life' set out by the 1995 Nolan Committee on Standards in Public Life and now included in a code of ethics in the *Ministerial Code.* They are selflessness, integrity, objectivity, accountability, openness, honesty and leadership. Allegations of financial sleaze brought about the resignations of ministers under Major (e.g. Neil Hamilton in the 1994 'cash for questions' case) and Blair. Peter Mandelson and David Blunkett both left the Blair cabinet twice after allegations about their private interests and/or conduct in office. Peter Hain stood down in 2008 while the police examined donations to

David Blunkett

his Labour deputy leadership campaign, but rejoined the cabinet after the case was dropped. Cecil Parkinson resigned in 1983 following revelations about his private life, but others (e.g. John Prescott) have survived personal scandal.

Table 8.4 Ministerial resignations over individual responsibility: examples

Date	Minister	Post	Reason for resignation
1963	John Profumo	Minister of war	*Personal misconduct* — sex scandal and lying to House of Commons
1967	James Callaghan	Chancellor of the exchequer	*Policy failure* — devaluation of sterling
1972	Reginald Maudling	Home secretary	*Personal misconduct* — financial affairs
1982	Lord Carrington (and two junior ministers)	Foreign secretary	*Policy failure* — misjudgements before Argentina invaded the Falkland Islands
1983	Cecil Parkinson	Secretary of state for trade and industry	*Personal misconduct* — extramarital affair
1986	Leon Brittan	Secretary of state for trade and industry	*Political pressure* — leak of letter in Westland affair
1992	David Mellor	Secretary of state for national heritage	*Personal misconduct* — extramarital affair and financial dealings
1994	Neil Hamilton	Minister of corporate affairs, Board of Trade	*Personal misconduct* — 'cash for questions'
1998	Peter Mandelson	Secretary of state for trade and industry	*Personal misconduct* — financial affairs

Date	Minister	Post	Reason for resignation
2001	Peter Mandelson	Secretary of state for Northern Ireland	*Personal misconduct* — allegations of abuse of office
2002	Stephen Byers	Secretary of state for transport	*Political pressure* — disputes in Department of Local Government, Transport and the Regions, and policy problems
2002	Estelle Morris	Secretary of state for education and skills	*Political pressure* — criticism of her performance and policy problems
2004	David Blunkett	Home secretary	*Personal misconduct* — allegations of abuse of office
2005	David Blunkett	Secretary of state for work and pensions	*Personal misconduct* — broke *Ministerial Code* on private sector job
2008	Peter Hain	Secretary of state for work and pensions; secretary of state for Wales	*Personal misconduct* — police investigation into political donations
2010	David Laws	Chief secretary to the treasury	*Personal misconduct* — past expense claims

There are, then, no hard-and-fast rules on individual ministerial responsibility. Resignations often result from cumulative pressure rather than a single incidence of failure. The prime minister, House of Commons, political party and media can all apply pressure on underperforming ministers. A minister is unlikely to remain in office if the prime minister considers ongoing media publicity too damaging or has lost faith in them.

Weblinks

www.cabinetoffice.gov.uk — click on 'Codes of Conduct', then select 'Ministerial Code'.

Concepts explained

Collective responsibility

The convention that all members of the government are responsible as a group. It has three main elements:

➤ Discussions in government should be kept secret.

➤ Decisions made in government are binding on all ministers.

➤ The government as a whole must resign if defeated on a vote of confidence in parliament.

Individual ministerial responsibility

The convention that ministers are accountable to parliament for their personal conduct, the general conduct of their department and the policies they pursue, the actions of officials within their department, and their own personal conduct. Governments have redefined the convention so that ministers should *not* be held personally responsible for:

➤ decisions made in their department that they had no knowledge of

➤ operational matters handled by officials in departments or executive agencies

Ministers and civil servants

Government departments are staffed by **civil servants**: that is, officials appointed by the Crown. Civil servants provide policy advice to ministers. In doing so, they may have a number of advantages over ministers, such as experience, expertise and access to information. Civil servants are required to provide impartial advice, but they can define which policy options are practicable and affordable.

Criminal and civil law

Distinguish between

Ministers	Civil servants	Special advisers
➤ MPs and peers.	➤ Officials appointed by the Crown.	➤ Political appointments made by ministers.
➤ Make policy decisions.	➤ Advise on policy options.	➤ Advise on policy options.
➤ Required to support government policy.	➤ Politically neutral.	➤ Politically partisan.
➤ Accountable to parliament.	➤ Anonymity.	➤ Accountable to ministers.
➤ Bound by *Ministerial Code*.	➤ Bound by *Civil Service Code*.	➤ *Code of Conduct* provides guidance on role.
➤ Temporary.	➤ Permanent.	➤ Temporary.

Concerns that senior civil servants had too great an influence in the policy process were frequently aired in the 1970s and 1980s. Tony Benn, for example, complained that civil servants had frustrated his policies when he was a minister. The 1980s BBC television comedy *Yes Minister* caught the mood of the times with its depiction of a senior civil servant who manipulates his often hapless ministerial boss (but often gets his comeuppance).

Special advisers and spin doctors

By the late 1990s, ministers had tilted the balance back in their favour. Rather than simply relying on advice from officials, they employed **special advisers** while many civil servants were engaged in more mundane activities. Special advisers are not career civil servants, but political appointments. They carry out policy advice or media liaison roles, with those in the latter category known as **spin doctors**. In 2009, there were 74 special advisers working in government, 23 of them in Number 10. This marked a fall from the peak of 84 reached under Blair, but was still more than double the number employed in the early 1990s. The BBC comedy *The Thick Of It* reflected the changed times by pitching spin doctors against ministers and civil servants.

Special advisers have the status of 'temporary civil servants' and their role is set out in a code of conduct. But they have proved controversial. They are allowed to convey instructions to civil servants and commission work from them. Two of Tony Blair's most prominent advisers, chief of staff Jonathan Powell and communications director Alasdair Campbell (1997–2003), were also given the power to issue instructions to civil servants. Gordon Brown removed this power.

Brown's media adviser, Damian McBride, resigned in 2009 when emails making unfounded allegations about Conservative politicians became public. In 2001–02, a dispute between advisers and civil servants spiralled out of control in the Department of Transport, Local Government and the Regions. Secretary of state Stephen Byers, his media adviser Jo Moore and Martin Sixsmith, the civil servant in charge of the department's communications, all lost their jobs.

Weblinks

www.civilservice.gov.uk — the civil service website, with information on the structure and values of the civil service.

Key terms

➤ **Civil servant** An official employed in a civil capacity by the Crown, responsible for policy advice or policy implementation.

➤ **Special adviser** A temporary political appointment made by a government minister.

➤ **Spin doctor** A special adviser employed to promote the image of the minister and his or her policy in the media.

Civil service reform

Principles of the civil service

The civil service is a **bureaucracy** that operates according to a clear set of procedures and has a hierarchical structure. It has traditionally operated according to four principles:

➤ **Impartiality.** Civil servants serve the Crown rather than the government of the day. They are expected to be politically neutral and not become involved in overtly party political tasks.

➤ **Anonymity.** Individual civil servants should not be identified as the author of advice to ministers. Some may be called before parliamentary committees, but they give evidence under the direction of ministers. All civil servants sign the Official Secrets Act.

➤ **Permanence.** Civil servants stay in their posts when there is a change of government.

➤ **Meritocracy.** Civil servants are not political appointments. Instead, the civil service is staffed by generalists, recruited through competitive exams and interviews.

Concepts explained

Bureaucracy

A bureaucracy is a large organisation that enacts policy and operates according to a clear set of rules and procedures. The role of each official within a bureaucracy is defined by these rules, and appointments are based on merit. There is a hierarchy of positions, with junior officials responsible to senior officials. A bureaucracy is impersonal: officials act on behalf of the organisation rather than in a private capacity.

Weblinks

www.civilservant.org.uk — an independent site detailing the work of the civil service and its reform.

Reforms since 1988

Significant reforms of the civil service have been introduced by Conservative and Labour governments since a report called *Next Steps* was produced in 1988. The report argued that the civil service was too big, lacked innovation and was not providing quality policy advice or effective policy delivery. The main reforms have been as follows:

- **Executive agencies.** The policy-making and policy implementation roles of the civil service were separated after *Next Steps*. Civil servants working in **Whitehall** continue to advise ministers, but policy implementation functions and the delivery of public services were transferred to **executive agencies** (e.g. HM Prison Service and JobCentre Plus). These operate at arm's length from government departments. A chief executive is responsible for their day-to-day operations.
- **Marketisation.** Many activities of government departments and executive agencies were contracted out to the private sector, which, it was claimed, would provide cheaper and more efficient services. Private sector finance has been used to fund public projects through the Private Finance Initiative.
- **Managerial culture.** Private sector management techniques have been introduced into departments and executive agencies. These include efficiency drives, performance measures and changes to pay and working conditions. The size of the civil service has been cut (from 732,000 in 1979 to 483,000 in 2008) and jobs relocated outside London.
- **Recruitment.** More outsiders have been recruited, particularly those with experience in the private sector or with specialist skills (e.g. in IT or communications).
- **Diversity.** Senior ranks of the civil service were, into the 1980s, largely made up of white, middle-class men who had a public school and Oxbridge education. By 2008 women made up 31% of the senior civil service and ethnic minorities 4%.

Key terms

- **Executive agency** An agency responsible for the delivery of government policy that is subordinate to a government department but enjoys significant autonomy in its day-to-day operations.
- **Marketisation** The extension of market mechanisms into government and the public sector: for example, by the transfer of the provision of public services to the private sector.
- **Whitehall** The UK civil service and government departments, named after the area of London in which many departments are based.

Concerns about impartiality

These radical changes to the structure, functions and character of the civil service have prompted concerns that the principles of impartiality, anonymity and permanence are under threat. The main concerns are:

➤ **Fragmentation.** The separation of the policy advice and service delivery functions of the civil service has brought fragmentation and problems of control and coordination.

➤ **Markets and agencies.** Critics argue that market forces and new managerial practices have eroded the public service ethos of the civil service. Although many executive agencies have brought greater efficiency and improved service delivery, there have been some notable failures (e.g. the Child Support Agency).

➤ **Accountability.** The creation of executive agencies has blurred the lines of accountability. It is not clear whether agency chief executives or government ministers should be held ultimately responsible for policy failures. Ministers have used the distinction between policy and operations to escape direct responsibility for policy delivery problems.

➤ **Politicisation.** Governments have been criticised for exerting too much political pressure on the civil service. The use of special advisers, the role that civil servants have played in promoting government policy, and senior appointments based in part on political considerations are said to have undermined the impartiality of the civil service.

Theories of executive power

Cabinet government versus prime ministerial government

For much of the twentieth century, the main debate about executive power was whether the UK still had a system of **cabinet government** or had developed one of **prime ministerial government**. In his classic text *The English Constitution* (1867), Walter Bagehot described a system of cabinet government in which the prime minister was 'first among equals' (or *primus inter pares*) but decision making was a collective endeavour.

Concepts explained

Cabinet government

A system of government in which executive power is vested in a cabinet whose members exercise collective responsibility, rather than in a single office. Within the cabinet, the prime minister is 'first among equals'. Although the prime minister has institutional resources (e.g. patronage) that other ministers do not have, he or she cannot act unilaterally. In the UK, the executive and legislative branches are 'fused' rather than separate. Cabinet members are accountable to parliament, but must also be members of it.

Prime ministerial government

A system of government in which the prime minister is the dominant actor in the executive. The prime minister sets the direction of government, makes the major decisions and intervenes decisively in policy areas of his or her choosing. The cabinet is able to advise and warn the prime minister, but does not decide policy.

By the second half of the twentieth century, however, the cabinet had been weakened and the powers of the prime minister had expanded. Proponents of the prime ministerial government thesis argued that the prime minister was now the dominant actor and frequently bypassed the cabinet when taking key decisions.

The core executive model

The term **core executive** covers those organisations and actors that coordinate central government activity, including the prime minister and his or her advisers, the cabinet and its committees, and coordinating bodies such as the Prime Minister's Office and Cabinet Office (see Figure 8.2).

The core executive model argues that the debate on whether the UK has either prime ministerial government or cabinet government is flawed. Power is not located inevitably in one or the other; instead it is shared between actors who are mutually dependent. The decline in the power of the cabinet does not inevitably mean that the prime minister is dominant. The key actors in the core executive all have resources, but to achieve their goals they need to cooperate and exchange resources with each other. Power is based on dependence, not command. A prime minister needs the support of cabinet ministers and officials to achieve his or her objectives. If this cooperation is not forthcoming, success will be difficult.

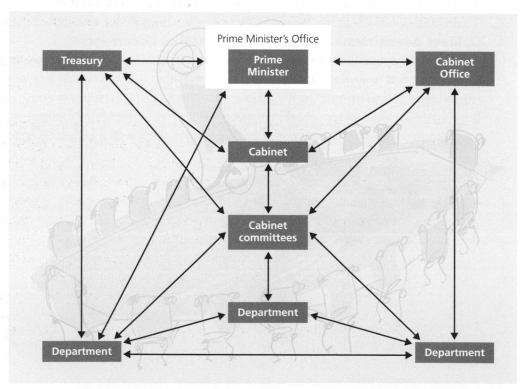

Figure 8.2 The core executive

The prime minister has considerable resources at his or her disposal. However, the powers of the prime minister are not fixed but depend on a number of variables. These include external factors (e.g. policy success, parliamentary majority, government popularity) and the strategies of resource exchange (e.g. the leadership style) adopted by the prime minister. Cabinet ministers also have resources. Most head a government department, giving them authority and policy knowledge. They may also enjoy policy success and support within their party. Departmental civil servants are also significant actors, having detailed knowledge and experience as well as links with colleagues across Whitehall.

Martin Smith argues that Margaret Thatcher's downfall was inevitable, given her failure to recognise her dependence on the support of cabinet ministers at a time of wider political difficulties. By contrast, John Major recognised that in difficult times a prime minister needs the support of other actors within the core executive.

The core executive model recognises that the resources available to the prime minister have increased in recent years. The Prime Minister's Office has been strengthened and the prime minister's media profile has increased. However, other developments have made it more difficult for the prime minister to command policy. These include:

- the devolution of power to new institutions in Scotland, Wales and Northern Ireland
- the continued transfer of policy competences to the European Union
- the decision to grant the Bank of England's Monetary Policy Committee the power to set interest rates
- privatisation and the transfer of functions to executive agencies, which make policy coordination more difficult

Prime ministerial predominance

Richard Heffernan has developed the core executive model by describing a system of prime ministerial predominance. The prime minister is the predominant figure within the core executive. They have the potential to exercise leadership by utilising their institutional resources (e.g. leadership of the government allows them to set the policy agenda) and making judicious use of their own personal skills (e.g. being a good media performer). The more institutional and personal power resources the prime minister has, the more likely they are to be predominant. The prime minister cannot have a monopoly of power, however. They have to work with ministers because government is a collective endeavour, and they must also respond to parliamentary and public opinion.

The prime minister, then, leads but does not command the executive, and directs rather than controls its policy agenda. The political context is also important: policy success, public popularity and high standing in the party strengthen the prime minister's position, but policy failure and bad luck will damage it.

A British presidency?

Michael Foley has argued that the office of prime minister has become more

> **Concepts explained**
>
> **Core executive**
>
> The core executive is the heart of government, consisting of those organisations and actors who coordinate central government activity, including the prime minister, cabinet, cabinet committees, bilateral meetings between the prime minister and ministers, the Prime Minister's Office, coordinating departments (e.g. the Cabinet Office and Treasury) and top civil servants. The core executive model claims that power is based on dependence rather than command.
>
> **Presidentialism**
>
> The idea that UK prime ministers have taken on some of the characteristics of presidents because of the emergence of a personalised form of leadership. It is characterised by spatial leadership (the distancing of the prime minister from his or her government) and public outreach (the tendency of the prime minister to reach out to the public directly). The concept of presidentialism does not claim necessarily that the office of UK prime minister is becoming the same as that of US president.

'presidential': that a 'de facto British presidency' has emerged. Three trends are central to **presidentialism**:

> ➤ **Personalised leadership.** The prime minister is expected to be a dominant political personality who stamps his or her imprint on the government, and imposes a personal vision. Thatcher was a conviction politician whose ideology set the political agenda, while Blair was the architect of 'New' Labour. They, rather than the government as a whole, were personally associated with major policy initiatives. The personalisation of leadership is also evident in election campaigns and party organisation. Election victory is proclaimed as a personal mandate by the prime minister. The televised leadership debates held during the 2010 general election campaign reinforced this focus on party leaders.
>
> ➤ **Public outreach.** Political leaders have become public commodities. The political and media spotlight falls on the prime minister to a far greater extent than any other minister. He or she becomes communicator-in-chief for the government. The prime minister is also expected to connect with the popular mood and act as spokesperson for the nation. He or she claims to represent the public interest, and takes his or her message directly to the public through the popular media (e.g. on 'soft format' chat shows rather than heavyweight political programmes).
>
> ➤ **Spatial leadership.** A sense of distance has been created between the prime minister and his or her government and party. The prime minister relies more on his or her own inner circle of advisers than on the cabinet system, as was the case in Blair's 'sofa government'. Blair presented himself as an outsider when he claimed that his efforts to reform the public sector had been frustrated by the machinery of government, leaving 'scars on my back'.

The leadership stretch that characterises presidentialism has strengthened the position of the prime minister. But it can also create problems. Just as the prime minister gains credit for policy success, so he or she is blamed personally for policy failure. Blair eroded the institutional foundations of prime ministerial power and developed instead an individual power base. But his position became exposed after the invasion of Iraq, when trust in his leadership declined and his leadership style was questioned. Brown was also blamed personally for the declining fortunes of his government, and faced additional criticism about his inability to connect with the public and communicate a clear vision.

View point   Is there a 'British presidency'?

YES
- Leadership in the executive is personalised, with the prime minister expected to impose his or her personality and agenda upon it.
- Prime ministers rely on a close circle of (often unelected) advisers and pursue 'sofa government'.
- Prime ministers have created a 'strategic space' between themselves and their governments, distancing themselves from other actors in the executive.
- Prime ministers appeal to the public directly, through the media, and claim a personal mandate from the electorate.
- Prime ministers have additional authority as party leaders, where they are elected by MPs and members, and exercise personalised leadership.

NO
- The prime minister leads but cannot command the executive, and directs rather than controls the agenda.
- Senior ministers enjoy support from government departments and have their own special advisers.
- The prime minister needs the support of ministers and officials to achieve his or her objectives.
- The prime minister's position is strong only if he or she enjoys policy success and popular approval, and makes effective use of his or her own personal abilities
- Support from the party is not unconditional, and unpopular leaders face concerted attempts to remove them.

Criticisms of the presidential model

Critics argue that the notion of a British presidency misrepresents the nature of power within the core executive, overstating the room for manoeuvre that a prime minister has and underestimating their dependence on cabinet ministers and their party. Crude versions can also be criticised for ignoring the significant differences between the British and US political systems (see US/UK comparison).

Foley's presidentialism thesis does not claim, however, that the office of British prime minister is becoming the same as, or even a pale imitation of, that of the US president. Nor has the UK become a presidential system of government. Important institutional differences between the British prime minister and the US president remain. The prime minister is indirectly elected, is accountable to the legislature and is head of a collegial executive. But a British prime minister also has greater resources than a US president, given that the former is leader of a disciplined political party and the British system allows for executive dominance whereas the separation of powers is a guiding principle of the US Constitution.

▶ What you should know

- ❯ The prime minister is the predominant actor within the executive branch. He or she has significant institutional resources. The prime minister appoints and dismisses members of the government; chairs the cabinet and directs discussion within it; and is supported by the Prime Minister's Office and Cabinet Office. Leadership of the largest party in the House of Commons brings additional authority.

- ❯ However, prime ministerial power does not automatically flow from this. The powers of a prime minister are tempered by constraints: for example, the need to placate senior colleagues and the party when appointing the cabinet. The prime minister has the potential to exercise leadership, but this depends upon effective use of these institutional resources, a favourable context (e.g. policy success) and the prime minister's own leadership skills.

- ❯ The position of the prime minister has been strengthened in recent decades, to the extent that some scholars claim that we have seen its 'presidentialisation'. Leadership has become more personalised, and prime ministers turn to their inner circle of favoured ministers and advisers rather than to the formal institutions of the cabinet system.

- ❯ But no prime minister can monopolise power. They can lead but not command, and direct rather than control policy. Other individuals (e.g. cabinet ministers) and institutions (government departments) also have resources. The cabinet discusses major issues but tends to ratify decisions that are made elsewhere. Nonetheless, to achieve his or her goals, the prime minister needs the support of senior cabinet ministers. Prime ministers who face a difficult environment and troubled relations with colleagues in government and their party may have only a tenuous grip on office.

UK/US comparison

The prime minister and the president

- ➤ The US president is head of state as well as head of government. Many of the powers of the president are set out in the US Constitution. It places significant limits on presidential power. The queen is head of state in the UK. The powers of the prime minister are not set out in statute law.

- ➤ The US president is directly elected and can claim a personal mandate. Fixed-term elections take place every 4 years. The British prime minister is not directly elected; he or she is leader of the largest party in the House of Commons.

- ➤ In the USA, the separation of powers means that the executive does not dominate the legislature. The president cannot force Congress to accept his will, although he does have some powers to veto legislation. The legislature cannot dismiss the president. In the UK, the executive exercises significant control over the legislature. But the government must resign if it loses a vote of confidence in the Commons.

➤ The US executive branch serves the president. The US cabinet is an advisory body subordinate to the president; it does not share executive power with him. The Executive Office of the President provides strong institutional support. Presidents also appoint many of the officials working within their administration. The British prime minister is the predominant figure in the executive, but needs the support of senior cabinet colleagues. The British civil service is impartial and is not politically appointed.

➤ The US president's nominees for key posts, such as cabinet members and Supreme Court judges, are subject to approval by the legislature. Most key appointments made by the British prime minister are not subject to parliamentary approval.

➤ The US president is head of his political party, but parties are loose organisations whose members often act independently. The British prime minister is also leader of his or her party, but enjoys much greater control over it.

Further reading

Fairclough, P. (2007) *The Prime Minister and the Cabinet (Advanced TopicMaster)*, Philip Allan Updates.

Foley, M. (2009) 'The presidential controversy in Britain', *Politics Review*, Vol. 18, No. 3, pp. 20–22.

Heffernan, R. (2008) 'Prime-ministerial predominance', *Politics Review*, Vol. 17, No. 3, pp. 2–5.

Heffernan, R. (2010) 'Gordon Brown as prime minister', *Politics Review*, Vol. 20, No. 1.

Riddell, P. (2006) 'Tony Blair: prime minister or president?', *Politics Review*, Vol. 15, No. 3, pp. 30–33.

Smith, M. (2000) 'The core executive', *Politics Review*, Vol. 10, No. 1, pp. 2–5.

Exam focus

Short-answer questions (around 5 minutes each)

Explain, using examples, the meaning of each of the following terms:

1 *Primus inter pares*
2 Cabinet government
3 Royal prerogative
4 Collective responsibility

Mid-length questions (around 10 minutes each)

Outline two arguments 'for' and two arguments 'against' each of the following:

1 Special advisers
2 Coalition government
3 Bilateral meetings
4 Cabinet committees

Mini-essays (around 25–30 minutes each)

Write a mini-essay in response to each of the following questions:

1 'The limitations on the power of the prime minister are insufficient.' Discuss.
2 'Senior civil servants and not ministers are the key players at the heart of central government.' Discuss.
3 'Cabinet government is dead.' Discuss.
4 Discuss the view that the UK has seen the rise of a 'presidential prime minister'.

Chapter 9

Judges and civil liberties

Key questions answered in this chapter

➢ What is the judiciary?

➢ How are senior judges appointed?

➢ How powerful is the UK judiciary?

➢ How has the creation of a UK Supreme Court changed things?

➢ What are civil liberties?

➢ How effectively are civil liberties protected in the UK?

➢ Does the UK need a Bill of Rights?

What is the judiciary?

In its simplest sense, the term 'judiciary' refers collectively to all UK judges, from lay magistrates and those serving on tribunals right up to the 12 senior justices sitting in the UK Supreme Court. Indeed, in a wider sense the term might even be seen as encompassing all of those who are directly involved in the administration and application of justice.

Figure 9.1 An outline of the judiciary in England and Wales

UK Supreme Court

Court of Appeal (Criminal and Civil Divisions)

High Court

Crown Court and County Courts Magistrates' Courts and Tribunals

It is important to remember that the UK judiciary does not exist as a single body — Scotland and Northern Ireland operate under different legal arrangements than those in place in respect of England and Wales. The one feature common to all three systems is the part played by the UK Supreme Court, which acts as the highest court of appeal from the High Court of Justiciary and Court of Session in Scotland, the Court of Judicature in Northern Ireland and the Court of Appeal in England and Wales.

Although the judiciary in all three territories is broadly hierarchical in structure (see Figure 9.1, for example), the picture is in fact a good deal more complicated than it might appear to be at first sight. This complexity results, in part at least, from the fact that there are different legal pathways for cases involving different types of dispute, with the most obvious division coming between those cases brought under **criminal law** and those rooted in **civil law**.

Criminal and civil law

Distinguish between

Criminal law

➤ Criminal law deals with crimes by an individual or group against the state (e.g. violent behaviour, serious fraud or burglary). Such cases are normally brought by the state and can lead to fines and imprisonment.

Civil law

➤ Civil law is concerned with interrelationships between different individuals and groups. Civil cases generally involve matters such as wills or contracts. Cases under civil law are generally brought by individuals rather than the state and they tend to result in compensation awards as opposed to prison sentences.

The system of courts operating in England and Wales, our primary focus in this chapter, is shown in detail in Figure 9.2.

Weblink

www.judiciary.gov.uk — the Judiciary of England and Wales site.

What do judges actually do?

➤ Judges at all levels are involved in ensuring that justice is done and the law is properly applied.

➤ At the lower levels of the judiciary, the main role of judges is to preside over trials, give guidance to the jury and impose sentences.

➤ At the High Court level, judges hear more serious cases and can also hear cases on appeal from lower courts.

➤ At the Court of Appeal level and above, judges are generally concerned with clarifying the meaning of the law, rather than simply applying it. These courts can establish legal precedent (i.e. common law).

➤ Cases heard at the Court of Appeal normally result from confusion in the lower courts regarding the meaning of a law. The Court of Appeal also deals with major cases arising under the 1998 Human Rights Act (HRA).

➢ The UK Supreme Court — located in Middlesex Guildhall, Westminster — generally hears cases on appeal from the Appeals Court. In recent years, such disputes have often been brought under the HRA (1998) or under EU law.

While it is helpful to have an awareness of the judiciary in its broader sense, the higher levels of the judiciary (i.e. the top two tiers of our simplified pyramid) are of most concern to students of politics. This is because it is these higher tiers that have the power to set legal precedent establishing **common law** through their use of **judicial review**. In short, these higher courts clarify the meaning of the law as opposed to simply applying the letter of the law.

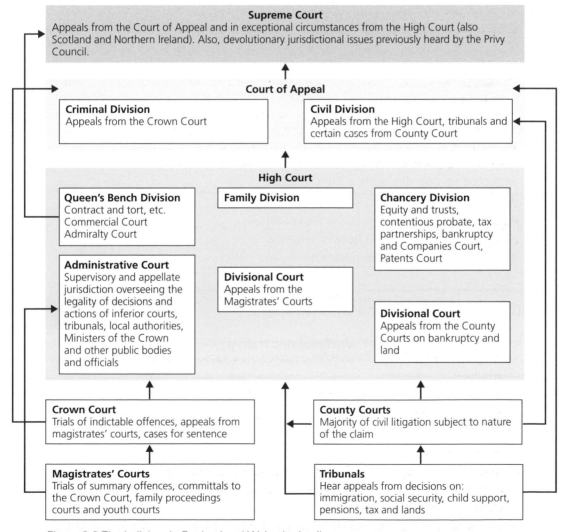

Figure 9.2 The judiciary in England and Wales in detail

Concepts explained

Judicial review The process by which judges review the actions of public officials or public bodies in order to determine whether or not they have acted in a manner that is lawful. This process often requires senior judges to clarify the legal meaning of a particular law or regulation. Judicial review may also involve reviewing on appeal cases heard previously at lower ('inferior') courts.

The doctrine of parliamentary sovereignty and supremacy of statute law means that judicial review in the UK is generally seen as being less significant that in the USA, where the US Supreme Court can strike down pieces of regular statute that are judged to have violated the provisions of the US Constitution.

In the UK, judicial review traditionally involved little more than judges determining whether or not a public official had operated beyond the authority granted to them under the law (i.e. acted ultra vires), as opposed to questioning the basis of the law itself.

The passing of the Human Rights Act (1998) and the power given to UK courts in respect of EU legislation in recent years have seen a change in the nature and scope of judicial review in the UK.

Judicial independence and judicial neutrality

Judges at all levels of the UK judiciary are expected to operate with a high level of independence and dispense justice with a degree of neutrality. However, it is important to draw a clear distinction between judicial independence and judicial neutrality.

Key terms

> **Common law** The body of legal precedent resulting from the rulings of senior judges. Sometimes referred to as case law or judge-made law, it is an important source of the UK constitution.

Judicial independence and neutrality

Distinguish between

Judicial independence

> Judicial independence is the principle that those in the judiciary should be free from political control. Such independence allows judges to 'do the right thing' and apply justice properly, without fear of the consequences.

Judicial neutrality

> Judicial neutrality is where judges operate impartially (i.e. without personal bias) in their administration of justice. Judicial neutrality is an essential requirement of the **rule of law**.

> The absence of judicial independence will threaten judicial neutrality because, if judges are subject to external control, their impartiality will be compromised. However, judicial independence does not guarantee judicial neutrality because judges may still allow their personal views to influence their administering of justice.

How is the independence of the judiciary maintained?

Judicial independence in the UK is based upon six main pillars:

> **The security of tenure enjoyed by judges.** Judges are appointed for an open-ended term, limited only by the requirement that they must retire by the age of 75. This means that politicians cannot seek to bring influence to bear by threatening to sack or suspend them.

Concepts explained

Rule of law A key principle of the UK constitution under which justice is guaranteed to all. A. V. Dicey saw the rule of law as one of the 'twin pillars' of the constitution; the other being parliamentary sovereignty.

According to Dicey the rule of law has three main strands:

> **No one can be punished without trial.** While this principle makes good sense in theory, it is not always maintained in practice. As we will see later in this chapter, terrorist suspects have been subject to a range of punishments without trial under measures passed since 2001, including indefinite detention, the imposition of control orders and the freezing of their assets.

> **No one is above the law and all are subject to the same justice.** Again, while this would appear to be a principle that would hold true in all liberal democracies, there have always been those who are effectively above the law in the UK: for example, the monarch, foreign ambassadors and MPs. In the case of the latter, a number of MPs even tried to use parliamentary privilege as a way of ending legal proceedings taken against them over their expenses.

> **The general principles of the constitution (e.g. personal freedoms) result from the judges' decisions rather than parliamentary statute.** While the decisions of judges (i.e. case law or common law) certainly have a part to play in defining the UK's constitutional arrangements, parliament remains sovereign and statute law reigns supreme: any legal precedent can be overturned by the means of a simple Act of Parliament.

Security of tenure It is extraordinarily hard for judges at High Court level and above (i.e. the 'senior judiciary') to be removed. Indeed, this can only take place as a result of impeachment proceedings requiring a vote in both houses of parliament. However, those in more junior ranks of the judiciary can be removed by the Lord Chancellor and the Lord Chief Justice. For example, on 17 May 2008 the *Guardian* reported the results of a Freedom of Information Act (2000) request confirming that two junior judges had been dismissed for misconduct in 2005.

> **Guaranteed salaries paid from the Consolidated Fund.** The salaries of judges cannot be altered with the aim of putting pressure on them because control of judges' pay has been placed beyond everyday political control. As a result, judges are free to make decisions as they see fit without fear of financial penalty, and politicians are unable to offer judges financial inducements to make the decisions they want.

Key term

➤ **Consolidated Fund** A government bank account used to pay the salaries of judges and certain other officials. The fund, managed by the Bank of England, receives all government tax revenues. Judges' salaries are classified as 'standing services' and are therefore paid from the fund automatically. The fact that the payment of such salaries is not part of the regular budgetary planning process means that politicians are unable to manipulate judges' salaries as a way of controlling them.

➤ **The offence of contempt of court.** Under sub judice rules, the media, ministers and other individuals are prevented from publicly speaking out during legal proceedings. This requirement is designed to ensure that justice is administered fairly, without undue pressure being brought to bear by politicians or the public in general.

➤ **A growing separation of powers.** The downgrading of the post of Lord Chancellor and the creation of a new UK Supreme Court has enhanced the separation between the senior judiciary and the other branches of government. Prior to these changes, the most senior judges, the Law Lords, sat in the House of Lords and the Lord Chancellor held significant roles in all three branches of government: executive, legislature and judiciary.

➤ **An independent appointments system.** The Constitutional Reform Act (2005) saw the creation of an independent Judicial Appointments Commission. This brought greater transparency to the process of judicial appointments and served to address concerns that the system in place previously had been open to political bias.

➤ **The training and experience of senior judges.** Most senior judges have served an 'apprenticeship' as barristers and come to the bench having achieved a certain status within their chosen profession. It is argued that such individuals take considerable pride in their legal standing and are therefore unlikely to defer to politicians or public opinion, where this would be seen to compromise their judicial integrity.

How is judicial neutrality guaranteed?

In simple terms, of course, it is impossible to guarantee judicial neutrality; judges are human, after all, and they will inevitably bring some degree of personal bias to their work. However, the promise of a universal application of the law under the doctrine of the rule of law requires that such bias is not allowed to colour judicial decisions.

There are four main ways in which this goal is achieved:

➤ **The relative 'anonymity' of senior judges.** Judges have traditionally operated away from the public eye. Until recently, judges rarely spoke out publicly on issues of law or public policy, and senior judges are still expected to avoid being drawn into open defence of their rulings, or criticism of those in government.

➤ **Restriction on political activity.** As with many senior civil servants, judges are not supposed to campaign on behalf of a political party or a pressure group.

Although judges retain the right to vote, their political views or outlook should not become a matter of public record.

- **Legal justifications of judgments.** Senior judges are generally expected to offer an explanation of how their decisions are rooted in law. This requirement that decisions be clearly rooted in the law makes it less likely that senior judges will be guided be personal bias.

    Note that in the case of the UK Supreme Court, decisions are published in full on the court's official website, along with press summaries of significant cases.

- **Training.** Judges are part of a highly trained profession, regulated by the Law Society. Senior judges have commonly served for many years as barristers before taking to the bench, and their elevation to the higher ranks of the judiciary would normally reflect a belief that they are able to put any personal bias they might hold to one side when administering justice. Although the security of tenure enjoyed by senior judges makes it difficult to remove those whose neutrality is open to question, additional guidance and training can be required in such cases, and individual judges might also be moved away from more serious cases while their performance is monitored.

Threats to judicial neutrality

The main question mark over judicial neutrality comes from the narrow recruiting pool from which senior judges have traditionally been drawn, with most of those appointed to the higher tiers of the judiciary being privately schooled, Oxbridge-educated, white, middle-class men, who are beyond middle age. How, it is argued, can judges be truly neutral when their own life-experiences are so very different from most of those who are brought before them? As we will see later in this chapter, the creation of the Judicial Appointments Commission appears to have done little to address this problem, and the composition of the UK Supreme Court, although determined under entirely different procedures, is similarly unrepresentative.

Critics also point to the way in which senior judges have been drawn into the political fray in recent years, the suggestion being that the passage of measures such as the Human Rights Act (1998) has resulted in a **politicisation** of the judiciary. However, while some see this growing public profile and increased conflict between senior judges and politicians as posing a threat to judicial neutrality, it could just as easily be seen as evidence of growing independence and neutrality — not least because senior judges appear increasingly willing to take on the political establishment in defence of civil liberties.

Concepts explained

Politicisation The process by which individuals traditionally regarded as being beyond the party political fray are drawn into it. Politicisation of the judiciary is said to result from appointments being made on political grounds as opposed to being truly meritocratic. The way in which the UK judiciary was drawn into areas of political controversy in the wake of the Human Rights Act (1998) was also seen by some as evidence of politicisation.

Viewpoint · Has the UK judiciary become more politicised in recent years?

YES

- Politicians have often broken with convention by publicly criticising rulings handed down by senior judges.

- Measures such as the Human Rights Act (1998) have drawn senior judges into the political arena by requiring them to rule on the 'merit' of individual pieces of statute law as opposed to their 'application'.

- The Factortame case (1990) showed that UK courts are able to 'suspend' Acts of Parliament where they are found to contradict EU law.

- The decision to transform the Law Lords into justices of the Supreme Court and locate the new court in Middlesex Guildhall has brought the most senior UK judges into the public arena for the first time, subjecting them to greater scrutiny by the media and the general public.

NO

- The process by which senior judges are appointed in the UK has been made more transparent and less open to accusations of political interference — in part as a result of the creation of an independent Judicial Appointments Commission.

- Whereas the concept of 'politicisation' is often associated with a loss of judicial independence, the UK senior judiciary has in fact become more independent in the wake of the Constitutional Reform Act (2005), not least with the 'downgrading' of the role of Lord Chancellor.

- Increased conflict between judges and politicians is a 'good' sign, as it shows that the courts are challenging the government when it appears to be encroaching upon our civil liberties.

- The fact that senior judges still benefit from security of tenure and guaranteed salaries affords them a degree of 'insulation' from political pressure.

Appointments to the senior judiciary

Appointments to the **senior judiciary** were traditionally made by the monarch on the advice of the prime minister and the Lord Chancellor. The Lord Chancellor customarily consulted serving senior judges through a process known as **secret soundings**. Although lower-level vacancies in the senior judiciary (e.g. for High Court judges) were advertised from the 1990s, the Lord Chancellor was under no obligation to fill vacancies by selecting his appointees from the ranks of those who had formally applied. It was said that this system

Key terms

➤ **Senior judiciary** The senior judiciary comprise justices of the Supreme Court (formerly the Lords of Appeal in Ordinary, or Law Lords); heads of divisions; Lords Justices of Appeal; High Court judges; and deputy High Court judges.

➤ **Secret soundings** The informal and secretive way in which most senior UK judges were once appointed. The phrase described the way in which the Lord Chancellor consulted in secret with close associates and those already serving in the senior judiciary. The resulting lack of transparency in appointments led to accusations of elitism.

lacked transparency, compromised the separation of powers, and resulted in a senior judiciary drawn almost exclusively from a very narrow social circle: public school and Oxbridge educated, white, male and beyond middle age.

Reform of the process under New Labour

In 2003 Labour announced plans to reduce the power of the Lord Chancellor and place most senior judicial appointments into the hands of a new, independent Judicial Appointments Commission (JAC). It was hoped that this change, brought into law under the Constitutional Reform Act (2005), would enhance the separation of powers and result in a senior judiciary that was more socially representative of the broader population. In spite of this second stated desire, early indications based upon the work of the JAC suggested that the process of creating a judiciary that 'looked like the UK' might take longer than originally anticipated.

On 28 January 2008, the *Guardian* reported that the new JAC had approved 21 individuals to become High Court judges, with ten of those approved having been appointed to positions on the High Court. Of these ten appointees:

- All were white, male, former barristers.
- Six of the nine who were educated in the UK went to leading independent schools.

In evidence to the Justice Select Committee in 2008, the justice minister Jack Straw conceded that in 2006–07, the JAC's first year of operation, only 8% of those recommended for appointment were from black or Asian backgrounds (down from 14% the previous year) and only 34% were women (down from 41%).

In responding to such criticisms, the JAC has maintained its commitment to appointing 'on merit and merit alone [using] selection processes that are open and fair to all applicants, regardless of their gender, race or background'. This defence echoes the commission's self-proclaimed guiding principle in making appointments: 'diversity in the field, merit in the selection'.

Appointments to the UK Supreme Court

Founding members of the UK Supreme Court

Justices of the UK Supreme Court are appointed under a different system from that used in respect of all other appointments to the senior judiciary. The founding justices of the new Supreme Court were those active Law Lords in-post on 1 October 2009 (see Table 9.1). Under the Constitutional Reform Act (2005) the most senior of the 12 at that time, Lord Phillips of Worth Matravers, took on the role of president of the court, with the second most senior, Lord Hope of Craighead, assuming the role of deputy president.

Although these former Law Lords themselves remained members of the House of Lords, they were barred from sitting and voting in the upper chamber for as long as they remained Justices of the Supreme Court. Under the Constitutional Reform Act (2005) those appointed to the court subsequently are not automatically elevated to the Lords.

Table 9.1 The make-up of the first UK Supreme Court (October 2009)

Justice	Date of birth	University	Retires
Lord Phillips of Worth Matravers President of the Supreme Court	21/01/1938	Kings College, Cambridge	2013
Lord Hope of Craighead Deputy president	27/06/1938	St John's College, Cambridge University of Edinburgh	2013
Lord Saville of Newdigate Justice of the Supreme Court	20/03/1936	Brasenose College, Oxford	2011
Lord Rodger of Earlsferry Justice of the Supreme Court	18/09/1944	New College, Oxford University of Glasgow	2019
Lord Walker of Gestingthorpe Justice of the Supreme Court	17/03/1938	Trinity College, Cambridge	2013
Baroness Hale of Richmond Justice of the Supreme Court	31/03/1947	Girton College, Cambridge	2022
Lord Brown of Eaton-under-Heywood Justice of the Supreme Court	09/04/1937	Worcester College, Oxford	2012
Lord Mance Justice of the Supreme Court	06/06/1943	University College, Oxford	2018
Lord Collins of Mapesbury Justice of the Supreme Court	07/05/1941	Downing College, Cambridge Columbia Law School, New York	2011
Lord Kerr of Tonaghmore Justice of the Supreme Court	22/02/1948	Queen's University, Belfast	2023
Lord Clarke of Stone-cum-Ebony Justice of the Supreme Court	13/05/1943	King's College, Cambridge	2018
Lord Neuberger of Abbotsbury	10/01/1948	Christ Church, Oxford	2009

Note that at the time that it began its work on 1 October 2009, only 11 of the 12 places on the UK Supreme Court were filled. This was because one of the former Law Lords, Lord Neuberger of Abbotsbury, had taken up the position of Master of the Rolls in preference to making the move across Parliament Square to Middlesex Guildhall.

Profile of justices

One would hardly expect a superior court such as the UK Supreme Court to be socially representative of the broader population, but the membership of the new court left it open to accusations of elitism:

➢ Ten of the 11 justices who were on the UK Supreme Court at the time it opened for business had attended Oxford or Cambridge.
➢ Nine of the 11 had attended independent secondary schools.
➢ Ten of the 11 were men.
➢ The justices had an average age of 67.8 years.

Qualifying to sit in the UK Supreme Court

In order to be considered for appointment as a justice of the Supreme Court, candidates must have either:

> held high judicial office for at least 2 years, or
> been a **qualifying practitioner** for a period of 15 years

Selection commission

Vacancies in the court are filled by an ad hoc selection commission as opposed to the JAC. According to Schedule 8, part 1 of the Constitutional Reform Act (2005), this five-member commission comprises:

> the president of the Supreme Court
> the deputy president of the Supreme Court
> one member of the Judicial Appointments Commission (JAC)
> one member of the Judicial Appointments Board for Scotland
> one member of the Northern Ireland Judicial Appointments Commission

Appointments process

Although the appointments process still involves the minister who formally retains the title of Lord Chancellor (i.e. the justice minister), his role is greatly reduced.

Nomination

> A vacancy arises.
> A five-member selection commission is convened to consider possible nominees and make a 'selection' based on merit.
> The commission submits a report to the Lord Chancellor identifying a nominee.

Confirmation

The Lord Chancellor may:

> accept the selection by 'notifying' the prime minister
> reject the selection, or
> require the commission to reconsider its selection

Once 'notified', the prime minister must recommend the approved candidate to the queen. The appointment is confirmed once the monarch has issued letters patent.

Although on paper this appears to leave the Lord Chancellor with considerable power in appointments to the new court, the reality is rather more complicated as he or she is not permitted repeatedly to reject names put forward by the commission.

The power of the UK judiciary

Whereas the US Supreme Court can declare Acts of Congress unconstitutional, thereby striking them down, UK courts have no such power in respect of parliamentary statute.

This is because statute law remains the supreme source of constitutional law in the UK. Despite this reality, however, senior courts in the UK still wield considerable power when reviewing the actions of the government or government officials.

Ultra vires cases

Traditionally the most significant cases were those where senior courts reviewed the actions of government officials in order to decide whether or not they have acted unlawfully or **ultra vires**.

In recent years, however, the power of the UK judiciary has been enhanced by two key developments: the growing importance of EU Law; and the impact of the Human Rights Act (1998).

EU membership and judicial power

Under the European Communities Act (1972), the UK incorporated the Treaty of Rome into UK law. The effect of this simple change was to give European laws precedence over conflicting UK statutes, whether past or present. For many years this simply meant that the UK government could be called to account at the European Court of Justice. However, in the wake of the **Factortame** case (1990), UK courts have also been able to 'suspend' UK statutes that appear to be in violation of EU law.

> ### Key terms
> ➤ **Ultra vires** From the Latin, meaning 'beyond the authority' or 'beyond one's powers'. The process of judicial review can be used to determine whether or not a minister or other government officer has acted ultra vires: that is, beyond the authority granted to them in law.

Concepts explained

'Factortame' A case in which the European Court of Justice established the precedent that UK courts can suspend UK statute law where it appears to violate EU law, at least until the European Court of Justice is able to make a final determination as to the legality of the statute in question.

The case took its name from a Spanish-owned fishing company, Factortame Limited, which had challenged the legality of the Merchant Shipping Act (1988) under European law.

The Human Rights Act and judicial power

Before 1998 cases brought under the European Convention on Human Rights were heard at the European Court of Human Rights in Strasbourg. Under the Human Rights Act (HRA, 1998), the convention was incorporated into UK law, meaning that UK citizens can now have their cases heard in UK courts. Under the HRA, UK courts are able to issue a declaration of incompatibility where a parliamentary statute appears to violate the rights guaranteed. Crucially, however, parliament is not obliged to amend the offending statute. Note that the scope and extent of power afforded to the judiciary under the HRA will be dealt with in more detail later in the chapter when considering the protection of civil liberties.

How has the UK Supreme Court changed things?

Why was the court established?

The UK Supreme Court was established under the Constitutional Reform Act (2005) in response to a number of longstanding concerns:

- concerns over the incomplete separation of power — or 'fusion of powers' — present in the UK system: specifically, the position of the Lord Chancellor and the presence of the Law Lords in the upper chamber of the legislature
- criticisms of the opaque system under which senior judges such as the Law Lords were appointed
- widespread confusion over the work of the Law Lords — specifically, a widespread failure to understand the distinction between the House of Lords' legislative and judicial functions

All of this was compounded by the fact that the Appellate Committee of the House of Lords, which served as the highest court of appeal before the creation of the new Supreme Court, was largely a mystery to most of those it existed to protect. As the BBC's Chris Summers noted back in 2007, 'Ask any tour guide in Washington DC and they will be able to direct you to the US Supreme Court. Make the same enquiry of a London guide about the UK version and they would be left scratching their head.'

Powers assigned to the UK Supreme Court

In November 2008, the soon-to-be president of the UK Supreme Court, Lord Phillips, offered his thoughts on the role of new court in a speech to the Law Society.

> Our Supreme Court is attracting huge interest worldwide. One question that I am repeatedly asked is, 'What difference is it going to make?' In theory, it need not make much. The change is [largely] one of form rather than of substance...[but] it is plain that there are many who are hoping that the move across Parliament Square will prove a catalyst for change.

Lord Phillips' comments highlighted the paradox apparent in the media coverage of the new court: namely, that a body that was to be given no new powers was nonetheless widely expected to assume a more pivotal role within the UK system.

Under the Constitutional Reform Act (CRA, 2005) the new UK Supreme Court simply took on most of those roles previously performed by the Law Lords:

- acting as the final court of appeal in England, Wales and Northern Ireland
- hearing appeals on issues of public importance surrounding arguable points of law
- hearing appeals from civil cases in England, Wales, Northern Ireland and Scotland
- hearing appeals from criminal cases in England, Wales and Northern Ireland (with the High Court of Justiciary retaining jurisdiction over criminal cases in Scotland)

Early cases before the court

The sense that the creation of a new UK Supreme Court was more a change in form than in substance was reinforced by the early cases heard by the new court, few of which represented a significant departure from what the Law Lords had done hitherto. For example, the court's ruling in the case of those suspected terrorists who had had their assets seized without trial under the new anti-terror regime (see Box 9.1) was not so very different in tone or scope from those handed down previously in respect of the indefinite detention of terrorist suspects at Belmarsh under the Anti-terrorism Crime and Security Act (2001) or the use of control orders introduced under the Prevention of Terrorism Act (2005).

> ### Box 9.1 The Supreme Court finds against the Treasury's seizure of the assets of suspected terrorists
>
> On 27 January 2010, the Supreme Court ruled that the UK Treasury had acted ultra vires when implementing parts of the Terrorism (United Nations Measures) Order 2006 (TO) and the Al-Qaida and Taliban (United Nations Measures) Order 2006 (AQO).
>
> These measures had been introduced by the Treasury as 'Orders in Council' (laws passed without parliament) as a way of fulfilling the UK's commitments under United Nations Security Council resolutions.
>
> Under the TO, an individual's assets could be frozen if there was a 'reasonable suspicion' that they were involved in terrorist activities. Under the AQO, individuals whose names appeared on the UN Security Council's 'Consolidated List' were to have their assets frozen automatically. In both cases, those whose assets were frozen would have no real right to reply. The Supreme Court ruled that the Treasury's use of such Orders in Council encroached upon fundamental rights and was beyond the authority granted it under statute.

In simple terms, therefore, the court was doing little more than using those powers that had been available to the Law Lords previously in respect of ultra vires rulings, declarations of incompatibility and disputes arising under EU law.

Impact of the UK Supreme Court

The UK Supreme Court is still in its infancy and any conclusions we offer at this stage must therefore be tentative.

Already apparent

- **Appointments and composition.** The appointments process set up in respect of the new Supreme Court is significantly more independent and less opaque than the system under which Law Lords were appointed previously. This may, in time, have a knock-on effect on the composition of the court.
- **Power.** The move across Parliament Square to Middlesex Guildhall has not been accompanied by any change in the roles or power of the court.
- **Judicial independence.** On the face of it, judicial independence has been enhanced, not least as a result of a clearer separation of powers. However, evidence of increasing friction between the judiciary and leading politicians ahead of the creation of the

new court suggests that the highest tier in the UK judiciary was already functionally independent.

Less tangible

➤ **Importance of a physical separation.** The move to Middlesex Guildhall has a significance beyond simply taking the active Law Lords out of the Palace of Westminster. Giving the new court its own building is likely to raise its profile, engender greater public interest in the court and allow it to develop a distinctive identity and character.

➤ **Lifting of restrictions on television cameras.** The likelihood of regular televised sessions should demystify the senior judiciary and might well result in the emergence of a new relationship between the media and senior judges.

➤ **Changes in the way rulings are delivered.** The court's website already carries downloadable texts of its rulings along with press summaries of many judgments. This will allow for greater public scrutiny of the workings of the court and those it finds against.

➤ **Relations between the court and government.** It is likely that the changes outlined above will affect the way in which the other branches of government view the new court and their relationship with it.

Weblinks

www.supremecourt.gov.uk — the official site of the UK Supreme Court.

Civil liberties in the UK

Often seen as synonymous with the term **rights**, **civil liberties** are those fundamental freedoms enjoyed by citizens under the style of limited government practised in liberal democracies such as the UK and the USA. As Paul Floyd has noted, such liberties may 'concern the freedom to do or to have something, such as the right to assemble, to privacy, to ownership of property or to a fair trial', or instead 'be about freedom from things, such as oppression, arbitrary arrest, slavery or imprisonment without trial'. In theory, at least, government should only encroach upon — or 'abrogate' — such liberties in time of war or when facing other emergencies.

Key terms

➤ **Civil liberties** The fundamental freedoms enjoyed by citizens in a liberal democracy, properly limited only by those laws established for the common good.

➤ **Rights** Legal or moral entitlements to have something or behave in a particular way.

What civil liberties are protected in the UK?

The main liberties available to UK citizens are no different from those afforded to citizens living under other western liberal democratic systems of government: the right to life; freedom of expression; freedom of religion and conscience; freedom of movement;

Demonstrators during a May Day rally in Edinburgh in 2010, protesting about the war in Afghanistan and cuts to public services

freedom of association; the right of protest; freedom from arbitrary arrest; freedom from torture; the right to fair trial; political rights, such as the right to vote (the franchise); and property rights.

Where are civil liberties set out in the UK?

The uncodified nature of the UK's constitutional arrangements has traditionally made it hard to determine precisely 'where' civil liberties are set out. Historically, the UK has had neither a codified constitution, nor — prior to 1998 at least — anything analogous to the US Bill of Rights. The constitution and the statutory framework have instead evolved over time, with citizens remaining free to do anything that is not prohibited in statute; a system characterised by **negative rights** as opposed to **positive rights**.

Positive and negative rights

Distinguish between

Positive rights
➤ Those explicitly assigned to citizens, often being entrenched as a part of a codified constitutional settlement — as is the case in the USA.

Negative rights
➤ Those liberties that are not explicitly set out, but exist in the absence of any law forbidding individuals from exercising them.

According to the nineteenth-century constitutional lawyer A. V. Dicey, such freedoms are protected:

➤ through the actions of a sovereign, independent and robust parliament, which will act quickly to address perceived injustices

➤ by the fact that public opinion will not stand for encroachment on longstanding freedoms

> through the laying down of judge-made case law — often called common law or ordinary law

These three factors combined created a system under which the rights of UK citizens were protected by an overlapping web of provisions, some rooted in convention, some afforded statutory footing and others resulting from legal precedents established in the courts. This can be seen, for example, in the protection afforded to the 'right to life'. Long established in common law, the right to life has also been recognised in parliamentary statutes such as the Offences Against the Persons Act (1861), the Murder (Abolition of Death Penalty) Act (1965) and the Crime and Disorder Act (1998), as well as a number of international treaties and conventions — for example, Protocol 13 (2002) of the European Convention on Human Rights and the United Nations Convention on the Rights of the Child (1989).

The UK's new 'rights culture'

It was the absence of a clear and authoritative summary of the rights available to UK citizens that prompted New Labour to bring three new pieces of legislation to the statute books following its return to office in 1997: the Human Rights Act (1998), the Freedom of Information Act (2000) and the Data Protection Act (DPA 1998), the first two measures having been included in the party's manifesto at the 1997 general election:

> We will by statute incorporate the European Convention on Human Rights into UK law.

> [This] will establish a floor, not a ceiling for human rights. Parliament will remain free to enhance these rights, for example by a Freedom of Information Act.

Some commentators argue that the passage of these measures has resulted in the emergence of a new culture of positive rights in the UK — something more akin to that embedded in US political culture.

Human Rights Act (1998)

The Human Rights Act (HRA) came into force in October 2000. It incorporated most of the articles of the **European Convention on Human Rights** (ECHR) into UK law, thereby allowing citizens to pursue cases under the ECHR through UK courts as opposed to having to go directly to the European Court of Human Rights in Strasbourg.

Key terms

> **European Convention on Human Rights (ECHR, 1950)** The ECHR was established by the Council of Europe, an intergovernmental body that is separate from the European Union and not to be confused with the EU's Council of Ministers or European Council. Alleged violations of the ECHR are investigated by the European Commission on Human Rights and tried in the European Court of Human Rights, based in Strasbourg. Again these bodies are not to be confused with the EU's European Commission and European Court of Justice.

European Court of Human Rights and European Court of Justice

Distinguish between

European Court of Human Rights

- ➤ The European Court of Human Rights was established by the Council of Europe
- ➤ It hears cases brought under the European Convention on Human Rights.
- ➤ It is based in Strasbourg but is not an EU institution.

European Court of Justice

- ➤ The European Court of Justice is the 'supreme court' of the European Union.
- ➤ It hears cases arising under EU law
- ➤ It is based in Luxembourg.

Box 9.2 **The scope of the HRA**

The HRA (1998) came into force in October 2000. It incorporated the 18 Articles of the European Convention on Human Rights (1950) into UK law.

Article 1 commits all signatories to protecting the rights included in the convention.

Article 2 protects the right to life.

Article 3 prohibits torture and degrading or inhuman treatment.

Article 4 outlaws slavery and involuntary servitude.

Article 5 secures liberty and security of the individual against arbitrary arrest and imprisonment.

Article 6 guarantees a fair trial.

Article 7 prevents legislation that criminalises acts retrospectively.

Article 8 promotes respect for the individual's private and family life.

Article 9 protects the freedom of thought, conscience and religion.

Article 10 enshrines the right to freedom of expression.

Article 11 protects the rights of association and assembly: for example, the right to form a trade union.

Article 12 protects the right of men and women to marry and start a family.

Article 13 allows for the redress of grievances where convention rights have been violated.

Article 14 prohibits discrimination in the application of rights guaranteed in the convention.

Article 15 allows for suspension or 'derogation' of some of the rights guaranteed by the convention in times of national emergency.

Article 16 permits restrictions on the political rights of foreign nationals.

Article 17 prevents rights protected in the convention from being used to limit other convention rights.

Article 18 holds that the 'get out clauses' included in some articles of the convention should not be abused as a way of limiting those rights protected in more general terms.

As the HRA is based on the Council of Europe's ECHR, rather than on EU law, it is not superior to parliamentary statute, as EU laws are under the Treaty of Rome. That said, the HRA (like the ECHR) has a 'persuasive authority' that has enhanced the protection of individual rights in the UK (see Box 9.2).

Freedom of Information Act (2000)

New Labour's manifesto at the 1997 general election included an explicit commitment to introduce freedom of information legislation — a response both to the allegations of sleaze that had affected the dog-days of John Major's Conservative administration and to a more widespread perception that there needed to be greater transparency in government.

The Freedom of Information Act (FOI) received the royal assent on 30 November 2000, but did not come into force until 1 January 2005 (see Box 9.3). This delay in implementation was supposed to provide public authorities an opportunity to prepare for the anticipated avalanche of requests for information.

> **Box 9.3** **The Freedom of Information Act in outline**
>
> ➤ The FOI (2000) came into force in January 2005.
> ➤ It gave citizens a right to access information held by public authorities.
> ➤ It required public bodies seeking to deny requests for information to show that the public interest warrants an exemption under the Act.
> ➤ It established a new Information Commissioner and Information Tribunal.
> ➤ It required public authorities to adopt a scheme for the publication of information.

Data Protection Act (1998)

The Data Protection Act (DPA), though often overshadowed by the HRA (1998) and the FOI (2000), nonetheless provides some significant guarantees.
- It places restrictions on the storage of personal data.
- It limits the sharing of such data between different organisations.
- It requires that information is held securely.
- It gives individuals the right to see any information that relates to them and to have factual inaccuracies corrected.

The status of rights in the UK

As we have seen, UK courts cannot declare an Act of Parliament unconstitutional as a result of the supremacy of statute law. The power of senior judges is therefore limited to declaring that a government official has acted beyond the authority given to them under statute (ultra vires), suspending UK statutes where they appear to violate EU law (since the Factortame case) or issuing a declaration of incompatibility where the measures in question appear to violate the HRA (1998).

The HRA in action

As we have seen, the HRA does not have the same legal status as EU law or the US Bill or Rights, with the latter being both entrenched and superior to regular statute. As a regular piece of statute, the HRA can be amended, 'suspended' (**derogated**) — in its entirety or in part — or simply repealed, like any Act.

While the courts cannot strike down parliamentary statute under the HRA, they can make a declaration of incompatibility and invite parliament to reconsider the offending statute (see Box 9.4). Furthermore, where statute is silent or unclear, the courts can make even greater use of the HRA by using its provision to establish legal precedent in common law. In addition, we should remember that the HRA also has a hidden influence through the process by which draft legislation is now examined by parliament's Joint Committee on Human Rights in order to ensure that it is HRA compatible.

The coverage of early cases brought under the HRA was fairly comprehensive, taking in the full range of rights protected (see Box 9.4). However, recent years focus far more on the way in which the HRA sits with the government's efforts to protect UK citizens from the threat of terrorism (see Box 9.5).

> **Concepts explained**
>
> **Derogation** A process by which a country is exempted, perhaps temporarily, from observing a law or regulation it has previously agreed to abide by. Under Article 15 of the European Convention on Human Rights (ECHR), national governments are permitted to derogate some of the convention's articles in times of national crisis.

Box 9.4 Early cases under the HRA

➤ **The killers of James Bulger.** The court imposed a lifetime ban on revealing the new identities of Thompson and Venables, the two boys convicted of killing toddler James Bulger in 1993. The ban was granted on the grounds that identifying them might threaten their right to life (Article 2) and could also result in their being subjected to inhuman and degrading treatment (Article 3). The court also held that such a ban might protect the boys' right to private and family life (Article 8). Newspapers had argued that the freedom of expression protected under Article 10 gave them the right to publish detail; the court disagreed.

➤ **The 1997 'two strikes and you're out' legislation.** A case was brought by four men imprisoned for life under legislation requiring mandatory life sentences for those convicted of serious offences for a second time. The men argued that the legislation violated their right to liberty (Article 5), was inhuman and degrading (Article 3) and fell foul of the Article 7 ban on making laws retrospective. The Court of Appeal ruled that judges should be able to use their discretion when sentencing — as they had done prior to the Act being passed — rather than being forced to impose a life sentence in such cases.

➤ **Treatment of mental patients.** A paranoid schizophrenic killer detained at Broadmoor argued that the Mental Health Act (1983) reversed the burden of proof by requiring him to prove that he was cured before he could be considered for release. The Court of Appeal ruled that the Act violated both Article 5 and Article 6 of the convention.

➤ **Right to remain silent.** A woman charged after admitting being drunk in charge of a vehicle argued that section 172 of the Road Traffic Act (1988) had violated her right to silence (Article 6) by making it an offence for her to refuse to name the driver of a vehicle. Section 172 also applied to vehicles caught on speed cameras. Scotland's High Court threw out the prosecution against her on the grounds that the Act undermined her right to a fair trial (Article 6).

Box 9.5 **The Courts, the HRA and the detention of terrorist suspects**

Part 4 of the UK's Anti-Terrorism Crime and Security Act (2001), which allowed the indefinite detention of foreign terrorist suspects, was only passed into law after the government chose to derogate Article 5 of the European Convention on Human Rights on the grounds that there was a 'public emergency threatening the life of the nation'. This was the form of words required to meet the requirements for derogation under Article 15 of the European Convention on Human Rights.

In the landmark case *A and Others* v *Secretary of State for the Home Department* (2004), an appellate committee of nine Law Lords ruled (8:1) that the **indefinite detention** of suspects under the Anti-terrorism, Crime and Security Act (2001) was incompatible with Articles 5 and 14 of the HRA.

In June and August 2006, the High Court found that the use of **control orders** allowed under the Prevention of Terrorism Act (2005) also violated Article 5, as such restrictive measures amounted to imprisonment without trial.

Key terms

➢ **Control order** A form of close house arrest allowed under the Prevention of Terrorism Act (2005). It was introduced after the indefinite detention of foreign terrorist suspects, which was sanctioned under the Anti-terrorism, Crime and Security Act (2001), was declared incompatible with the ECHR incorporated into UK law under the Human Rights Act (1998).

➢ **Indefinite detention** The right to hold foreign terrorist suspects indefinitely without trial, as authorised by the Anti-terrorism, Crime and Security Act (2001). Suspects were famously held at Belmarsh Prison in London. Indefinite detention was ruled incompatible with the Human Rights Act (1998) in the case *A and Others* v *Secretary of State for the Home Department* (2004).

The FOI in action

In much the same way as the HRA (1998) initially failed to live up to its billing, the FOI (2000) did not lead to the anticipated avalanche of requests for information. Public authorities ranging from government departments to local police and fire authorities had spent 5 years preparing for 'information D-day' on 1 January 2005. Indeed, in many cases additional staff had been taken on specifically to deal with requests from the public.

Most early requests for information under the Act came not from individual citizens but from media organisations that saw the Act either as a means of tying up loose ends on earlier stories or as an additional tool when engaged in investigative journalism. By 2010, however, the FOI had been used more widely and was increasingly seen as an effective means by which the government and elected officials could be held to account.

In no area was the use of the FOI more apparent than in the case of the furore over MPs' expenses. Although this scandal entered the broader public consciousness as a result of the *Daily Telegraph*'s decision to publish leaked details of MPs' expenses verbatim, we should remember that the chain of events that led to these disclosures began with a request by the Anglo-American journalist Heather Brooke made under the FOI.

The DPA in action

Although the DPA (1998) was designed to enhance the privacy of citizens in an information age, it has failed to deliver in a number of key areas. First, the Act has not prevented the emergence of massive national databases. Secondly, there is mounting concern regarding the way in which information is shared between state institutions. Thirdly, there have been numerous losses of personal data. Such problems were highlighted in a survey conducted by the Rowntree Trust in 2008 (see Box 9.6).

Box 9.6 Concerns over data protection

➤ A quarter of all the largest public database projects breach data protection and rights laws.

➤ A half have problems with privacy and could fall foul of a legal challenge.

➤ Only 6 of the 46 database schemes 'get the green light'.

Source: Rowntree Trust, 2008.

Importance of political culture

One should not underestimate the part played by **political culture** when assessing the extent to which a government is able to encroach upon individual liberties unchallenged.

It was unrealistic to think that UK political culture would be transformed overnight as a result of the passage of measures such as the HRA (1998) and the FOI (2000). It takes time for such Acts to enter the public consciousness and longer still before significant numbers of ordinary citizens are moved to employ those rights in legal action. Thus, whereas early cases saw the HRA being used largely by celebrities as a means of protecting their privacy — rather than by 'ordinary citizens' protecting their civil liberties — recent years have seen more widespread and ground-breaking use of the Act.

The prevailing political culture is also shaped by factors beyond the control of government and parliament, such as the state of emergency that followed the attacks of 9/11 (2001) and 7/7 (2005). These events saw most if not all UK citizens accept restrictions on their civil liberties that would previously have been considered unthinkable. Such a willingness to defer to the government in a crisis should come as no great surprise; even the philosopher John Locke (1632–1704) acknowledged that in times of emergency, 'responsible leaders could resort to exceptional power'. However, it is equally significant that as the immediate terrorist threat appeared to recede after 2008, the opposition to government measures that threatened individual civil liberties grew. This can be clearly seen in the battle over New Labour's national ID card scheme.

Key terms

➤ **Political culture** The opinions, attitudes and values that shape political behaviour. A nation's political culture consists of the citizens' collectively held attitudes towards the political system and their place in it.

Threats to civil liberties post-9/11

The lack of entrenchment afforded to civil liberties in the UK has been underlined by the extent to which individual liberties were eroded in the face of the increased terrorist threat perceived after 9/11.

Caught between the need to protect the lives of UK citizens and a desire to protect other civil liberties, the government's legislative programme often appeared to prioritise the former over the latter (see Table 9.2).

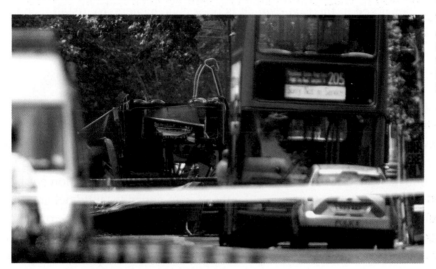

The remains of a double-decker bus after the terrorist attack in London, July 2005

Table 9.2 Civil liberties under threat post-9/11

Act	Year	Key provisions
Anti-terrorism, Crime and Security Act	2001	Allowed the indefinite detention of foreign terrorist suspects.
Proceeds of Crime Act	2002	Allowed the confiscation of the assets of suspected terrorists without prosecution.
Regulation of Investigatory Powers Act	2002	Empowered the police and local authorities to undertake covert surveillance.
Criminal Justice Act	2003	Limited the right to trial by jury in some cases.
Anti-social Behaviour Act	2003	Allowed the imposition of curfews.
Prevention of Terrorism Act	2005	Introduced control orders.
Serious Organised Crime and Police Act	2005	Restricted protests in the vicinity of parliament.
Identity Card Act	2006	Provided for the phased introduction of a compulsory national biometric ID card scheme.
Terrorism Act	2006	Made it an offence to 'glorify' acts of terrorism.
Counter-terrorism Act	2008	Allowed the police to restrict photography in public places as well as extending the rights of policy to take DNA evidence and monitor those suspected of involvement in terrorist activity.
Coroners and Justice Act	2009	Allowed inquests into deaths relating to terrorist activities to be held in secret.

It is perhaps inevitable that citizens will defer to government in times of national emergency: accepting restrictions on their civil liberties that they would surely never countenance in the normal course of events. Once passed into law, however, it is largely up to the authorities to determine precisely how such powers are applied and when (if ever) they are rescinded. The open-ended nature of many of those measures which have found their way on to the statute books in recent years presents a clear and present danger to civil liberties in the UK. As the American cryptographer and computer expert Bruce Schneier noted in the *Guardian*, 'It is poor civic hygiene to install technologies that could some day facilitate a police state.'

Does the UK need a formal Bill of Rights?

Controversy over the Human Rights Act (1998)

Supporters of the HRA argue that it simply brings into British law those freedoms and rights previously available to British citizens under the European Convention on Human Rights. However, the application of these guarantees since the HRA came into force in October 2000 has given cause for concern. A particular bone of contention has been the extent to which the Act has been used by those who engender little public sympathy, specifically criminals and foreign nationals facing deportation. The case of the Afghan hijackers in 2006 provides a clear illustration of this point. Originally arrested and charged with a range of offences in connection with the hijacking of a passenger airliner, nine Afghans who claimed to have fled from the Taliban were ultimately allowed to remain in the UK and seek employment after the government was found to have denied them their rights under the HRA.

The reaction of many politicians and the broader public to cases such as this, while being entirely understandable, strikes at the very heart of what the HRA is supposed to do in terms of making fundamental rights available universally. The whole point of codifying such rights in this way is to protect those who might be denied their liberty under a more arbitrary set of arrangements.

It is true that the HRA has seen the senior judiciary coming into conflict with government ministers more regularly than was previously the case in the UK, but this is an inevitable consequence of an emergent rights culture. Although the anti-terror legislation that came in the wake of the attacks on 9/11 and 7/7 has raised serious questions regarding the proper relationship between the judiciary and politicians, the key function of an independent judiciary is to protect citizens from a government that seeks to erode their rights and encroach upon their freedoms.

This observation is particularly true of the judicial criticism of indefinite detention without trial of terrorist suspects under the Anti-terrorism, Crime and Security Act (2001) and the imposition of control orders under the Prevention of Terrorism Act (2005). Both measures struck at the heart of the presumption of innocence, the right to a free and fair trial, and freedom from arbitrary arrest and imprisonment. While the belief of successive Labour home secretaries that the judges 'don't get it', as John Reid put it, or are 'confused on rights', as Charles Clarke claimed, reflects their genuine concern and frustration, it also betrays a failure to see the bigger picture.

Ultimately, of course, the government is not required to give way under pressure from judges. Declarations of incompatibility issued under the HRA only invite parliament (and, by implication, the government) to reconsider its position, allowing a 'freedom to differ' that has been apparent over control orders. The UK government can also apply to derogate those guarantees enshrined in the ECHR in times of national emergency.

Calls for a UK Bill of Rights

Concerns over the operation of the HRA helped to create a situation in which both of the major UK political parties were calling for a new Bill of Rights in the UK by 2009 (see Box 9.7).

Box 9.7 **Party positions on a Bill of Rights in 2009**

Labour: 'A Green Paper to examine the case for developing a Bill of Rights and Responsibilities. A dialogue with the British public about how we might develop and articulate an inclusive view of our shared values.'

Conservative: 'Replace the Human Rights Act, which has undermined the government's ability to deal with crime and terrorism, with a British Bill of Rights.'

One would hardly expect the Labour government to abandon the HRA — given that it was a Labour government that introduced the measure back in 1998. However, declining public confidence in the Act, and the apparent popular appeal of the Conservatives' promise to scrap it and offer a uniquely British replacement, forced the government to reconsider its position — to the disappointment of many of those on the liberal-left.

The Conservative leader, David Cameron, offered a more root-and-branch approach to tackling the perceived deficiencies of the HRA. Although initially suggesting that a Conservative government would 'reform, replace or scrap' the Act, in 2006 he made a commitment to replacing, as opposed to amending or developing, the existing HRA (see Box 9.8). In 2010 part of the agreement on the formation of the coalition was to retain ECHR rights in UK law.

Box 9.8 **Cameron on the case for a new Bill of Rights**

We need a new approach:

The Human Rights Act has made it harder to protect our security;

It is hampering our fight against crime and terrorism;

It has done little to protect out liberties; and

It has helped create rights without responsibilities.

Source: David Cameron, 'Balancing freedom and security — a modern British Bill of Rights', 26 June 2006.

Problems in establishing a new UK Bill of Rights

What should be included in the new bill?

The US Bill of Rights — the first ten amendments to the US Constitution — is often championed as a model of how fundamental rights can be codified and protected. In reality, however, it is a rather disparate document that combines guarantees of basic freedoms such as those outlined in the First Amendment (see Box 9.9) with other measures that today appear at best anachronistic (e.g. the Third Amendment) and at worst rather unhelpful (e.g. the Second Amendment). Moreover, the US Bill of Rights did not prohibit slavery (only added with the Thirteenth Amendment) or give a guarantee of equal protection under the law (later included in the Fourteenth Amendment).

Box 9.9 **Extracts from the US Bill of Rights (1791)**

First Amendment
Congress shall make no law respecting an establishment of religion, or prohibiting the free exercise thereof; or abridging the freedom of speech, or of the press, or the right of the people peaceably to assemble, and to petition the Government for a redress of grievances.

Second Amendment
A well regulated Militia, being necessary to the security of a free State, the right of the people to keep and bear Arms, shall not be infringed.

Third Amendment
No Soldier shall, in time of peace be quartered in any house, without the consent of the Owner, nor in time of war, but in a manner to be prescribed by law.

The question of precisely what should be included in a new UK Bill of Rights is likely to prove similarly difficult to resolve. The beauty of the UK's Human Rights Act was that it effectively sidestepped the need for a discussion over the fundamentals of what should and should not be included simply by bringing a pre-existing list of rights and liberties — the European Convention on Human Rights — into UK law.

How will the broader public be consulted on the proposals?

Both major parties have suggested a kind of 'national conversation' or, as Labour put it, 'a dialogue with the British public'. Quite what this would mean in practice is unclear in a nation of over 60 million souls. A formal consultation along the lines that normally accompanies a Green Paper would surely fall way short of the kind of popular engagement and participation that both parties are looking to encourage, as such processes are invariable dominated by organised interests. The alternative, some kind of democratically appointed constitutional convention of the type employed at Philadelphia in 1787, appears equally improbable.

How will a new Bill of Rights square with UK commitments under the ECHR?

The repeal of the HRA would not, of course, deny UK citizens access to the rights it guarantees, because these rights are enshrined in the European Convention on Human

Rights (ECHR), on which the HRA was based and to which the UK has been a signatory since 1950. Repealing the HRA would do little more than turn the clock back a decade to a time when UK citizens had no option but to take their grievances to the European Court of Human Rights in Strasbourg. Although there is nothing to prevent the UK from withdrawing from the ECHR entirely, such a course of action would be problematic, for while remaining a party to the ECHR is not a legal requirement of EU membership, all 27 EU member states were signatories in 2010.

The issue of entrenchment

As a regular piece of statute law, the HRA can be amended or repealed like any other. As we have seen, national governments can also apply to derogate some or all of the convention's articles in times of national emergency.

Although the creation of a new UK Bill of Rights would remove the second problem, as it would be entirely separate from the ECHR, the first problem would remain under the doctrine of parliamentary sovereignty. In the absence of the kind of 'higher law' provided by a properly codified and entrenched constitution, parliament would always be free to alter or suspend the freedoms and liberties set out in any new Bill of Rights. Back in 2006, David Cameron suggested that a degree of entrenchment might be achieved by adding a Bill of Rights to the list of measures that the House of Commons cannot force through the House of Lords under the authority of the Parliament Act. Such an obstacle, he argued, would not absolutely prevent a government from encroaching upon the rights of citizens, but it would offer an additional level of protection for the measure.

Some commentators take a different line entirely, arguing that concerns over a lack of entrenchment are largely unfounded. This view is generally rooted in a belief that the House of Commons will be reluctant to encroach upon citizens' rights for fear of provoking a public backlash. In this way, the new Bill of Rights might in time become so embedded in the public consciousness that no government would dare to tamper with it, even though parliament would ultimately retain the authority to do so. Although some argue that this line of reasoning relies rather too heavily on the Commons checking themselves, evidence of this kind of 'governmental restraint' has already been seen in the Labour government's decision to defer to the courts over indefinite detention and to the Lords over the proposed 42-day detention of terrorist suspects.

Viewpoint   Does the UK need a formal Bill of Rights?

- A properly entrenched Bill of Rights would give enhanced constitutional protection to those rights considered fundamental.
- A Bill of Rights would serve to limit the power of the state.
- A UK Bill of Rights would reinforce the rule of law.
- A Bill of Rights could build upon rather than replace the guarantees offered under the HRA (1998).
- The presence of a formal Bill of Rights would help to raise public awareness of rights, thus contributing to the emergence of a rights culture.
- A Bill of Rights could link the concept of rights to the responsibilities and duties of UK citizens.

NO

- A Bill of Rights is unnecessary given the protection already afforded under the ECHR, common law and regular parliamentary statute.

- Entrenching rights would undermine the doctrine of parliamentary sovereignty.

- It would be difficult to entrench the Bill of Rights properly in the absence of a codified and entrenched constitution.

- It would be difficult to decide what to include and what to leave out.

- A codified and entrenched document might serve to undermine other rights set out elsewhere but not included in the new Bill of Rights.

- Some supporters of a UK Bill of Rights are motivated more by a desire to weaken the guarantees provided under the HRA (1998) than by a commitment to protecting civil liberties.

◗ What you should know

◗ The term 'judiciary' refers collectively to all judges in the UK, from lay magistrates all the way up to justices of the UK Supreme Court. However, students of politics are primarily concerned with the senior judiciary.

◗ The senior judiciary comprises justices of the Supreme Court (formerly known as Lords of Appeal in Ordinary or 'Law Lords'); heads of divisions; Lords Justices of Appeal; High Court judges; and deputy High Court judges.

◗ Judges at the Appeals Court level and above have the power to establish legally binding precedent or 'common law' using the power of judicial review. This role is particularly significant where statute law is ambiguous or unclear, or where the laws passed by parliament conflict with European law or are deemed incompatible with the Human Rights Act (1998).

◗ Under the doctrine of the rule of law, UK judges are expected to operate under the twin principles of judicial independence and judicial neutrality. Judicial independence requires that judges are able to apply the law as they see fit, free from external political controls. Judicial neutrality demands that justices set aside personal bias when applying the law.

◗ In recent years, the independence of the UK judiciary has been enhanced as a result of reforms to the judicial appointments process and the greater separation of powers achieved following reforms to the role of the Lord Chancellor, and the creation of a new UK Supreme Court.

◗ The Supreme Court is likely to grow in status and authority in the coming years, although it was not afforded any significant powers beyond those held by the Appellate Committee of the House of Lords, which it replaced in October 2009.

◗ Civil liberties are those fundamental freedoms enjoyed by citizens in a liberal democracy, limited only by those laws established for the common good. They include the right to life and liberty, and the freedom of speech.

◗ Traditionally, the UK was said to be characterised by the concept of negative rights — that citizens were free to do all that was not prohibited in law. In recent years there has been a move towards the setting out of positive rights, such as those included in the Freedom of Information Act (2000) and the guarantees incorporated into UK law under the Human Rights Act (1998).

◗ The courts can defend the rights of citizens by making ultra vires rulings where government officials have acted beyond their authority, by finding that UK law violates EU law, or by issuing a declaration of incompatibility under the Human Rights Act.

❍ The lack of a codified and entrenched constitutional settlement makes the rights of UK citizens vulnerable to change. This fact and the controversy surrounding the application of the Human Rights Act have led to calls for a UK Bill of Rights.

UK/US comparison

Judiciary and rights in the USA

➤ Under the US Constitution, the 50 US states are free to organise their own state-level judiciary largely as they see fit. As a result, UK/US comparisons tend to focus on the higher levels of the US (i.e. federal) judiciary in the USA and the senior judiciary in the UK.

➤ The US judiciary, like the UK judiciary, is broadly hierarchical in structure. The US Supreme Court sits above 13 US Federal Circuit Courts of Appeal, with US District Courts, the US Claims Court and the US Court of International Trade at the lowest tier.

➤ Whereas the UK Supreme Court comprises 12 members (the president of the court, the deputy president of the court and 10 justices of the court), the US Supreme Court has numbered 9 justices since 1869 (with one chief justice and 8 associate justices).

➤ The role and powers of the US Supreme Court are set out in Article 3 of the US Constitution, but the court's main power — that of judicial review — is not clearly enumerated. This power was instead 'discovered' by the court in the case of *Marbury* v *Madison* (1803) and extended in a number of landmark cases thereafter.

➤ The power of judicial review allows the US Supreme Court to strike down regular Acts of Congress where they violate constitutional provisions. This makes the US Supreme Court significantly more powerful than its UK counterpart — which has the doctrine of parliamentary sovereignty and the supremacy of statute law to contend with.

➤ US courts, like their UK counterparts, are expected to operate with high levels of judicial independence and judicial neutrality. Judges on both sides of the Atlantic must rely on other state institutions to enforce their judgments.

➤ Whereas the UK has traditionally operated under a system of negative rights, the USA has a long-established rights culture based upon explicit guarantees. The first ten amendments to the constitution, known collectively as the Bill of Rights (1791), offer entrenched protection to a range of fundamental freedoms and rights.

➤ The US Bill of Rights is far harder to change or ignore than the UK Human Rights Act (1998), which can easily be repealed or derogated in times of national emergency. Subsequent amendments to the US Constitution have offered citizens further guarantees: for example, the Thirteenth Amendment (1865) prohibits slavery and the Fourteenth Amendment (1868) guarantees equal protection under the law.

> As in the UK, the rights of US citizens are also protected under regular law (e.g. the US Civil Rights Act (1964) and the US Freedom on Information Act (1966)) and through legal precedents established by judicial interpretation (e.g. *Brown* v *Board of Education* (1954), which outlawed racial segregation in schools, and *Roe* v *Wade* (1973), which prevented states from banning abortion outright.

Further reading

Fairclough, P. and Magee, E. (2009) 'Civil liberties: do we live in a national security state?', *UK Government and Politics Annual Survey 2009*, chapter 4, Philip Allan Updates.

Fairclough, P. and Magee, E. (2010)'Goodbye Human Rights Act, hello Bill of Rights?', *UK Government and Politics Annual Survey 2010*, chapter 7, Philip Allan Updates.

Fairclough, P., Kelly, R. and Magee, E. (2006) 'A new rights culture and a more independent judiciary for the UK?', *UK Government and Politics Annual Survey 2006*, chapter 12, Philip Allan Updates.

Fairclough, P., Kelly, R. and Magee, E. (2007)'The Human Rights Act: why so controversial?', *UK Government and Politics Annual Survey 2007*, chapter 8, Philip Allan Updates.

Gearty, C. (2006) 'Civil liberties in the United Kingdom', *Politics Review*, Vol. 16, No. 2.

Le Sueur, A. (2009) 'Judges in the modern British constitution', *Politics Review*, Vol. 18, No. 3.

Simpson, M. (2006) 'Freedom of information: worth the wait?', *Politics Review*, Vol. 15, No. 3.

Wildbore, H. (2008) 'Does Britain need a bill of rights?', *Politics Review*, Vol. 17, No. 4.

Exam focus

Short-answer questions (around 5 minutes each)

Explain, using examples, the meaning of each of the following terms:

1 Judicial review
2 Ultra vires
3 Factortame
4 Judicial Appointments Commission (JAC)

Mid-length questions (around 10 minutes each)

Outline two arguments 'for' and two arguments 'against':

1 The Human Rights Act (HRA)

Outline the main differences between:

2 The HRA and a US-style Bill of Rights
3 Judicial independence and judicial neutrality
4 The European Court of Human Rights and the European Court of Justice

Mini-essays (around 25–30 minutes each)

Write a mini-essay in response to each of the following questions:

1 'The senior judiciary in the UK is neither independent nor neutral.' Discuss.
2 To what extent did New Labour's period in office (1997–2010) result in an erosion of civil liberties?
3 'A loud sounding nothing.' Assess this verdict on the UK Supreme Court.
4 'Politicians wearing wigs.' To what extent would you accept this view of senior judges in the UK?

Chapter 10

Devolution and local government

Key questions answered in this chapter
- ➤ Why did demands for devolution emerge?
- ➤ What powers do the devolved bodies have?
- ➤ What are the main implications of devolution for British politics?
- ➤ What functions does local government have?

The UK is a multinational state made up of four nations: England, Scotland, Wales and Northern Ireland. For all but the final year of the twentieth century, the UK was one of the most centralised states in western Europe. Labour's 1997 general election victory, however, brought major changes to the territorial politics of the UK as power was devolved to new institutions in Scotland, Wales and Northern Ireland in 1999. **Devolution** has brought significant changes to the politics of these nations and to the wider UK political system.

Key terms
- ➤ **Devolution** The transfer of political power from central government to subnational government.

The Union

The official title of the British state is the 'United Kingdom of Great Britain and Northern Ireland'. Great Britain is an island consisting of three nations: England, Scotland and Wales.

England is the largest of the UK's four nations with a population of 49 million (83.5% of the UK population). It is also the wealthiest of the four nations and home of the UK's capital city, London. Scotland has a population of 5 million, Wales 3 million and Northern Ireland 1.6 million people.

The nations of the UK joined a union with England at different times and in different circumstances.

➤ Wales entered the Union in 1536 when England completed its conquest of the principality. It was governed from London but retained a distinctive culture despite Anglicisation. The 2001 census reported that 28% of people in Wales had one or more skills in the Welsh language.

➤ Scotland was an independent state with its own parliament until the 1707 Act of Union. This international treaty saw Scotland join the Union but retain its legal system, education system and local government. Scottish identity continues to draw upon the history of independent statehood and a robust civil society.

➤ The six counties that make up Northern Ireland chose to remain part of the UK when the rest of the island of Ireland formed the Irish Free State in 1922. Ireland had joined the Union in 1800 through an Act of Union. The Union was a troubled one with the 'Irish Question' becoming one of the longest-running and most difficult issues in British politics. Demands for home rule eventually led to the partition of Ireland in 1922. The Irish Free State became the Republic of Ireland, an independent state, in 1949.

Unitary or union state?

Prior to devolution, the United Kingdom was usually described as a **unitary state**. A unitary state is a centralised state in which political power is located at the centre in national institutions. There is a high degree of centralisation and homogeneity

---

Distinguish between

Direct and representative democracy

Unitary state
➤ A unitary state is a highly centralised state in which political power is concentrated at the centre.
➤ Central government has ultimate authority over subnational institutions.
➤ The centre dominates the political, economic and cultural life of the state.
➤ All areas of the state are governed in the same way and there is a very high degree of administrative standardisation.

Union state
➤ A union state is a state whose component parts have come together through a union of crowns or by treaty.
➤ There is a high degree of administrative standardisation, but the component nations retain some of their pre-union features (e.g. separate churches or legal systems).
➤ Political power is concentrated at the centre, but the component nations have some degree of autonomy (e.g. through devolution).

Federal state
➤ A federal state is a state in which the constitution divides decision-making authority between national (federal) and regional (state) tiers of government.
➤ The different tiers of government are protected by the constitution: one tier cannot abolish the other.
➤ The regions within the state have a distinctive political, and often cultural, identity.

Key terms

➤ **Federalism** The sharing of power, enshrined in a constitution, between national (federal) and regional (state) authorities.

➤ **Union state** A state in which there are cultural differences and where, despite a strong centre, different parts of the state are governed in slightly different ways.

➤ **Unitary state** A homogeneous state in which power is concentrated at the political centre and all parts of the state are governed in the same way.

— all parts of the state are governed in the same way. In the UK, parliamentary sovereignty means that Westminster can make law on any subject of its choosing and this law cannot be overturned by any higher institution. Aside from the Stormont Parliament (1922–72) in Northern Ireland, the other parts of the UK did not have their own parliaments.

The centralisation found in a unitary state contrasts with the division of powers that characterises federal systems. In federal states such as the USA and Germany, power is divided between the national government (the federal government) and regional (state) governments. The constitutions of federal states allocate policy competences to the different tiers and give the states protected status.

Not all political scientists accepted the description of the UK as a unitary state. James Mitchell argued that the term did not reflect the character of the multinational UK. He preferred to describe the UK as a **union state**. In a union state, important political and cultural differences remain after union. Although there is a relatively high degree of administrative standardisation, differences in the way that parts of the state are governed have persisted.

Administrative and legislative devolution

Two types of devolution have been found in the UK:

➤ **Administrative devolution.** Political power is concentrated at the centre, but special arrangements are made to take account of distinctive regional interests and identities. Prior to 1999, Scottish and Welsh interests were catered for through distinctive procedures at Whitehall and Westminster, but Scotland and Wales did not have their own parliaments.

Concepts explained

Administrative devolution

A form of devolution in which political power is concentrated at the centre but special arrangements are found in the executive and legislature to take account of the distinctive interests and identities of various nations or regions. These nations and regions do not, however, have their own assemblies.

➤ **Legislative devolution**. This involves the creation of separate parliaments with legislative powers. It existed in Northern Ireland during the Stormont period (1922–72). In 1999, power was devolved from Westminster to new legislative assemblies in Scotland, Wales and Northern Ireland.

> **Concepts explained**
>
> **Legislative devolution**
>
> A form of devolution in which separate parliaments are established in the nations or regions of a state. Policy-making powers are transferred from the centre to the devolved assemblies, but the state-wide legislature retains ultimate authority and can overrule or abolish the devolved bodies.

Administrative devolution

During the period of administrative devolution, a number of special arrangements existed for the government of Scotland and Wales:

➤ **Territorial ministries in UK central government.** The Scottish Office was established as a government department in 1885, and the Welsh Office in 1964. They were responsible for a range of government activities (e.g. agriculture, education and health) in their respective nations. A secretary of state sat in the UK cabinet. The territorial ministries represented the interests of their nations in central government, but were also responsible for implementing UK government policy. By the 1980s, it was becoming difficult to marry these roles and many people in Scotland felt that the Scottish Office was not protecting their interests effectively.

➤ **Over-representation at Westminster.** Scotland and Wales were over-represented in the Commons, having more MPs per head of population than England. In the House of Commons, a Scottish Grand Committee and Welsh Grand Committee discussed matters in those countries. They consisted of all MPs representing Scottish and Welsh constituencies respectively.

➤ **A preferential formula for public spending.** The **Barnett formula**, agreed in 1978, translates changes in public spending in England into equivalent changes in the block grants for Scotland, Wales and Northern Ireland, calculated on the basis of population. Under the formula, Scotland, Wales and Northern Ireland receive more public spending per head of population than England.

> **Key terms**
>
> ➤ **Barnett formula** A formula devised by Joel Barnett MP in 1978 which determines the relative levels of public spending in England, Scotland, Wales and Northern Ireland.

Towards legislative devolution

Demands for legislative devolution have a long history. In the early twentieth century, the 'Irish Question' prompted brief interest in 'Home Rule all round' under which each **nation** would have had its own parliament in a federal state. **Nationalism** found political expression in the Welsh nationalist party Plaid Cymru, founded in

1925, and the Scottish Nationalist Party (SNP), which was founded in 1934. They campaigned for independence and the recognition of their national cultures. The nationalists made electoral breakthroughs at Westminster in the 1960s and 1970s, helped by dissatisfaction with the British political system and a popular revival of Scottish and Welsh identities.

Concepts explained

Nation

A group of people who inhabit a historic territory, share common traditions and culture, and regard themselves as a distinctive political community. A nation may also share a common language or religion.

Nationalism

A political ideology or movement that regards the nation as the main form of political community, and believes that humanity is divided into distinctive nations and that nations should be self-governing. National self-determination is the right of the nation to govern itself and have its own independent state. Two variants of nationalism are commonly identified: civic or political nationalism, which views the nation as the citizens of a territory who share a political culture, and upholds the rights of nations to govern themselves; and ethnic or cultural nationalism, which defines the nation in terms of ethnic descent and shared culture, and is often chauvinist or aggressive in character.

The nationalists' success posed difficult questions for Labour and the Conservatives. The Conservatives reacted in 1968 by supporting a Scottish Assembly. But this policy was not implemented by the Heath government of 1970–74, which introduced local government reform instead. Margaret Thatcher reversed the party's support for legislative devolution in 1979.

Historically, Labour had focused on class politics and opposed nationalism, but it now saw its electoral dominance in Scotland and Wales threatened. Opponents of devolution feared that it would undermine the equitable provision of public services and make the break-up of the UK more likely. But supporters of devolution within the Labour Party argued that it would cement support for Labour and reduce the appeal of the nationalists.

The 1979 referendums

The Labour government of James Callaghan (1976–79) introduced bills to establish legislative assemblies in Scotland and Wales. These were not, however, to come into force unless the proposed assemblies were supported in referendums in Wales and Scotland. It was also stipulated that the Scottish Assembly had to gain the support of 40% of the total Scottish electorate.

The 1979 Welsh referendum produced a decisive 'no' when only 20% of those who voted backed an assembly. In Scotland, 52% of those who voted supported devolution, but the 40% threshold was not reached as only 33% of the total electorate voted 'yes'. The

Labour government fell and was replaced by a Conservative administration opposed to devolution.

Demands for legislative devolution gathered momentum from the late 1980s. They were fuelled by the four consecutive elections won by the Conservatives despite their low (and declining) support in Scotland and Wales. A further concentration of power in Whitehall and the perceived insensitivity of the Thatcher government to Scottish distinctiveness also increased support for devolution. John Major's government sought to bolster support for the Union by giving the Scottish Office limited new powers, but he could not turn the pro-devolution tide.

Crucial to the prospects of devolution was Labour's conversion to the cause, particularly under the leadership of John Smith (1992–95). Devolution was now seen as the optimal way of preserving the Union, and was part of a wider constitutional reform agenda. A Scottish Constitutional Convention set up in 1989 proposed a Scottish Parliament with legislative and tax-raising powers. It also claimed that sovereignty lay with the people of Scotland, rather than at Westminster.

The 1997 referendums

Tony Blair maintained Labour's support for devolution but insisted that referendums be held in Scotland and Wales to approve the creation of the new institutions. The referendums followed within months of Labour's 1997 election victory. In Scotland, the referendum asked voters whether they supported (1) a Scottish Parliament and (2) tax-varying powers for the parliament — 74.3% supported a Scottish Parliament and 63.5% supported tax-varying powers. The decisive vote reflected elite and popular support for devolution in Scotland, and gave the new Scottish Parliament legitimacy from the outset.

The result of the referendum asking voters in Wales if they supported a Welsh Assembly was very close: 50.3% voted 'yes' and 49.7% 'no' on a turnout of 50.1%. Much of western Wales, where there is a higher proportion of Welsh speakers, supported the assembly but eastern Wales did not.

Devolution in Scotland and Wales

The Scottish Parliament and Welsh Assembly began their work after the first elections to the new institutions in May 1999. Labour's devolution settlement has been one of **asymmetric devolution**: that is, each of the devolved institutions has different powers and distinctive features. The Scottish Parliament has legislative and tax-varying powers whereas the Welsh Assembly has only executive powers. The former is solely responsible for law-making in devolved matters, but the latter merely determines how Westminster legislation is implemented in Wales.

Key terms

Asymmetric devolution
A form of devolution in which the political arrangements are not uniform, but differ from region to region.

The Scottish Parliament

The Scottish Parliament has 129 members (MSPs) elected by the additional member system. Seventy-three MSPs (57% of the total) are elected in single-member constituencies using the first-past-the-post system; the remaining 56 MSPs (43%) are 'additional members' chosen from party lists. They are elected in eight multi-member regions, each of which elects seven members using the list system of proportional representation. These seats are allocated to parties on a corrective basis so that the distribution of seats reflects the share of the vote won by the parties (see Chapter 2). Elections are held every 4 years.

It has primary legislative powers in a range of policy areas, including law and order, health, education, transport, the environment and economic development (see Table 10.1). Westminster no longer makes law for Scotland on these matters. The Scottish Parliament also has tax-varying powers: it can raise or lower the rate of income tax in Scotland by up to 3% (i.e. 3p in the pound), but has yet to use this power. Funding comes from a Treasury block grant (£23 billion in 2008) determined by the Barnett formula.

The Scotland Act (1998) places a number of limits on the Scottish Parliament's legislative powers. It specifies several policy areas in which the Scottish Parliament has no legislative authority. These 'reserved powers' remain the sole responsibility of Westminster. They include the UK constitution, economic policy, foreign policy and relations with the European Union. The Act also states that Westminster remains sovereign in all matters, but has chosen to exercise its sovereignty by devolving legislative responsibility to a Scottish Parliament without diminishing its own powers. Westminster retains the right to override the Scottish Parliament in areas where legislative powers have been devolved. It may also legislate to abolish the Scottish Parliament, although an attempt to do so would be hugely controversial.

The Scottish executive, renamed the Scottish government by the SNP after it took power in 2007, draws up policy proposals and implements legislation passed by the

The Scottish Parliament buildings at Holyrood, Edinburgh

Roger Pilkington/Fotolia

parliament. The first minister, usually the leader of the largest party at Holyrood, heads the Scottish government and appoints the cabinet.

Weblinks

www.scottish.parliament.uk and www.scotland.gov.uk — websites of the Scottish Parliament and Scottish government.

The Welsh Assembly

The National Assembly for Wales, commonly known as the Welsh Assembly, has 60 members elected by the additional member system. Forty members are elected in single-member constituencies using the first-past-the-post system, and 20 in five multi-member regions using the list system.

The assembly is considerably weaker than the Scottish Parliament: it has only executive and secondary legislative powers, not primary legislative power. It determines how legislation passed by Westminster on a range of Welsh issues should be implemented. If Westminster leaves significant scope for interpretation, the assembly can play an important role in determining policy in Wales. But if Westminster legislation is tightly drawn, the prospects for assembly initiative

The Senedd, National Assembly for Wales building on Cardiff Bay waterfront

Chris Howes/Wild Places Photography/Alamy

are reduced. The Government of Wales Act (1998) specified the policy areas in which the assembly has executive power. They include education, health, transport, the environment and economic development (see Table 10.1). Funding comes from a Treasury block grant (£12 billion in 2008) determined by the Barnett formula. The assembly decides how to allocate this money and can alter the basis of local taxation, but it does not have tax-varying powers.

The Welsh Assembly government formulates and implements policy. The first minister, who is normally the leader of the largest party in the assembly, heads the assembly government and appoints the cabinet.

Weblinks

www.assemblywales.org and www.wales.gov.uk — websites of the Welsh Assembly and the Welsh Assembly government.

Table 10.1 Powers of the devolved administrations and reserved powers

Scottish Parliament	Welsh Assembly	Northern Ireland Assembly	Powers reserved to Westminster
Law and home affairs	Economic development	Law and order	UK constitution
Economic development	Agriculture and fisheries	Economic development	Defence and national security
Agriculture and fisheries	Education and training	Agriculture and fisheries	Foreign policy, including relations with the EU
Education and training	Local government	Education and training	Fiscal, economic and monetary systems
Local government	Health	Local government	Common market for British goods and services
Health	Housing	Health	Employment legislation
Housing	Environment	Housing	Social security
Environment	Transport	Environment	Transport safety
Transport	Culture, the Welsh language and sport	Transport	Media
Culture and sport		Culture and sport	Protection of borders
Tax-varying powers of 3p in the pound			

Further powers

The creation of the devolved assemblies marked a beginning not an end. The former secretary of state for Wales, Ron Davies, recognised that devolution is a 'process not an event'. Both the Scottish Parliament and the Welsh Assembly are likely to be given further powers in the next few years.

The Government of Wales Act (2006) enabled the Welsh Assembly to ask Westminster to transfer more competences. Further devolution is thus occurring on an incremental basis. The Act also paves the way for the assembly to gain primary legislative powers like the Scottish Parliament. For this to happen, two-thirds of assembly members would have to vote for a referendum on new powers, as would both Houses of Parliament, and Welsh voters would have to deliver a 'yes' vote in a referendum. The three main parties at Westminster support a referendum on further devolution, as did the 2009 All Wales Convention report.

Weblinks

www.ucl.ac.uk/constitution-unit/research/devolution/devo-monitoring-programme.html — select 'Research' then 'Devolution' and then click on 'devolution monitoring reports' for regular reports on devolution developments from the Constitution Unit at UCL.

Independence or more devolution?

The SNP government's 2009 *Your Scotland, Your Voice* White Paper set out three main options:

- **The status quo.**
- **Extending devolution.** Powers currently reserved to Westminster would be transferred to the Scottish Parliament. These could include consumer protection, energy policy and some taxation powers. 'Full devolution' would mean fiscal autonomy, with the Scottish Parliament given substantial tax and spending powers. Defence, foreign relations and the UK currency would remain reserved matters.
- **Independence.** The SNP's preferred option would see the Scottish Parliament and government take full responsibility for all reserved areas, ending the UK Parliament's powers to legislate for Scotland and the UK government's competence for executive action in Scotland. The White Paper envisages independence being enacted by legislation at both Westminster and Holyrood. The SNP government has pledged to hold a referendum on the principle of independence by 2011. If this produced a 'yes' vote, the SNP government would demand negotiations on independence with the UK government.

The UK government and the other main parties in the Scottish Parliament set up the Calman Commission on Scottish Devolution to consider further devolution — but not independence. Its 2009 report concluded that devolution had been a success and that the Union was beneficial to Scotland, particularly in economic terms. It made the following recommendations:

- **Greater tax-varying powers.** The Scottish Parliament should be able to vary the standard and upper rates of income tax by up to 10p in the pound. It should also be responsible for stamp duty, land tax, landfill tax and air passenger duty. In turn, the block grant from the UK Treasury should be reduced, although the Barnett formula should remain in place. The Scottish government should also be able to borrow money.
- **Further devolution.** Further powers should be devolved to the Scottish Parliament, including airgun and drink-driving legislation, animal health and responsibility for Scottish elections.
- **Return of some powers to Westminster.** Laws on food labelling, charities, the regulation of health professionals and the winding up of companies should be reserved to Westminster.

The three main parties at Westminster accepted many of Calman's recommendations. Surveys commissioned by the BBC to mark a decade of devolution showed public support for increasing the powers of the Scottish Parliament and Welsh Assembly (see Tables 10.2 and 10.3). Asked how they would vote in a referendum on independence, 38% of Scots said they would vote in favour and 54% against. Only 13% of those surveyed in Wales supported independence.

Weblinks

www.commissiononscottishdevolution.org.uk — the Calman Commission.

Table 10.2 Views on the future government of Wales

Option	Total support (%)
Wales should become independent, separate from the UK and the EU	5
Wales should become independent, separate from the UK but part of the EU	8
Wales should remain part of the UK with its own elected parliament which has law-making and taxation powers	34
Wales should remain part of the UK with its own elected parliament which has law-making but no taxation powers	10
Wales should remain part of the UK with its own elected assembly which has limited law-making powers only	21
Wales should remain part of the UK and the assembly should be abolished	19

Source: BBC Wales/ICM poll, February 2009.

Table 10.3 Views on the future government of Scotland

Option	Total support (%)
Scotland should become independent of the rest of the UK, with the Scottish Parliament able to make all decisions about the level of taxation and government spending in Scotland	28
Scotland should remain part of the UK, with the Scottish Parliament able to make some decisions about the level of taxation and government spending in Scotland	47
Scotland should remain part of the UK, with decisions about the level of taxation and government spending in Scotland made by the UK government	22

Source: BBC Scotland/ICM poll, June 2009.

The impact of devolution

Devolution has had a significant impact on politics in Scotland and Wales, and on the UK political system as a whole. This section examines:

➤ a new politics
➤ multi-party politics
➤ minority and coalition governments
➤ policy divergence
➤ funding
➤ intergovernmental relations
➤ Westminster and the English Question
➤ Britishness

A new politics

Hopes were high in Scotland and Wales that legislative devolution would usher in a different style of politics. Whereas Westminster politics was seen as adversarial and elitist, the hope was that post-devolution politics would be consensual and more democratic. This was always likely to prove over-optimistic, and the new institutions have not been free of scandal. But there is a different atmosphere in the Scottish

Parliament and Welsh Assembly. Two examples are:

➤ **Representation of a broader range of society.** Women constitute a higher proportion of the Scottish Parliament (33%) and Welsh Assembly (47%) than is the case at Westminster.

➤ **Greater opportunity for public participation in the legislative process.** A petition helped persuade MSPs to press ahead with a ban on smoking in public places.

Multi-party politics

A casual observer might be forgiven for thinking that elections in Scotland and Wales are not very competitive. Labour won 41 of 59 seats (69.5%) in Scotland and 26 of 40 (65%) in Wales at the 2010 general election, but on 42% and 36% of the vote respectively. The elections to the devolved bodies provide a more accurate reflection of multi-party politics in these nations. The nationalist parties perform better in these elections than at Westminster, while support for Labour is lower. The additional member system has produced more proportional outcomes than are found at Westminster, with small parties such as the Greens and Scottish Socialists winning seats in the Scottish Parliament.

Minority and coalition governments

The three rounds of elections to the Scottish Parliament and Welsh Assembly held in 1999, 2003 and 2007 produced different types of government. Elections to the Scottish Parliament led to:

➤ Labour–Liberal Democrat coalitions following the 1999 and 2003 elections. These were based on formal policy agreements and a division of ministerial posts between the two parties.

➤ A minority Scottish National Party government after the 2007 election. The SNP beat Labour in both votes and seats, but needed the allocation of regional list seats to take it to 47 seats, one ahead of Labour (see Table 10.4). Alex Salmond formed a minority administration, relying on the support or abstention of Green and Conservative MSPs to get key measures through the parliament. But the SNP had to shelve some of its proposals (e.g. a local income tax).

Welsh Assembly elections have produced complex outcomes:

➤ Labour formed a minority government after the 1999 election, before forming a 'partnership' with the Liberal Democrats in 2000.

➤ Labour won 30 of the 60 seats in the assembly in 2003 but had a technical majority because the Presiding Officer and his deputy were from other parties. This disappeared in 2005 when Peter Law left Labour to sit as an independent.

➤ Labour lost four seats in 2007 but remained the largest party (see Table 10.5). Negotiations on a 'rainbow coalition' of Plaid Cymru, Conservatives and Liberal Democrats broke down. Labour then formed a minority administration but soon agreed a coalition with Plaid Cymru.

Table 10.4 Elections to the Scottish Parliament, 2007

	Constituency contests		Regional lists		
	Share of vote (%)	Seats won	Share of vote (%)	Seats won	Total seats
Con	16.6 (+0.0)	4 (+1)	13.9 (−1.6)	13 (−2)	17 (−1)
Lab	32.2 (−2.4)	37 (−9)	29.2 (−0.1)	9 (+5)	46 (−4)
Lib Dem	16.2 (+0.8)	11 (−2)	11.3 (−0.5)	5 (+1)	16 (−1)
SNP	32.9 (+9.1)	21 (+12)	31.0 (+10.1)	26 (+8)	47 (+20)
Green	0.1 (+0.1)	0 (+0)	4.0 (−2.9)	2 (−5)	2 (−5)
Others	2.0 (−7.5)	0 (−2)	10.6 (−5.1)	1 (−1)	1 (−9)

Note: figures in brackets refer to change since 2003.

Table 10.5 Elections to the Welsh Assembly, 2007

	Constituency contests		Regional lists		
	Share of vote (%)	Seats won	Share of vote (%)	Seats won	Total seats
Con	22.4 (+2.5)	5 (+4)	21.5 (+2.3)	7 (−3)	12 (+1)
Lab	32.2 (−7.8)	24 (−6)	29.6 (−7.0)	2 (+2)	26 (−4)
Lib Dem	14.8 (+0.7)	3 (+0)	11.7 (−1.0)	3 (+0)	6 (+0)
Plaid Cymru	22.4 (+1.2)	7 (+2)	21.0 (+1.3)	8 (+1)	15 (+3)
Others	8.3 (+3.5)	1 (+0)	16.3 (+4.5)	0 (+0)	1 (+0)

Note: figures in brackets refer to change since 2003.

Policy divergence

Devolution has allowed governments in Scotland, Wales and Northern Ireland to adopt policies which differ from those pursued by the UK government in England. Notable examples of policy divergence are found in health and education (see Table 10.6). The Scottish executive introduced free long-term personal care for the elderly, while prescription charges have been either reduced or abolished.

Policy differences can be seen as a positive development because the devolved bodies reacted to the concerns of their electorate. Policies developed in Scotland and Wales — such as the ban on smoking in public places in Scotland and the creation of a Children's Commissioner — were taken up subsequently by the UK government. However, policy divergence may undermine the principle of equal rights for UK citizens if it widens disparities in welfare provision.

The extent of policy divergence should not be exaggerated. The UK civil service and EU law promote policy convergence, and the budgets of the devolved institutions are not large enough to allow them to increase public spending greatly. There have been few major disputes between the UK governments and the devolved administrations. The most controversial issue was the decision by the Scottish executive in 2009 to free the Lockerbie bomber Abdelbaset Ali Al-Megrahi from a Scottish prison.

Funding

The devolved administrations are funded by block grants from the UK Treasury, the size of which is settled by the Barnett formula. This needs-based formula, agreed in

Table 10.6 Examples of policy divergence (health and education)

Scotland	Wales	Northern Ireland
Reduction and phasing out of prescription charges	Abolition of prescription charges	Abolition of prescription charges
Free long-term personal care for the elderly	Free school milk for children under 7	Free fares for the elderly
Ban on smoking in public places takes effect before ban elsewhere in UK	Abolition of SATs for 7, 11 and 14-year-olds	Abolition of school league tables
Abolition of up-front tuition fees for university students	Piloting of Welsh baccalaureate	Establishment of Children's Commissioner
Abolition of ban on 'promoting homosexuality' in schools	Establishment of Children's Commissioner	

1978, translates changes in public spending in England into equivalent changes in the block grants for Scotland, Wales and Northern Ireland, calculated on the basis of population. Scotland, Wales and Northern Ireland receive more public spending per head of population than England. For 2008/09, if the UK level was taken as 100, then government funding for England would be 97, for Wales 111, for Scotland 116, and for Northern Ireland 122. In other words, government funding per head of population is 16% higher in Scotland than in the UK as a whole.

Critics claim that this amounts to an English subsidy of the rest of the UK. Despite their favourable allocation and increased funding since 1999, Scotland and Wales have, however, seen their share of public spending squeezed. An independent review of the operation of the Barnett formula in Wales (2009) called for a new system and greater funding.

Intergovernmental relations

The Scotland Office, Wales Office and Northern Ireland Office represent the interests of their respective nations in Whitehall. Secretaries of state for Scotland, Wales and Northern Ireland sit in the cabinet, but the holder of the first two posts also held other portfolios for part of the first decade of devolution.

New mechanisms to handle relations between the UK government and the devolved bodies (i.e. **intergovernmental relations**) have been established to foster cooperation and resolved disputes:

> **Concordats.** Concordats are formal agreements setting out the rules governing the relationship between UK government departments and the devolved administrations.

> **Joint Ministerial Committee.** Meetings are held between UK ministers and those from the devolved administrations to discuss policy in devolved matters and resolve disputes.

Key terms

> **Intergovernmental relations** Relations between the UK government and devolved administrations.

> **Supreme Court.** This is the final arbiter in cases where legal disputes about the competences of the devolved administrations arise. Before it started work in 2009, this role was carried out by the Judicial Committee of the Privy Council.
> **British–Irish Council.** Created by the Good Friday Agreement, this promotes the sharing of ideas between the UK and Irish governments, the devolved administrations in Scotland, Wales and Northern Ireland, plus the Isle of Man, Jersey and Guernsey.

Despite these bodies, coordination across the post-devolution UK has been characterised by pragmatism and ad hoc arrangements rather than clear rules of the game.

Westminster and the English Question

Devolution required procedural changes at Westminster. MPs at Westminster can no longer ask parliamentary questions on solely devolved matters. 'Sewel motions' enable the Scottish Parliament or Northern Ireland Assembly to delegate responsibility for legislating on devolved matters back to Westminster on a case-by-case basis.

The **West Lothian Question** asks why MPs representing Scottish constituencies at Westminster should be permitted to vote on purely English matters (e.g. local government in England) when English MPs have no say over matters devolved to the Scottish Parliament. It was named after Tam Dalyell, MP for West Lothian, who raised it during debates on devolution in the 1970s. Legislation on foundation hospitals and university tuition fees in England in 2003–04 would not have passed without the votes of Labour MPs from Scotland. The reduction in the number of Scottish MPs from 72 to 59 in 2005 was a partial response to the question, but it has yet to be resolved fully.

> **Key terms**
> **West Lothian Question.** Why should Scottish MPs be able to vote on English matters at Westminster when English MPs cannot vote on matters devolved to the Scottish Parliament?

The West Lothian Question becomes more pressing if the governing party at Westminster has a majority of seats in the UK as a whole, but does not have a majority of seats in England. Labour polled fewer votes in England than the Conservatives in 2005 but won 92 more seats. In 2010, the Conservatives won 297 seats in England compared to Labour's 191, but had only one MP in Scotland.

These issues are part of a broader 'English question' about how England should be governed within the post-devolution Union. Underpinning it is a sense that English interests and identity are not recognised explicitly. Four main solutions to the English question have emerged:

> **Elected regional assemblies in England.** The Blair governments proposed that directly elected regional assemblies with limited executive functions be created in the eight English regions outside London. The policy was scrapped after a 'no' vote in a referendum on a regional assembly for northeast England in 2004. Regional Development Agencies, created in 1999 to promote economic development, remained in place although the Conservatives pledged to abolish them. Few English regions have a strong sense of identity.

➤ **Regional select committees at Westminster.** The Brown government established regional select committees for nine English regions in 2009. But they achieved little as Conservative and Liberal Democrat MPs refused to attend. New regional ministers were also created.

➤ **English votes for English laws.** In 2001 the Conservatives proposed a system in which bills would be designated 'English-only' and MPs representing Scottish constituencies would not be permitted to vote on them. In 2010 the Conservative suggestion was that only English MPs should be allowed to amend bills on English matters. Critics note that bills dealing with public spending in England still matter to Scotland because of the way the Barnett formula calculates funding.

➤ **An English parliament.** This would have powers, similar to those of the Scottish Parliament, over domestic English issues. But there is only limited elite and public support for this option.

All these proposed solutions have problems. The status quo thus emerges as a fifth option because the 'answer' to the English question may be as problematic as the question.

Britishness

Britishness is an umbrella identity that provides a common bond between the peoples of the UK, but which also enables them to retain their distinctive national (i.e. English, Welsh, Scottish and Northern Irish) identities. British identity has been built around symbols of the British state, such as the monarchy, parliament and the National Health Service. Until the second half of the twentieth century, the British Empire was also an important element in British identity.

The number of people describing themselves as exclusively Scottish, Welsh or English or as having a dual identity (e.g. Scottish and British) has risen since 1997. This is particularly true in Scotland. But most people still feel British to some extent. Surveys show that support for Scottish and Welsh independence has not increased greatly since devolution. Opinion polls also suggest that the English see the West Lothian Question and Barnett formula as unfair, but that these issues do not matter greatly to voters.

View point   **Has devolution weakened the union?**

YES

● The piecemeal approach to devolution has meant that problems (e.g. the West Lothian Question and the future of the Barnett formula) have not been addressed effectively.

● Insufficient attention has been paid to the purpose and benefits of the Union and Britishness in the post-devolution UK.

● The rules of the game on policy coordination and the resolution of disputes are not clear enough.

● Policy divergence has undermined the idea of common welfare rights in the UK.

● The SNP's promise of a referendum on independence and the increase in Scottish identity have made the break-up of the Union more likely.

● There is growing unease in England about the perceived unfairness of the devolution settlement.

NO

- Devolution has answered Scottish, Welsh and Northern Irish demands for greater autonomy, bringing decision making closer to the people.
- The first decade of devolution has proceeded smoothly and there have not been major disputes between the British government and the devolved bodies.
- Policy divergence reflects the different interests of the nations of the UK and has allowed initiatives that have proved successful in one nation to be adopted elsewhere.
- Most people in the UK still feel British to some degree, and only a minority in each nation favour independence.
- The prospects for peace and power sharing in Northern Ireland are stronger than ever before.

Northern Ireland

From 1922 to 1972, the Stormont Parliament and executive was responsible for the government of Northern Ireland. It was dominated by unionist politicians who represented the Protestant majority and pursued policies that discriminated against the Catholic minority. The civil rights movement and the Irish Republican Army (IRA) took up Catholic grievances in the 1960s. British troops were sent to the province in 1969, but as 'the Troubles' escalated, Edward Heath's Conservative government suspended the Stormont Parliament in 1972. **Direct rule** from London was imposed: UK government ministers and Northern Ireland Office officials took policy decisions, not local politicians. Subsequent British governments introduced a series of unsuccessful initiatives to bring about **power-sharing devolution**, but the IRA's terrorist campaign continued. The Good Friday Agreement of 1998 proved a significant breakthrough.

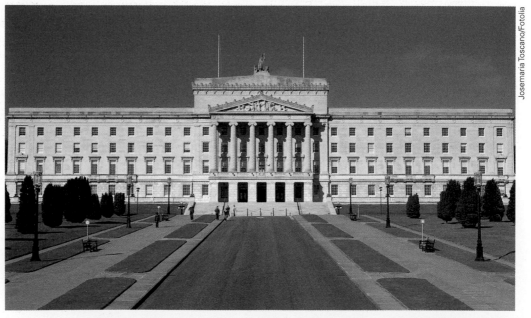

Stormont Castle, Belfast was the home of the Stormont Parliament from 1922 to 1972. Now the Northern Ireland Assembly sits here

Key terms

➤ **Direct rule** The government of Northern Ireland from London, through special procedures at Westminster.

➤ **Power-sharing devolution** A form of devolution in which special arrangements are put in place to ensure that both communities in a divided society are represented in the executive and that they assent to legislation on sensitive issues.

A place apart

British governments have treated Northern Ireland as 'a place apart' in UK territorial politics. Special circumstances have applied to Northern Ireland:

➤ **Conditional status.** Northern Ireland's status as a part of the UK is conditional on a majority of its population wishing to remain within the UK. At present, a majority support the constitutional status quo. The UK government depicts itself as a neutral broker in the search for a peaceful solution.

➤ **Separate administration.** Northern Ireland has been governed differently from the rest of the UK. Between 1922 and 1972, it was the only part of the UK to have its own parliament with legislative and executive powers. After 1972, under direct rule, the secretary of state for Northern Ireland had greater policy-making powers than the secretaries of state for Scotland and Wales. Policy was made through Orders in Council rather than primary legislation at Westminster. Devolution in Northern Ireland has also been distinctive because it has been designed so that unionist and nationalist parties share power.

➤ **The 'Irish dimension'.** Since the 1980s, the UK government and the government of the Republic of Ireland have worked together to find a peaceful settlement in Northern Ireland. The Anglo-Irish Agreement (1985) gave the republic a formal role in the search for a settlement.

➤ **Communal conflict.** The main political divide in Northern Ireland is that between **unionists** and **nationalists**. Unionists want Northern Ireland to remain part of the UK. Nationalists favour constitutional change, such as a united Ireland or a greater role for the Irish republic in the affairs of Northern Ireland. Unionists identify with the British state and tend to be Protestant, whereas nationalists identify themselves as Irish and tend to be Catholic. Catholics made up 40% of the Northern Ireland population in 2001.

Key terms

➤ **Nationalist** An adherent of a political position in Northern Ireland that supports constitutional means of achieving improved rights for Catholics, and the eventual incorporation of the six counties of Northern Ireland into the Republic of Ireland.

➤ **Unionist** An adherent of a political position in Northern Ireland that supports the continued union between Great Britain and Northern Ireland.

> **Distinctive party system.** Communal divisions shape Northern Irish politics. Elections are contested between unionist and nationalist parties; the main electoral issue is the constitutional status of Northern Ireland. The main UK parties have tended not to field candidates in Northern Ireland elections, but the Conservatives formed an alliance with the Ulster Unionist Party for the 2010 general election.

> **Security.** Terrorist campaigns by republican and loyalist paramilitary organisations posed security problems. British soldiers patrolled the streets for several decades. The IRA has been on ceasefire for much of the period since 1995, but the breakaway Real IRA — which killed 29 people in the 1998 Omagh bombing — remains active.

The Good Friday Agreement

Years of negotiations between the UK and Irish government, and (some of) the Northern Irish political parties, resulted in the 1998 Good Friday Agreement (the 'Belfast Agreement'). It created a number of institutions:

> **Northern Ireland Assembly.** The assembly consists of 108 members, elected by the single transferable vote system of proportional representation (see Chapter 2). It has primary legislative powers in a range of policy areas, but does not have tax-raising power (see Table 10.1). Some measures require cross-community support from both unionist and nationalist parties.

> **Northern Ireland executive.** This is led by a first minister and deputy first minister. The first minister is the leader of the largest party in the assembly, and the deputy first minister is drawn from the second largest party. Ministerial posts are allocated on a proportional basis according to party strength in the assembly. The agreement thus ensures power sharing, with both unionists and nationalists represented in government.

> **North–South Ministerial Council.** In this body, the Northern Ireland executive and Republic of Ireland government cooperate on cross-border issues.

> **British–Irish Council.** Here the UK and Irish governments, the devolved administrations in Scotland, Wales and Northern Ireland, plus the Isle of Man and Channel Islands, exchange policy ideas.

> **British–Irish Intergovernmental Conference.** In this body, the UK and Irish governments discuss the situation in Northern Ireland.

The agreement also required the UK and Irish governments to amend their constitutions to clarify the status of Northern Ireland. It paved the way for a new Police Service of Northern Ireland and the early release of prisoners.

However, the UK suspended the devolved institutions and reimposed direct rule on four separate occasions as the lack of trust between the two communities continued. Parades by the Protestant Orange Order, paramilitary activity, policing issues and, most importantly, decommissioning all threatened to derail the peace process. The IRA, the main **republican** paramilitary body, did not fully decommission its arms or declare explicitly that its conflict was over until 2005. Most **loyalist** paramilitary groups have also disarmed.

The pro-Good Friday Agreement centre 'hollowed out' as unionists in particular lost faith in the peace process. The Ulster Unionist Party (UUP) and Social Democratic and Labour Party (SDLP) had been key players in the agreement and shared the top positions in the Northern Ireland executive. But by the 2003 assembly elections, they had been overtaken by their rivals. Ian Paisley's Democratic Unionist Party (DUP), which had initially opposed the agreement, became the main representative of the unionist community. Sinn Fein, a republican party with strong ties to the IRA and led by Gerry Adams, became the main voice of nationalists.

In a remarkable turn of events, however, the DUP and Sinn Fein agreed to work together. Former enemies Ian Paisley, dubbed 'Dr No' for his refusal to share power with Sinn Fein, and Martin McGuinness, one time IRA commander in Derry, became first minister and deputy first minister in 2007. Paisley retired the following year and was succeeded by Peter Robinson. After tense negotiations, responsibility for law and order was transferred to the assembly in 2010.

Key terms

➤ **Loyalist** An adherent to a variant of unionism that has supported the use of political violence to defend the union between Great Britain and Northern Ireland.

➤ **Republican** An adherent to a variant of Irish nationalism that has supported the use of political violence to end British rule in Northern Ireland.

Northern Ireland first minister Ian Paisley and deputy first minister Martin McGuinness in 2007 after the DUP and Sinn Fein agreed to work together

Weblinks

www.niassembly.gov.uk and www.northernireland.gov.uk — websites of the Northern Ireland Assembly and the Northern Ireland executive.

A quasi-federal UK

Devolution has created a new relationship between the UK's component nations. It provides institutional recognition of the distinctiveness of these nations while reflecting their desire to remain part of the Union. The post-devolution UK no longer fits the criteria of a highly centralised unitary state, but nor is it a federal state with power constitutionally divided between autonomous institutions.

Professor Vernon Bogdanor characterises the UK as a **quasi-federal** state that has some federal characteristics but retains some of the features of a unitary state. When William Gladstone sought to recognise the multinational character of the UK state by devolving power to a legislative assembly in Ireland in the late nineteenth century, constitutional theorist A. V. Dicey argued that there could be no halfway house between parliamentary sovereignty and separatism. More than a century later, Labour's devolution settlement has taken the UK into this middle ground. The main features of quasi-federalism are:

> **Parliamentary sovereignty is limited.** In legal terms, Westminster remains sovereign because it can overrule or abolish the devolved bodies. In practice, however, Westminster is no longer sovereign over domestic matters in Scotland and Wales — it does not have unlimited power. Although sovereignty has been formally delegated rather than devolved, Westminster has accepted that it will not impose legislation in areas devolved to the Scottish Parliament. A UK government that sought to abolish the Scottish Parliament or Welsh Assembly without holding a referendum would provoke a constitutional crisis.

> **Westminster is a quasi-federal parliament.** Westminster operates as an English parliament in the sense that it makes domestic law in England; it makes primary legislation in Wales; and it is a federal parliament for Scotland and Northern Ireland because it retains reserved powers on major UK-wide matters. MPs from Scotland and Northern Ireland have few constituency responsibilities and deal mainly with economic and foreign affairs issues in the House of Commons.

> **Supreme Court.** The UK Supreme Court can resolve disputes over competences by determining if the devolved bodies have acted within their powers.

Concepts explained
Quasi-federal
A quasi-federal state is one in which the central government of a unitary state devolves some of its powers to subnational governments. It has some of the features of a unitary state and some of a federal state. Legally, there is a supreme legal authority located at the centre, as in a unitary state. But in practice, the centre no longer makes domestic policy for some parts of the state and it would find it difficult politically to abolish the subnational tier of government.

Multi-level governance
The UK has moved away from a system of centralised government to one of **multi-level governance**. Central government remains the single most important actor, but it does not monopolise decision making because a number of bodies operating at different levels have policy competences. These include:

> supranational level: the European Union (see Chapter 11)
> UK level: the Westminster Parliament and UK government
> regional level: the devolved institutions, the mayor of London and the London Assembly
> local level: elected local authorities and local quangos

Local government

Local authorities are the lowest level of government in the UK, and in England are the only elected branch of government below central government. **Local government** is not protected by the uncodified constitution, allowing central government to change its structure and functions. The last 30 years have seen two main trends that have brought about a decline in the power of local government:

> **Centralisation.** Central government has taken over or redistributed some of the functions of local authorities, and has exercised a tight grip on their finance.
> **Local governance.** Rather than local authorities providing most local services directly, there is now a system of local governance in which a range of bodies are involved in decision making at local level.

Key terms

> **Local governance** A system in which a range of bodies and networks are involved in the provision of local services.
> **Local government** A system in which elected local authorities provide many local services directly, and are accountable to voters at local elections.
> **Multi-level governance** A system of decision-making in which policy competences are shared between local, regional, national and supranational institutions.
> **Quangos** Quasi-autonomous non-governmental organisations; unelected public bodies responsible for the funding or regulation of certain areas of public policy.

Structure

The 1974 reorganisation of local government in England established a uniform two-tier structure in which the provision of local services in an area was divided between two authorities. This became more complex in the 1990s with the creation of unitary authorities (i.e. a single tier of local government) in some parts of England. Scotland and Wales moved to a uniform system of unitary authorities. In 2010, the structure of local government in England was:

> 56 unitary authorities, responsible for a full range of local services
> 27 county councils, responsible for some local services (e.g. education, social services, policing and transport) in the shires
> 201 district councils, responsible for some local services (e.g. housing, leisure and refuse collection) in the shires

➤ 36 metropolitan districts, responsible for a full range of local services in urban areas

Different arrangements apply in London, where the Greater London Authority has strategic responsibility for economic development, transport, planning and policing. It consists of a directly elected mayor and a 25-member London Assembly. The mayor sets the budget and determines policy. The main initiative taken by the mayor has been the congestion charge introduced by Ken Livingstone in 2003.

The Blair governments hoped that other local authorities would also have directly elected mayors. Referendums on moving to this system were held in 37 areas outside London, but only 12 voted for an elected mayor. Stoke-on-Trent held a second referendum in 2008 that abolished the post. A number of independents and minor party candidates were successful in mayoral elections. Most local authorities have an indirectly elected leader who heads a cabinet of councillors.

Weblinks

www.direct.gov.uk/en/DI1/Directories/Localcouncils/index.htm — gateway to the websites of local authorities.

Funding and functions

Local government expenditure accounts for over a quarter of all public spending in England. Funding comes from three main sources:

➤ **Grants from central government.** This makes up 55% of local authority income, but central government determines what proportion of this funding can be spent on individual services.

➤ **Local taxation on domestic properties.** The council tax accounts for 25% of local authority income. Levels are set by local authorities but are subject to capping by central government. The council tax is based on the value of a property, with a 25% discount for single householders. It replaced the community charge, commonly known as the poll tax, in 1993. This was paid by most citizens at a flat rate.

➤ **Local taxation on business properties.** The national non-domestic rate accounts for 20% of local authority income. It is set and collected by central government.

Local authorities are responsible for many of the services used by citizens on a day-to-day basis, including:

➤ education (e.g. primary and secondary schools)
➤ social services (e.g. residential care and care in the community)
➤ housing (e.g. public housing)
➤ roads (e.g. maintenance and regulation of smaller roads) and public transport (e.g. bus services)
➤ planning (e.g. decisions on planning applications)

> environmental health (e.g. refuse collection and recycling)
> leisure services (e.g. libraries and leisure centres)

Local authorities do not provide all of these services directly. Instead, they have been transformed into **enabling authorities** that oversee the provision of services by other bodies. Rather than providing services directly, local authorities now organise, supervise, regulate and fund the provision of services by others. Services such as refuse collection are often provided by private companies. Other services that used to be provided by local authorities are now delivered by housing associations, heath trusts and foundation schools.

The three main parties propose further localism, with local community bodies given a greater role in shaping priorities and delivering programmes (e.g. to tackle poverty and crime). With turnout in local elections low, this offers an alternative model of **local democracy** in which local authorities are required to promote democracy by fostering participation in community groups.

> **Key term**
> **Enabling authorities**
> Local authorities that set the framework in which other bodies provide local services, but do not provide all these services themselves.

Weblinks

www.lga.gov.uk — website of the Local Government Association, with information on the role and structure of local government.

Viewpoint Is local government still important?

YES
- Local government has overall responsibility for many of the local services that people use on a regular basis.
- Local authorities are responsible for 25% of public spending.
- Local authorities are major players in local governance, shaping policy and enabling others to provide effective service delivery.
- Local authorities play a leadership role in promoting community action and participation.
- Elected local authorities are directly accountable to voters.

NO
- Local government has lost much of its autonomy in the last three decades and its structure has been changed frequently.
- Central government determines how local authorities raise and spend most of their money.
- Local services that used to be delivered by local authorities (e.g. education and housing) are now delivered by other bodies.
- Turnout in local elections is very low, and those who do vote often do so on national rather than local issues.
- Local government operates in a system of multi-level governance in which more decisions are now taken at regional or EU level.

Concepts explained

Local democracy

The traditional perspective on local democracy is that elected local authorities should be responsible for the provision of local services. They are held accountable to voters in local elections. But this model became problematic because of low turnout in local elections and the reduction in the power of local authorities to collect and spend money. The enabling authority model sees local citizens as consumer of services. Service providers are held accountable through contracts and regulatory frameworks, leaving local councillors responsible for strategic decisions. Local authorities have a statutory duty to promote democracy by encouraging, for example, participation in community groups.

◗ What you should know

◗ The UK was a highly centralised state for most of the twentieth century. A system of administrative devolution provided some recognition at the centre for the distinctive interests of Scotland and Wales. But Northern Ireland (1922–72) was the only part of the UK to have its own assembly.

◗ The Labour government elected in 1997 implemented legislative devolution in which policy-making powers were transferred from Westminster to a Scottish Parliament, Welsh Assembly and Northern Ireland Assembly. These began work in 1999. The new system is asymmetric: the devolved bodies had different powers and institutional arrangements. Devolution is also an ongoing process, with further powers expected to be transferred to the devolved bodies.

◗ Devolution has already brought about significant changes in UK territorial politics. Elections to the devolved bodies have produced minority and coalition governments, which have introduced policies on health and education that differ from those pursued by the UK government in England. It has also posed questions about the government of England which have yet to be answered fully.

◗ Devolution is an important element in the emergence of multi-level governance in the UK, with policy-making competences held by institutions at supranational, national, regional and local levels. Local government is relatively weak and has lost functions to both central government and unelected local bodies. However, local authorities remain responsible for many of the services used by citizens on a daily basis.

UK/US comparison

Federalism in the USA

➤ The USA is a federal state in which law-making power is divided between two tiers of government: the federal government (located in Washington DC) and the governments of the 50 states of the USA. The UK is a unitary state, but since devolution it has taken on some quasi-federal features.

➤ The two tiers of government in the USA are protected by the constitution. Their powers are inalienable. One tier of government cannot abolish the other tier of government. The division of powers can only be altered by amendment to the constitution, which requires special procedures. In the UK, Westminster retains parliamentary sovereignty and can overrule or abolish the devolved bodies. In practice, parliament has recognised that it no longer has authority over devolved policies.

➤ Powers that are reserved to the US federal government include defence, foreign policy, the US currency and the US single market. Relatively few powers are reserved exclusively to the states (e.g. local taxes), but power is shared between the federal and state governments in many areas (e.g. criminal and civil law, health and education). Westminster also has reserved powers over defence, foreign policy, the constitution, the UK currency and the single European market.

➤ There is significant policy divergence between the 50 states of the USA (e.g. on the death penalty and drug laws). Devolution has produced limited policy divergence between the four nations of the UK.

➤ The US Supreme Court makes binding judgments where disputes arise about the distribution of powers between federal and state governments. The UK Supreme Court can pronounce on whether the devolved bodies have acted within their powers, but it cannot strike down an Act of the Westminster Parliament.

➤ The nature of US federalism has changed over time, with the USA becoming a more centralised nation than was envisaged in the Constitution. The policy-making scope of the federal government expanded, notably with the 1930s New Deal and 1960s Great Society programmes, and it exercised more control over state funding. Some policy responsibilities were returned to the states under the Reagan administration in the 1980s, but funding was also cut. The UK was highly centralised for much of the twentieth century, but power was devolved to new institutions in three of its component nations in 1999, creating a quasi-federal system.

Further reading

Bogdanor, V. (2007) 'The English question', *Politics Review*, Vol. 17, No. 2, pp. 2–5.

Bogdanor, V. (2010) 'Sovereignty and devolution: quasi-federalism?', *Politics Review*, Vol. 19, No. 3, pp. 12–15.

Bradbury, J. (2007) '2007 Welsh Assembly elections', *Politics Review*, Vol. 17, No. 2, November, pp. 13–16.

Deacon, R. and Sandry, A. (2007) *Devolution in the United Kingdom*, Edinburgh University Press.

Denver, D. (2007) '2007 Scottish Parliament elections: a historic moment?', *Politics Review*, Vol. 17, No. 1, pp. 19–21.

Jeffrey, C. (2009) 'Devolution in the UK: what's wrong with the status quo?', *Politics Review*, Vol. 18, No. 4, pp. 14–16.

Tonge, J. (2007) 'The return of devolved power-sharing to Northern Ireland', *Politics Review*, Vol. 17, No. 2, pp. 8–12.

Exam focus

Short-answer questions (around 5 minutes each)

Explain, using examples, the meaning of each of the following terms:

1 Unitary state
2 Devolution
3 West Lothian Question
4 Quasi-federalism

Mid-length questions (around 10 minutes each)

Outline two arguments 'for' and two arguments 'against' each of the following:

1 English votes for English laws.
2 The importance of local government.

Outline the main differences between:

3 Primary legislative powers and secondary legislative powers.
4 Unitary and federal systems of government.

Mini-essays (around 25–30 minutes each)

Write a mini-essay in response to each of the following questions:

1 'Devolution has resulted in the UK moving from a unitary to a quasi-federal form of government.' Discuss.
2 'Devolved institutions in Scotland are significantly more powerful than those in Wales.' Discuss.
3 'The devolution programme pursued by New Labour has left England's interests under-represented.' Discuss.
4 Critically assess the case in favour of 'English votes for English laws'.

Chapter 11

The European Union

Key questions answered in this chapter

➤ How has the European Union developed?

➤ What are the roles and powers of the European Union institutions?

➤ What policies have British governments pursued in the European Union?

➤ How has membership of the European Union affected the British political system?

The United Kingdom joined the European Economic Community (EEC) — later to become the European Union (EU) — in 1973. Since then, the EU has enlarged and taken on more policy responsibility. Membership of the EU has had a significant impact on the British political system, and the UK's relationship with the EU is a major issue in contemporary politics.

Weblinks

http://europa.eu/index_en.htm — official website of the European Union.

Development of the European Union

The origins of the European Union lie in the aftermath of the Second World War (1939–45) when six western European states sought closer economic cooperation. They were France, West Germany, Italy, Belgium, the Netherlands and Luxembourg ('the Six'). The 1950 Schuman Plan proposed a European Coal and Steel Community (ECSC). Set up in 1952, this was a **supranational** body with its own policy-making authority, budget and laws. It differed from **intergovernmental** bodies in which states cooperated voluntarily and could veto proposals.

Concepts explained

Supranational

A supranational organisation is one in which nation states transfer sovereignty to institutions which then have their own independent authority to create laws that take precedence over national laws. The EU has a number of supranational features. It has exclusive competence in some policy areas (e.g. competition policy). EU law takes priority over national law, and is interpreted by the independent Court of Justice. The European Commission acts in the interests of the EU as a whole rather than that of individual member states. The European Parliament is directly elected by EU citizens. In many policy areas, national governments do not have a veto.

Intergovernmental and supranational organisations

Distinguish between

Intergovernmental organisations

➤ National governments are the dominant actors in decision making.
➤ Nation states retain sovereignty, cooperating on a voluntary basis.
➤ Decisions are taken by unanimity — states have the right to veto proposals.

Supranational organisations

➤ Nation states transfer decision-making authority to a higher body whose institutions have authority independent of their member states.
➤ Nation states pool their sovereignty and accept supranational laws that take priority over national law.
➤ Decisions are taken by majority or qualified majority votes — states do not have veto rights.

In 1957 the Six signed the Treaties of Rome, establishing the supranational European Economic Community (EEC) and European Atomic Energy Community (EURATOM). They began operating in 1958. The EEC agreed a Common Agricultural Policy (CAP) in 1962 and completed a customs union in 1968 by removing internal tariff barriers and establishing a common external tariff. The 1965 Merger Treaty brought together the existing bodies to form the European Community (EC).

The pace of **integration** slowed in the mid-1960s as the French president Charles de Gaulle blocked plans to strengthen the EC's supranational elements. He also twice vetoed British membership of the EC. The 1970s brought only limited policy advances. The most significant was the creation of the European Monetary System in 1979. Central to this was the exchange rate mechanism (ERM), a currency grid in which the values of currencies were fixed against each other. The EC expanded to nine members when the UK, Ireland and Denmark joined in 1973. Three further states joined in the 1980s: Greece (1981), Spain and Portugal (both 1986).

Key terms

➤ **Integration** The process of coordinating the activities of different states through common institutions and policies.

Box 11.1 The European Union: a chronology

1950 Schuman Plan proposes a European Coal and Steel Community (ECSC).

1952 ECSC is established.

1957 Treaty of Rome, establishing the European Economic Community (EEC), is signed by Belgium, France, West Germany, Italy, Luxembourg and the Netherlands.

1958 EEC is established.

1960 Seven states, including the UK, establish the European Free Trade Association (EFTA).

1961 UK applies for EEC membership (vetoed by France in 1963).

1962 Common Agricultural Policy agreed.

1965 Merger Treaty establishes the European Community (EC).

1967 UK reapplies for EEC membership — vetoed by France again.

1968 Customs union completed.

1973 UK, Ireland and Denmark join the EEC.

1979 European Monetary System established. First direct elections to the European Parliament.

1981 Greece joins the EEC.

1985 Single European Act agreed (comes into force in 1987).

1986 Spain and Portugal join the EEC.

1989 Collapse of Communist regimes in central and eastern Europe.

1990 German unification.

1991 Maastricht Treaty agreed (comes into force in 1993).

1992 UK leaves the exchange rate mechanism.

1993 European Union (EU) is established.

1995 Austria, Finland and Switzerland join the EU.

1997 Amsterdam Treaty agreed (comes into force in 1999).

1999 Stage III of Economic and Monetary Union begins with 11 member states.

2000 Treaty of Nice agreed (comes into force in 2003).

2004 Cyprus, Czech Republic, Estonia, Hungary, Latvia, Lithuania, Malta, Poland, Slovakia and Slovenia join the EU.

2005 EU Constitutional Treaty shelved after 'no' votes in French and Dutch referendums.

2007 Bulgaria and Romania join the EU. Lisbon Treaty is agreed (comes into force in 2009).

2009 Herman van Rompuy becomes first president of the European Council.

Single market to single currency

The Single European Act (SEA), which was agreed in 1985 and came into effect in 1987, revived European integration. It created a single European market by the end of 1992. This is 'an area without internal frontiers in which the free movement of goods, services, persons and capital is ensured'. Three main barriers were removed:

➢ **Physical barriers**: customs checks at borders were scaled back.

➤ **Technical barriers**: under a system of 'mutual recognition', goods that met minimum standards in one member state could be freely traded in another. Professional qualifications would also be accepted across the EU.

➤ **Fiscal barriers**: new VAT procedures were introduced.

The single market led to a greater EC role in social and regional policy. France, Germany and the European Commission also pushed for **economic and monetary union** (EMU) and further political union, but the UK opposed them. The Maastricht Treaty was agreed in 1991 and came into force in 1993. Its key features were:

➤ the creation of the European Union, comprising of three pillars: the existing EC; an intergovernmental pillar on Common Foreign and Security Policy (CFSP); and an intergovernmental pillar on Justice and Home Affairs (JHA)

➤ EMU, with a single currency to be established by 1999 for those member states meeting specified 'convergence criteria'

➤ the principle of **subsidiarity**, under which the EU should act only where member states are unable to do so effectively

Key terms

➤ **Economic and monetary union** The creation of a single currency, central bank and common monetary policy.

➤ **Opt-out** An exemption negotiated by a state, and set out in a treaty or law, which means that it does not have to take part in a specific policy.

Concepts explained

Subsidiarity

The principle that decisions should be taken as close as possible to the citizen. It has been a principle of EU law since the Maastricht Treaty — the EU should not act unless it can do so more effectively than national, regional or local government. Actions should not go beyond what is required to achieve the policy objective: decisions should be proportional.

The British government won two exemptions:

➤ an **opt-out** from EMU — the UK did not have to join the single currency; parliament was free to decide whether or not to participate at a future date

➤ an opt-out from the social chapter which extended cooperation in social policy — although the UK would accept the social chapter in 1997

Deepening and widening

Since Maastricht, the EU has been engaged in both 'deepening' (further integration) and 'widening' (**enlargement**). Developments occurred in three main areas:

Key terms

➤ **Enlargement** The expansion of the EU to include new member states.

➤ economic and monetary union

➤ eastward enlargement

➤ treaty reform

Economic and monetary union

The Eurozone included 16 states by 2010. Eleven states — Austria, Belgium, Finland, France, Germany, Ireland, Italy, Luxembourg, the Netherlands, Spain and Portugal — formed the 'first wave' at the launch of the single currency in 1999. The UK, Denmark and Sweden opted out. Greece joined in 2001, followed by Slovenia (2007), Cyprus and Malta (2008), and Slovakia (2009). The values of the currencies of states adopting the euro were fixed. Their national currencies were then abolished and replaced by the euro.

EMU brings a number of benefits, including an end to exchange rate uncertainty and the elimination of transaction costs on cross-border trade. But it also involves a loss of monetary sovereignty. Interest rates in the Eurozone are set by the independent European Central Bank. The Stability and Growth Pact was designed to ensure budgetary discipline by monitoring economic performance and imposing sanctions on states with excessive deficits. Some EMU states ran up large debts in 2009–10, with Greece required to take drastic measures to cut its deficit.

Weblinks

http://ec.europa.eu/economy_finance/euro/index_en.htm — the European Commission's site on the euro.

Eastward enlargement

Austria, Finland and Sweden joined the EU in 1995. But the accession of 12 former Communist states from central and eastern Europe was the most ambitious and difficult in the EU's history. In the early 1990s, these states were only slowly developing into liberal democracies with market economies — key criteria for EU membership. Each had to adopt existing EU law in its entirety, requiring years of political and economic reform.

Ten states became EU members in 2004: Cyprus, the Czech Republic, Estonia, Hungary, Latvia, Lithuania, Malta, Poland, Slovakia and Slovenia. Bulgaria and Romania joined in 2007. Croatia is expected to join in the near future. Accession negotiations with Turkey and Macedonia are under way. Albania, Bosnia-Herzegovina, Iceland, Kosovo, Montenegro and Serbia have also applied for membership.

Weblinks

http://ec.europa.eu/enlargement/index_en.htm — information on applicant states and negotiations on EU enlargement.

Treaty reform

The EU's institutions and policies had to be reformed for a 27-member Union to function effectively. Since 1993, four new treaties have been agreed — Amsterdam, Nice, the Constitutional Treaty (which never came into force) and Lisbon.

Figure 11.1 Map of the European Union

Amsterdam Treaty

The Amsterdam Treaty was agreed in 1997 and came into force in 1999. It transferred many policies from the intergovernmental Justice and Home Affairs pillar to a supranational 'area of freedom, security and justice'. The UK gained opt-outs or opt-ins for some of these policies. Flexibility clauses in the treaty, which allow a majority of member states to pursue further integration without the need for all states to participate, have not yet been used.

Nice Treaty

The main innovation of the Nice Treaty (agreed in 2001, came into force in 2003) was a European Security and Defence Policy under which the EU would develop a common defence policy and undertake limited military action. Nice also signalled post-enlargement changes to the EU institutions.

Constitutional Treaty

The Treaty establishing a Constitution for Europe — often called the Constitutional Treaty or 'EU Constitution' — was signed in 2004 and included major institutional reforms. It could not enter into force until it was approved by all member states. But 'no' votes in referendums in France and the Netherlands in 2005 halted the ratification process.

Lisbon Treaty

The Lisbon Treaty, the successor to the Constitutional Treaty, was agreed in 2007. It brought about:

➢ the merging of the different pillars into one legal entity, the European Union
➢ a full-time president for the European Council, serving a 2½-year term
➢ a High Representative of the Union for Foreign Affairs and Security Policy
➢ a 'team presidency' system for the Council of Ministers
➢ a 'dual majority' system of **qualified majority voting**
➢ the extension of qualified majority voting and co-decision
➢ a clearer definition of the competences of the EU and its member states
➢ procedures that allow a move from **unanimity** to qualified majority voting without a treaty amendment

Key terms

➢ **Qualified majority voting** A voting arrangement in which proposals must win a set number of votes (more than 50%) to be approved.
➢ **Unanimity** A voting arrangement in which states can veto proposals.

The main differences between the Lisbon Treaty and the Constitutional Treaty are as follows:

➢ It is an 'amending treaty', amending existing treaties rather than replacing them with a constitution.
➢ The title 'High Representative of the Union for Foreign Affairs and Security Policy' is used, rather than 'Union Minister for Foreign Affairs'.
➢ The UK and Poland secured assurances that the Charter of Fundamental Rights did not extend the power of the European Court of Justice or create new rights.

Ten states were scheduled to hold referendums on the Constitutional Treaty, but only Ireland did so on the Lisbon Treaty — and it produced a 'no' vote in 2008. Lisbon finally came into force in December 2009 after its approval in a second Irish referendum.

Weblinks

http://europa.eu — click on 'Lisbon Treaty' for the official EU webpage on the Lisbon Treaty.
http://news.bbc.co.uk/1/hi/in_depth/europe/2003/inside_europe/default.stm — BBC 'Inside Europe' site, with news and analysis of the UK and the EU.

The institutions of the European Union

The EU's institutional architecture is unique. It includes intergovernmental bodies in which national governments meet (the Council of Ministers and European Council) and supranational bodies with their own authority (the European Commission, the European Parliament and European Court of Justice).

European Commission

The European Commission is the executive body of the EU. It is based in Brussels. As a supranational body, it acts in the general interests of the Union and is independent of member states. The president of the commission and the College of Commissioners are its political face. But the commission also acts as a civil service for the EU, employing some 23,000 officials — far smaller than most national bureaucracies.

Key parts of the European Commission

President of the European Commission

The commission president is appointed by a qualified majority vote in the European Council, and must also be approved by a vote in the European Parliament. The president and other commissioners serve a 5-year term. Jose Manuel Barroso became president in 2004 and was reappointed for a second term in 2009.

The president allocates portfolios within the College of Commissioners, can reshuffle posts and demand the resignation of a commissioner. He or she provides leadership within the commission, but needs support from member states to lead the EU.

College of Commissioners

Commissioners meet in the college to finalise legislative proposals and discuss developments. There are currently 27 commissioners, one nominated by each national government. But commissioners are not national representatives and must swear an oath of independence. The European Parliament votes to approve the college as a whole. It does not have the formal power to reject individual commissioners, but after expressing concerns about some nominees, it did bring about changes in 2004 and 2010. Each commissioner is given a portfolio covering an area of EU activity. The British national in the college is Catherine Ashton, who is the High Representative of the Union for Foreign Affairs and Security Policy.

Directorates-general

The commission is divided into administrative units called directorates-general, which cover particular policy areas (e.g. agriculture) or services (e.g. translation). There are 23 policy and external relations directorates-general.

Functions and powers

The European Commission has a number of powers:

> ➤ It has the sole right to initiate draft legislation in most areas of EU activity (except common foreign and security policy).

> It executes and administers EU legislation and programmes.
> It administers EU expenditure and collects revenue.
> It acts as a 'guardian of the treaties', ensuring that EU law is applied properly.
> It represents the EU on the world stage, notably in international trade negotiations.

The commission has both a bureaucratic and a political role. Much of its work involves technical and administrative tasks similar to those performed by a national civil service. But it relies on national bureaucracies to monitor the implementation of **European Union law** and on the Court of Justice to punish transgressors.

Key terms

> **European Union law** The laws of the European Union, contained in treaties, secondary legislation and decisions of the Court of Justice.

The commission played a significant agenda-setting role under Jacques Delors. But its standing was damaged by the allegations of nepotism and fraud that led to the resignation *en masse* of the Santer Commission in 1999. Jose Manuel Barroso has a higher profile than many of his predecessors, but his capacity to influence EU affairs has been limited by the desire of large member states to set the agenda.

Weblinks

http://ec.europa.eu/index_en.htm — website of the European Commission, including information on major EU policy areas.

Council of Ministers

The Council of Ministers is the main decision-making body of the EU. It is also referred to as the 'Council' or the 'Council of the European Union'. Based in Brussels, the Council of Ministers is the institution in which government ministers from the 27 member states take key decisions on EU legislation. It is the scene for intensive bargaining and negotiation.

The council consists of ten sectoral councils dealing with specific areas of EU activity. The most important are:

> **General Affairs.** Made up of national foreign ministers, this council deals with issues that cut across policy areas (e.g. enlargement).
> **Foreign Affairs.** Made up of national foreign ministers and chaired by the High Representative, this deals with foreign, security and defence policy.
> **Economic and Finance Affairs (Ecofin).** Made up of national finance ministers, this covers budgetary and financial matters.
> **Agriculture and Fisheries.** This council deals with the largest area of EU expenditure.

Much preparatory work is done by national delegations, headed by a Permanent Representative. They hold weekly meetings in the Committee of Permanent Representatives (COREPER), which takes decisions on technical issues.

The presidency of the Council of Ministers is held by member states rather than an individual. The Lisbon Treaty created a 'team presidency' system for the Council of Ministers, in which groups of three states share the presidency for 18 months. This replaced the previous rotating presidency in which member states took it in turns to hold the presidency for a 6-month term. The UK will next hold the presidency in 2017 (with Estonia and Bulgaria). The state holding the presidency chairs council meetings but will be criticised if it pushes its own interests at the expense of consensus.

Functions and powers

The Council of Ministers has a number of functions:

➤ It is part of the EU legislature, although it shares legislative power with the European Parliament and legislative proposals must originate from the European Commission.

➤ It coordinates the broad economic policies of member states.

➤ It takes key decisions on common foreign and security policy.

Many decisions in the council are made by consensus, but votes are also held regularly. Voting procedures vary from policy to policy. There are three main procedures:

➤ **Unanimity.** Here a proposal will fail if at least one member state vetoes it. An abstention does not count as a veto. Unanimity now applies only for major or sensitive policies.

➤ **Simple majority.** This applies to a limited number of technical decisions.

➤ **Qualified majority voting (QMV).** QMV now applies to most areas of EU activity. Each member state is allocated a set number of votes roughly according to their population (see Table 11.1). To be approved, a proposal must be backed, first, by a majority of member states, and secondly, by 255 votes from a total of 345. Under the Lisbon Treaty,

Table 11.1 Votes allocated to member states under QMV

Member state	QMV votes	Population (millions)
Germany	29	82.2
France	29	63.8
United Kingdom	29	61.1
Italy	29	59.6
Spain	27	45.3
Poland	27	38.1
Romania	14	21.5
Netherlands	13	16.4
Greece	12	11.2
Portugal	12	10.6
Belgium	12	10.6
Czech Republic	12	10.3
Hungary	12	10.0
Sweden	10	9.1
Austria	10	8.3
Bulgaria	10	7.6
Denmark	7	5.5
Slovakia	7	5.4
Finland	7	5.3
Ireland	7	4.4
Lithuania	7	3.4
Latvia	4	2.2
Slovenia	4	2.0
Estonia	4	1.3
Cyprus	4	0.8
Luxembourg	4	0.5
Malta	3	0.4

weighted votes will from 2014 be replaced by a 'double majority' system in which a qualified majority is reached when at least 55% of member states, representing at least 65% of the population of the EU, vote for a proposal. A blocking minority will require at least four states.

QMV is an efficient way of taking decisions in a 27-member EU. But problems will arise if states find that they are forced to adopt policies they opposed. The Council of Ministers thus seeks consensus where possible.

Weblinks

www.consilium.europa.eu — click on 'Council of Ministers' for the Council of Ministers site, with a link to the European Council website.

European Council

Set up in 1974, the European Council is the meeting place of the heads of government (and, in the cases of France and Finland, the heads of state) and foreign ministers of member states. The president of the European Council and the president of the European Commission also attend. The European Council is a political rather than legislative body. It was formally separated from the Council of Ministers by the Lisbon Treaty.

The European Council meets at least four times per year. It used to be chaired by the state holding the presidency of the Council of Ministers. But the Lisbon Treaty created a permanent post of president of the European Council, held by an individual selected by the European Council for a renewable 2½-year term. Belgian prime minister Herman von Rompuy is the first person to hold the post. Early indications are that the post will be largely administrative, with von Rompuy's role being restricted to chairing meetings. Leaders of the large states did not want to see the president of the European Council emerge as a rival who could determine the political direction of the EU. They thus preferred a low-profile politician to candidates such as Tony Blair.

The functions of the European Council include:

> discussing major issues in the EU and in international affairs
> setting the agenda and political direction for the EU
> making key decisions on foreign policy and on the economic situation in the EU
> launching new policy initiatives and agreeing treaty change

The European Council has established itself as the EU's key strategic body, enhancing the power of member states and reducing the political influence of the European Commission.

European Parliament

The European Parliament is the EU's only directly elected institution. The first direct elections were held in 1979. They take place at fixed 5-year intervals. Each member state uses a version of proportional representation. Turnout in European Parliament elections is lower than for general elections.

Members of the European Parliament meeting in Strasbourg in March 2009

Seats in the European Parliament are allocated to member states roughly according to their population. A total of 736 Members of the European Parliament (MEPs) were elected in 2009, but the number will increase to 751.

MEPs sit in transnational party groups based on ideology rather than nationality. The rewards of group membership include funding and access to important posts within the European Parliament. The centre-right European People's Party (EPP) is the largest group. Labour and the Liberal Democrats sit in the social democratic and liberal groups respectively. The Conservatives were members of the EPP from 1992 to 2009, but were uncomfortable with its federalist ethos. They formed the smaller European Conservatives and Reformists group in 2009.

The European Parliament has three locations: Strasbourg (where most plenary sessions are held), Brussels (where committee meetings are held) and Luxembourg (where the Secretariat is based).

Functions and powers

The European Parliament has a number of powers.

Legislative power

The European Parliament shares legislative power with the Council of Ministers. It cannot, however, initiate legislation. The influence of the European Parliament varies according to the legislative process being used. There are three main legislative routes for EU legislation:

> **Ordinary legislative procedure (formerly the co-decision procedure).** The European Parliament's power is greatest here, as it can both amend and block proposed legislation. It is now used for most areas of EU activity.
> **Consultation procedure.** The European Parliament is asked for its opinion on a legislative proposal, but the Council of Ministers and the European Commission are not obliged to take account of it. Before the Single European Act, this was the main legislative procedure. It is now used only in limited policy areas (e.g. competition law).
> **Consent procedure (formerly the assent procedure).** The European Parliament holds a simple majority vote. It is used to approve the accession of new EU members.

Budgetary authority

The European Parliament shares budgetary authority with the Council of Ministers and can influence EU spending. It can request amendments to the draft budget and veto the final budget. Parliament's refusal to approve the budget contributed to the resignation of the Santer Commission in 1999. EU spending is monitored by a parliamentary committee.

Democratic supervision

The European Parliament oversees the activities of the European Commission. It holds hearings to approve the commission president and College of Commissioners. It can also censure the commission. Although this power has not been used, investigations of financial mismanagement brought about the resignation of the Santer Commission. The European Parliament forced the withdrawal of two nominees to the commission in 2004, and one in 2010.

The European Parliament questions commissioners, and members of the Council of Ministers are also questioned in parliament. Parliament can also set up committees of inquiry (e.g. on the extraordinary rendition of terrorist suspects by the US Central Intelligence Agency in 2006).

Weblinks

www.europarl.europa.eu — click on 'English' for information on the European Parliament, including the UK's MEPs.

Court of Justice

The Court of Justice of the European Union, located in Luxembourg, is the EU's judicial body. It consists of three courts:
> the Court of Justice
> the General Court (formerly the Court of First Instance)
> the Civil Service Tribunal

The first of these is the most significant. It consists of one judge from each member state. Most cases are heard by only three or five judges. The Court of Justice upholds EU law, ensuring that it is applied uniformly and effectively. It decides cases involving member states, EU institutions, businesses and individuals. National courts can ask the Court of Justice for a preliminary ruling on a matter of EU law.

Decisions by the court have had an important impact on the EU, extending its policy role and strengthening its institutions. In *Costa* v *ENEL* (1964), for example, it ruled that Community law could not be overridden by national law. In the 1979 Cassis de Dijon case, the court ruled that goods that are lawful in one member state — in this instance, a French blackcurrant liqueur — cannot be prohibited by another. This established the principle of mutual recognition and paved the way for the single European market.

The Court of Justice should not be confused with the European Court of Human Rights in Strasbourg. The latter is associated with the Council of Europe, an intergovernmental organisation set up in 1949, and is not an EU institution.

Weblinks

http://curia.europa.eu — click on 'en' (English) for the European Court of Justice webpages.

The EU political system

It is difficult to fit the EU's institutions neatly into the categories of executive, legislature and judiciary because they tend to differ from national institutions. But we can broadly classify them by their function (see Figure 11.2). The Court of Justice is the EU's independent judicial branch. Much EU activity concerns economic and related policies (e.g. the single European market, agriculture). Here the EU legislative branch has the equivalent of two 'houses'. The Council of Ministers is the equivalent of an upper house where national governments are represented, and the European Parliament is the equivalent of a lower house with member states represented roughly according to their population.

The European Commission can be seen as the executive branch of the EU. It does not have the power of national cabinets, but it resembles them in that each commissioner is responsible for a particular policy portfolio. It is also like an executive in that it makes proposals to the legislative branch and is responsible for implementing laws. But the

Figure 11.2 The EU system of government

Council of Ministers also performs some executive functions (e.g. influencing the EU's strategic direction).

Where does power lie?

It is helpful to distinguish between two different types of EU activity:

- ➢ 'history-making decisions' (e.g. treaty changes), which are the result of bargains between the EU's most powerful member states and are decided in the European Council
- ➢ 'day-to-day decisions' (e.g. single market legislation on mobile 'phone charges), where the European Commission, Council of Ministers and European Parliament are the major actors in decision making

The democratic deficit

The **democratic deficit** refers to the transfer of policy competences from national governments, which are accountable to national legislatures and electorates, to the EU, where decision-makers are less accountable to voters or elected bodies. National parliaments have been weakened because they cannot hold the European Commission accountable and national ministers may ignore their domestic legislature or find themselves outvoted in the Council of Ministers.

The main executive body of the EU, the European Commission, is not directly elected. However, commissioners are nominated by national governments and the commission is accountable to the European Parliament. The European Parliament enjoys greater power than in the past and shares legislative power with the Council of Ministers in many policy areas, but it cannot propose legislation. The sharing of power between the EU institutions ensures that there are checks and balances.

The EU is also regarded as complex and remote from its citizens. Few citizens understand how the EU works. Decision making is often secretive, particularly negotiations in the Council of Ministers. When citizens have delivered a negative verdict on integration in referendums on EU treaties, the EU has often responded by stepping up its communications efforts ahead of a second vote. It is worth noting, though, that the EU's supranational institutions have most autonomy in technical areas which operate at arm's length from the democratic process in nation states as well. Decisions on interest rates, for example, are made by the European Central Bank in the EU and by the Bank of England in the UK. The EU has little power over taxation and spending, and its budget is relatively small. It also relies on national governments to implement EU policy.

Addressing the democratic deficit

Direct election of the president of the European Commission and a strengthening of the European Parliament are sometimes proposed as solutions to the democratic deficit. But critics argue that the model of the democratic nation state cannot be transposed to the European level. Democracy remains rooted within the nation state; relatively few citizens identify with the EU or, indeed, with Europe. The European Parliament enjoys neither the authority nor the legitimacy of national parliaments. Turnout in parliamentary elections is also low, falling to just 43% across the EU in 2009, and campaigns are dominated by national rather than European issues.

The Lisbon Treaty included some measures to address the democratic deficit:

- The power of the European Parliament was extended, with co-decision extended to a further 40 areas and established as the standard legislative procedure.
- If one-third of national parliaments believe that a proposal from the European Commission breaches the principle of subsidiarity, they can ask it to reconsider.
- More decisions taken in the Council of Ministers will be made public.
- Under the 'Citizens' Initiative', 1 million citizens from across the EU can call on the European Commission to launch a policy proposal.
- A secession clause sets out how a member state can leave the EU.

Concepts explained

Democratic deficit

The erosion of democratic accountability that occurs when decision-making authority is transferred from institutions that are directly accountable to ones that are not. National parliaments and voters are less able to hold decision-makers accountable. The democratic deficit also refers to the perceived distance between the EU and its citizens. Citizens do not identify with or fully understand the EU, and have opposed important developments in the integration process.

Viewpoint Is there a democratic deficit in the EU?

YES
- Legislation is initiated by the European Commission, which is not directly elected.
- National governments can be outvoted under qualified majority voting, and this may mean that the will of the electorate is thwarted.
- The directly elected European Parliament is not sufficiently powerful.
- Elections to the European Parliament are dominated by national issues and turnout is low.
- Citizens do not understand or identify with the EU — it is too distant and complex — and have opposed key developments (e.g. the Constitutional Treaty).

NO
- The European Commission is accountable to the European Parliament, and its key personnel are nominated by national governments.
- The EU's supranational institutions have greatest autonomy in technical matters (e.g. competition policy, central banking).
- National governments are represented in the Council of Ministers and the European Council, where bargaining is the norm.
- The European Parliament shares legislative power with the Council in most policy areas — a system of checks and balances operates in the EU.
- The EU does not have power in key areas of national life, such as taxation, social security and education.

Understanding European integration

The EU has some of the characteristics of an international organisation and some of a federal state, but cannot be described accurately as either. Classic international organisations (e.g. the United Nations) and regional trade bodies (e.g. the North American Free Trade Area) are intergovernmental organisations in which nation states are the primary decision-makers. States cooperate voluntarily and retain the right to veto decisions they oppose: they retain sovereignty. But the EU has important supranational elements. The European Commission has independent authority and EU law is binding upon member states. States pool sovereignty when joining the EU: they give up some sovereignty but share in the greater capacity to act that this delivers.

Federalism

The EU is often compared to a federal system. **Federalism** is a political system in which the constitution divides power between two autonomous tiers of government: a federal (i.e. national) government and state (i.e. subnational) governments. Federalist ideas inspired the pioneers of European integration in the postwar period, while some commentators also speak of the contemporary EU in terms of federalism. In the UK, Euro-federalism is often associated with the creation

Key terms

➤ **Federalism** A political system in which power is constitutionally divided between federal and state (regional) authorities.

of a supranational EU 'state', whereas in continental Europe it refers to a constitutional sharing of power between the EU and its member states.

The EU has some of the features of a federal system:
➤ The EU treaties set out the powers held by different levels of government.
➤ EU law has primacy over national law.
➤ It has authority in many areas of public policy, including trade, monetary policy and agriculture.
➤ It has its own budget.
➤ It has its own currency, the euro.
➤ The European Commission negotiates trade treaties on behalf of member states.
➤ EU citizens are directly represented in the European Parliament.

To be a fully fledged federal system, however, the EU would have to be equivalent to a federal government, while the governments of member states would have powers equivalent to regional governments. This is not the case:
➤ States retain their distinctive political systems.
➤ Citizens primarily identify with their nation states and European identity is weak.
➤ Except for the European Parliament, the EU's major institutions derive their authority from national governments. The European Council and Council of Ministers are run by national governments; the key figures in the Commission and Court of Justice are appointed by them.

> The EU does not have substantial authority over areas such as taxation, health and defence policy.

Integration theory

Different theories have been put forward to explain the European integration process. The most significant are:

> neo-functionalism
> intergovernmentalism
> supranationalism
> multi-level governance

Neo-functionalism

Neo-functionalism was the prevalent theory of European integration in the 1950s and 1960s. It claims that interest groups and supranational bodies are the most important actors in the integration process. Integration is a dynamic process, with cooperation in one area (e.g. coal and steel) producing 'spillover' into others (e.g. trade). Neo-functionalism assumed that political and economic elites would then transfer their loyalties to supranational bodies.

The theory fell out of favour in the 1970s when national governments reasserted their authority. But it was revived in the 1980s by scholars who argued that the European Commission and business interests were responsible for pushing for the single European market and EMU. Critics argue that it ignores the power of national governments in 'history-making decisions'.

Intergovernmentalism

Intergovernmentalism claims that national governments are the most important actors in the EU. They determine the EU's development by agreeing to cooperate in areas of mutual benefit but defending their sovereignty in other areas. This perspective argues that EMU came about because the most powerful member states saw it as being in their national interest, and the details were thrashed out in bargaining between them. A variant of this approach, liberal intergovernmentalism, notes that prior to EU negotiations, governments form their policies in response to pressures from groups and institutions in the national arena. Critics argue that intergovernmentalism downplays the influence of supranational bodies and is more suitable in explaining 'history-making decisions' than routine policy formation.

Supranationalism

The theory of supranationalism (which is distinct from the concept of a supranational organisation) claims that major developments in the EU come about as a result of the formation of supranational coalitions. In the case of the Single European Act, it points to the importance of commission president Delors and lobbying by multinational corporations that were concerned by the relatively poor performance of the European economy compared to Japan and the USA.

Multi-level governance

The EU is a system of **multi-level governance** in which a range of actors are involved in decision making. National governments remain the most important actors: they have authority in the major policy areas and are the key players in big decisions in the EU (e.g. treaty change and common foreign and security policy). But national governments do not monopolise decision making. Supranational actors such as the European Commission have their own authority and are the most important actors in technical areas of policy (e.g. single market rules). Subnational governments such as the Scottish government also have policy-making powers.

> **Key terms**
> **Multi-level governance**
> A system of decision making in which subnational, national and supranational institutions all have policy competences.

A system of multi-level governance operates in the UK, with decisions taken at different levels of government:

> the EU (e.g. the operation of the single European market)
> central government (e.g. income tax and social security)
> subnational government — the devolved bodies (e.g. education in Scotland)
> local government (e.g. local transport)

The UK and the European Union

The UK did not join the EEC at the outset, as the government feared the loss of sovereignty that would result from membership. It saw the UK operating in 'three circles' in world affairs: the Commonwealth, the 'special relationship' with the USA, and intergovernmental cooperation in Europe. The UK also supported free trade rather than a customs union and joined the European Free Trade Association (EFTA) in 1960.

Harold Macmillan's Conservative government applied for EEC membership in 1961. The change in policy was a result of:

> the declining political and trading importance of the Commonwealth
> the UK's declining influence in world affairs, illustrated by the 1956 Suez crisis
> the successful development of the EEC, which prompted fears that the UK would be left behind
> pressure for British entry from the US government

The UK still did not support supranationalism but hoped to defend its sovereignty from within the EEC. But French president de Gaulle vetoed the application in 1963 and did so again in 1967 when Labour prime minister Harold Wilson applied for entry.

Membership negotiations proved successful under Edward Heath's Conservative government and the UK joined the EEC on 1 January 1973. In 1975, the Labour government called a referendum which produced a two-to-one vote in favour of continued membership.

Margaret Thatcher at a European Council meeting in Brussels in the 1980s

The Thatcher and Major governments (1979–97)

In its early years, Margaret Thatcher's Conservative government sought to reduce British contributions to the EEC budget and reform the Common Agricultural Policy. It then became a leading supporter of the single European market, which dovetailed with the Thatcherite commitment to the free market. But by the late 1980s, Thatcher was a staunch opponent of further European integration, particularly the Social Charter and EMU. Divisions on Europe emerged in the cabinet, and concern about Thatcher's views on Europe contributed to her downfall in 1990.

John Major had been instrumental in taking the UK into the ERM in the final weeks of Thatcher's premiership. He promised a more cooperative approach and presented the Maastricht Treaty as a good deal for the UK, given the opt-outs on EMU and the social chapter. But **Eurosceptics** argued that it meant an unacceptable loss of sovereignty and opposed EMU as a matter of principle, particularly after sterling's exit from the ERM in 1992. Major maintained his non-committal 'wait and see' policy on EMU, but struggled to hold the Eurosceptic and **pro-European** wings of the Conservative Party together. Policy became more Eurosceptic, notably in the policy of 'non-cooperation' pursued after the EU banned British beef exports during the BSE crisis.

Key terms

➢ **Eurosceptic** Concerned about the extension of supranational authority in the EU and hostile to further integration.

➢ **Pro-European** Supportive of further European integration and a leading role for the UK in the EU.

The Blair and Brown governments (1997–2010)

The Blair government agreed the Amsterdam Treaty in 1997, signing the social chapter and framing an EU employment strategy that balanced labour market flexibility with effective social protection. In the Amsterdam, Nice and Lisbon treaties, Blair accepted an extension of QMV but preserved the veto on issues of 'vital national interest', such as taxation, treaty change and defence.

Conflict in Kosovo persuaded Blair that the EU had to develop a more effective defence and security role. The UK was a pivotal player in the creation of a European Security and Defence Policy. But the 2003 invasion of Iraq damaged British influence in this area. The government maintained British border controls but supported EU action on organised crime, illegal immigration and asylum.

The Blair government supported British membership of the Eurozone if the economic conditions were right. It would hold a referendum if the cabinet decided to join. Chancellor Gordon Brown set out five 'economic tests' against which entry would be judged:

➢ sustainable convergence between the UK economy and the Eurozone
➢ sufficient economic flexibility
➢ the impact on investment in the UK
➢ the impact on financial services
➢ the impact on employment

Brown announced in 2003 that only one of the tests (financial services) had been met. This ended the prospect of the UK joining the euro in the medium term, and an issue that had dominated British politics for a decade fell off the agenda.

Blair bowed to pressure and agreed to hold a referendum on the Constitutional Treaty. But this was not held because the treaty was shelved after the French and Dutch referendums. Blair and Brown refused to hold a referendum on the Lisbon Treaty, arguing that it did not have the significance of the EU Constitution. Brown was not as pro-European as Blair, but his premiership saw little change in policy. Climate change, competitiveness and economic reform were key priorities.

Blair had hoped to increase British influence in, and domestic support for, the EU. On defence, internal security and economic reform, the UK played an active role in the EU. But the invasion of Iraq and non-participation in EMU limited British influence. Domestically, Blair was unable to turn back the tide of Eurosceptic opinion. Yet with Gordon Brown and David Cameron adopting more Eurosceptic positions, the period 1997–2003 is likely to be seen as a high-water mark of British pro-European policy.

Weblinks

www.fco.gov.uk — click on 'Global issues', then select 'International institutions' and 'Britain in the European Union' for information on current UK policy in the EU from the Foreign Office website.

An awkward partner

Professor Stephen George described the UK as an 'awkward partner' within the EU. This does not imply that the UK is the only country to oppose further integration or fight for its national interest. But the UK is less enthusiastic about European integration than most other member states. Factors contributing to British 'awkwardness' include:

> **A distinctive history and culture.** The UK's historical development differs from that of continental Europe. It has had a global outlook and a close relationship with the USA, and it has not experienced the major political upheavals seen in other European states.

> **Wariness of further integration.** British governments have tended to be less enthusiastic about (and often hostile to) further integration. The UK has supported intergovernmental cooperation rather than extensive supranational authority; a single market rather than EMU. Great importance has often been attached to the defence of **national sovereignty**.

> **Limited influence in EU negotiations.** On some key EU policies (e.g. EMU), British governments have not set the agenda but have reacted to proposals from others by attempting to slow the pace of integration or limit its impact. The UK has often been in a minority of states opposed to change and has not developed durable alliances to rival the Franco-German alliance. But it has been influential on some issues, notably the single market and defence.

> **Weak elite consensus.** The UK does not have the strong elite consensus on the benefits of the EU found in many other member states. Labour and the Conservatives have often taken adversarial positions on Europe, and the issue has also caused divisions within the main parties.

> **Limited popular support.** Levels of public support for EU membership and integration are lower in the UK than in most other member states (see Table 11.2). UK citizens are also less knowledgeable about the EU and less likely to feel European. Sovereignty issues are prominent in the British debate and many newspapers take a populist Eurosceptic position. Euroscepticism is prominent in the Conservative Party as well as in smaller parties such as the UK Independence Party (UKIP).

Key term

> **National sovereignty**
> Ultimate decision-making authority is located in the nation state.

Table 11.2 UK public opinion and EU membership

Question: 'If there were a referendum now on whether Britain should stay in or get out of the European Union, how would you vote?

Year	Stay in (%)	Get out (%)
1977	47	42
1980	26	65
1983	36	55
1987	48	39
1990	62	28
1991	60	29
1992	52	35
1993	46	39
1994	52	36
1996	44	40
1997	49	35
1998	47	40
1999	51	41
2000	49	44
2001	48	43
2003	49	41
2007	51	39

Source: Ipsos MORI, www.ipsos-mori.com.

The EU and British politics

Membership of the EU has had a significant impact upon the British political system. The EU is the main actor in many areas of public policy (see Table 11.3). Much legislation in policy fields such as agriculture and the standards of goods and services emanates from the EU.

Table 11.3 Policy competences of the EU (selected)

Areas where the EU has exclusive competence	Areas where the EU and member states share competence	Areas where member states retain competence
Customs union	Single European market	Taxation
Competition policy	Social and employment policy	Social security
Monetary policy (in the Eurozone)	Regional policy	Education
Trade	Agriculture	Health
Fisheries conservation	Freedom, security and justice	Defence

Sovereignty and the EU

An institution is generally understood to be sovereign if it has final legislative authority and can act without undue external constraint. The term 'sovereignty' is used in different ways in the debates on Europe, for example:

➤ **national sovereignty** — the idea that final decision-making authority should reside within the nation state, with the national government determining law for its own territory

➤ **parliamentary sovereignty** — the doctrine that the Westminster Parliament is the supreme legislative body within the UK

➤ **popular sovereignty** — the idea that the electorate should choose decision-makers

➤ **economic sovereignty** — the idea that national governments should have the authority to determine economic and monetary policy

Key term

➤ **Parliamentary sovereignty**

Parliament is the supreme law-making body.

Eurosceptics and pro-Europeans offer different interpretations of the nature of sovereignty and the implications of EU membership. Eurosceptics tend to define sovereignty in absolute terms, seeing it as ultimate decision-making authority. They argue that the supranational EU has undermined British sovereignty.

Eurosceptics differ on how 'lost' sovereignty can be regained. Some favour UK opt-outs on policies such as EMU, while others would like to renegotiate the treaties so that some EU powers (e.g. on fisheries) are returned to national governments. Others view withdrawal from the EU as the optimal means of restoring sovereignty.

Pro-Europeans reject claims that EU membership has had negative consequences for British sovereignty. Instead of viewing sovereignty as a legal concept concerned with ultimate law-making authority, they define sovereignty in terms of effective influence and a practical capacity to act. The UK has not lost sovereignty; rather it has **pooled sovereignty** — it has shared sovereignty with other EU member states in order to increase its influence and capacity to act.

> **Key term**
> ➤ **Pooled sovereignty** Member states transfer decision-making authority to a supranational organisation, combining their sovereignty to achieve their interests.

Viewpoint Has EU membership eroded British sovereignty?

YES
- EU law has primacy over national law, meaning that UK law can be overturned.
- The UK has lost its right of veto in policy areas where qualified majority voting is used.
- The EU has extended its competences into crucial areas such as immigration, defence and monetary policy.
- Parliament and voters have few opportunities to hold EU decision-makers accountable.

NO
- By pooling sovereignty, the UK has achieved policy objectives (e.g. the single market) that it could not have achieved alone.
- The UK has more influence in European and world affairs as a member of a strong EU.
- **Globalisation** means that no state can act independently on issues such as the environment, migration and economic policy.
- The UK Parliament can repeal the European Communities Act, and the Lisbon Treaty sets out how a state could leave the EU if it chooses.

> **Key term**
> ➤ **Globalisation** The process by which states and peoples become more interdependent and interconnected.

Parliamentary sovereignty

The doctrine of parliamentary sovereignty is a central element of the British constitution. It has three elements:

➤ Legislation made by parliament cannot be overturned by any higher authority.
➤ Parliament can legislate on any subject of its choosing.
➤ No parliament can bind its successors.

But EU law has primacy: in cases of conflict between national law and EU law, the latter takes priority. The European Communities Act (1972) gave future EU law legal force in the UK and denied effectiveness to national legislation which conflicts with it. This was illustrated in the 1990 Factortame case. The Merchant Shipping Act (1988) had prevented non-British citizens from registering boats as British in order to qualify for the UK's quota under the Common Fisheries Policy. But the House of Lords, following a ruling from the European Court of Justice, decided that the Act was incompatible with Community (now EU) law and should be 'disapplied'. Compensation was subsequently paid to the Spanish fishermen who brought the case.

This would appear to undermine parliamentary sovereignty, as parliament cannot legislate on any subject of its choosing and legislation made by parliament can be overturned by another authority. However, we cannot say that parliamentary sovereignty is now meaningless. The Factortame case concerned legislation that was not intended as a deliberate breach of EU law. In *Thoburn* v *Sunderland City Council* (2002), the Law Lords ruled that there was a hierarchy of Acts of Parliament: 'ordinary' statutes and 'constitutional' statutes. Constitutional statutes (e.g. the European Communities Act) should only be repealed when parliament does so by express provisions, rather than as an unintended consequence of a new law. Ultimately, parliament still retains ultimate legislative authority, as it has the right to repeal the European Communities Act.

Policy making

Within central government, the lead actors in developing British policy towards the EU are the prime minister, the Cabinet Office and the Foreign and Commonwealth Office. The prime minister shapes the key policy objectives and attends European Council meetings. In this respect, EU membership has strengthened the position of the prime minister. But cabinet divisions on Europe undermined the authority of Thatcher and Major, while Blair ceded significant responsibility for policy on EMU to the Treasury.

Within the cabinet system, a cabinet committee undertakes detailed policy work. A European adviser is based in the Prime Minister's Office. The European Secretariat, based in the Cabinet Office, coordinates policy so that all departments fall in line with the agreed negotiating position. The Foreign and Commonwealth Office also coordinates policy and takes the lead in EU negotiations. The foreign secretary attends key meetings of the Council of Ministers and European Council. The Treasury is the lead department on EMU and keeps EU-related spending in check.

Government departments and local authorities implement EU legislation, and the UK courts enforce EU law. Some local authorities have benefited from money available to poorer regions through the EU Structural Funds. Councils may have offices in Brussels or members on the EU Committee of the Regions.

The EU has policy competence in many of the areas (e.g. agriculture) devolved to the Scottish Parliament, Welsh Assembly and Northern Ireland Assembly. But responsibility for the UK's relations with the EU is 'reserved' to the UK Parliament. The devolved administrations are consulted on British policy in the EU, but once the British government's single negotiating line has been settled, they are bound by it.

Political parties and the EU

The UK's role in the EU is an important issue in contemporary politics. But it is one that political parties have found difficult to handle. Reasons for this include: changes in the positions of the main parties, internal divisions and the problems of exploiting the issue for electoral advantage.

Policy change

The two main parties have swapped positions on Europe. The Conservatives were the more pro-European from the 1960s to the late 1980s. They applied for membership (1961), achieved EEC entry (1973) and agreed the Single European Act (1985). But Euroscepticism escalated after Maastricht and became the dominant creed in the Conservative Party after 1997. Many Conservatives saw further European integration as a threat to national sovereignty and their free market economics. By 2010, Kenneth Clarke was the only pro-European to hold a senior position in the Conservative Party.

In 2010, the Conservatives sought the return to Westminster of some EU social and employment policy competences, and wanted further safeguards on the Charter of Fundamental Rights and EU action on criminal law. They also proposed legislation requiring British governments to hold a referendum on any future treaty that handed further powers to the EU, and a Sovereignty Bill that would make it clear that Westminster retained ultimate sovereignty.

Labour opposed EEC membership in 1961, applied for entry in 1967, then opposed the membership terms agreed by the Conservatives in 1971–72. Labour called for withdrawal from the European Community in its 1983 manifesto. A pro-European conversion began in the late 1980s when Labour supported the Community's social and regional policy agenda. Labour has been the more pro-European of the main parties since then, particularly under Tony Blair's leadership. Blair believed that, in an era of globalisation, economic and social reforms had to be pursued at European as well as national level.

Internal divisions

The most pronounced differences on Europe have often been found *within* the two main parties rather than between them. Internal divisions create difficulties for party leaders. Adopting a firm pro-European or Eurosceptic position risks exposing divisions, so leaders often strike compromises which are acceptable to many, but which do not fully satisfy those with convinced views. Major's 'wait and see' policy on EMU was an example. Party leaders have also tried to quell dissent by removing the issue of Europe from the political agenda. Tony Blair promised a referendum on the single currency to head off criticisms of his pro-European position.

Serious divisions on the issue of Europe arose in the Labour Party in the 1970s and early 1980s. The Conservative government of Edward Heath only secured parliamentary backing for EEC entry when 69 Labour MPs defied the whip to support it. Harold Wilson held a referendum on continued membership of the EEC in 1975 to manage these divisions. Cabinet ministers were permitted to take opposing sides in the campaign. Later, Labour's policy of withdrawal from the European Community was an important factor in the defection of pro-European MPs to the breakaway Social Democratic Party in 1981. Labour's switch to a pro-European position did not bring large-scale dissent, but 66 Labour MPs voted against the Maastricht Treaty. Only 18 Labour MPs voted against ratification of the Lisbon Treaty.

Europe provoked the most serious dissent in the recent history of the Conservative Party in the 1990s. The ratification of the Maastricht Treaty saw large, well-organised rebellions in which 20% of Conservative MPs defied the whips. Since then, the Conservatives have become an almost uniformly Eurosceptic party. David Cameron has, though, experienced some dissent from 'hard' Eurosceptics who demand a fundamental renegotiation of the UK's relationship with the EU, or withdrawal.

Party competition

Debates on Europe have often been characterised by adversarial politics in which the two main parties take opposing positions. The simple plurality electoral system and two-party system encourage this. Partisanship has sometimes resulted from pronounced differences between the parties: for example, in the 1983 and 2001 elections. On other occasions, the parties have broadly agreed on the benefits of membership of an intergovernmental EU but have differed on particular policies. The Conservative and Labour parties broadly supported the Maastricht Treaty, but Labour voted against it because the government had not signed the social chapter.

The issue of Europe appeared a potential vote winner for the Conservatives in the 2001 general election because their policy was more popular than Labour's. But it did not figure prominently among the concerns of voters and an excessive focus on Europe made the Conservatives appear out of touch. Since then, Labour and Conservative leaders have downplayed the issue and it hardly featured in the 2005 and 2010 elections.

The issue has a higher profile in European Parliament elections. The UK Independence Party (UKIP) won 16% of the vote in both the 2004 and 2009 European elections, coming second ahead of Labour in the latter. It wants the UK to leave the EU. But UKIP fares less well in general elections when voters look at a range of issues and are less inclined to cast a protest vote.

❯ What you should know

- ❯ The European Union has changed significantly since the UK joined what was then the EEC back in 1973. It now has 27 members and has extended its policy competence into areas such as economic, internal security and foreign policy. The EU's supranational institutions have also grown in importance. The EU, then, looks less like an organisation of sovereign nation states than the EEC did, but nor is it a fully fledged federal state. Nation states still shape the development of the EU in crucial ways and retain significant powers in major policy areas, such as taxation, social security and defence.

- ❯ The UK is still regarded as an 'awkward partner' in the EU. Successive governments have sought to defend national sovereignty and have opted out of major EU policy developments such as EMU. The Blair governments had a more pro-European outlook than the Conservative governments of Thatcher and Major, but did not join the euro. British governments have, however, also been influential agenda setters in areas such as the single European market.

- ❯ EU membership has had a significant impact on British politics. Many areas of public policy are now determined in the EU. EU law takes priority over national law. Political parties have changed positions on Europe, and both Labour and the Conservatives have experienced damaging internal divisions. Euroscepticism is more prevalent in the British party system, public opinion and the media than in many other EU member states.

UK/US comparison

Federalism in the USA and EU

➤ The USA is a federal state in which law-making power is divided between two tiers of government: the federal government (located in Washington DC) and the governments of the 50 states of the USA. The European Union has some of the characteristics of a federal system, but is a hybrid of intergovernmental and supranational elements.

➤ The US federal system is enshrined in the US Constitution. The 13 original states initially agreed the Articles of Confederation (1777) which created a union of sovereign states. These were replaced by the Constitution of the United States in 1787. The Tenth Amendment states that powers that are not delegated to the federal government nor prohibited to the states are reserved to the states or to the people. The division of powers can only be altered by amendment to the constitution. The EU was created by international treaty and its member states remain sovereign under international law. The distribution of powers between the EU and its member states is set out in the EU treaties, which can be amended with the unanimous support of the member states.

➤ A clear separation of powers exists between the executive, legislative and judicial branches of the US federal government. In the European Union, there is no clear distinction between executive, legislative and judicial functions. The EU's major decision-making institutions, the Council of Ministers and European Council, derive their authority from national governments.

➤ Powers reserved to the US federal government include defence, foreign policy, the US currency and the US single market. Few powers are reserved exclusively to the states (e.g. local taxes), but power is shared between the federal and state governments in many areas (e.g. criminal and civil law, health, education). The EU has substantial power in areas such as trade, but lacks power over taxation, social security and defence.

➤ The US Constitution does not contain a secession clause: there is no automatic right for a state to leave the USA. Eleven southern states declared secession in 1860–61 but were defeated in the American Civil War. The Treaty of Lisbon includes a secession clause that sets out how a member state might leave the EU.

Further reading

Geddes, A. (2004) *The European Union and British Politics*, Palgrave.

Jones, A. (2007) *Britain and the European Union*, Edinburgh University Press.

Lynch, P. (2004) 'British politics and Europe', *Politics Review*, Vol. 13, No.4, pp. 17–19.

McCormick, J. (2008) *Understanding the European Union*, 4th edn, Palgrave.

Whitaker, R. and Lynch, P. (2009) 'Where does power lie in the European Union?', *Politics Review*, Vol. 18, No. 1, pp. 10–13.

Exam focus

Short-answer questions (around 5 minutes each)

Explain, using examples, the meaning of each of the following terms:

1 Supranational
2 Subsidiarity
3 Qualified majority voting (QMV)
4 Democratic deficit

Mid-length questions (around 10 minutes each)

Outline two arguments 'for' and two arguments 'against' each of the following:

1 Qualified majority voting (QMV)
2 The idea that EU membership undermines the doctrine of parliamentary sovereignty

Outline the main differences between:

3 Supranationalism and intergovernmentalism
4 European integration and European enlargement

Mini-essays (around 25–30 minutes each)

Write a mini-essay in response to each of the following questions:

1 'Those EU institutions that hold the most power are those which are the least democratically accountable.' Discuss.
2 'EU membership presents a major threat to UK sovereignty.' Discuss.
3 'The twin processes of EU integration and enlargement have gone too far.' Discuss.
4 'In recent years all three main UK parties have adopted similar positions on the question of UK relations with the European Union.' Discuss.

Index